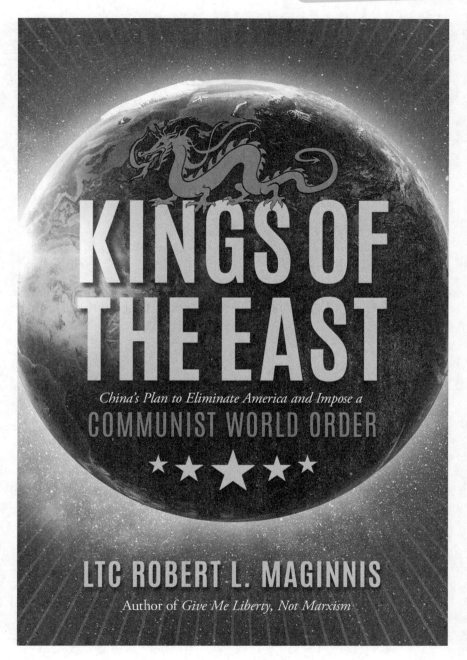

KINGS OF THE EAST

China's Plan to Eliminate America and Impose a
COMMUNIST WORLD ORDER

★★★★

LTC ROBERT L. MAGINNIS

Author of *Give Me Liberty, Not Marxism*

DEFENDER

CRANE, MO

*Kings of the East: China's Plan to Eliminate America and Impose a
Communist World Order*
LTC Robert L. Maginnis

Defender Publishing
Crane, MO 65633
© 2022 LTC Robert L. Maginnis
All Rights Reserved. Published 2021.

Printed in the United States of America.

ISBN: 9781948014595

A CIP catalog record of this book is available from the Library of
Congress.

Cover design by Jeffrey Mardis.

All Scripture quoted is from the King James Version unless otherwise
noted.

耿耿

Dedicated to China's Christians who bravely evangelize their
countrymen and worship their Savior albeit while under the
totalitarian boot of the Chinese Communist Party.

Acknowledgments

I gratefully acknowledge...

...my wife, Jan, who is always supportive of these writing efforts to address very tough issues, albeit at some sacrifice given that throughout this writing I had a "day" job. She's a comfort and a supporter through these troubled times.

...my dear friend Don Mercer, who provided welcomed recommendations and insights about the prophetic implications of Communist China's moves on the world stage and what they might mean for the prophetic end times.

...finally, like all my previous works, my Lord Jesus Christ, who gave me the thoughts, skills, and breath to complete this effort, and I pray it serves His purpose. All the glory is to Him.

Robert Lee Maginnis
Woodbridge, Virginia

Contents

Acknowledgments iv
Preface vii

Section I
China's History, Leadership, and Ambitious Plans for the New World Order

1: Review of Chinese History 3
2: Communist-Revised History and Myths about China 25
3: President Xi, the Hand Behind Him,
    and the Plan for a New World Order 45

Section II
China's Five-Part Framework to Create a New World Order

4: China Dream: An Economic New World Order 81
5: Seeking China's Ideological New World Order 107
6: Role of China's Military in Creating a New World Order . . 147
7: Kings of the East: Geopolitical Agenda 177
8: Kings of the East: Technology 211

Section III
What to Do: China's New World Order Ambitions and Prophetic Implications of the Communist Regime's Hegemony

9: The China We Wanted and the One We Got:
    Resetting That Relationship 243
10: China's Prophetic End-Times Role:
    How Should We Then Live? 283

Afterword 309
Notes 315

Preface

In 2018, I wrote *Alliance of Evil: Russia, China, the United States and a New Cold War.* At the time, many security experts balked at the view that Russia and China were our adversaries, much less that we were in a new cold war.[1] However, recently we've seen mounting evidence of the emergence of a new cold war with the Communist People's Republic of China (PRC) demonstrated by indicators similar to the original Cold War (1947–1991) between the US and the former Union of Soviet Socialist Republics. In fact, the aggressive rise of Beijing's global tyranny alongside aggressive Russia, its growing economic leverage, ideological campaign, and sophisticated security capabilities enhanced by mostly stolen Western technologies presents a true existential threat for America and the West—not that different from the frightening darkness that shrouded the world during the first Cold War.

A simple majority of Americans confirms this perceived threat posed by the PRC. A fall 2021 survey found that "fifty-two percent of Americans name China when asked which country they see as the greatest threat to the United States, while only 14% say Russia." This is more than a twofold increase among Americans who named Communist China as the top threat in 2018, while 30 percent at that time picked Russia. A range of issues is identified for the perceived threat attributed to the Chinese regime: unfair trade practices, rampant espionage, malign influences inside the US, security threats posed by Chinese technology, growing overt military and political threats against democratic Taiwan, Chinese military personnel activity in the Middle East, and human-rights abuses against religious minorities like the Uyghurs and Hong Kong residents.[2]

Rising Communist China's multifaceted threat became especially sobering in 2014 when Chinese President Xi Jinping outlined his hegemonic vision for the world and articulated his total rejection of Western liberal ideals. Specifically, Mr. Xi told the leadership of the Chinese Communist Party (CCP) at the time there will be no place in China for Western-style democracy and "well-fed foreigners who have nothing better to do than to lecture us." Rather, the Communist leader told the CCP's Plenum (meeting of the Communist Party's Central Committee) he seeks a rules-based authoritarian system in which the regime's bureaucracy serves the "masses" unchallenged. Translation: Chinese Marxist totalitarianism must reign at home and across the globe.[3]

President Xi's strategy aims to achieve what he calls "the great rejuvenation of the Chinese nation," a goal to surpass America's global influence by revising the international order to advantage Beijing's authoritarian (read "Marxist-Leninist") system and interests. Mr. Xi called for national "rejuvenation" that harkens back to the language of his imperial forbearers intending to unite modern China with a nationalist credo.[4]

To realize the dictator's "great rejuvenation" guiding principle, there must be success of economic reform, resilient politics, and strategic confrontation with the West—specifically, the United States. As President Xi reminded his fellow Communists at the Plenum, China is special among all nations. "Several thousand years ago, the Chinese nation trod a path that was different from other nations," explained Mr. Xi. Today, he seeks to retrace a similar (contrarian) path to create a different world order, not one characterized by the West's ideologies of democracy, capitalism, and globalization, but one that relies on the renaissance of the warlike Qing Dynasty's Manchu ethos.[5]

Manchu culture is promoted by the contemporary CCP, and its Manchu-like leadership once again forms one of the most socioeconomically advanced minorities within China and especially among the ruling Chinese (read "Communist") elite. The original Manchu, also called Man, lived centuries ago in Manchuria (Northeast China) and descended from peoples called the Tungus and Juchen, who established a kingdom that blossomed into a great dynasty. By the seventeenth century, the Juchen embraced the name "Manchu" and then gained complete control, using its military might to bring all sections of China under the rule of the Qing Dynasty, China's final of fifteen imperial empires that reigned from 1644 to the early twentieth century (1911).[6]

The Qing Dynasty under Manchu leaders was arguably China's heyday, a time of expansion and great prosperity. It is therefore little wonder that President Xi, the son of Xi Zhongxun (1913–2002), a Communist revolutionary and former chief of the CCP's propaganda department, as well as most of the CCP leadership, uses the successes of the Qing Dynasty and the Manchu elite as a rallying cry to resurrect nationalist feelings necessary to achieve Xi's "great rejuvenation" and presumably global dominance.[7]

Kings of the East: China's Plan to Eliminate America and Impose a Communist World Order characterizes President Xi's Manchu-inspired "rejuvenation" announcement as a harbinger of trouble ahead for the world, and one anticipated by some Western leaders. Specifically, nearly two hundred years ago, French Emperor Napoleon Bonaparte warned about the inevitable return to greatness of the Chinese to the world stage: "China is a sickly, sleeping giant. But when [not "if"] she awakes the world will tremble."[8]

Yes, twenty-first century China under the tyrant Mr. Xi and the CCP leadership is very much awake, as the French emperor warned, and thanks to two former US presidents, Franklin D. Roosevelt and Richard Nixon. President Roosevelt elevated Communist China out of post-World War II insignificance to grant it the elevated status of a world power with a veto at the Security Council in the United Nations. That decision angered British Prime Minister Winston Churchill, who labeled Roosevelt's move an "affectation."[9]

President Nixon further elevated China when he traveled to Peking (now Beijing) in 1972 to welcome that brutal Communist regime into the modern world, a move that resulted in awakening the Chinese "sleeping giant" to rise to shake the world today—and many people across the globe are justifiably "trembling."

Just prior to Mr. Nixon's trip to China, the former president explained his rationale for that bilateral meeting. He said that he intended to avoid future confrontation, especially "when they [the PRC] become a super power, a nuclear super power."[10] Then, upon his return to Washington from China, Mr. Nixon further pointed out that "we [the US and the PRC] are on a collision course," and he hoped his bilateral discussions with Mao Tseung (Zedong) would create a "better chance that we will not have that collision course years ahead."[11]

Little did the former president know at the time that China would become a "super power" as predicted, a nuclear power, and his warning about the "collision course years ahead" was rather prophetic. However, the blame for China's rise shouldn't all be put at President Nixon's feet for opening the door to the Communist giant. No, there are a host of other well-meaning American leaders from all walks of life who, over the past half-century-plus, encouraged the Communist Chinese to join the international community. In fact, those leaders provided the regime plenty of financial help, market access, and technology, albeit while ignoring the regime's crimes against humanity by naively believing the PRC would eventually become a reliable, healthy member of the family of nations.

Unfortunately, efforts to recruit Beijing to the international community backfired on those well-wishers who idealistically expected China to inevitably shed its Marxist ideology and totalitarian ways for capitalism and democracy. Rather, the tyrants in Beijing took our goodwill and resources and became a much more powerful and cancerous despotic regime, which today is rapidly seeking to reverse our fortunes and freedoms using its robust national powers.

Kings of the East in three sections profiles that nation's current leadership and long-term goals, then examines the regime's instruments of national power that just might lead the PRC to become the uncontested global superpower, replacing the US with a totalitarian system of world governance and perhaps leading to the biblical end times.

Section I outlines the regime's history (chapter 1), which influences key contemporary Chinese leaders, especially President Xi, who are the driving force behind the Communist government's ambitious charge to world dominance, a fact recognized broadly. For example, Britain's MI6 intelligence agency chief, Richard Moore, said Communist China poses a "serious challenge" to global peace and has become the "single greatest priority" for his organization.[12]

"The Chinese Communist Party increasingly favors decisive action justified on national security grounds," Moore explained. "The days of Deng Xiaoping's 'hide your strength, bide your time' are long over," he said soberly. China "does not share our values and often their interests clash with ours," and Mr. Xi is "very clear that we are now in a more assertive stage with China."[13]

Indeed, and further, chapter 2 elaborates on Mr. Xi's modern-day Manchu agenda and his forceful (tyrannical) personality, which is often compared to that of one of the PRC's originators, Mao Tseung (Zedong), the blood-soaked founding dictator. The section concludes (chapter 3) with an overview of the CCP's employment of key national powers to attain his lofty new-world-order aim by the year 2049, the 100th anniversary of the PRC.

The second section in five chapters outlines how the regime harnessed its economic might to garner a front-row seat in the global economy and now uses that power to commercially manipulate many sovereign nations and perhaps ultimately the world.

Present-day China built a productive economy that tethered itself to the world through trade and dependency, but with a very different aim than the West ever anticipated. Chapter 4 demonstrates that Beijing leverages its financial prowess using President Xi's 2013 Belt and Road Initiative (BRI) to take captive entire countries and regions and build a foreign infrastructure that fits its long-term military requirements, leverages new raw material sources no matter the cost to savaged countries, and creates a world of dependent entities that serve the Communist regime's nefarious ambitions.

Chapter 5 outlines the PRC's governing dogma—Chinese Marxism-Leninism—and how the CCP not only ideologically dominates the 1.4-plus billion Chinese people but also seeks to control, through its various efforts, much of the world.

The CCP has a long history of manipulating the masses. Chairman Mao cleansed the Chinese people ideologically with a Cultural Revolution (1966–1976), which in many ways continues even today under the guise of Mr. Xi's "rejuvenation" revolution that advances its Marxist poison of Chinese totalitarianism demanding total dominance and promoting the regime as the people's only "god"—the Communist government. And there's no room for those who refuse to bow to the regime's Communist "god," especially people of contrary faiths like Christians and Muslims. Further, those who resist are subjected to severe retribution, which identifies the PRC as one of the most immoral regimes in history because it kills, tortures, and incarcerates opponents in great numbers.

By extension, the CCP uses it poisonous ideological mindset to garner leverage across the entire world to include the American public. Yes, it is a verifiable pariah state responsible for deliberately spreading the highly transmissible COVID-19 virus that claimed more than six million lives across the world,[14] and the PRC's near-total surveillance state mechanisms allow that tyrant government to know fully well that Chinese criminal gangs profit from the production of fentanyl compounds that killed more than one hundred thousand Americans in 2021, according to the US Centers for Disease Control and Prevention.[15]

The sixth chapter presents the PRC's rapid march from being a weak, regionally focused armed force to a global military power with the latest sophisticated weapons that seeks to dominate the world across all domains by mid-century (year 2049).

Of course, Marxists like President Xi survive only at the mean end of the rifle, which explains the necessity to maintain a strong Chinese armed forces. Over the past two decades, Beijing poured trillions of dollars and considerable intellectual power into building the soon-to-be world's-most-powerful armed force in terms of sheer numbers and technological sophistication. It could outmatch the US military inside the next two decades (by 2035) and is already a tool of Beijing's foreign policy used to wrap a growing number of nations into its security orbit, and any future conflict with China could lead to a mutually assured destruction outcome.

The seventh chapter of *Kings of the East* addresses the PRC's geopolitical means to grasp ever more control over the entire world. It leverages international bodies like the United Nations and coerces many sovereign nations to its camp using its economic BRI and coercive foreign policy. Further, the People's Liberation Army (China's armed forces) is now a primary foreign-policy tool that is joined at the hip with the regime's economic strategy to intimidate, coerce, and/or buy off every nation's leadership to force them into Beijing's orbit.

Chapter 8 exposes the PRC's technological ambitions and how it uses its growing sophisticated scientific efforts to transform every aspect of human life and eventually to dominate much of the world.

A major aspect of President Xi's "rejuvenation" revolution is the fusion of all Chinese technological centers to greatly benefit its armed forces. All military, business, scientific, and academic enterprises in China work collaboratively to advance the nation's technological edge to become the world's dominant high-technology state using every modern invention: artificial intelligence, autonomous systems, advanced computing, quantum-information sciences, biotechnology, and advanced materials and manufacturing. What Beijing can't achieve with the fusion of all elements of national power, and its collaboration with other nations, it will buy or steal from the West through espionage, thanks to its global enterprise of agents and cyber warriors.

The third section of *Kings of the East* begins by outlining how the US—and, by association, the balance of the Western world—ought to respond to the hegemonic Chinese Communist regime. We start with a glimpse of how the West over the years contributed to the creation of the Frankenstein-like monster in Beijing, and then chapter 9 outlines what the US and the balance of the West ought to do to respond to the PRC's present use of all means of national powers outlined in this section.

Most important, the third section concludes with chapter 10, which addresses the PRC's possible biblical end-times role. Is China a key biblical end-times player? Or will Beijing's economic and military might fade, to be replaced by another, more sinister, tyrant? Is President Xi's "rejuvenation" aim a reflection of the Qing Dynasty's Manchu ethos that stirs, as Napoleon said, to "trembling" not just the Chinese people but a broad swath of the world—a true Antichrist-like entity? Alternatively, is the CCP regime a precursor that sets the stage for the coming Antichrist? Perhaps President Xi is the Antichrist himself—or might the Antichrist be a yet-identified Communist Chinese leader or a European surrogate?

After confirming that China is likely an end-times player, we examine the current state of affairs for Christians under the heel of the Communist regime. Specifically, I answer the question: Why is Christianity growing so rapidly as the level of official discrimination, persecution, becomes so acute? Then I conclude with what the Christian community must do to support the Chinese believers until the Lord's return.

Kings of the East: China's Plan to Eliminate America and Impose a Communist World Order is a sobering examination of the Communist giant, its authoritarian leadership, and how the tyrants in Beijing are employing powerful instruments of change to create a new world order in their image—and, worse, potentially usher all of humanity to the biblical end times.

Section I

CHINA'S HISTORY, LEADERSHIP, AND AMBITIOUS PLANS FOR THE NEW WORLD ORDER

During the civilization and development process of more than five thousand years, the Chinese nation has made an indelible contribution to the civilization and advancement of mankind.[16]
—Communist Party General Secretary Xi Jinping, at the Politburo Standing Committee Members' meeting at the Great Hall of the People in Beijing. (The Politburo is the CCP's principal policy-making body.)

Kings of the East: China's Plan to Eliminate America and Impose a Communist World Order begins (chapter 1) by examining the "Middle Kingdom's" long, dynastic march through thousands of years of history that ended in the early twentieth century with the fall in 1911 of the Qing Dynasty thanks to the Wuchang Uprising and the abdication by Puyi, the last emperor. On January 1, 1912, Sun Yat-sen formally established the Republic of China (ROC), ending over three and a half thousand years of imperial rule in China.[17]

The ROC controlled the country until its fall in 1949, when it was taken over by the CCP, which founded the People's Republic of China (PRC). At that time, the ROC government retreated to the island of Taiwan,[18] also known as the "Kuomintang's Retreat" or the "Great Retreat," where it remains today. Meanwhile, the influence of the last imperial dynasty, the Qing Dynasty (especially its Manchu elite), continues to play a larger-than-life role among contemporary CCP leaders. This chapter examines that influence and the implications that it has for Beijing's goal of a new world order in its image.

Chapter 2 dispels widely held and naïve Western views (myths) about contemporary Communist China. Then, as promised, I elaborate on the rise of contemporary Chinese leaders who seek to spark nationalism by resurrecting attributes of the former Qing dynastic period and especially the Manchu legacy.

Chapter 3 examines how President Xi Jinping—and the CCP leadership, by association—intends to realize a new world order made in their ideological image. That plan is then developed in the subsequent sections of *Kings of the East,* and this volume concludes by interpreting the possible prophetic implications of China's ambitious new world order.

1

Review of Chinese History

The Chinese people are a great people; they are industrious and brave, and they never pause in pursuit of progress.[19]
—Xi Jinping, Nineteenth National Congress of the Communist Party of China, 2017

In late 2021, the Chinese Communist Party (CCP) rewrote history to elevate President Xi Jinping to a stature alongside founder Mao Zedong (1893–1976) and Deng Xiaoping (1904–1997), the Party's chief economic architect. The CCP's communique on the topic states that, under Mr. Xi's leadership, China has "made historic achievements and undergone a historic transformation" in terms of economics, foreign policy, and even the deadly COVID-19 virus.[20] The CCP's updated, official history went on to claim that Mr. Xi had brought China "closer to the center of the world stage than it has ever been. The nation has never been closer to its own rebirth."[21]

China's "rebirth" under the leadership of President Xi should concern not just the Chinese people, but, more broadly, every free, sovereign nation. Likely, that "rebirth" is a reference to the regime's ambition to ignite Chinese nationalism and resurrect the former greatness China knew during the former Qing Dynasty as well as avoid the "Century of Humiliation" it suffered in the nineteenth century at the hands of foreigners. The possible implication is that the CCP will become like the Manchus who once ran the Qing Dynasty, a hegemonic cadre that boasted of their superiority.

This chapter begins by reviewing China's long, mostly imperial history to appreciate this proud people, the world's oldest continuous major civilization. It concludes with an analysis of the Qing Dynasty, the final of fifteen main dynasties spanning 3,500 years, to provide insights about the possible characteristics of China's "rebirth" that President Xi and the CCP seek for both the People's Republic of China (PRC) and the world, which they plan to dominate.

WORLD'S OLDEST CONTINUOUS MAJOR CIVILIZATION

China was ruled by fifteen successive dynasties dating back 3,500 years, beginning with the Xia Dynasty, which ruled from 2,070 to 1,600 Before Christian Era (BCE).[22] China's dynastic structure produced a mostly agrarian civilization, but it was not necessarily unsophisticated. During the period of the Han Dynasty (206 BCE–AD 220 [*Anno Domini*, Latin, "in the year of the Lord"]), the Chinese developed the Confucian ideology that gave strength and structure to their civilization, such as ideals of government and a civil service, as well as technological inventions such as paper and much more.[23]

China's dynastic period was also known for repeated conquests across much of Asia, such as by the Mongols in the thirteenth century and the Manchus in the seventeenth century. Importantly, these non-Chinese conquerors almost always adopted key aspects of Chinese civilization, which preserved much of China's ancient culture.

On a broader level, dynastic China has a long, storied history of launching invasions around its periphery, such as the Han Dynasty, which assaulted and then occupied northern Korea (in 108 BC, era

Before Christ) for four hundred years and, more recently, millions of Chinese troops invaded the Korean Peninsula in November 1950 to support their Communist ally in Pyongyang, North Korea.[24]

Multiple Chinese dynasties invaded Vietnam and ruled that country for a thousand years until the Vietnamese won their freedom in AD 938 (*Anno Domini*, "in the year of the Lord"). Once again, the Ming Dynasty invaded Vietnam until they were overthrown in AD 1428 by the Le Loi's Lam Son (*Khởi nghĩa*) uprising. More recently, in AD 1970, China invaded Vietnam, but suffered significant casualties and retreated.[25]

China twice attempted to conquer Japan using Korea as a stepping stone to that island kingdom. In both AD 1274 and AD 1281, Chinese fleets reached Japanese shores, but were quickly defeated and withdrew.[26]

By now, it is obvious to the reader that ancient Chinese history is full of violence, rebellion, and war at home and fighting abroad. In fact, the Chinese were experts in warfare, which led them to think and write about how to wage war. Most notable, from about 500 BC, Sun Tzu, a Chinese general, strategist, writer, and philosopher, wrote the now famous book on the topic, *The Art of War*. This classic is about how to use bribery, spying, alliances, deceit, and psychological warfare to conquer one's enemy. For example, Sun Tzu wrote, "To subdue the enemy without fighting is the acme of skill." *The Art of War* is one of the most-studied strategy books by military professionals across the modern world.[27]

China's history also includes a Confucian concept for the "peaceful transition of power" called *shanrang* (禪讓), which started before the Xia Dynasty (2070–1600 BCE). However, actual peaceful transitions of power based on merit were rare for a civilization with a history that includes literally hundreds of rebellions, wars, and invasions.[28]

The Qin Dynasty (221–206 BCE) was the first true imperial dynasty of China and was founded by Qin Shi Huang (personal name Ying Zhen), who proclaimed himself the "First Sovereign Emperor" and claimed his dynasty would last "10,000 generations." He unified China by defeating the Zhou Dynasty (1050–771 BCE) then conquered the other six of the seven warring states—i.e., the Three Jins (Han, Wei, Zhao), Qi, Chu, and Can. Although the Qin Dynasty ruled for the shortest period of all major dynasties (fifteen years), its influence shaped the Han Dynasty and started the imperial system that endured until AD 1911, when the Qing Dynasty fell.

Ying Zhen, aka Qin Shi Huang, was very ambitious, as evidenced by his rapid changes. He established a fully centralized administration, abolished the territorial feudal power, forced wealthy aristocratic families to relocate to the capital (Xianyang), divided the country into thirty-six districts administered by military and civil officials, standardized measurements like weights, constructed road networks and canals, and even built the now world-famous Great Wall.[29]

Emperor Qin Shi Huang lived a life of isolation; he was virtually inaccessible in giant palaces and survived three assassination attempts, which might explain the isolation and his distrust of those near him. Further, his enormous funerary compound speaks volumes about the man as well. Specifically, that compound was hewn out of a mountain "in conformity with the symbolic patterns of the cosmos." Modern excavation indicates his necropolis covered thirty-eight square miles, surrounded by a moat of mercury and guarded by eight thousand life-sized terra-cotta soldiers and horse figures guarding the dead king, a much-visited tourist site today.[30]

The final—and, arguably, the most important—Chinese dynasty was the Qing (Ch'ing), established in 1644. It, too, came into being via invasion. Nomadic Manchus assaulted and overthrew the Ming Dynasty. Eventually, the Qing empire crumbled, albeit after 267 years, thanks to a combination of economic challenges and the associated social unrest that spawned a revolution, but also because numerous foreign interventions played a role in the eventual demise of the dynasty.

Foreigners first came to trade, but then used their modern weapons of war to defeat the Qing army. The Qing's first notable conflict with a foreign power is attributed to the British insistence on compromising many Chinese by trading massive quantities of the addictive drug opium.

The British illegally exported opium from India to China beginning in the early eighteenth century, but that trade grew dramatically after 1820. Meanwhile, addiction to opium became a widespread problem across China, causing serious social and economic challenges. Although the Qing government eventually prohibited the opium trade, the British pushed back against the dynasty, which resulted in two wars.[31]

The Chinese lost the First Opium War (1839–1842), and as a result, the United Kingdom took advantage of the Qing Dynasty by occupying Chinese territories, especially lands with navigable ports along the country's massive coastline. One of the most noteworthy war-based territorial acquisitions was a byproduct of the 1842 Treaty of Nanking, which ceded Hong Kong to the British for ninety-nine years.[32]

The Second Opium War pitted the Qing Dynasty against both the United Kingdom and France (1856–1860), and, like in the first war, modern European technology (steam power, iron ships, rocket launchers, breech and magazine-loading rifles) gave Western forces a decisive advantage over the technologically backward Chinese, earning the Europeans additional trade concessions, reparations, and more territory.[33]

The Qing Dynasty's defeat at the hands of modern Western forces sparked a reformist effort among some Chinese officials. However, tradition died slowly in dynastic China because the Qing government initially rejected reformist ideas while clinging to its ancient ways and antiquated technologies.[34]

The rejected Chinese reformists turned to a revolutionary citizen, Sun Yat-sen (1866–1925), who called for the overthrow of the Qing Dynasty and the establishment of China's first republic. Eventually, that movement sparked a military coup that ended the monarchy system in 1911. Meanwhile, Sun Yat-sen founded the Kuomintang (KMT), translated "China's National People's Party," traditionally referred to as the Chinese nationalists.[35]

Once Sun Yat-sen toppled the government, he wisely allowed senior

Qing officials to retain their positions in China's new republic, a move intended to prevent a civil war. However, the KMT failed to achieve complete control over the country at the time, and had to compromise by giving the presidency to General Yuan Shikai (1859–1916), who played a significant role in the revolution that toppled the Qing Dynasty.[36]

Yuan Shikai's tenure was short-lived due to his abuse of power that ignored the newly minted constitution as well as his attempt to restore the hereditary monarchy for himself. That abuse led to a "Second Revolution," which failed to depose Yuan and was quickly followed by a crackdown by Yuan that forced the dissolution of the KMT and the exile of the Party's leadership to Japan. Subsequently, Yuan had himself crowned as the Honqxian Emperor (Chinese: 洪憲皇帝), which ended with his death in 1916 just after his abdication. At that juncture, the country quickly fractured into regions that fell under the control of various warlords.[37]

The Warlord Era (1916–1928) found China divided among former military cliques of the Beiyang Army (a Western-style Imperial Chinese Army established by the Qing Dynasty) and other regional factions. Warlords filled the power vacuum left by Yuan's death. This period was marked by constant civil war between competing factions; the largest was the Central Plains War (1929–30), which involved one million combatants.[38]

Hoping to reunite the nation, and with the support from the Soviet Union, Sun Yat-sen reorganized the KMT, the Chinese Nationalist People's Party, and aligned itself with the Chinese Communist Party (CCP) to fight the warlords. That alignment ended the Warlord Era, although some warlords continued to maintain influence as late as the 1940s.

Once the KMT-CCP coalition defeated the warlords, they turned on one another. Prior to the defeat of the warlords, Sun died (1925) and his successor, Chiang Kai-shek (1887–1975) arrested and executed key CCP leaders. That action sparked a renewed nationwide civil war that sent many of the Communists fleeing to China's southeastern mountain region.[39]

After faltering in the civil war with the KMT in the southeast, the CCP relocated to northwestern China via what came to be called the "Long March" that terminated at Yan'an, the city that became the center of the Chinese Communist Revolution from 1935 to 1947, and the location Mao Zedong became the CCP leader.[40]

The KMT-CCP civil war was put on hold after the Japanese invasion of China in 1937. Evidently, their common interests (ejecting a foreign power) permitted them to put aside their differences to create a united front against the Imperial Japanese occupation, which lasted until the end of Second World War.[41]

After Japan's surrender in September 2, 1945, the KMT and CCP resumed their civil war, and this time, Chiang's forces were defeated in a number of decisive battles in 1948. So, by 1949, Chiang Kai-shek's KMT government and his army retreated to the island of Taiwan, where Chiang imposed martial law, presided over social reforms, and spurred economic prosperity. Meanwhile, the CCP founded the People's Republic of China (PRC) on October 1, 1949, which continues to rule to this day.[42]

At the PRC's founding, Mao proclaimed that a Marxist-Leninist single party would control China, the CCP. Mao wasted no time reconstructing the nation exhausted by years of civil war and drained of resources by both a long civil war and the Japanese occupation. Perhaps not surprising, the Communists enjoyed widespread support across the population, primarily due to Mao's promises of a return to peace and normalcy. That exchange allowed the CCP time to consolidate its control over all aspects of society.[43] For example, Mao's tight grip on the country came thanks to land reform, the campaign to suppress counterrevolutionaries, the "Three-Anti and Five-Anti Campaigns,"[44] and through a psychological victory in the Korean War (1950–1952), even though the fighting claimed hundreds of thousands of Chinese lives.[45]

Mao's early efforts mirrored a Soviet-style political and economic model. However, the failings of that model soon became evident, leading Mao to initiate what came to be called the "Great Leap Forward," a social and economic strategy intended to transform China from an agrarian economy into a developed socialist economy through rapid industrialization and collectivization. The new economic program included the creation of communes (cooperatives) established in the countryside and in the cities, and Mao seeded "backyard" factories as well. As a result of these socialist efforts, agricultural production plummeted to the point that basic food needs weren't met—and besides, the concept of forced labor proved to be unproductive across the country's backyard factories as well.[46]

Mao's Great Leap Forward turned into a total disaster. The factories produced little of value, and the food-production levels practically starved the population. Then, bad weather in 1959–1961, combined with the failed harvests, resulted in widespread famine, often labeled the "Great Chinese Famine."[47]

The Great Chinese Famine is regarded as one of the most significant man-made disasters in human history, as it claimed the lives of tens of millions. Mao's Great Leap Forward policies were blamed for the famine because they created inefficient distribution of food; fostered poor agricultural techniques; disrupted the ecosystem with his "Four Pests' Campaign,"[48] which created a political culture that encouraged over-reporting of grain production; and unwisely ordered millions of farmers to abandon agriculture for steel production. Surprisingly, in 1962, Liu Shaoqi, the second chairman of the PRC, admitted that most (70 percent) of the Great Chinese Famine was attributed to man-made (read "Mao's") errors (三年大饥荒 ; literally: "three years of great famine").[49]

The setbacks from the Great Leap Forward-induced famine were soon tackled by PRC President Liu Shaoqi and CCP General Secretary Deng Xiaoping, who adopted economic policies that aided recovery. However, their policies came to be labeled as "capitalist" (culturally translated as "foreign-inspired") by some, but it was undeniable they boosted their personal prestige among the people, arguably surpassing even that of founder Mao.[50]

In 1966, Mao launched yet another Marxist-inspired movement

known as the "Great Proletarian Cultural Revolution," an obvious formula that questioned Liu and Deng's "capitalist" (read "foreign-inspired") policies. At the time, Mao employed radical youth known as the "Red Guards" to attack Liu and Deng, which resulted in Liu's imprisonment and eventual death. Deng was sent packing to a forced labor camp in a remote region of China, but not for long.[51]

The late 1960s were especially turbulent times, as China's political scene stabilized and former leaders were forced out of power, in part by Mao's Red Guards. By 1971, word of a coup surfaced, and the principal organizer, Lin Biao, fled the country and later died in a plane crash in neighboring Mongolia. The coup-related trauma led to a PRC reorganization and the resurrection of former officials such as Deng Xiaoping, who was appointed vice premier and a member of the CCP's Politburo in 1973.[52]

Soon, Chairman Mao's wife, Jiang Qing, challenged Deng's new authority. She and three associates, who came to be known as the "Gang of Four," attacked Deng's policies, an obvious attempt to garner more control for themselves. These efforts again contributed to Deng's second exit from power, albeit temporary once again.[53]

On September 9, 1976, Mao Zedong died, which sparked a succession struggle between the Gang of Four and other CCP officials. In early October, Hua Guofeng, the minister of public security, became the CCP chairman and premier. One of his first official acts was to arrest the Gang of Four, and then, at the August 1977 11th Party Congress, Deng Xiaoping was reinstated.[54]

In 1978, Deng introduced a series of economic reforms aimed at increasing rural incomes and enhancing incentives, encouraging autonomy, and reducing centralized government control. He also encouraged direct foreign investment and more overseas economic cooperation.[55]

Deng's economic reforms introduced freedoms for the Chinese people, and there was even a period that Mao's Cultural Revolution (1966–1976) was openly criticized, a temporary boon to public free speech. Further, thanks to Deng's reforms, most citizens realized improved living standards as well. However, that period of economic and civil liberty prosperity was short-lived, because by the mid-1980s, social problems began to raise their ugly head as inflation increased and security issues came to haunt the population and diminish their liberties.[56]

Those years also saw a rise in corruption among senior government officials, sparking calls for reform. By 1987, Hu Yaobang, the CCP's general secretary, became the fall guy for the growing dissatisfaction with government. He was replaced by Zhao Ziyang (1919–2005), who became the CCP general secretary, and Li Peng (1928–2019) became the premier at the time.[57]

Unfortunately for China, Zhao Ziyang sought further restructuring of the economy, once again fueling more inflation. That outcome compelled officials to enact greater centralization through economic controls, which was coupled with slow reforms and corruption, and together those changes exacerbated the growing dissatisfaction among the masses.[58]

Soon Chinese citizens took to the streets in protest. Some came to Beijing's Tiananmen Square to demand reforms, more freedom, and democracy. Most of the protestors were university students who camped at the square where many staged fasting protests.

(Tiananmen Square is the city square in the center of Beijing, located near the central business district and named after the eponymous Tiananmen ["Gate of Heavenly Peace"], a monumental gate. The square is also a national archive area, like Washington's Mall, that hosts the mausoleum of Mao Zedong and the "Great Hall of the People,"[59] as well as the National Museum of China.[60])

The Tiananmen Square protesters ignored government calls to leave, prompting officials to declare martial law on May 20, 1989. The students ignored those calls to abandon their protests; this led to the most emblematic standoff in China's twentieth century. On the early morning of June 4, 1989, Chinese troops opened fire on the students, not just against those gathered at Tiananmen Square but against protests that engulfed some four hundred cities across the country. Some reports indicate thousands of dissenters died that day.[61]

The bloody outcome of the Tiananmen standoff led to more political strife across China. Student leaders and others were imprisoned and "reeducated." Eventually, Zhao Ziyang stepped down from his position as Party general secretary, and Jiang Zemin (1926) took the reins.[62]

The trauma associated with the Tiananmen incident healed slowly, and by 1992, China stepped up the pace of reform thanks to young pro-reform leaders. Those reforms came gradually as President Jiang Zemin stepped up to govern for the ailing Deng Xiaoping under the guise of what came to be known as the "Third Generation Leadership."[63]

The Third Generation Leadership under Jiang Zemin, who was replaced in 2003 by Hu Jintao, made significant economic reforms, including opening its economy to the outside world, and especially thanks to President Bill Clinton's facilitation of the PRC's eventual membership in the World Trade Organization (2001). Further, at the time, Beijing moved many formerly state-owned enterprises into private hands. Additionally, there were efforts to downsize the central government's bloated bureaucracy and launch a campaign against government corruption.[64]

By 2010, China became the world's second-largest economy, and a few years later (2014), Beijing reportedly surpassed the US in that economic metric. Meanwhile, social issues mounted just as the "Fourth Generation" leaders retired and new blood entered, such as CCP General Secretary Hu Jintao and Premier Wen Jiabao, who steered China in a new direction by creating what came to be called a "socialist harmonious society." That process favored rural development, a populist measure. Meanwhile, the Hu-Wen government began to restrict personal freedoms such as the expression of political views on the Internet.[65]

The PRC's global prominence soon increased, as did scrutiny, especially of its hosting of the 2008 Summer Olympics in spite of justifiable criticism for the regime's human-rights abuses. Similarly, Beijing earned considerable criticism for its genocidal actions against Muslims in the Xinjiang Uygur Autonomous Region leading up to the 2022 Winter Olympics, which resulted in a number of countries such as the US expressing their dissatisfaction with diplomatic boycotts of the event and earning the label for those games as the "Genocide Olympics."[66]

Predictably, the Communist regime denied the genocide allegations and rejected the diplomatic boycotts as a "farce," which helped the CCP fuel anti-foreign feelings and stoke an intense wave of socialist patriotism (nationalism).[67]

Today, China is living under the leadership of what's known as the "Fifth Generation." President Xi is the undisputed Fifth Generation leader known for his Belt and Road Initiative, the China-US trade war, the Hong Kong protests, Uygur genocide and reeducation camps, and the global COVID-19 pandemic.

The next chapter in *Kings of the East* takes a deep dive into President Xi's rise to power and his agenda for the PRC. However, at this point, it's clear that China's history is notable for catastrophic dysfunction: unending violence; massive corruption; willingness to attack its own people; factions held together by force, which occasionally erupts in violence; multiple pagan religions; little Christian influence; leadership highly subject to assassination and violent overthrows; and a history of disregarding basic human and civil rights.

QING AND MANCHU INFLUENCE

What is so unique about the Qing Dynasty, China's last of fifteen lines of hereditary rulers, and in particular the dynasty's overlords, the ethnic Manchus? What made that dynasty so successful and yet vulnerable to foreign invasions? Why do leaders like President Xi want to emulate the Manchus and the Qing Dynasty?

For a number of reasons, the Qing Dynasty and the Manchu leadership might be President Xi's leadership template. After all, Yale University historian Jonathan Spence claims that Mr. Xi echoes the governance style of traditional Qing-era emperors in his consolidation of power and "majesty of his undertakings," such as the global Belt and Road Initiative. Specifically, Qing emperors Kangxi and Yongzheng, two of the most capable rulers in China's dynastic history, provide case studies in leadership that appear to be endorsed by President Xi.[68]

Professor Spence compares Mr. Xi to Kangxi, who ruled in 1661–1722 and inherited an unstable empire. "Likewise, President Xi has a huge expanse of problems—foreign policy, colossal water and pollution issues, corruption and deciding on the best people for various portfolios," Spence said. Mr. Xi evidently also took a page out of Kangxi's leadership book with his far-reaching anti-corruption campaign, removing nearly one hundred thousand CCP members.[69]

One of the first acts of Emperor Yongzheng (1722–1735), who succeeded Kangxi, was to reform the corruption-prone tax system. The emperor created a process that encouraged officials to report directly to him, and he "appointed new men to key offices," explained Professor Spence. Those efforts reduced the level of corruption.[70]

Mr. Xi appears to have also followed Yongzheng's example. "I assume that Xi," explained Spence, "has good knowledge of the investment opportunities that his own officials can exploit. Emperor Yongzheng had good, close advisers, but he was always suspicious of them. He kept his communications confidential, and would keep a watch on them, file and revise the information he knew of them repeatedly." Evidently, President Xi is known to do much the same.[71]

The Qing Dynasty and especially its Manchu emperors may well inform us about Mr. Xi's leadership style and ambitions for the future. After all, President Xi said he seeks "the great rejuvenation of the Chinese nation," and the CCP's new (2021) official history alleges "the nation has never been closer to its own rebirth."[72]

Are Xi's "rejuvenation" and the CCP's "rebirth" calls for a return to China's former greatness arguably referring to the time of the Qing Dynasty? Do President Xi and the CCP view the Qing Dynasty and the empire's Manchu leadership as a template for them to realize China's new world order?

To answer these questions, we must first better understand Qing history and Manchu leadership by elaborating on the earlier Qing portion of this chapter. Second, I will draw from this further to report some possible lessons, indicators, and characteristics of the Qing era that might influence President Xi's "rejuvenation" and the CCP's promised "rebirth."

The Qing empire, officially the Great Qing (大清), lasted almost three hundred years (1644–1911) and put in place the geographic boundaries of present-day China. It became the fourth-largest empire ever in terms of total territory and oversaw the largest population in the world at the time.[73]

Briefly consider the circumstances that ushered in the Qing Dynasty and the Manchus. In the late sixteenth century, Nurhaci, the leader of the House of Aisin-Gioro,[74] organized what came to be known as "banners," military-social units populated by Manchu, Han, and Mongol peoples. By 1616, leader Nurhaci united these banners (clans) to create what came to be known as the Manchu ethnic identity. Then in 1636 Nurhaci's son, Hong Taiji, declared the Qing Dynasty into existence. However, he first had to depose the Ming Dynasty.[75]

The Ming Dynasty (明朝, míngcháo) came to power through rebellion after overthrowing the Mongol-dominated Yuan Dynasty (元朝, yuáncháo), which brought the ethnically Han Ming rulers to power.

The great Ming emperor, Yongle, expanded China's frontiers and moved the capital to Beijing. He resurrected the crumbling Great Wall of China, the significant 5,500-mile-long Chinese engineering marvel. Further, Ming rulers launched the largest exploratory naval fleet the world had ever seen, reaching foreign lands throughout the Indian Ocean and even the eastern coast of Africa.[76]

The Ming Dynasty, like the thirteen previous dynasties, was not immune to the cyclical tale of dynastic rise and fall. By the sixteenth century, peasants across the empire rose up against their local governments mostly due to failing economic policies.

By 1644, Ming control collapsed as Hong Taiji-led rebels conquered Beijing. However, fighting between Ming loyalists and rebels continued until 1683. At that point, Emperor Kangxi (1661–1722), the reigning Qing monarch, took total control and permanently installed the Manchu identity.

The name "Manchu" was the invention of Qing rulers intending to obscure their relationship with the Jurchen people who had previously been subject to the Ming emperor. The Manchus eventually abandoned their nomadic ways for agriculture by the time they joined the campaign to dethrone the Ming. Their contribution to the war effort was especially significant because they were outstanding fighters due to their legendary skill as mounted archers.

The newly minted Qing emperor, Shunzhi, who reigned 1644–61, was quite cunning and shrewd in the way he pacified former Ming officials. Shunzhi quickly embraced the Ming's systems of administration and then appointed former Ming government agents to help manage six ministries that oversaw key government programs such as revenue and personnel matters. However, there was one major difference from the previous Ming government. All key government positions were jointly occupied by one Manchu leader and one Han (former Ming) Chinese. While the Chinese appointee did the substantive work, the Manchu always had the final say to ensure loyalty to Qing rule. (This is much like the former Soviet style of a military leader and the second in command, the Zampolit [Party official (hack)]). However, outside of the capital region, Han Chinese personnel filled most key positions except for those in the military's command.[77]

A major aspect of the Manchus' assimilation into mainline Chinese life was their retention of many Ming cultural institutions. For example, they continued the Confucian court practices and temple rituals.[78] The Manchus also maintained their ethnic autonomy, even while overseeing the Qing Dynasty. Specifically, they kept their own language and dress and only married fellow Manchus. Further, Han Chinese could not migrate into the Manchu homeland (notably northeast China, Manchuria), and Manchus were prohibited from engaging in manual labor.[79]

The so-called High Qing Era (1683–1839), sometimes referred to as the "Prosperous Age of Kangxi, Yongzheng and Qianlong," was a time of prolonged economic and political stability, and is perhaps the period President Xi thinks about when he calls for "rejuvenating" the modern Chinese nation.[80]

The High Qing Era was also notable as the time when the dynasty reached its greatest territorial extent in the latter half of the eighteenth century. At that time, the Qianlong Emperor, who reigned from1735 to 1796, the fifth emperor of the Qing Dynasty, led "Ten Great Campaigns" into inner Asia to extend the Qing's dominion well beyond China's previous borders. Those campaigns into the landlocked regions brought Tibet, Hainan, Mongolia, the Russian far east, and Siberia under the empire's domain, making the dynasty the fourth-largest union in history—stretching from the Himalayas (mountains) to the Gobi (great desert), encompassing 450 million souls.[81]

Part of the Qing's empire included nations that were part of the tributary system, an arrangement inherited from the Ming Dynasty, which influenced China's foreign influence. That system required countries that desired a relationship with China to acknowledge presumed Chinese cultural superiority. Foreign nation acceptance of that arrangement came in the form of envoys coming to the royal court to kowtow (prostrating, kneeling, and/or bowing) to the emperor, thus acknowledging his superiority as well as paying tribute or giving gifts to the imperial leader. The tribute system had four main functions: 1) it maintained the preeminence of the Chinese dynasty, 2) it constituted a political means of dynastic self-defense, (3) it was a means of foreign trade, and (4) it provided a way of conducting diplomacy.[82]

Of course, the tribute system differed across the many subject countries. Vietnam and Korea were tightly controlled by the emperor; essentially, they became vassal states while others, countries much farther away like Afghanistan, were less controlled and maintained the relationship as long as they sent tributary gifts and acknowledged the sovereignty of the Qing emperor.[83]

The tribute system began to fade by the mid-eighteenth century, however. There were seventeen missions from Western nations during the Qing Dynasty between 1655 and 1795. The last mission was led by British Ambassador Lord Macartney (1793), and, like those who came before him, he performed the kowtow before the Chinese emperor. However, this form of tribute mostly ended for foreigners with the defeat of the Chinese in the First Anglo-Chinese (Opium) War, although it persisted between China and its nearby vassal states like Korea until the late nineteenth century.[84]

The empire's fortunes also turned less favorable by the nineteenth century. In that new century, the Manchus faced major changes, both at home and from threats coming from overseas. Domestically, there was the Taiping Rebellion (1850–1864), an indicator that the empire was fracturing from within. That rebellion was led by Hong Xiuguan, a charismatic man who claimed to be the brother of Jesus Christ and was allegedly in receipt of visions from God directing him to build a utopian society, what came to be called a "Kingdom of Heavenly Peace," for the benefit of the Chinese peasants.[85]

Hong's rebellion was opposed by the Qing Dynasty, which mounted a war against the Kingdom of Heavenly Peace and, in the process, turned much of China into a wasteland—but the Qing generals did regain total control for the emperor. That fourteen-year war became the bloodiest in human history, claiming as many as thirty million lives.[86]

By the late nineteenth century, the Qing Dynasty came to rule over the world's largest population, an estimated three hundred million souls just within China proper, and by all accounts, it was the world's wealthiest country. Further, thanks to foreign influence, the outsized empire began to crumble, primarily because it failed to keep pace with the industrialized West.[87]

The Manchus held tight to the old order rather than use the nation's plentiful resources to industrialize like much of the outside world. Part of their problem was the well-cemented mindset of imperial neo-Confucian scholars who advanced the view of cultural superiority and rejected foreign influence. That nationalist arrogance resulted in the rejection of foreign ideas, mostly about industrialization, which were treated by rank-and-file Qing aristocracy as heresy.[88]

The nineteenth-century Manchus came to regret their anti-modernization views, which spelled trouble for the dynasty—domestically and especially when Chinese soldiers faced modern foreign warriors. Further, the nation's limited industrial infrastructure at the time and mostly agricultural-based economy failed to tap the empire's growing labor surplus, which led to widespread discontent. Couple that with government corruption and widespread urban impoverishment, and it is little wonder that large swaths of unemployed, hungry young men began to revolt. Soon, secret societies like the White Lotus and the Triad Society leveraged widespread discontent that was mostly directed to anti-Manchu (Qing) subversion.[89]

These early nineteenth-century tensions weren't enough to push the country into outright civil war, however. Rather, the West's intrusion into China beginning as early as the sixteenth century—albeit subtly, first with Christian missionaries and eventually with merchants and soldiers of fortune—seeded significant national insecurities. In fact, over time, Western nations came to dominate many of China's port cities and pushed imports like the drug opium that eventually led to two Opium Wars in the mid-nineteenth century.[90]

The Qing Dynasty lost both Opium Wars, which led to Britain, France, Japan, and other foreign nations to further divide the country's coast for exploitation. However, the West's arrival also fueled massive unemployment, as noted above, and festering anti-foreign sentiment contributed to the founding of the group Taiping Tianguo—the "Heavenly Kingdom of Great Harmony." Hong Xiuuqan, the group's zealous Confucian leader from the south of China who claimed to be the brother of Jesus Christ (as previously stated) and allegedly in receipt of visions from God directing him to build a utopian society, believed he had been chosen to conquer China and "destroy the demon Manchu rulers." He recruited from among the poor and outcast youth to build an army that eventually swept across China. What came to be known as the "Taiping Rebellion" (1850–1864) became so strong that it took the Qing Dynasty fifteen years to defeat and, in the process, turned much of China into a wasteland.[91]

In the late nineteenth century, the Qing Dynasty suffered further humiliation at the hands of the Japanese. The Sino-Japanese War (1894–1895) was in part a response to China's use of the tributary system across Asia. However, Japan modernized its military by the late nineteenth century and used its well-armed forces to contest China's grip on the Korean Peninsula and Taiwan. Following that war, the Qing ceded Taiwan to the Empire of Japan.[92]

China's military proved to be no match for the technologically modern Japanese forces. Worse, Japan's quick victory proved to other adversaries, especially Western colonial powers, that the Qing Dynasty wasn't up to the task of resisting foreign intrusions, inviting yet another bold intrusion by Western forces.[93]

Meanwhile, the nineteenth-century Western Industrial Revolution sobered China and fueled its internal efforts to modernize. However, industrialized foreign powers continued to slice up China's coast until yet another rebellion erupted across the country: the "Boxers Rebellion." Anti-foreigner and disenfranchised, poor peasants trained in the martial arts and members of the Righteous and Harmonious Fists (义和拳 *yìhéquán*), were a secret society that took matters into their own hands.[94]

The Boxers focused on purging their homeland of foreigners, especially Christians. Initially, the Boxers' ranks swelled to almost one hundred thousand when, in 1900, they marched on Beijing, intending to expel all foreigners from the city. At that time, Qing Empress Dowager Cixi joined the Boxers and formally declared war on the foreigners.[95]

An eight-nation alliance—America, Austro-Hungaria, Britain, France, Germany, Italy, Japan, and Russia—reacted to the Boxers' threat by assembling an army of twenty thousand soldiers that crushed the Boxers and entered Beijing. Meanwhile, Empress Dowager fled before their arrival, but was eventually forced to sign the "Boxer Protocol," a document that allowed for the permanent posting of foreign troops in Beijing, the execution of officials who aided the Boxers, and payment of reparations.[96]

The Qing Dynasty survived a decade past the Boxers Rebellion, and to its credit began modernizing—but those efforts came much too late to save the empire. After all, ancient practices die slowly, and the empire's inability to correctly respond to repeated nineteenth-century security challenges resulted in failure. By 1911, the province of Wuchang declared independence from the Qing Dynasty, and quickly all eighteen Chinese provinces voted to secede. Puyi, the last emperor, abdicated the throne on February 12, 1912, ending the Qing Dynasty, China's multi-millennia-long imperial period, and ushering in the Republic of China.[97]

CONCLUSION

What did we learn from this short history about the Qing Dynasty and Manchu leadership? What are the insights from that period that may influence future Chinese actions if in fact President Xi and the CCP do perceive the Qing era as a template for their planned rebirth and rejuvenation of China?

Consider the following Qing, Manchu characteristics President Xi may well seek to emulate:

- **Arrogance and nationalism:** The Manchus embraced the view that the Chinese are superior to all other people.
- **Willingness to compromise in order to leverage others:** After conquering the Mings, the Manchus embraced Chinese culture and their administration to avoid civil war. They recruited Ming experts to do the work, but were overseen by Manchu minders.
- **Belief that China is the center of the world:** The Qing Dynasty promoted the ancient view that China is the center of the world,

in part because it is one of the oldest cultures, dating back thousands of years. Further, the view that China is the Middle Kingdom dates to the Chou Dynasty (1122–221 BC), which believed they occupied the middle of the earth, surrounded by barbarians.

- **Militaristic and hegemonic actions:** The Manchus conquered the Ming and many other nations, and killed millions of Chinese citizens to remain in power—e.g., the Taiping Rebellion.
- **Use of the tribute system to control foreign nations:** The Qing Dynasty effectively used the tribute system to control other nations.
- **Demonization of foreigners to promote nationalism:** At every turn, the Manchus opposed foreigners, using the threat of outside influence among Chinese citizens to spur nationalism.
- **Autocratic rule:** The Manchus were autocratic at home and hard-nosed totalitarians with all foreigners.
- **Deceptive actions:** The Qing created the Manchus to obscure their relationship with the Jurchen people, who had previously been subject to the Ming emperor.
- **Too much confidence in traditional ways:** The Manchus refused to modernize their industry and military even though Western powers consistently won military victories.
- **Trust only in Manchus:** The Manchus only trusted their own with major decisions, which included command of military troops.
- **Close monitoring of all people:** They maintained ethnic autonomy and controlled the movement of all people and countered corruption within their ranks.

Today, the Manchu people are China's fourth-largest ethnic minority, and they predominately live in northeast China in four provinces: Liaoning, Hebei, Jilin, and Heilongjiang.[98] They enjoy special status thanks to the CCP.

In fact, the Communist PRC has encouraged the revival of Manchu culture that includes traditional storytelling, music, falconry, and ethnic holidays. Further, most ethnic Manchus speak Mandarin Chinese as well as continue their efforts to preserve the Manchu language, a Tungusic tongue.[99] Of course, the emphasis on sustaining elements of the Manchu culture is a potential weakness to exploit in terms of propaganda to the rest of the Chinese people.

The cultural preservation of the Manchus is marginally important, however. What's significant for this volume is whether modern Chinese rulers like President Xi view the lessons from the Manchu-led Qing Dynasty as a template to create a new world order. The next chapter explores President Xi's plans for China and, more broadly, for its new world order. You will see that some of President Xi's past actions and future plans do indeed reflect Qing, Manchu characteristics that defined that dynasty and are indeed worthy of what he seeks: "the great rejuvenation of the Chinese nation."

2

Communist-Revised History
and Myths about China

Our responsibility is to rally and lead the whole party and the Chinese people of all ethnic groups, take up this historic baton and continue working hard for the great renewal of the Chinese nation, so that we will stand rock firm in the family of nations and make fresh and greater contribution to mankind.[100]

—Xi Jinping
New General Secretary of the CCP (2012)

Few Westerners study Chinese history in school, which is why I began this volume with a review of China's rich, 3,500-year record. That historical review ended with the suggestion that President Xi intends to use as a template the legacy of the Manchu-led Qing Dynasty to "rejuvenate" China and then create a new world order. We begin with the evidence of that suggestion and then demonstrate just how naïve and gullible most Westerners are about China by exploring five common myths about the Middle Kingdom.

REWRITING HISTORY TO EMPOWER THE CCP'S HOLD

German historian Leopold von Ranke encouraged his peers to write about the past "as it actually happened," and let the reader understand the past "on its own terms." The CCP violates that principle in order to shape public opinion and remain in power.[101]

The CCP, according to Pulitzer Prize-winning journalist Ian Johnson, "does not just suppress history, it recreates it to serve the present."[102]

This is precisely what happened in 2021. The CCP rewrote history for the third time in its century-long record to serve the new leader's agenda. The first time it rewrote history was to help Mao Zedong by providing a "correct" analysis and a new program that contributed to winning the Chinese Civil War with the KMT. Years later, Deng Xiaoping offered yet another revised history that called for "reform and opening up" designed to connect the previously autarchical PRC to the international economy. Now, the Party issued yet another revised history to bolster President Xi's agenda.[103]

The revised histories are really about preserving the CCP, not about serving the Chinese people. After all, President Xi perceives today's ninety-five-million-member CCP to be positioned similarly to the then two million Manchus who ruled the Qing Dynasty. During the Dynasty's period, the Manchus ruled over three hundred million mostly Han Chinese, and today's Communists hold power over 1.4 billion mostly non-Communist people. Like the Manchus who ruled an expansive, diverse dynasty, today's CCP struggles as did the Manchus to govern a population characterized by ethno-religious "splittism," "reactionaries," and "anti-patriotic" sentiments. Meanwhile, the Communist Party seeks to recruit all "Chinese" to the central idea of "One China," a call for nationalism and a single, unifying identity under their watchful rule.[104]

How can the CCP accomplish its One China feat and thus protect the Party's position? It rewrites history. So, "to destroy a people," or more specifically, to advance a One China identity, "You must first destroy their history," wrote Manchu-era reformer Gong Zichen. That's exactly what the CCP is doing with its One China plan to Sinicize the population, especially among dissenting minorities like the Muslim Uighurs.[105]

That brings us to President Xi's use of the Qing Dynasty and the Manchus leadership as a template for "rejuvenating" by Sinicizing (to make Chinese in character) the population. In 2019, Mr. Xi spoke to Party loyalists about "hostile forces at home and abroad" promoting "historical nihilism," which he said is a mortal threat to the Party, and the only response was to fiercely struggle for survival in the "ideological domain" by once again rewriting history.

So, for the Party to survive, it must co-opt a piece of history to win widespread support. Understand that "China" is a place, a civilization, and the PRC is a ruling arrangement (government) set up in 1949 by Communists as a tool to monopolize power and retain the empire. The Party's primary purpose, according to Leninist doctrine, is to maintain control, and that includes rewriting history to serve its aim. Leninism is a political ideology created by the Russian Marxist Vladimir Lenin (1870–1924), the founder of the Soviet Union, who proposed the dictatorship of the proletariat (working class) led by a revolutionary (Communist) Party.[106]

Years ago, the CCP portrayed the Manchu Qing Dynasty as colluding with European powers and Japan against the Chinese people. That arrangement led to the Century of Humiliation, described in the previous chapter. That series of tragedies is now rewritten to fit the Party's contemporary narrative/interests because today the history of the Qing Dynasty and the Manchus' leadership approach serves President Xi's One China policy.

CCP REWRITES QING AND MANCHU HISTORY TO EMPOWER PRESIDENT XI'S AGENDA

In October 2018, President Xi chose his tour of Manchuria much like Mao Zedong visited the countryside to be seen among the proletariat (peasants)—a propaganda ploy. Mr. Xi called his Manchuria visit an "inspection tour" that portrayed him as a "leader who is of the people, who dreams of a better China and a better life for all Chinese." He used the heritage home of the Manchus to call for the "great rejuvenation of the Chinese nation," an area rich in history—albeit one marred by wars and sagas, used and then abandoned.[107]

Manchuria was the birthplace of China's fifteenth and final imperial dynasty, the Qing, and it was led by Manchus. That memory and history is what Mr. Xi hopes to leverage to advance his "rejuvenation" plan for the One China policy.

President Xi's trip and other recent activities are intended to have strategic and historical resonance. Of particular interest to the Communist regime is the Qianlong emperor, a man of formidable intellect and will who ruled China from 1736 to 1795—arguably the high point of the Qing Dynasty.[108]

The CCP also rewrites the history of ancient Chinese leaders to fit its agenda. Wang Xuedong, the head of the Palace Museum in Beijing (the Forbidden City), described past Chinese emperors as hardworking statesmen who "wanted their empire to be stable and prosperous," a self-serving interpretation of history.[109]

Not all depictions of dynastic leadership serve the regime's interests. There was a Chinese television drama series set in Qianlong's court, a Qing-era emperor, but the CCP removed the program from the air in 2019 after state media complained about the "negative impact" of imperial sagas that celebrated poisonings, betrayals, and extravagant living. Mr. Wang labeled the Qing dramas as "cultural pollution," then suggested television ought to show good governance by the emperor.[110]

Evidently, tributes to favored emperors are now commonplace for the Communist regime, mostly rewritten history to suit the regime's message. We've seen this approach in the 1980s and 1990s, when Maoist propaganda intended to stir Chinese nationalism was replaced by programs about Qianlong, which portrayed the ancient emperor as a nation-builder. Of course, as outlined in the previous chapter, eighteenth-century Qing emperors, especially Qianlong, added vast territories to the empire, notably Tibet and Xinjian, by the edge of the sword. Qianlong's reign was arguably the high point of the dynastic period, albeit noteworthy for its use of military force.

The CCP sees value in presenting itself as the heir to the greatness of emperors like Qianlong, but of course the Communists rewrite history to ignore what has become known as the Century of Humiliation—as referenced earlier, a term used in China to describe the intervention and subjugation of the Qing and Republic of China by foreign powers from the mid-nineteenth to mid-twentieth centuries. However, the CCP refers to that period only when it comes to boasting that it made China strong once again.

Predictably, Communist flacks present the CCP as heir to the Man-chu-led Qing Dynasty. For example, Mr. Wang, a Communist official of vice-ministerial rank, explained: "If you did not have 5,000 years of civiliza-tion, you would not have socialism with Chinese characteristics." He then called the CCP "a loyal inheritor and protector" of that glorious past.[111]

Chinese leaders reinforce the Qing-CCP association. In August 2021, President Xi visited a site dear to the newly minted CCP icon Qianlong, the imperial summer retreat at Chengde, north of Beijing. At the site, Mr. Xi visited Puning Temple, a Buddhist complex that cel-ebrates Qianlog's victory over Mongol nomads. While touring, Mr. Xi is said to stress one of his One China priorities: the need to Sinicize religions, which means to make them Chinese in orientation so to bet-ter conform to and serve the needs of a socialist (read "Communist" Chinese) society.[112]

Mr. Xi also visited a new-at-that-time exhibit at the Chengde Museum, one that praises Qianlong in rhetoric similar to that of the CCP's media mouthpiece, the *People's Daily*. In fact, signs at the museum explain that Qianlong "improved the Qing central government's man-agement of Tibet, quelled multiple bouts of conflict by separatists in Xingang, and further unified this multi-ethnic country."[113]

The museum presents Qianlong as the epitome of a virtuous Chi-nese ruler who honored ancestral rites and promoted policies that "unify all ethnicities." The museum also boasts reproductions of Mandarin-language calligraphy and images of Qianlong in Chinese imperial robes, even though the emperor was a Manchu, like all Qing emperors.[114]

The CCP's rewritten history ignores the nature of Manchu rule. Specifically, I previously established that the Qing toppled the Ming, and Qianlong, like other emperors of that dynasty, sought to preserve the traditions of his martial ancestors, calling it "the best way to train Manchus." Honest history also indicates the dynasty was open to Manchu nobles and soldiers, and Qing institutions were closed to Han, the majority Chinese nationality. In fact, the Han lived as subjects in a Manchu-led empire; they were barred from marrying Manchus and often lived in separate city districts.[115]

These divisions complicate the CCP's move to leverage the Manchu heritage, which might explain the rewrite of history. However, the CCP is very effective at rebranding itself. For example, Communist historians claim the Qing, in their rewrite of history, admired the Han culture and quickly assimilated, thus even the Manchus were the latest in an unbroken line of Chinese rulers dating back five thousand years.

Another exhibit at the Chengde Museum reflects an example of rebranded, revisionist history. Specifically, there is a wall sign that praises the Qing's "historic feats" of "pacification and consolidation of the border regions." Of course, the unfiltered truth is the term "consolidation" is the CCP's spin on history, a claim that Tibet and Xinjian have always been part of China, not conquered by Manchus.[116]

What's clear from the CCP's view of history is that the Qing Dynasty is to be emulated and that Qianlong was a wonderful leader, a man who reflected the boldness, skill, and love for One China.

Much as China's rewritten history fits the CCP's remain-in-power agenda, it also coopts the laudatory parts of the Manchu-run Qing history to demonstrate that the present-day Beijing regime is truly the heir apparent of China's great dynastic past.

Yes, the modern Chinese government not only rewrites history to persuade its citizens to rally behind the CCP, but the regime also manipulates Westerners' understanding of the Beijing regime by promoting myths that must be debunked.

SETTING THE RECORD STRAIGHT: A REALITY CHECK FOR WESTERNERS

In 2019, former Speaker of the US House of Representatives, Newt Gingrich, admitted in a *Newsweek* article: "It has become more and more obvious that our strategies for dealing with China don't work." He went on to state: "Our strategies are failing because they are based not on reality but on…myths."[117]

The Speaker explained that "our misreading" is based on "our own arrogance and wishful thinking and part on a deliberate Chinese strategy of deception." Indeed. We've been ignorant of history, played as the fool, and embraced propaganda (myths) rather than cold, hard facts about the Chinese Communists.[118]

Mr. Gingrich illustrated Western naivety by citing the use of a picture of the smiling Chinese revolutionary and statesman Deng Xiaoping (1904–1997) boasting a cowboy hat while enjoying a Texas rodeo. That image was intended, according to Gingrich, to dissuade the American audience about warnings that Xiaoping was a hard-nosed Communist, someone devoted to totalitarianism, not someone who would embrace Western-style democracy. Evidently, according to Gingrich, Americans fell for the Communist ruse. After all, the Communist Chinese want Americans to believe China is receptive to liberal values, rule of law, and open markets. This perspective, which runs contrary to realist warnings, fooled most Americans—and, by association, the West—about the true nature of the Beijing tyrants.[119]

Yes, Washington fell for the Communists' propaganda about their true objective. Therefore, we granted the Communist regime unfettered access to our academy (the education establishment) and economy. Soon, tens of thousands of Chinese students flooded American colleges and universities, and our political masters were practically giddy about the prospect that the academy would infect Chinese coeds with Western ideas of liberty. We didn't stop there. No, we admitted China to the World Trade Organization (2001), convinced the regime would become more law-abiding and would fall in line with the West to protect, not steal, intellectual property.

We were so wrong, and today we have come to rue these misplaced decisions and our collective stupidity. America and much of the West were flummoxed by a distorted picture of Chinese history, culture, and the Middle Kingdom's true intentions: world domination.

Let's examine some common misconceptions, myths about the People's Republic of China, to appreciate the Communists' manipulation of Western thought.

We begin with two myths identified by the former Speaker. Then we will consider three quite different myths that resonate around the notion that political freedom will follow economic freedom in China.

1. "China intends to change."

Speaker Gingrich's first myth is: "China intends to change." Not true. The PRC will remain a totalitarian, Leninist dictatorship, but will compromise, albeit temporarily, to gain leverage and then return to its hard-nose ways.[120]

President Xi is the most powerful leader in China—a smart, tough, and driven man who is the general secretary of the CCP, chairman of the military commission, and president of the PRC. His power base is the CCP, and the People's Liberation Army (PLA) is an instrument of the Party. Mr. Xi has ninety-five million Party members scattered across China in literally every company, involved in every community.

There is nothing in the West to compare with the CCP. It is a Leninist organization, which is why it is so dangerous. Understand that Vladimir Lenin was a hardened revolutionary who took his intellectual doctrine from Marxism and translated it into a formula for a totalitarian police state. Doctrinally, the Party has one supreme leader, and he uses all means to accomplish its ends. Joseph Stalin, the Soviet dictator after Lenin was known for massive brutality, perfected Lenin's totalitarian system, and millions of Russians died as a result.

The Chinese Communists long ago embraced Leninism. Mao and the other founders studied Lenin and were influenced by Stalin's *History of the Communist Party of the Soviet Union: Short Course*, a book Speaker Gingrich said was chiseled into every Soviet Communist mind. Let there be no misunderstanding, however. The same brutal Leninism of the Soviet era is at the very core of the Chinese Communist system today.

President Xi, like Deng Xiaoping and Jiang Zemin before him, uses his chairmanship over the PLA and the CCP to advance his Leninist ambitions. The PLA is integral to the operations of state and is at the chairman's direct disposal to ruthlessly purge dissenters as it did in 1989 at Tiananmen Square.

2. "China is inherently peaceful."

Second, there is a misleading view (a myth) that China is inherently peaceful. Chinese history makes clear that nation's 3,500-year record was not peaceful.

The first chapter of this volume documents China's history as soaked in blood. The account of the fifteen dynasties is filled with every sort of war, rebellion, and violence—domestic and overseas. Even the prosperous periods were marked with war-based expansion by the emperors. Then, once China shed the dynastic system (1911), it repeatedly found itself in either a foreign war or civil war, and that record continues today.

The CCP is among the worst offenders of peace. For the past century, it used its power to kill millions of Chinese and earn the reputation as a tyrant, a bloody oppressor in order to maintain its stranglehold of power.

Consider a brief history of the CCP's century of violence.

Land-reform campaign: In 1950, the CCP launched a nationwide "land reform" campaign, which called for peasants to rise up against landlords. During this period, between one hundred thousand and two hundred thousand landlords died, and others were tortured alongside their families.[121]

Movement to suppress counterrevolutionaries: In 1950, the CCP issued an order to suppress people viewed as a threat, including KMT (Kuomintang) officials, bandits, religious entities, and other groups. Most of those killed in cities were former KMT officials, businessmen, former employees of Western companies, and intellectuals. Chiang Kai-shek, the KMT leader and president of the Republic of China, claimed that as many as 3.83 million non-Communist people were executed by the CCP between February 1951 and February 1952.[122]

Persecution of intellectuals: Chairman Mao said, "The more knowledge one has, the more counter-revolutionary one is." The CCP launched the "anti-rightists' movement" in 1957, which encouraged intellectuals to voice their views to "help the CCP rectify itself." However, that effort was a trick to "lure the snakes out of their holes." Soon, tens of thousands of intellectuals were caught in the Communist trap. They were jailed or sent for "thought reform" through hard labor. In 1958, the CCP's Politburo announced it caught 3,178,470 "rightists" in their trap, and most were never heard from again.[123]

China's Great Famine: China's Great Famine (1959–61) claimed an estimated thirty-six million Chinese lives during Chairman Mao's Great Leap Forward. The CCP was especially harsh by first falsely exaggerating production yields and then by taxing the people on the inflated yields, leaving them nothing to live on. Also, when the people were found hiding food, they were often "tied up, hung-up, beat-up while being criticized in public."[124]

Mao's Cultural Revolution—astronomical death toll: Mao's decade-long Cultural Revolution (1966–1976) destroyed countless ancient books, cultural relics, and places of historical significance. He set loose the young hoodlums known as Red Guards to ransack enemies of the state. In 1978, a CCP spokesman said in a speech:

It is estimated that 20 million people died during the cultural revolution, over 100 million people were subjected to political persecution, accounting for 1/9 of China's entire population, and 800 billion yuan [currency] was wasted.[125]

Denial of the 1989 Tiananmen Square massacre: The June 4, 1989, bloody massacre shocked the world, yet the CCP claimed that "no one was killed when the PLA cleared out the square, not a single shot was fired." A 2017 declassified United Kingdom document indicated that at least ten thousand people were killed by the PLA during the June 4 massacre.[126]

Persecution of Falun Gong: Since 1999, the CCP has killed more than four thousand practitioners, and upwards of three million were arrested, with many sent to brainwashing centers and labor camps.

The CCP cover-up of the COVID-19 pandemic: The CCP played a direct role in the devastating coronavirus pandemic that, by early 2022, killed more than six million people.[127]

The CCP's genocide against the Muslim Uyghurs: The US State Department found the PRC guilty of genocide against the Uyghurs in the northwestern Xinjian Uygur Autonomous Region. At least one million Uyghurs are also held against their will in "reeducation camps," and hundreds of thousands of others have been sentenced to prison terms. There is evidence many are in forced labor camps, and women are being forcibly sterilized.[128]

The above litany of CCP-related violence conclusively demonstrates that the Party is not peaceful. It is vicious, and uses its power to maintain a tight hold on the population.

POLITICAL PROSPERITY WON'T FOLLOW ECONOMIC PROSPERITY

The next three myths address the misguided view that political freedom will follow economic freedom in China. All we need to do, so goes this view, is expose the Chinese to our academy, our freewheeling economic ways, and our open Internet. That openness, we naively believed, would persuade the Beijing tyrants to abandon their ways, according to Rana Mitter, a professor of the history and politics of modern China at Oxford University, Cambridge, United Kingdom, and Elsbeth Johnson, a senior lecturer at the Massachusetts Institute of Technology's Sloan School of Management. They outline three myths in "What the West Gets Wrong about China," an article in the May/June 2021 edition of *Harvard Business Review.*[129]

> Westerners in general and especially the political and business classes continue to hold to false assumptions [myths] about modern China. Why? Mostly because they have little knowledge about China's history and culture, which encourages them to apply Western thinking to embrace deeply flawed analogies between communist China and other countries.[130]

3. "Economics and democracy are two sides of the same coin."

There are three myths (flawed analogies) that influence Western thought regarding China, according to Mitter and Johnson. First, "Economics and democracy are two sides of the same coin."[131]

"Many westerners assume," they say, "that China is on the same development trajectory that Japan, Britain, Germany, and France embarked on in the immediate aftermath of World War II." Not true. China started much later, after Mao's cultural revolution (1966–1976), but even with that delay, many in the West assume eventually China would "move toward a more liberal model...as did those countries."[132]

The view that a Western-style outcome was inevitable for China was shared by former President William "Bill" Clinton. "By joining the WTO [World Trade Organization]," Mr. Clinton said, "China is not simply agreeing to import more of our products, it is agreeing to import one of democracy's most cherished values: economic freedom. When individuals have the power to realize their dreams, they will demand a greater say."[133]

President Clinton's argument ignores fundamental differences between China and the Western nations, which enjoyed post-World War II "pluralist democracies with independent judiciaries." For the West, economic prosperity accompanied social progress. By comparison, the collapse of the former Soviet Union in 1991 welcomed that nation's integration into the global economy along with Mikhail Gorbachev's political reforms (*glasnost*).[134]

Unlike Russia, China prospered without abandoning its Marxist-based ideology, which argues that democratic rule and economic prosperity are not mutually dependent. In fact, Mitter and Johnson suggest Beijing's economic successes such as poverty reduction and infrastructure investment came about because of China's centralized, authoritarian (Leninist) form of government.[135]

There is also the parallel belief that an authoritarian regime inhibits innovation. Contrary evidence shows that China is now a leader in artificial intelligence, biotechnology, and space exploration. Interestingly, Mitter and Johnson point out that "much of the technological progress has come from a highly innovative and well-funded military that has invested heavily in China's burgeoning new industries." In fact, military investments bolstered China's consumer applications such as Alibaba, Huawei, and TikTok.[136]

The view that economic prosperity is possible under an authoritarian regime is also supported by other facts. A July 2020 poll conducted by the Ash Center at Harvard's Kennedy School of Government found that the vast majority (95 percent) of Chinese citizens are satisfied with their government. Of course, any poll taken in China ought to be suspect, but according to Mitter and Johnson, their anecdotal contacts with average Chinese citizens confirmed that they "don't feel that the authoritarian state is solely oppressive."[137]

Communist Chinese leaders evidently also share the view that economic reform is possible without liberalizing politics. That view is supported by the fact that China is today an economic titan, a leader in technology, a military superpower—all while remaining authoritarian.[138]

The lesson that authoritarian leadership as well as economic and military prosperity are simultaneously possible tracks back to the 1930s and Germany. Adolf Hitler became the German chancellor in 1933, promising to right that nation's economic problems. But there was more to Hitler's agenda, according to Richard Overy, in his article, "An Economy Geared to War." The new German leader wanted the "complete control of [the] national economy," an autocratic ambition, because he believed it would ensure victory in a future war.[139]

"Hitler's priority in the early 1930s was economic recovery, the key to political stabilization and social peace after the chaos of the [post-World War I] slump," wrote Overy. However, once Germany was on the road to economic recovery, Hitler announced his comprehensive strategy, written in August 1936, which called for a massive rearmament effort. At the time, the German authoritarian argued that the much-anticipated future great war required a dual front, not only "military rearmament," but also "economic rearmament and mobilization…in the same tempo."[140]

The evident conclusion by both the Communist Chinese and the Nazi ruler was that authoritarianism can indeed produce economic prosperity, which called into question Gorbachev's abandonment of the USSR's Communist authoritarianism in favor of liberalization. In fact, decades later, the current Russian president, Vladimir Putin, has increased Kremlin control and reversed much of the post-Cold War liberalization, especially regarding civil liberties. However, Russia's economy today is performing poorly, perhaps because it is overly dependent on energy (40 percent of its GDP), and is not diversified, as is the Chinese economy.[141]

One of the reasons Westerners misread China's authoritarian-like economic prosperity is by design. The Communist regime likes to compare itself to commercial brands with which "Westerners are familiar." For example, Mitter and Johnson call out the United Kingdom's 5G infrastructure rollout, delivered by the giant Chinese firm Huawei, which the firm labeled the "John Lewis of China," an effort to associate with the popular British department store known for trusted brands.[142]

Contrary to the myth that democracy is necessary for an economy to prosper, China demonstrates that authoritarian governance can realize prosperity.

4. "Authoritarian political systems can't be legitimate."

The second myth, according to Mitter and Johnson, is that "authoritarian political systems can't be legitimate." To the contrary, the Communist Chinese believe their totalitarian form of government is both legitimate and successful. However, as Mitter and Johnson observe, the West fails to appreciate that even authoritarian governments can play many legitimate political and economic roles—such as investor, regulator, and intellectual property owner—and still enjoy prosperity.[143]

China has a long history of centralized control, as examined in chapter 1. As Mitter and Johnson observe, "China has often had to fight off invaders and, as is rarely acknowledged in the West, fought essentially alone against Japan from 1937 until 1941, when the US entered World War II." Of course, as explained earlier, once the Japanese surrendered, the CCP and KMT restarted their civil war, which resulted in KMT leader Chiang Kai-shek retreating to Taiwan and the CCP establishing its legitimacy and authority by forming the People's Republic of China.

Most Chinese believe their long history of centralized government control is appropriate for the modern world and more effective than those found in the West. Further, the Chinese way is different than other authoritarian regimes because it isn't just Marxist, but also Leninist, a significant distinction. "A Marxist system is concerned primarily with economic outcomes," Mitter and Johnson rightly explain. However, China's government controls the political as well. Specifically, Leninism is essentially a political doctrine; "its primary aim is control." Therefore, as Mitter and Johnson explain, "a Marxist-Leninist system [PRC] is concerned not only with economic outcomes but also with gaining and maintaining control over the system itself."[144]

A Marxist-Leninist system is uniquely different from the typical authoritarian regime, especially when it comes to issues of business. That means the PRC welcomes foreign businesses and investors committed to mutually beneficial economic growth, but the Leninist system requires political control as an aspect of any joint venture. Specifically, when a Western firm seeks access to a Chinese market, it must transfer ownership of its intellectual property to the Chinese company, a firm condition, and permit political control as well.[145]

The Leninist approach is also used by the CCP to select future leaders. The Party cultivates competent leaders through a progressive training system that begins small, like running a town, and successful leaders advance to the province with the most effective serving on the Politburo. In other words, observe Mitter and Johnson:

> You can't become a senior leader in China without having proved your worth as a manager. China's leaders argue that its essentially Leninist rule book makes Chinese politics far less arbitrary or nepotistic than those of many other, notably Western, countries.[146]

Keep in mind, Leninist doctrine is a significant aspect of China's modern culture. CCP membership and getting into the university require applicants to take courses in Marxist-Leninist thought. Even social media such as apps like *Xuexi Qiangguo* (translated "Study and Make the Nation Great"[147]) teaches the basics about Marx, Lenin, and Comrade Xi, and so does the Chinese app "Xi Jinping Thought," the most popular smartphone app in China, which intends to immerse the Communist cadres in political doctrine.[148]

The PRC's authoritarian model builds trust across the citizenry unlike anything we in the West might understand. Mitter and Johnson illustrate the point by calling out actions by the Chinese city of Rongcheng. That municipality uses government data gained through surveillance to award "social credit scores." These "scores" are open doors to citizens according to their political and financial virtues. For example, a good financial score gives the citizen access to certain loans, and a good social score grants the citizen access to the best transportation options. Westerners are appalled by such a system, but for the Chinese, it's part of their social contract with the state.[149]

The authoritarian Marxist-Leninist system, according to Mitter and Johnson, is widely embraced in China and deemed effective for economic and political outcomes.[150]

5. "The Chinese live, work, and invest like Westerners."

The third myth, "The Chinese live, work, and invest like Westerners" is misleading as well.

Chinese citizens and their state approach to decision-making is quite different from Westerners, in terms of time and risk. Mitter and Johnson argue this myth is the least understood by Westerners.[151]

The Chinese and their government both tend "to apply a higher discount rate to potential long-term outcomes than to short-term ones," Mitter and Johnson explain. Not that the Chinese aren't concerned about long-term outcomes, but their risk tolerance tends to diminish with time. Therefore, this cultural phenomenon influences their long-term commitments.[152]

This is contrary to Western thinking, especially when it comes to investments. Unlike American investors, Chinese consumers prefer short-term gains in the stock market than investing in long-term equities. That is borne out in a 2015 survey that found four in five (81 percent) of Chinese investors trade at least once a month, even though frequent trading is invariably riskier. That compares with only 53 percent of US individual investors who embrace riskier paths. This suggests that for the Chinese investor, long-term unpredictability is less preferred than taking the short-term payoff.[153]

Individual and CCP decisions about investment really echo Chinese civilizational issues concerned with security and stability in an unpredictable world. This mindset tracks back to China's turbulent, violent history. The Chinese psyche resonates with the past threat posed by foreign powers, such as the two Opium Wars with the more modern United Kingdom and France, and the occupation by Japan (1937–1945) that contributed to what is known as China's earlier-mentioned Century of Humiliation. That history colors Chinese foreign policy and its obsession with "the inviolability of its sovereignty."[154]

So, Chinese history explains why both citizens and the CCP operate on a very different decision clock compared to their peers in the West. They are taught about their past that denied them control, which influenced them to make choices in a much more short-term way. Meanwhile, Chinese policymakers, mostly Leninists, look for ways to gain more control over the future; as a result, they play a much longer game than do Western nations. Both individual and government approaches favor an authoritarian system, one in which control is key.[155]

By comparison, many in the West accept without reservation the view that China presents, and that it almost always uses, propaganda to hide the truth about the CCP. What's clear is that since the beginning of the Chinese Communist regime (the PRC) in 1949, it plays a central role in every Chinese institution and the lives of its citizens. It is an authoritarian, Marxist-Leninist government. Unless we in the West begin to understand the truth about Communist China, we will continue to misunderstand our primary adversary, a clear violation of the ancient Sun Tzu's principle of knowing your enemy.

CONCLUSION

President Xi and the CCP style themselves as modern-day Manchus who are charged with bringing together a vast multicultural and otherwise diverse population. They rewrite history to make the Qing Dynasty template help them spawn nationalism that "rejuvenates" the Chinese into One China, an outcome the Qing emperors were able to accomplish, albeit as they used the sword to expand the empire's geographic boundaries.

Chapter 3 examines President Xi's aim to create a new world order. What does it mean, and what's his plan to accomplish that outcome?

3

President Xi, the Hand Behind Him, and the Plan for a New World Order

Corruption could lead to the collapse of the Party [Communist Party of China] and the downfall of the state [People's Republic of China].[156]

—Xi Jinping (2013)

We begin with an introduction of President Xi and his source of power, the CCP. How does that relationship work, and why? We then consider Xi's/the Party's view of the current world order and outline their vision for China's new world order and the ingredients of that plan.

UNDERSTANDING XI IN THE CONTEXT OF THE CCP

A Westerner would read a biography about a leader to understand his or her motivation. However, reading Mr. Xi Jinping's biography wouldn't help without first appreciating the role the CCP played in his development and the fact that President Xi is more of a servant to the evil nature of Chinese Leninism than the dictator of Communist China.

The Western press doesn't help us understand that distinction. Rather, most Western journalists report on Mr. Xi as they would on the chief executive of any European country. However, he isn't at all like his European peers.

Consider the reporting that emerged about Mr. Xi from the CCP's one hundredth birthday celebration on July 1, 2021.

President Xi addressed more than seventy thousand of the faithful gathered at Beijing's Tiananmen Square to mark the CCP's centennial birthday. He spoke in strident tones to rouse patriotic passions about the Party's successes both at home and abroad, such as eliminating rural poverty and resisting imperialist aggression.

On that occasion, Mr. Xi was dressed in a characteristic Mao tunic suit as he spoke from a podium atop the Gate of Heavenly Peace, the main gate at Tiananmen Square. The Chairman used the opportunity to promise that never again would China be humiliated by foreign powers, as it was during the nineteenth and twentieth centuries in what many attending the celebration recalled as the Century of Humiliation, the earlier-mentioned time when Europeans and Japanese conquered China and extracted heavy reparations. No, Mr. Xi explained, the Chinese people "will never [again] allow any foreign force to bully, oppress, or enslave us." Then he outlined the consequences should they try to repeat that humiliation. They "shall be battered and bloodied from colliding with a great wall of steel forged by more than 1.4 billion Chinese people using flesh and blood," Xi soberly warned.[157]

President Xi also spoke to China's diaspora to encourage them to contribute to the "great rejuvenation of the Chinese nation," his nationalist credo. It's his view that China's authority extends across the world, especially to those whose hearts pump Chinese blood.[158]

The centennial celebration showcased Xi's achievements as the chief executive of the world's most populated country that confronts a host of domestic and foreign challenges. But the occasion was about more than touting past accomplishments; it was also about charting Xi's path ahead and cementing his presumed third term as Party chief (chairman) and PRC president. Therefore, it was an opportunity for Xi to spin the narrative of his indispensability to China's future success and cast himself as the pilot for the PRC's alternative to the West's international order.[159]

Ultimately, Mr. Xi spoke over the heads of those at Tiananmen Square and the millions watching on television. His intended audience was the Communist Party's ninety-five million members—especially the power brokers who set the course for the Party and, in particular, his selection for a third term as general secretary of the CCP (and as president of China), an unprecedented decision since founder Mao's death in 1976. As of this writing, his third term is scheduled to begin in November 2022.

It did appear, based on the intensive preparations for the 100th anniversary, that Xi's third term is a foregone decision, as is the necessity for the Party to use such occasions to shape the public's perception of China's leaders. After all, Mr. Xi reminded the audience of his deep family roots in the Party's revolutionary heritage and his repulsion for liberal (read "Western") values, but there was no mention in his speech of the regime's many setbacks, such as Mao's deadly Cultural Revolution and the 1989 Tiananmen Square massacre.[160]

"Long live the Chinese Communist Party, great, glorious and correct," Mr. Xi said to conclude his speech before flag-waving patriots as military jets roared overhead. "Long live the Chinese people, great, glorious and heroic."[161]

The celebration was about sending messages and Party rule. However, the CCP's assembly is far more substantive and secretive regarding the future of President Xi and the Party. In early November 2021, the CCP hosted the Sixth Plenum, a four-day meeting of the Party's leadership. That conference issued, as mentioned in the previous chapter, the Party's third-ever resolution on its (rewritten) history, which upheld President Xi's leadership and reiterated support for his reforms, a tacit endorsement for a third term in office.[162]

The rewritten Party history elevates Xi to a stature alongside founder Mao Zedong and Deng Xiaoping, the Party's chief economic architect.

The CCP's communique from the Sixth Plenum states that under Mr. Xi's leadership China has "made historic achievements and undergone a historic transformation" in terms of economics, foreign policy, and even containment of the deadly COVID-19 virus.[163]

The message of the revised Party history confirmed that Mr. Xi is its irreplaceable core leader and downplayed his challenges while lauding a century of Party accomplishments and touting socialism as the best course for China's future.

The communique also echoed the revised history to lavishly praise Mr. Xi's policies, especially since his taking the Party's reigns in 2012. It called out his efforts to retool the economy, reduce pollution and poverty, and attack corruption. The statement from the CCP leadership said Xi has shown "enormous political courage."[164]

The rewritten history and a glowing communique appear to confirm that President Xi will get a third term. However, it doesn't mean that he is like Mao. In fact, Xi's hold on power is not a given. After all, consider that the summary of the 2021 Plenary Session was delayed almost a week, which is quite unusual for that publication. Why? Some scholars indicate there is an ongoing struggle—infighting among CCP factions—that caused the delay.

"Xi Jinping wants to be the second Mao Zedong," explained Feng Chongyi, a professor at the University of Technology Sydney, Australia. Unlike Mao, Mr. Xi has many enemies. Professor Chongyi continued: "The officials, who are loyal to [former CCP leaders] Jiang Zemin and Hu Juntao, are in strong opposition and are trying their bests [sic] to prevent Xi's next possible term."[165]

Lee Yeautarn, a professor at the Graduate Institute of Development Studies at National Chengchi University, PRC, is skeptical as well. "It's not confirmed that Xi Jinping can take another term," argued the professor. He continued, "Before the 20th CCP rubber stamp conference, his priority is fighting his political opponents." However, other scholars disagree.[166]

Tang Jingyuan, a US-based China affairs commentator, said the content of the Plenary's summary portrayed Xi in a positive light. Tang is confident in a third term for President Xi because "he agreed to give some powers to the opponents."[167]

What is clear is that the Sixth Plenary Session, November 8–11, 2021, in Beijing, was characterized as a struggle. In fact, state-run media described it as a "hot debate." Professor Feng said the use of the word "debate" is serious and likely means the factions could not agree on key issues facing the CCP. The session's summary report explains the context of the inter-party tension—"debate"—when it describes the "extremely heavy and hard tasks to control the COVID-19 pandemic and develop the economy and society inside China."[168]

On November 8, 2021 the *People's Daily*, the CCP's mouthpiece, published a front-page editorial citing corruption among officials as one of the Party's challenges. President Xi is quoted in that article as stating: "There's no 'iron-cap prince' when it comes to anti-corruption," a reference to an official who has so much power that he is never held accountable. Mr. Xi continued, "The corruption is getting worse and worse, and will definitely disintegrate our Party and our regime in the end."[169]

"Xi worries far more about the political conflicts than the Chinese people's livelihood and foreign affairs," Professor Lee explained. He continued, "Any intensified conflicts will worsen the factions' strugglings." Evidently, Lee understands the forces gathering steam against Mr. Xi.

In early 2022, President Xi really began to worry about his personal future because he has genuine opposition within the Party elite. Gregory Copley, president of the International Strategic Studies Association, said Xi has an "enormous array of domestic enemies." After all, Mr. Xi created that opposition in exchange for the CCP chairmanship. He took power from others and, in the process, jailed tens of thousands of Communist Party opponents in his purge, what he called "anti-corruption" campaigns.[170]

Recently, Mr. Xi used the COVID pandemic to leverage more power. Mr. Copley wrote, "Xi's 'zero COVID' policy is, indeed, less about stopping the spread of COVID and more about suppressing his internal enemies, both in the public and in the Party." However, he is most vulnerable in his handling of the country's economy, which could end up being the reason he doesn't get a third term in Beijing.[171]

There is genuine panic in Beijing about the sagging economy, as evidenced by the regime's decision to inject almost $1 trillion in new credit in January 2020. And, as Gordan Chang, a China expert, wrote, Chinese technocrats used "shadow stimulus" to provide "local governments and their entities in order to allow the central government [PRC] to avoid reporting spending."[172]

China's troubled economic situation has the attention of many within the CCP elite. We got a glimpse of that distress in an article, "An Objective Evaluation of Xi Jinping," subtitled, "The Ark and China," or "Fang Zhou and China" (方舟與中國). That January 2022 piece is attributed by Mr. Chang to be the work of "several members of the Communist Party's Shanghai Gang faction, headed by former leader Jiang Zemin."[173]

Predictably, "Fang" attacked Xi for ruining the Chinese economy. "Xi will be the architect of his own defeat." Further, according to Fang, "His [Xi's] style of governance is simply unsustainable; it will generate even newer and greater policy missteps." Geremie Barme with the Asia Society agrees with Fang: "Xi's policies have been retrogressive and derivative, his successes minor and his blunders numerous."[174]

Could a flagging economy be the reason the CCP pulls the plug on granting Xi a third term as general secretary? After all, it's uncommon for the CCP elite to air dirty laundry in public, which is no doubt the reason Xi sees that he is in a real struggle and his future might be in doubt.[175]

That doubt could also become the spark that plunges all of us into a new war. Gordon Chang suggests that Xi is indeed targeting the United States, and he quotes an August 2021 article in the *People's Daily* that accuses America of launching "barbaric" attacks on China. The same Chinese tabloid published an earlier article that suggests the US was working with China's "enemies," no doubt a reference to Taiwan's democratic government.[176]

Such saber-rattling isn't new. In 2019, the CCP declared in the *People's Daily* a "people's war" on America, an effort being fanned today because Mr. Xi needs a distraction at home away from his performance and political detractors.[177]

Besides a troubled economy, Chairman Xi has a range of other difficulties: the ongoing US-China trade dispute, South China Sea sovereignty disputes, unifying Taiwan, transforming Hong Kong into a Communist city, and many more.[178]

The Party also faces growing international opposition. Yen Chien-Fa, the deputy executive officer of Taiwan Foundation for Democracy, said: "The Chinese regime is more and more isolated in the international community. Not only the United States, [but] the whole world is against it."[179]

All the fanfare about President Xi and the crises twirling around his political future and Beijing really miss the point, however. After all, Mr. Xi is not China's latest emperor, much less another Chairman Mao. No, at best, he is China's chief servant answerable to the Communist Party's elite, the real power source in Beijing, a perspective worth exploring.

Consider that unique perspective about Xi, the CCP's chief servant, as explained by Kerry Brown, the director of the Lau China Institute at King's College London and an associate for Chinese affairs at Chatham House, an independent policy institute in London. Mr. Brown lived in China for thirty years working in education, business, and government. His 2017 *Asian Affairs* article, "The Powers of Xi Jinping," introduces a seldom-heard perspective on the topic of President Xi and the CCP.

Mr. Brown argues that "Xi's powers are intrinsically linked with the organization that he leads and which his power is sourced in—the Party itself." Translation: Mr. Xi is not a modern emperor like Mao; rather, the CCP "acts as the all-seeing, all-powerful rule. In this model, Xi is its servant, not its master."[180]

You will recall from chapter 2 that I argued Xi seeks to emulate Qianlong, one of the great Qing Dynasty emperors, and to associate with the best aspects of that dynasty's Manchu leaders. Even former President

Barack Obama praised Xi's greatness, stating that China's president is "the most powerful leader modern China has seen since Mao Zedong." Yet other leaders named Mr. Xi "the chairman of everything," and he is frequently granted the ultimate accolade, one as powerful as Mao Zedong, which is a gross distortion of CCP history.[181]

A quick study of Mao's record disputes the compliments too often attributed to Xi. Mao was present at the first CCP Congress in 1921, he survived the Party's 1927 purge, and, as the Party leader, he fought in terrible wars, such as against the Japanese occupation that claimed twenty million Chinese lives. Then he guided the Party in the civil war against the KMT nationalists and emerged victorious to found the People's Republic of China in 1949.[182]

Xi is a nobody without the CCP. Brown states, "He is there because he is its servant." No doubt Xi worked hard and long to earn his position—"since his late teens," explained Brown. He spent his childhood interacting with his father who, at one point, was a high-level government official in the PRC's propaganda department. However, his father was arrested and spent two decades in house arrest. Meanwhile, Mr. Xi applied ten different times before he was admitted to the Communist Party in 1973. Since his admission, Mr. Xi has remained a faithful Party servant.[183]

Mr. Brown wisely cautions the reader:

Instead of asking who Xi is, what does he stand for, what does he believe in, it is best to take a step back and ask what is the party he belongs to, what does it stand for, what does it believe in?[184]

It is Brown's view that the CCP operates as a corporate body. "It has an identity, a culture, a discourse, [it is] a world within a world." That's not just Brown's view, but the perspective of one of China's current members of the Politburo Standing Committee of the CCP.[185]

Liu Yunshan is one of the seven members of the CCP's Standing Committee. His entire career has been the management of the CCP's propaganda apparatus, which puts him in the position to understand the Party and how it operates. Liu explained the CCP, according to Brown, "is a repository of the hopes and aspirations of the Chinese people. It is the expression of the cultural, social and political values of Chinese society, a force with a historic mission to deliver China to a moment of historic rectification, when the century of humiliation from the First Opium War after 1839 would be rectified and China return to its place at the center of world affairs." He continued, according to Brown, by stating that it is "not like a political party in the West." Liu explained the CCP is able to embrace the left and the right, the high and the low. It is "almost like a world within a world."[186]

The CCP, to some Western analysts, was a "state within a state," because it was a "subterfuge," a "victimized entity" that had to "create its own support structures, and protective walls," writes Brown. In the 1930s, under Mao's tutelage, the CCP differentiated itself from the Soviet Union's Marxist-Leninist approach because, unlike mostly urbanized Russia, China's population at the time was agrarian. According to Brown, the Chinese adapted their form of Marxism-Leninism to a *sui generis* nature: "a rule, in many ways, to itself."[187]

The CCP experienced significant and rapid change, first as the victor in the civil war with the KMT (1949), then it had to figure out how to govern—morphing from revolutionary to a governing entity. However, despite this transition, as Brown explains, Mao "never quite lost the zealous desire for social mobilization and change," such as his nineteen mass movements culminating in the Cultural Revolution (1966–1976)—or, as Chinese writer Ba Jin wrote to label Mao's work, "a spiritual holocaust."[188]

Everyone, especially the Party elite, suffered under Mao's ongoing "holocaust," and meanwhile, the state within a state, the CCP, became ruler over a vast society.[189]

Brown asks at this point: "What is the [Chinese] Communist Party in the 21st century?" It didn't follow the same path as the Soviet Union's Communist Party, which succumbed in 1991. No, the Chinese

Communist Party was always different from its Soviet counterpart. Those differences are reflected in the Chinese psyche, Brown explains.[190]

That unique psyche allowed the Party and, by association, the Chinese people to make a radical turn after 1978, a turn from a mostly agrarian, socialist economy to "embrace the free market, foreign capital and entrepreneurialism," what Brown calls "a stupendous money-making machine." That society by the mid-2000s morphed seemingly overnight from a dictatorship of the proletariat to "the most phenomenal wealth-creation organization the world has ever seen." The transformation was staggering, and once China entered the World Trade Organization (2001), its productivity "went truly ballistic." Its economy "quadrupled in size over the next two decades."[191]

Into the abyss of abundance, Chinese society slid, however. Literally, the transformation was earth-shaking, as Brown described how "at one point, Shanghai had more [construction] cranes than the rest of the world put together, putting up 2,000 tower blocks over 20 stories high." The rapid change to material enrichment muted the influence of Marxism-Leninism, said Brown, and the "Party's ethical basis" took a fall.[192]

Those were "the fat years," a time of incredible decadence with new billionaires who "had so much money they could paper their walls with it." At that time, when the Party was "swamped in material excess," corruption also became "endemic" to the point, explains Brown, "when Chinese officials are not corrupt, everyone else regards them with suspicion, and wonders what is wrong with them."[193]

That reality created a steep cost to the Party—a collapse of public trust. Corruption was endemic at the time because everyone was on the take, writes Brown. There were reports that the family of then-Premier Wen Jiabao offloaded state enterprises for billions of dollars, and meanwhile, capital vanished as it flowed out of the country to secret bank accounts. Brown explained that sectors like telecoms, energy, and housing became personal fiefdoms, and the Party became more like a coalition of business networks—a Chinese mafia—with no evidence of its founding mission.[194]

It was into this context that Xi Jinping entered the political stage, amidst great wealth, which was beginning to dry up by 2012. At that point, Premier Li Keqiang said the "country had to rebalance its model." It needed, according to Li, to "wean itself off export-oriented manufacturing for foreign markets" and "start to service the 'spaces of growth' within the country." Mr. Xi's task was to "do something urgently about equity and efficiency—the gross imbalances between the rich and the poor." Catching its breath, the Party had to "start sounding, and acting, like it had a belief system and a moral order—even if it was creating this as much from scratch as the cities that were being thrown up across the country which were appearing from nowhere."[195]

The move to pull back, rebalance, was a decision by the CCP's collective leadership, not the decision of one man. The Fifth Generation of the CCP's leadership faced the task of transitioning from a badly damaged Party with little moral compass to a better place. That's where Xi comes to the rescue.

Mr. Brown writes about a truly cynical view of Xi—a naïve, faithful Marxist who believes in the CCP's original mission. After all, Mr. Xi never was a member of the Party's super-wealthy elite. No, as Brown writes, he was a "B-grader—a member of a secondary-level family, not one of the grand clans." In other words, Mr. Xi came from China's backwoods with his primitive belief in the Party's moral mission, a man who avoided the lure of big money that tainted so many of the elite CCP members.[196]

The big-money Communist elite needed someone like Xi, a true ideologue and squeaky clean from corruption. So, the Party found him, a man with "a naïve, visceral faith in its function, its purpose and its so-called historic mission."[197]

The Party recruited with Xi someone who would return the Party—and, by association, China—"back to basics"—sort of the Forrest Gump of the Chinese, someone who rose through the ranks, void of the allure of big money and a man who really believed in service.[198]

Part of Mr. Xi's solution for his wayward Party was a return to its ideological roots, Marxism-Leninism. He advocated forced indoctrination, and that began with the Party's own now nearly ninety-five million members via reeducation at the more than two thousand Party schools found across the country. It was regarded as such an emergency that those schools began inculcating the members with "a new ideological and moral mission."[199]

It doesn't matter whether the CCP members really hold those views deep in their soul, argued Brown. After all, most Party officials have only a modicum of understanding about Chinese socialism. No, what's important for the members is that they act as "a faith community" that reflects ideological unity and discipline. That was Deng's view as well. In his time, Deng explained that Marxism had a utility: "It created simplifying adherence and fidelity where there might, if relaxation happened, be the dreaded instability and chaos."[200]

It was the "faith community" aspect, all members embracing a "closed set of ideas," that mattered. Only then could the Party lift "China outside the highly tribal...social structure," a view once posited by Fei Xiaotong, the father of modern Chinese sociology. Chinese society, wrote Fei, was truly agrarian in nature, where everyone knew everyone else, a place where contracts and laws were not necessary. It was "a society of elastic bonds, with the individual, selfish, all-controlling, sitting at the center." This was a problem for the Communist elite because trust wasn't in the state, Party, or neighbors. Rather, four in five Chinese by far trusted only their family members, a feeling of family connectedness that, in Chinese, is *renqing* (人情, "human relationship").[201]

Destroying the *reinqing* was a problem for the CCP, as it was for the Soviet Communists. They wanted the Party to trump all other entities. However, its efforts to erode the family's influence failed. Campaigns beginning with Mao's Cultural Revolution and those of Deng, Jiang, and Hu attacked family links to limited success. Even Xi's anti-corruption efforts targeting debased families to create a society "ruled by law, not by men" proved unattainable.[202]

Here are the questions we must ask at this point: Is Xi's time in office an exception to the rule? Will his efforts to attack societal decay and chart a new path likely to result in a very different outcome?

The short answer is "No." Chances are that Mr. Xi's "Four Comprehensives," his formula to chart a new path, is a contrarian view for the political scientists watching modern China. After all, political science suggests that a one-party structure should collapse in the face of the Four Comprehensives, which are: build a moderately prosperous society; deepen reform; govern the nation according to law; and strictly govern the Party.[203]

So far, the one-party structure survives, and in the context of China, we better understand that Xi is little more than a servant political figure, Brown argues. Mr. Xi isn't a dictator like Mao, but the Party's front man kept on a tether, representing the CCP's elite core, which he serves well—like a pet monkey.

Further, and this is important to understand: Xi's CCP minders aren't myopically focused on economic performance alone, but on a grander vision of the future, their One China goal that addresses rejuvenation. That explains Xi's carefully choreographed speech at the 100th anniversary celebration and the Party's revised history.[204]

THE MAKING OF PAST WORLD ORDERS AND THE CCP'S ONE CHINA GOAL

We must consider the genesis of past world orders and how and why they emerged before considering President Xi's (albeit the CCP's) efforts to remake our current world order into the Communists' image.

The emergence of a world order has a spotty history. Michael Beckley, a professor at Tufts University, writes:

The strongest orders in modern history—from Westphalia in the seventeenth century to the liberal international order in the twentieth—were not inclusive organizations [nations] working for the greater good of humanity.

Quite the contrary. They were the construct of great powers to contain their rivals.[205]

"Today, the liberal order is fraying for many reasons," wrote Professor Beckley in *Foreign Affairs*. He continued, "but the underlying cause is that the threat [the current world order] was originally designed to defeat—Soviet communism—[which] disappeared three decades ago." The primary reason our current liberal world order is still around is that no new threat has emerged to force a change, perhaps until now, and that new threat is the Peoples Republic of China.[206]

The Communist Chinese are stirring the global cauldron, frightening countries and carving out more of the world to fit its authoritarian ambition. We haven't seen such a global threat since the old Cold War (1947–1991)—at least, not one that endangers our collective security, welfare, and way of life.

The PRC's bullying across the world is forcing democracies, mostly representative republics, to devise strategies to counter the hegemonic Chinese regime, and new coalitions and organizations are forming to push back at the authoritarian monster's rabid moves. That growing global response to the hegemonic regime in Beijing is a natural reaction, one intending to shut the Chinese out of the current, frayed liberal world order—a movement seen across much of recent history. Kyle Lascurettes, an international relations theorist at Lewis & Clark College in Portland, Oregon, wrote that the major orders of the past were "orders of exclusion" assembled by the major world powers to stiff-arm their rivals.[207]

The concept of shutting out a rival from a "world order" perhaps dates back to what's called the "Sallust's Theorem," which Professor Beckley explained is named "after the ancient historian [Gaius Sallustius Crispus (86–35 BC)] who argued that fear of Carthage held the Roman republic together." Carthage was the capital of the Carthaginian civilization, located on the Lake of Tunis in present-day Tunisia, in northern Africa.[208]

Fear of reprisal evidently is a powerful potion that drove states and people together for mutual protection, as evidenced across history. For example, "In 1648, the kingdoms that won the Thirty Years' War enshrined rules of sovereign statehood in the Peace of Westphalia to undermine the authority of the Catholic Church and the Holy Roman Empire," wrote Beckley. He also cited the 1913 Treaty of Utrecht to contain France; the Concert of Europe, the post-Napoleonic peace established in 1815; and the Treaty of Versailles, which created the post-First World War, interwar order to contain Germany and the upstart Bolshevik Russians.[209]

More recently, the Cold War (1947–1991) gave us a new world order that was created to exclude and "outcompete Soviet communism." During those years, the West created numerous international organizations to oversee cross-nation issues that excluded Russia, such as the International Monetary Fund, the World Bank, and General Agreement on Tariffs and Trade—all, as Professor Beckley wrote, "to rebuild capitalist economies and, later, to promote globalization."[210]

These international initiatives were aimed at defeating the former Soviet Union, which evidently worked. Once the Soviet Union collapsed in 1991, the victors of the Cold War kept their global-order formula in place, and for the subsequent decades, their institutions mushroomed into an international state of hyperglobalization.

Yes, the proponents of the post-Cold War liberal order evidently expected it to become the exception to the historical pattern. After all, G. John Ikenberry, a political scientist at Princeton University, said the global system's commitment to openness and nondiscrimination made it "hard to overturn and easy to join." Professor Beckley explained: "Any country, large or small, could plug and play in the globalized economy [world order]. ...[And it survived all these years because it] faced no major opposition" until now.[211]

Proponents of the current world order should have listened to the former Soviet official Georgi Arbatov, who warned an American audience in 1988: "We are going to do a terrible thing to you. We are going to deprive you of an enemy." Indeed, that's exactly what the Soviets did when they removed themselves from the global stage and thus unleashed, as Beckley wrote, "all sorts of nationalist, populist, religious, and authoritarian opposition" that disrupts the post-Cold War order.[212]

The demise of the Soviet threat and the hyper-globalized world order brought us to the first meaningful threat to the current global order—the hegemonic Chinese Communist Party. That Marxist-Leninist entity acting as the overlord for the largest single ethnic population hates the current liberal global order and is doing everything it can to change the international establishment into something better aligned with its interests.

CHINA CONFRONTS THE CURRENT WORLD ORDER

President Xi and his CCP-minders don't favor the current pro-West world order. They are trying to reshape it to their liking, and, as I will argue in the next section, their aim is to create a new world order in their image—a frightening prospect.

President Xi's ambition and China's global prominence are beyond dispute; many observers agree that Beijing's Communist tyrants want to reshape the international order, as evidenced by a host of actions.

So far, China's actions to reshape international order are defensive, in part to deflect criticism of their political system. After all, Mr. Xi seeks to reshape the international order to surpass the US, not just in the Asia-Pacific region but across the world.

The current world order is a formidable network of US alliances now more than seventy years old, however. It came about after World War II and was shaped by liberal democracies committed to universal human rights, the rule of law, free markets, and limited state intervention. Around that framework arose multilateral institutions and international law intended to promote these values as well as the technology to bolster them.[213]

Mr. Xi and his CCP bosses want that to change to a world order in which state (autocratic) control prevails. In that reshaped world, nation-states govern institutions, laws, and technology to limit individual freedoms and control markets as well as the flow of information. All this happens without an independent check on their power, a Marxist-Leninist outcome.

Beijing is making progress at reshaping the world to its liking. After all, it appears that much of the world believes "the east [China] is rising, and the West is declining!" a view attributed to Xi's vision of the world.[214]

You will recall at the 2021 People's Congress, Chairman Xi presented himself as a self-confident leader advancing the idea that much of the world was coming to his side, and his actions appear to reflect that confidence. That hubris is accompanied by a host of actions.

Like his Qing emperor role model Qianlong, Mr. Xi is redrawing the map of China. In October 2021, he said: "The historical task of the complete reunification of the motherland must be fulfilled and will definitely be fulfilled." That means he intends to assert sovereignty over regions much in the news: Hong Kong, the South China Sea, and Taiwan—his number-one priority. Therefore, the PRC's actions with Hong Kong, the South China Sea, and his significant saber-rattling regarding Taiwan evidence the Chairman's redrawing efforts.[215]

Beijing is also laying a foundation for China to supersede the US as the dominant force in the Asia-Pacific region. Chinese leadership already employs rhetoric that assumes outcomes such as the Asia-Pacific is a "big family"; "the region cannot prosper without China"; and "China cannot develop in isolation from the region." There is as well the widely stated view that the region is integrated, thanks to Chinese-powered trade, technology, infrastructure, and civilizational links.[216]

Keep in mind that China is already the largest trading partner with most Asian countries. Further, in 2021, the members of the Association of Southeast Asian Nations collectively ranked China as their top trading partner. There is also China's move to join the Comprehensive and Progressive Agreement for Trans-Pacific Partnership, the Tokyo-led free-trade agreement, and, if accepted, Beijing would become the dominant member in the region's two most important trade agreements, essentially sidelining the United States.[217]

China is rapidly making progress at positioning itself to be the region's undisputed security actor, once again by pushing the US to the side. After all, in 2014, Beijing proposed a new Asian security structure and then sent its defense minister across the region to advance the view that Asia-Pacific countries "should adhere to the principle that regional issues should be solved by the regional countries through consultation." Of course, success there would exclude the US and its post-Cold War-alliance infrastructure.[218]

The Communist regime is reshaping the post-Cold War order through its ambitious Belt and Road Initiative (BRI) as well. That program started with President Xi's announcement in 2013, which invests Chinese funds in foreign governments to build infrastructure to mutually address the hosts' needs but also to expand Beijing's overland and maritime corridors connecting Asia with Europe, the Middle East, Latin America, South America, and Africa—a modern version of China's ancient Silk Road.[219]

The BRI plants China squarely in an important place in the international system, where it can significantly influence physical, financial, cultural, technological, and political issues. In a way, Beijing is using BRI to redraw the world with fixed infrastructure—roads, bridges, fiber-optic cables, ports, and much more. BRI touches 140 countries at present, and that number is growing to eventually reach most countries, beginning with infrastructure projects that bring to those shores Chinese technology and influence as well.[220]

Predictably, Chinese propagandists travel the world physically and virtually to advance the regime's influence, which is helped by BRI. For example, President Xi champions the establishment of Confucius Institutes to promote Chinese-language and culture. The placement of these institutes is paid for by Beijing, which makes it an easy sell across much of the world.

Evidently, the costs associated with planting Confucius Institutes are worth it, according to Li Changchun, a member of the Politburo's Standing Committee. Li explained:

> The Confucius Institute is an appealing brand for expanding our culture abroad. It has made an important contribution toward improving our soft power. The "Confucius" brand has a natural attractiveness. Using the dogma of teaching Chinese language, everything looks reasonable.[221]

Beijing plants these Institutes strategically across the globe to advance its interests. Beijing sets the conditions for the Institutes' contracts to include who teaches and the curricula taught. Further, the Institutes often are used as a platform to help shape university policies and, of course, it's not a coincidence that, in the United States, Confucius Institutes tend to crop up where high-tech and especially defense work takes place, facilitating technology theft.[222]

China also uses its economic leverage to coerce international businesses. After all, for Beijing Communists, Leninists, they always mix business with politics. That's why Beijing threatens airlines, retail firms, and even Hollywood studios with financial repercussions when they fail to adhere to the regime's mercantilist and ideological views about issues like Taiwan, Hong Kong, and the use of Uighurs for slave labor. Agree with the regime's political aims or face being shut out of the giant Chinese economy.

China's draconian, Leninist views about free speech regarding its actions are much in the news, especially in 2021. The US and other allies decided to stage a "diplomatic boycott" of the China-hosted 2022 Winter Olympics because of widespread allegations of Chinese atrocities against the Uyghur community. In fact, the US accused China of genocide in the Xinjian region, which Beijing denied.

Chinese officials dismiss such criticism as "political posturing and manipulation" to discredit the regime. Further, in late 2021, China's foreign ministry spokesperson, Zhao Lijian, warned:

The US should stop politicizing sports, and stop disrupting and undermining the Beijing winter Olympics, lest it should affect bilateral dialogue and cooperation in important areas and international and regional issues.[223]

China even uses its financial leverage when high-profile individuals dare to call out the regime for its serial human-rights violations. The case of the tweet by Daryl Morey, then the National Basketball Association Houston Rockets' general manager who supported Hong Kong's pro-democracy demonstrators, illustrates the point. Almost immediately after Morey's tweet, Chinese stores pulled Rockets-branded products from their shelves, and the state-controlled China Central Television stopped broadcasting NBA games. The television network announced, "We believe that any remarks that challenge national sovereignty and social stability are not within the scope of freedom of speech." The regime's message is clear: They have the right to control speech anywhere in the world.[224]

The Beijing Communists also seek greater control over global institutions—another reshaping effort. The intent, according to President Xi, is to transform global governance and especially the liberal values and norms that underpin the international system. Mr. Xi wants these institutions to reflect Chinese preferences, not the values of liberal democracies that advance individual political and civil rights.[225]

Chinese officials even pressure international organizations to align with Beijing's national interests, such as trashing any favorable actions for the democratic nation of Taiwan. Chairman Xi called for transforming global norms concerning the Internet and human rights to elevate the interests of the state over individual freedoms. In fact, China takes the offensive in such matters by actively seeking leadership positions in international institutions that exercise influence over such policies. That explains why the United Nations is actively considering Chinese proposals that support state control of the flow of information to every network-connected device in the world.[226]

What's clear from the above examples is that China is trying to reshape the world order to its liking. PRC officials argue that the United States' leadership on the global stage, especially its democratic alliance system, is a historical aberration that must be replaced. Mr. He Yafei, China's former vice minister of foreign affairs, demonstrated that view when he said, "The end of Pax Americana, or the American century is in sight." In fact, Shen Dingli, a scholar at Fudan University, Shanghai, claims that China is now occupying the "moral high ground" in the international community, and is acting as "the leading country in the new era."[227]

President Xi agrees that "the end of Pax Americana…is in sight" and, in fact, China's "rejuvenation" is "a historic inevitability." That bullish view is thanks in part to the regime's success at reshaping many aspects of the world order as outlined above. However, the question before us is: Are China's reshaping actions sufficient to create a new world order in the regime's image?[228]

Mr. Xi says he wants China to be perceived as "credible, lovable, and respectable" to the international community. However, according to international public opinion polls, the CCP—and, by association, leaders like Xi—enjoys dismal levels of trust, and there's little desire for more global Chinese leadership.[229]

Can Xi curry more international trust? At this point, he appears unwilling to compromise, perhaps because he's the servant of his Leninist CCP bosses who won't surrender core political and strategic priorities. Meanwhile, Beijing is facing an international backlash, according to a Pew Research Center Survey. For example, groups like the European Union identify China as a "systemic rival," and the North Atlantic Treaty Organization (NATO) is forming a response to Beijing as well.[230]

At this point, Beijing's elite are not in the mood to change course. The Communists and their "leader" Xi are banking on their strength, the West's weakness. As a result, they're demanding that the world accommodate Beijing's preferences.

Obviously, based on the material outlined above, China's efforts to reshape the current world order aren't going all that well. After all, the world community of nations isn't as malleable as the Sixth Plenum, the committee that rewrote the Party's history hoping to extend President Xi's term of office. No, the regime's efforts to rewrite world order in its own image might take nothing less than a major war to realize its vision for the future, which at this point isn't out of the question.

It's appropriate here for a sidebar on the China-Russia relationship, because Beijing needs international partners to rewrite world order, and Moscow is a willing ally.

In 2018, I wrote a book about this emergent relationship, *Alliance of Evil: Russia, China, the United States and a New Cold War*, which makes the case that we are indeed in a new cold war pitting the US and much of the West against Communist China and its authoritarian Russian ally. I believe the evidence of that cold war is stronger today than it was a few years ago. Specifically, consider the US-China Economic and Security Review Commission's (USCC) findings regarding the deepening of the Sino-Russian relationship over the past couple of years.[231]

Since 2019, a number of factors contributed to the deepening of the China-Russia relationship, such as diplomatic and economic friction with the West, according to the USCC report. In October 2019, for example, Russian President Vladimir Putin acknowledged the relationship when he labeled ties with Beijing as an "allied relationship in the full sense of a multi-faceted strategic partnership," what the USCC explained as "stronger language than either side had used before to describe the bilateral relationship."[232]

There is plenty of evidence that Presidents Putin and Xi are strengthening their ties in tangible ways. In 2021, total China-Russia trade reached $146 billion, making China Russia's largest trading partner. That total is expected to grow to $250 billion by 2024.[233]

Much of that trade is in terms of energy. Moscow is China's second-largest source of energy, after Saudia Arabia, and may soon become Beijing's leading source, thanks to the inauguration of a key gas pipeline project, the Power of Siberia (2019), according to the USCC, which promises to deliver to China twenty-eight million tons of natural gas per year beginning in 2024.[234]

Sino-Russian military exercises are also becoming commonplace. The first such exercise took place in 2005, "Peace Mission 2005," and since that time, the frequency of bilateral maneuvers increased to include the "West-Joint-2021," an exercise with Russian soldiers disembarking from Chinese armored personnel carriers.[235]

It's noteworthy that President Putin also made a decree that 2020 would be the year of Sino-Russian science and technology cooperation, an effort to boost their cooperation on dual-use technologies, such as with artificial intelligence. Meanwhile, in March 2020, Chinese telecom giant Huawei partnered with one of Russia's largest banks, Sherbank, to provide a cloud-service platform, and also promised to build an "artificial intelligence ecosystem" in Russia by 2025.[236]

The two countries also committed to work on far-reaching space projects. In July 2020, their space agencies agreed to work on building a research base on the moon, beginning with joint manned-moon missions this decade. They claim the moon base will serve dual-use purposes, monitor deep space, and enhance remote sensing of the earth—likely spying.[237]

Beijing and Moscow are collaborating on ideological issues, such as on the diplomatic front as well as regarding disinformation and anti-American messaging. Diplomatically, China and Russia almost always support one another at the United Nations and in other international forums. For example, they support each other on issues over Syria's regime and on topics such as space arms control and many more.

On the misinformation and messaging front, the Chinese and Russians are mutually supportive. Throughout the COVID-19 global pandemic, Chinese and Russian actors spread disinformation about the US and other Western democracies in part to deflect criticism of their own response to the pandemic. For example, Moscow defended Beijing from Western criticism about being the source of the virus as well as promoting conspiracy theories that other countries such as the US were really the origin of COVID-19 virus.[238]

One of the strongest indicators of the new China-Russia alliance was announced in the shadows of the 2022 Winter Olympics in Beijing. Before the opening of the games, Presidents Putin and Xi met for three hours and, although the word "alliance" is not found in the 5,400-word statement issued after their February 4 meeting, it's clear the countries are in an alliance.[239]

That China-Russia bilateral statement reaffirms the "new inter-State relations" are indeed "superior" to both the political and military alliances of the "Cold War era." Further, the joint declaration also confirms there is no daylight between the two countries on significant geopolitical issues—i.e., "Friendship between the two states has no limits, there are no forbidden areas of cooperation." In fact, China sides with Moscow in its standoff with the West, including NATO expansion and weaponry deployments to Eastern Europe. Further, Russia reaffirmed "its support for the [O]ne China principle, [which] confirms that Taiwan is an inalienable part of China, and opposes any forms of independence of Taiwan."[240]

Behind the fanfare, the Xi-Putin joint statement proclaimed a far more grandiose view for all autocratic leaders across the world. Six times the statement mentions the US and, in that context, the document calls for a "redistribution of power in the world," aka a new world order.[241] In fact, the *Washington Post* admitted the meeting was "a bid to make the world safe for dictatorship."[242] And, perhaps more ominous, Kevin Rudd, a former prime minister of Australia, told the *Wall Street Journal*: "The world should get ready for a further significant deepening of the China-Russia security and economic relationship."[243]

A key leader in Europe shares the view that China and Russia are seeking to "replace the existing international rules" with their own. European Union chief Ursula von der Leyen accused Moscow of a "blatant attempt" to revamp global order beginning with his war on Ukraine. She said that Russia and China want to "replace the existing international rules—they prefer the rule of the strongest to the rule of law, intimidation instead of self-determination."[244]

So, if the above evidence is laid out and objectively analyzed, it should now be crystal clear there is a new China-Russia alliance, and that isn't good news for the present world order—especially for freedom-loving people.

A NEW WORLD ORDER IN CHINA'S IMAGE: GOING TOWARD THE MID-21ST CENTURY

Creating a new world order may require a war, perhaps just one of the cold varieties across a spectrum of functional areas. That war—China and its allies like Russia versus the West (especially the US)—is well underway and warrants detailed development in the coming chapters. For now, consider China's war talk, its war plans, and the battlefields it intends to engage to create a new world order in its image.

Perhaps you don't believe we are already at war. Then how do you explain President Xi's stark and threatening "bloody" statements in his address to the Party's 100th anniversary in Beijing's Tiananmen Square?

Mr. Xi spoke boldly to the crowd as he boasted of the "great rejuvenation of the Chinese nation." But what he said next is particularly alarming: China has "created a new model for human advancement," which it intends to spread across the world, and simultaneously it is raising an armed force to "world-class standards." That's a serious implied threat.[245]

China, under Mr. Xi's Leninist dictatorship, is a real threat to the democratic world, and not just to free Taiwan. After all, Beijing's Leninists have great ambitions as well as the necessary aggressiveness, means (economic and military), and self-confidence to pursue their goals, which may include kinetic operations, aka a shooting war.

Mr. Xi's speech to the faithful at the Party's birthday celebration in Beijing was laden with nationalist arrogance, reflective of China's newly revealed "wolf warrior" style of diplomatic thinking and engagement experienced firsthand by Biden administration representatives at their first bilateral meeting in March 2021, where the Communists disdain-fully lectured American diplomats about human rights. The "wolf war-rior" term is attributed to a 2015 Chinese movie, *Wolf Warrior*, a patriotic action film with the famous punchline: "Whoever offends China will be eliminated, no matter how far away [犯我中華者 雖遠必誅]."[246]

"We have never bullied, oppressed or subjugated the people of any other country," shouted Xi to that nation's 2021 birthday audience. Of course, to believe such rhetoric, one must ignore China's persecuted, such as the Tibetans, the pro-democracy people in Hong Kong, millions of Uyghurs peering out of barred windows at Beijing's concentration camps, and many others.[247]

President Xi's threat was clear: "We will never allow any foreign force to bully, oppress or subjugate us"—a reminder of the Century of Humiliation that resonates among the Chinese masses to this day and an era the regime constantly references to advance its authority and stoke nationalism. Then, Xi warned, "anyone who would attempt to do so will find themselves on a collision course with a great wall of steel... [those enemies will] have their heads bashed bloody." The blood threat was real, and not just for the democratic nation in Xi's crosshairs sitting across the Taiwan Strait.[248]

China's authoritarians see an opportunity to go far beyond just reshaping the current world order. After all, the West is fragmented and lacks strategic direction. Mr. Xi and his CCP minders believe China is poised strategically to take over the world.

Further, President Xi has a long-term strategic vision; the economic might; a growing global network, thanks to BRI; and a global, all-domain capable military—all backed up by an aggressive, wolf-warrior foreign policy.[249]

So, what is China's plan to create a new world order to advance its own interests? Will that war with Communist China be hot or cold, or perhaps both, with China playing a twenty-first-century version of the role performed by the former Soviet Union?

We know what the CCP wants, based on many official public statements, according to Professor Mitter, writing in *Foreign Affairs*. The regime intends, states the professor, to rein in Chinese society (exercise ideological control), bolster consumerism (sustain, grow economically at home and abroad), expand its global influence (geopolitical), and develop and export its technology (technological hegemony). I'd add to this list "security," a broad collection of the means to prevail at home and abroad. But, as Mitter argues, "To understand where China could be headed, observers must pay attention to the major elements of Chinese power and the frameworks through which that power is both expressed and imagined."[250]

That's a common-sense statement. So, if China is at war with the West, as I've long argued, and Chinese leaders' statements consistently agree, then, as Mitter alleges, we must "pay attention to the major elements of Chinese power and the frameworks." Then we have a template to better understand how China's new world order may evolve, as well as how we in the West might respond.

Below are some pieces of China's strategy applied to a five-part framework: economy, ideology, security, geopolitics, and technology.

This framework is outlined below, and provides the starting point for the following chapters that detail Beijing's strategy and numerous actions intended to carry out President Xi's plan for a new world order in the CCP's image.

Economy

The CCP's premier economic aim is China's ascendancy as the world's dominant producer of industrial goods. Of course, that nation is already an economic superpower and uses its global BRI network to develop infrastructure controlled or at least influenced by the regime. The massive program already touches 140 countries, tapping into most economic sectors of those nations—energy, communications, and raw material resources.

Cornering the global market on commodities is an important Chinese goal, much as it has a chokehold on rare earth metals, the heart of high-technology manufacturing. Should Beijing acquire control over more critical commodities, it will then have the means to manipulate even countries like the United States.

Another aspect of China's war to build a new world order is closely related to a variety of economic and financial issues. Specifically, financial warfare is a key tool the CCP uses to remain mercantilists, having already manipulated its currency, *renminbi*, which is usually abbreviated as RMB. But ultimately, Beijing seeks to supplant the US dollar with the Chinese RMB (also called *yuan*) as the world's primary reserve currency and all that implies.[251]

The RMB does have official reserve-currency status from the International Monetary Fund. However, its share in global payments and central bank reserves is only about 2 percent, according to Bloomberg.[252]

There is a path ahead for Beijing's efforts to replace the dollar with the RMB, and the BRI might be the road China uses to leverage up to 140 countries toward the Chinese currency. That's done by decoupling Western companies and banks from capital markets and money flows. Meanwhile, China will try to entice capital and financial institutions to China to make a city like Shanghai the banking and financial capital of the world.

China's economic and financial leverage is an important part of its new world order strategy. However, it must enjoy the reinforcement from the ideological campaign.

Ideology

The CCP intends to fundamentally change the world order by replacing liberal democracies with authoritarian-like rule over all nations. To accomplish that goal, Beijing will use several ideological tools in its quiver.

Psychological warfare focuses on softening up the enemy for a killing blow. The CCP's psychological warfare efforts are coordinated across the regime's leadership, diplomatic corps, state-run media, academic institutions, and foreign allies to impede or discourage their opposition. Actions in this category take on many forms: predatory trade practices, economic espionage, diplomatic pressure, rumors, false narratives, harassment, misinformation, and much more.[253]

Legal warfare is a CCP tool Beijing uses in its ideological campaign. The Heritage Foundation states, "Legal warfare, at its most basic, involves 'arguing that one's own side is obeying the law, criticizing the other side for violating the law [*weifa*], and making arguments for one's own side in cases where there are also violations of the law.'"[254]

The CCP uses this ideological tool to undermine the current international system, especially the West's "rule of law," by propagating an alternative Chinese legal framework. For example, the CCP extends its national security law to all ethnic Chinese, regardless of their location across the globe, arguing that legal framework supersedes international law for millions in the diaspora.

The CCP also engages in information warfare, the control of data and information used by a modern society. Of course, every sector of a contemporary society depends on the timely and accurate flow of information. What the Communist Chinese intend to do is corrupt that information by promoting misinformation to gain economic and geopolitical advantages.

Effective information warfare leads to dominance over an adversary in knowledge and understanding. It can be used in virtually any context to gain advantage over a competitor, such as by using misinformation to manipulate the outcome of an election, something I document in my 2021 book, *Give Me Liberty, Not Marxism*.

Ideological warfare often precedes kinetic fighting, the use of bullets and bombs. Let there be no doubt that the CCP is preparing in a massive way throughout the entire world to employ military power across all domains—air, sea, land, space, and cyberspace—to acquire a new world order.

Security

The Pentagon publishes an annual report to Congress on the Chinese armed forces. The 2021 report includes a host of sobering declarations about the People's Liberation Army (PLA, China's armed forces). Those findings conclusively demonstrate that Beijing has geopolitical and security ambitions far beyond Asia. Below are a few of those findings:

- China seeks to "complete PLA modernization by 2035." That means a global-capable, all-domain, sophisticated military fully prepared to contest the US military.[255]
- The "PLA [is] developing capabilities to conduct joint long-range precision strikes across domains, increasingly sophisticated space, counterspace, and cyber capabilities, and accelerating the large-scale expansion of its nuclear forces."[256]
- The CCP announced a new "milestone for PLA modernization in 2027 broadly understood as the modernization of the PLA's capabilities to be networked into a system of systems for 'intelligentized' warfare." The report indicates this would provide Beijing with "more credible military operations in a Taiwan contingency."[257]

This is just the tip of Beijing's ambitious national security strategy/plan. It has a host of foreign-policy implications and addresses the expansion of the PLA across the world, as well as fuses all research efforts (government, academy, business, and military) into a fusion-development strategy. The Communists are serious about rapidly expanding their armed forces and making them the best in the world.

The security sphere is very broad, to include areas of warfare well beyond tanks, ships, and airplanes. Cyber warfare is very important to China's national security. The US Department of Homeland Security states:

Malicious cyber activities attributed to the Chinese government targeted, and continue to target, a variety of industries and organizations in the United States, including healthcare, financial services, defense industrial base, energy, government facilities, chemical, critical manufacturing (including automotive and aerospace), communications, IT (including managed service providers), international trade, education, video gaming, faith-based organizations, and law firms.[258]

Biological warfare is another security tool used by the Chinese Communists. There is little doubt that the COVID-19 pandemic had CCP fingerprints all over it. Further, we know the PLA has been conducting biological warfare research for decades, and the 2021 Pentagon report, for the first time ever, states:

The PRC has engaged in biological activities with potential dual-use applications, which raise concerns regarding its compliance with the Biological and Toxins Weapons Convention (BWC) and the Chemical Weapons Convention (CWC).

The report goes on to state:

Based on available information, the United States cannot certify that the PRC has met its obligations under the Chemical Weapons Convention (CWC) due to concerns regarding the PRC's research of pharmaceutical-based agents (PBA) and toxins with potential dual-use applications.[259]

There is reason other than COVID-19 to believe that the PLA is very much involved in biological warfare efforts. Specifically, Chinese military researchers write about a new type of biological warfare discussed in the 2017 edition of "The Science of Military Strategy," an authoritative publication of China's National Defense University. That publication calls out what the researchers label as "specific ethnic genetic attacks," which employ pathogens that leave Chinese citizens immune but sicken and kill all others.[260]

Security capabilities go hand in glove with a nation's geopolitical strategy. Often, a nation's power structures lean forward in a coordinated way to realize the country's broader geopolitical outcomes, such as bringing foreign nations into compliance with its agenda.

Geopolitics

China's geopolitical ambitions begin with redrawing that nation's map. In his October 2021 speech at Beijing's Great Hall of the People, President Xi said: "The historical task of the complete reunification of the motherland must be fulfilled and will definitely be fulfilled." Most anyone who follows events in China knows he meant asserting sovereignty over contested territories—Hong Kong, the South China Sea, and, of course Taiwan, Mr. Xi's number-one priority.[261]

Mr. Xi looks around the Chinese mainland and claims the entire Asia-Pacific for the PRC. He calls that collection of island nations a "big family," and, as said earlier in this chapter, "the region cannot prosper without China."

China's BRI is a very useful geopolitical tool across the world as well. It uses the leverage it buys in exchange for infrastructure projects to advance its interests—economic, ideological, and security—and even with international organizations like the United Nations.

The UN is supposed to promote human rights and democracy, but Beijing uses its leverage at that international body to deny democratic Taiwan sovereignty and participation. Meanwhile, China is one of the world's leading abusers of human rights, and too often it gets a pass because of its global influence.

Expect that, much like Russia's claim of sovereignty over former Soviet Union client states like Ukraine and the Republic of Georgia, the

CCP aims to expand its influence beyond its borders. It already did so with Hong Kong and the South China Sea. Soon, expect Beijing to put Taiwan in its sphere, and then—Katy, bar the door!—the Communist regime will grow globally.

The CCP is using its leverage—via economics, security, finances, and membership in international organizations—through intimidation, coercion, bribing, and other means to build a global alliance of partners aimed at a new world order. Another aspect of the range of capabilities China brings to the table is its growing technological edge; it seeks to become the world's dominant force in that area.

Technology

The PRC aims to lead the world in technology, and that's especially evident in what the regime calls the military-civil, fusion-development strategy. The regime fuses its economic, social, and security development strategies to build an integrated national strategic system to serve multiple goals. It seeks to develop and acquire dual-use technology for military purposes and to serve a broader purpose of strengthening all instruments of national power, especially on the economic front.

It's no joke that China has overtaken the US in several technological areas and is quickly catching up in other areas. This fact has serious economic, security, and geopolitical implications.

China is arguably ahead of the US military in terms of its hypersonic missile program, which can strike anywhere on the globe with a nuclear weapon, and which no one can defend against. It certainly may soon edge out the US in areas like artificial intelligence and quantum computing as well.

Nicolas Chaillan, who spent three years on a Pentagon-wide effort to improve cyber security, said he left his job in 2021 because of the slow pace of the Pentagon's technological transformation. He told the *Financial Times* that Beijing was on its way to global dominance in AI, cyber, and machine learning. In fact, he described some of the cyber defenses in the US government as "kindergarten level."[262]

The International Institute for Strategic Studies (IISS) indicates the Chinese as compared to the United States dedicate significantly more military cyber forces to conducting attacks. The IISS evaluated military trends based on forces identified with a responsibility for cyberspace operations to report that 18.2 percent of Chinese military cyber forces are focused on effects compared to 2.8 percent of US cyber personnel. That report indicates that the term "effects" generally refers to actions to "deny, degrade, disrupt or destroy as well as those conducted by proxies in conjunction with a government actor." Those "effects" can include capabilities such as "research vulnerabilities, write or use malware, and maintain command and control through exploits."[263]

The global race for significant technologies is very serious. Should China win that race, it will have the means to accelerate its effort to build a new world order to its liking.

CONCLUSION

This chapter examines the role of President Xi within the CCP—a servant of China, not the sole dictator. Mr. Xi and his minders have tried with some success to reshape the post-Cold War international order. However, much more, perhaps a new war—hot and/or cold, engaged across a broad swath of areas (battlefields both real and virtual)—is necessary if the Beijing regime is to successfully create the new world order it seeks. At this point, Beijing is progressing rapidly toward that goal.

The following chapters in *Kings of the East*—addressing economy, ideology, security, geopolitics, and technology—develop the framework just outlined in greater detail, to include the CCP's many accomplishments and its strategy for building its new world order. Some pieces of that strategy are already in place, and yet others are emerging.

Section II

CHINA'S FIVE-PART FRAMEWORK TO CREATE A NEW WORLD ORDER

China will always remain the builder of world peace, a contributor to global development, and upholder of international order.[264]

—Xi Jinping
19th Congress of the Chinese Communist Party (2017)

This section, in five chapters, drills down across critical tools used by the Communist Chinese to create a new world order.

Chapter 4 addresses President Xi's "China Dream," an economic plan to make the PRC a great economic powerhouse and to position it to lead the world economically.

Chapter 5 explains how the CCP plans not only to control its expansive, 1.4-plus billion population, but to use its global ideological influence to gradually and then totally control the future world.

Chapter 6 outlines China's accelerating campaign to field the world's largest and most sophisticated armed force. Under President Xi's leadership, the People's Liberation Army (PLA; China's armed forces) will be the vessel by which the CCP comes to intimidate and then dominate the world.

Chapter 7 demonstrates how Communist China is shedding its isolationist shell to delve into the international community and leverage sovereign countries to support the regime's aim of establishing a new world order in the PRC's Marxist-Leninist image.

Finally, chapter 8 addresses the fifth tool at Beijing's disposal for creating a new world order: technology. The regime is hell-bent on leading the world by mastering the technological revolution that will change all our lives and then land the CCP in the driver's seat of the new world order.

4

China Dream: An Economic New World Order

You foreigners are all too anxious to wake us and to start us on a new road. And you will do it. But you will regret it, for once awakening and started, we shall go fast and further than you think. Much further than you want.[265]

—Manchu statesman Wenxiang (1865)

Communist China's ambition is to realize an economic new world order in its image. This chapter explores that possibility, beginning with a review of the PRC's recent economic history, how it dealt with past success, and the challenges ahead. The chapter concludes with an analysis of nine tactical practices that contribute to the regime's aim to realize an economic new world order in its image.

FACING DOWN CHINA'S ECONOMIC CHALLENGES AT HOME

Since becoming the leader of the CCP in 2012, Xi Jinping promoted the economic goal of realizing the "China Dream," according to Martin K. Whyte, an American sociology professor at Harvard University writing in the *Chinese Sociological Review*. That goal remains elusive, even though the nation previously enjoyed a meteoric economic rise beginning in 1978. However, now in the third decade of the twenty-first century, the circumstances that fueled the regime's previous dramatic economic growth no longer work, and China now faces serious challenges.[266]

The central meaning of Xi's goal, China Dream, is that the country "should continue the extraordinary successes in economic development achieved in recent decades so that the nation can eventually become, at a minimum, a moderately prosperous society, and at a maximum, can resume its rightful place as the richest country in the world, surpassing the United States, Japan, and advanced European countries."[267]

Professor Whyte sets the context to understand the challenges President Xi faces regarding the achievement of his China Dream. That begins with a review of the country's economic development history, its unexpected economic boom after 1978, and the major obstacles ahead.[268]

We begin with a review of China's historical setting leading up to the eighteenth century. At that point, according to Whyte, China was the "most advanced civilization on earth." However, as pointed out in chapter 1, beginning with the eighteenth century, China began to lag behind Western countries, which left the Middle Kingdom behind technologically.[269]

China's metaphorical nose was bloodied by the British and French in the two Opium Wars (1839–1842 and 1856–1860), and then again as a result of the 1895 Sino-Japanese War. After all, Japan and many Western countries became modern industrial powers while China clung to the past and, as a result, experienced the Century of Humiliation.

China suffered defeat at the hands of Japan and European nations because, according to Professor Whyte, the proud Middle Kingdom refused to abandon its ancient civilization's practices and embrace the innovations attributed to the West's industrial revolution. That failure to reform resulted in a very mixed economic record in the twentieth century.

Professor Whyte highlighted China's uneven economic development, beginning with Mao's socialist economy (1949–1976), which was characterized as "major successes and disastrous failure." Some of those efforts were outlined in previous chapters, not to be repeated here.

Fast forward from the Mao era to what Professor Whyte calls the "world's most dynamically growing economy for more than 40 years after 1978." The professor argues that China's economic boom after 1978 "had multiple causes and benefited from a serendipitous combination of factors and historical contingencies." He highlights those factors:

> …the benefits to China of the changing nature of the Cold War, the ability of China to ignore the experts and plot its own distinctive path to dismantling the planned socialist economy, and a clever if pernicious strategy to draw on China's "socialist serfdom" institutions to power economic growth from the 1980s onward.[270]

CAN PRESIDENT XI REALIZE HIS CHINA DREAM IN THE 21ST CENTURY?

Today, in 2022, China's red-hot economy is slowing to about half the growth rate of a decade ago. That's a challenge for President Xi, who faces several serious challenges at home in his pursuit of the China Dream.

Professor Whyte won't predict whether Mr. Xi can help China perform another economic miracle like the country did beginning in 1978. There are, according to the professor, at least three major challenges to realizing the China Dream in the twenty-first century. They are:

> …the shift backward toward favoring state over private firms, the rapid aging of the population, and the obstacles to growth now stemming from China's 'hukou' [household individual] system.[271]

RETURNING TO A DESTRUCTIVE SOCIALIST ECONOMIC MODEL

The post-Mao China abandoned the mostly destructive socialist economic model, according to Whyte, to allow "more efficient and productive private and foreign-investment firms to blossom and become the main engines of growth and providers of employment, goods, and services." However, it appears that President Xi is abandoning the "most dynamic sectors of the economy" that brought about previous high rates of economic growth.[272]

President Xi is systemically swinging back the economic pendulum to increase the prominence of state firms with government support and less emphasis on private firms and a reliance on market forces. Further, Xi appears to favor increased state controls over foreign firms and is discouraging further privatization of agricultural land. Professor Whyte critically suggests that China's current declining economic growth is directly correlated with Xi's policies, a view shared by economist Nicholas Lardy with the Brookings Institution, who wrote: "Unless this favoring of less productive state firms is reversed in years ahead, maintaining strong economic growth will be difficult."[273]

CHINA'S DAUNTING DEMOGRAPHY

Another major challenge for Xi's China Dream is the country's daunting demography—the Chinese "are aging much more rapidly than other societies." The underlying problem is: "China is growing old before getting rich."[274]

A society needs considerable infrastructure and associated wealth to support an aging population, things modern China lacks. Specifically, one study cited by Whyte projects that the cost of providing for its elders will rise to 23 percent of the country's gross domestic product (GDP) by 2050. Should that projection become a reality, then there will be far less funds to meet other needs such as economic growth.[275]

An aging population poses other challenges for Xi's China Dream as well. The CCP leader calls for shifting from an export-driven to a consumer-driven economy, but that transition is more difficult because older people spend and consume less than young people. Further, due to China's past (1980–2015) one-child policy, the nation is experiencing a decline in the number of young people entering the labor force, which means higher wages for the fewer willing workers. It also means China's export-oriented manufacturing firms have a smaller profit margin (if any), and a shrinking labor force means lower taxes for the government and less consumer demand.[276]

Meanwhile, China is experiencing a serious decline in its fertility rate that could lead to an extremely severe demographic problem for the regime. Specifically, demographers at Xi'an Jiaotong University, Shanghai, announced that China may lose half of its population in forty-five years, and certainly by the end of the twenty-first century, China could be a third of its present population.[277]

The best contemporary evidence of this demographic implosion is found at the province level, primarily because the Beijing central government keeps such information close-hold. For example, in the Chinese province of Anhui in 2021, the number of births tumbled 17.8 percent from 2020, which prompted local officials to declare that the number of newborns was "falling off a cliff."[278]

Anhui is China's ninth-most-populous province, which provides insight into the nation's overall declining fertility rate. "The population situation is extremely severe…[the number of births] shows the overall trend is falling off a cliff," states the provincial government's draft regulation on family planning.[279]

Other Chinese provinces report declines as well. For example, the southwestern province of Guizhou said its birth rate had been "going down year by year" since 2017. Alarm about the declining fertility rates has official attention, and governments across the nation are stepping up efforts to increase births. Some local governments are disbursing subsidies for couples who have at least two children. Others are subsidizing childcare, and still others are covering the medical insurance for couples for a third child.[280]

ABANDONING CHINA'S ANCIENT *HUKOU* SYSTEM

China must overcome the impact on human capital created by its long-held *hukou* system, which fueled the nation's dramatic post-1978 boom. That system promises to doom Xi's China Dream. Let me explain.

The hukou system dates to China's ancient times. However, the current form started with Mao's 1958 PRC Hukou Registration Regulation, which required the classification of each citizen either as an agricultural or non-agricultural (rural or urban) hukou. One's classification (hukou status) came with benefits, especially for the urban citizen.[281]

The hukou system was previously necessary to fuel the nation's demand for cheap labor while maintaining a glass ceiling for rural citizens. Specifically, a rural citizen could migrate to an urban area to work in a factory, but his/her accompanying children were limited in schooling options in the cities. For example, until recently, rural hukou youth who lived in the city with their migrant parents were forbidden to enroll in local public schools without paying a prohibitively high fee.

This discriminatory practice of denying migrant children access to free public education is changing across China. However, the hukou rural children are still segregated from urban students at public schools and are not allowed to enroll beyond middle school. There are exceptions to the rule, but they are very expensive for migrant families.

This old CCP economic policy objective was intended to maintain a working class to fuel the nation's low-paying industrial requirements. The impact was predictable. For example, a 2005 study found that 90 percent of fifteen- to seventeen-year-old urban youths had some high schooling, compared to only 43 percent of rural children. Not surprisingly, virtually all Chinese college students are still classified as urban hukou youth.[282]

Why does China's distinction between rural and urban hukou matter? Well, President Xi is attempting to shift the country from manufacturing inexpensive goods for export to become a nation driven by "domestic consumption and by the service sector, and toward the manufacture of higher value-added goods requiring advanced technology."[283]

This transition necessarily targets the "middle-income trap" for elimination. Professor Whyte explains:

> The middle-income trap refers to a general stage in the economic transition of formerly agrarian societies when they have moved from being a poor to a middle-income country primarily by transferring rural labor to more productive urban manufacturing and other non-agricultural work.

Thus, for the PRC to join the ranks of rich countries, which is Xi's China Dream goal, the nation must then escape the trap. Specifically, the PRC's past "reliance on low-cost, minimally educated labor from the countryside to perform low-skill manufacturing and other non-farm jobs will no longer suffice," Whyte explained.[284]

That is a significant challenge facing President Xi. For China to produce high-quality and technology-based manufacturing goods and services in a long-term, competitive global market, it must have a large, well-trained work force. The hukou system worked decades ago, but is now producing a serious human capital deficit. So, according to Professor Whyte, Xi must rapidly eliminate discrimination in schools so more of those with the necessary talents and creativity can be harnessed to fuel his high-tech China Dream.[285]

CAN XI ADDRESS CHINA'S ECONOMIC CHALLENGES?

At the present, the court of international public opinion is out regarding whether President Xi can put China on the glide path toward a robust, highly competitive economy, given the challenges outlined above. After all, in 2021, China's economic growth dropped to levels not seen in decades, and even when the COVID-19 pandemic is accounted for, the PRC's economic momentum declined with GDP in the third quarter of 2021 at the lowest point in three decades.[286]

Put aside for now whether Xi has another economic miracle up his sleeve. No doubt, Xi's Leninist agenda, much less his political survival, requires that he make economic progress at home. However, he must also make progress abroad if his China Dream has any chance of reaching his "maximum" goal of resuming "its rightful place as the richest country in the world."[287]

CHINA'S TACTICAL MOVES TO ATTAIN A NEW ECONOMIC WORLD ORDER

The Chinese Communists are economically aggressive across the world, using a variety of tools to realize a China-favoring new economic world order.

Below are nine economic tactical practices essential to China's plan to realize a new economic world order. Each is explained in terms of the ways the Communist regime uses it to attain the desired China-favoring outcome. In the third section of this volume, I will address how the US ought to counter these tactical practices.

Tactic #1: China seeks to garner the best intellectual property to then lead the manufacturing world. There are several ways a nation can address this tactic. It can incentivize domestic firms to be creative, or government can create think tanks to conduct research and development that leads to new technologies and applications. Alternatively, China does the above, as well as turn state agencies into a criminal enterprise to steal intellectual property.

The United States is the world's sole superpower and the preeminent target for industrial espionage by many countries—especially China. The PRC is the frontrunner in twenty-first-century economic espionage, and that country's Ministry of State Security runs operations to score trade secrets from the US and other Western countries. Since 1996, Chinese firms are charged in one-third (32 percent) of all US federal cases involving the Economic Espionage Act. More recently (2016–2019), China accounted for half of all charges related to economic espionage, and Federal Bureau of Investigation (FBI) Director Christopher Wray said that the US government views Chinese espionage as a growing threat. In fact, Wray said the FBI opens a new China-related counterintelligence case on average every ten hours, and nearly half of the Bureau's five thousand active cases are connected to China.[288]

The impact of China's economic espionage is significant. Nicholas Eftimiades, a senior fellow at the Atlantic Council's Scowcroft Center for Strategy and Security, estimates that Chinese economic espionage activities account for $320 billion in losses per year as of 2018, or 80 percent of the total cost of intellectual property theft to the US—estimated at $400 billion per year by the director of national intelligence.[289]

China's economic espionage is incentivized by top government officials. For example, part of Xi's China Dream goal includes "Made in China 2025," an industrial plan that aims to transition China's labor-intensive manufacturing economy to a more value-added technology production economy, one of President Xi's challenges outlined above. That plan calls for achieving 70 percent self-sufficiency in high-tech industries by 2025 and dominating the global high-tech marketplace by 2049.[290]

One of the Chinese programs that recruits foreign talent to help realize Made in China 2025 is Xi's "Thousand Talent Plan," which seeks to recruit scientists and a variety of industrial professionals to work in China to achieve its goals. Evidently, Chinese recruiters, according to US investigators, offer targeted employees cash bonuses to bring trade secrets from American firms when they relocate to China. For example, one US federal investigation accused a Chinese recruiter of offering a would-be US engineer more than $170,000 to bring secrets related to battery technology from his old company.[291]

Tactic #2: China seeks to monopolize critical commodities for self-enrichment and market manipulation. The twofold intent of this tactic is to enrich Chinese firms, but also to indirectly control foreign competitors by constraining their access to key commodities.

The Communist regime employs several tools/techniques to corner commodity, raw material markets. It subsidizes certain commodities and then dumps them on a foreign market to essentially chase out the competition, like its steel production. Another technique is to use President Xi's Belt and Road Initiative (BRI) to create a loan to a foreign nation and then, as many of those countries inevitably default, the regime moves in to strike a repayment contract that grants China control over certain critical commodities.

China also buys into commodity enterprises. It aggressively bought up raw materials in South America, essentially owning large swaths of some commodity suppliers. For example, Bolivia sold China a 49 percent stake in its lithium resources in 2019. In 2010, Ecuador sold the Chinese mineral and energy rights to its Amazon region. Meanwhile, Peru, the world's second-largest producer of copper, accepted China's $15 billion investment in that country's mining sector.[292]

Rare-earth metals represent the best-known example of China's efforts to corner the global market on a critical commodity. At present, China dominates the global market on rare-earth metals. In 2021, it produced 168,000 tons of these metals that are vital in many industries, including consumer electronics, green technologies, and defense. World-class militaries need these metals to produce weapons-guidance systems, jet engines, and laser weapons as well.[293]

China hasn't always dominated the rare-earth metal market, however. In the 1980s, the US led the world in the production of rare-earth metals—but no longer. Today, China controls 80 percent of the global production of the rare-earth metal supply, and it has previously used denying exports of those metals as a retaliatory tactic. For example, in 2010, after a China-Japan flare-up over the collision of a Chinese fishing boat with Japanese coast guard ships near the disputed Senkaku Islands, Beijing retaliated by imposing a ban on rare-earth metal exports to Japan.[294]

Understanding the export threat, the US tried to recapture some of the rare-earth metal supply chain, but China is outsmarting us. After all, these metals are found in Wyoming, Texas, and California. In 2017, a US company, MP Materials, purchased a mine in California with US taxpayer help. However, the company's largest customer and part owner is the Chinese company Shenghe Resources Holding, a PRC entity that ships the mining products to Asia for processing.[295]

Shenghe Resources Holding is owned in part (8 percent) by the state-owned China Geological Survey. Further, in 2019, Shenghe partnered with state-owned China National Nuclear Corporation, a nuclear-material producer linked to the Chinese military.[296]

The Biden administration is helping the PRC solidify their control of the rare-earth market as well. Specifically, on February 22, 2022, President Biden boasted that the Pentagon awarded a $35 million contract to MP Materials to boost rare mineral production. Of course, some of that money inevitably ends up in Chinese government hands because the PRC-owned Shenghe Resources Holding accounts for nearly all of MP Materials' $100 million annual revenue.[297]

James Kennedy, a rare-earth minerals industry consultant, expressed concern about the Pentagon's investment. He called Shenghe's investment in MP Materials a "geopolitical ruse" that helps the communist regime maintain its rare-earth monopoly.[298]

China continues to search for new sources of these metals. It is noteworthy that, after the Biden administration abandoned Afghanistan in August 2021, Beijing rushed into that country to strike a deal with the Taliban to extract some of the $3 trillion in rare-earth elements estimated to be hidden in that mountainous country. In fact, on April 29, 2022, the Beijing-Nangarhar Construction and Manufacturing Company signed a deal with the Taliban government to build a 650-acre industrial complex in Kabul's eastern district of Deb Sabz. This is China's first investment project in Afghanistan since the Taliban took over the country in August 2021.[299]

China also goes to the ends of the earth, even into the frigid Arctic, to access raw materials like rare-earth metals. Although China is not an Arctic nation like the United States, the Communist regime is very active in those cold waters, often sending flotillas of warships hugging America's Bering Strait (Alaskan) shores to enter the icy north to protect its "interests."[300]

"It doesn't matter where you look around the world, resources are becoming more scarce," said Ryan Burke, the co-director of the Arctic-focused Project 6633 at West Point's Modern War Institute. Nations like China feel pressured to acquire resources necessary to sustain themselves and their growth.[301]

The Arctic region harbors an array of natural resources—oil, natural gas, rare-earth metals, diamonds, and fish. China aggressively competes in that region to satiate its appetite for raw materials, but it doesn't end there.[302]

China is also interested in cornering the market on high-tech manufactured products, critical to the twenty-first-century economy. Specifically, Beijing is in a feverish race to capture the global market on semiconductors. China's 14th Five-Year Plan adopted in March 2021 singled out the semiconductor industry as one of seven strategic sectors to prioritize for investment. It is already targeting self-sufficiency in this product by 2025.[303]

It may be just a coincidence that the world's largest manufacturer of semiconductors is in next-door Taiwan, a democratic country Beijing promises to control either peacefully or through military action. Meanwhile, the Taiwan Semiconductor Manufacturing Company plans to invest another $100 billion over the next three years to increase its output. South Korea, which seeks part of that market, and which is the home of Samsung, also plans to spend $450 billion in semiconductor production over the next decade.[304]

Most telling about China's global economic ambition for resources is the CCP's decision to establish a large, wholly controlled global logistics group. On December 6, 2021, the China Logistics Group was created, which is managed by the PRC's state-owned Assets Supervision and Administration Commission of the State Council. This group will help the regime enhance its dominance in the global supply chain and maintain a monopoly on certain commodities and components across the world.[305]

Tactic #3: China employs any means necessary, including illegal, to obfuscate foreign inspection of its practices. The regime will cut corners and hide records to deceive its partners and foreign government regulators.

Chinese firms are fleeing this country to keep US regulators out of their books. Many Chinese companies listed in the US are retreating to Shanghai and Hong Kong rather than surrender their data to American regulators. Already, the New York Stock Exchange delisted China Telecom, China Mobile, and China Unicom. Why? The US banned all American investment in Chinese military-linked firms, which fuels the exodus.[306]

Evidently, Beijing is directing some firms to flee the States. They intend to keep their corporate data secret from regulators and investors, and the mass exodus lands most Chinese firms in Shanghai and Hong Kong, where the CCP controls everything.[307]

David Loevinger of the TCW Group, a California-based asset management firm, predicts that most Chinese companies once listed in the US will delist and move back to China. "I think for a lot of Chinese companies listed in US markets, it's essentially game over," Loevinger said. So far, firms like Alibaba, JD.com, Baidu, NetEase, and Weibo are among those moving to Hong Kong.[308]

The good news is that the migration of Chinese firms back to China will discourage many investors from capitalizing Chinese companies. After all, some of those companies have close ties to the Chinese military or other activities that only access to corporate records would reveal.[309]

Some Chinese maritime operators hide their location data because of suspected nefarious undertakings. Specifically, Chinese ships are hiding their geolocation data to prevent the US and other countries from seeing that they use commercial shipping for military purposes and for China's huge illegal fishing operations.[310]

Some Chinese ships turn off their Automatic Identification System (AIS) to hide what is known as "gray zone" tactics, the use of maritime (civilian) fishing boats as a militia to possibly seize islands, a practice called "cabbage" strategy. Also, some Chinese fishing trawlers turn off their AIS to violate other countries' exclusive economic zones in order to illegally harvest in sovereign waters.[311]

The AIS provides the geolocation data to the world to ensure ship safety, track location, and predict logistical movement. However, when these systems are turned off, it is unethical and often a violation of the UN Convention on the Law of the Sea. Further, restricting access to AIS data by maritime firms suggests criminality.[312]

On other fronts, China avoids paying tariffs and uses subsidized steel to cheat its way into saturated markets to earn future market share. US Trade Representative Katherine Tai called for updating trade law to reinforce anti-dumping duties, a means to cope with China's steel-making overcapacity. She told US steel-industry executives in Washington, "The tools that we have, we know how they can be effective, and we know where the limitations are."[313]

China tries to get around paying steel tariffs by subsidizing plants in other countries to facilitate the purchase of Chinese products, which are not currently subject to US punitive tariffs.[314]

Keep in mind that China makes up 60 percent of global steel production and ships government-subsidized, cheap steel from either domestic or partner-nation plants to crowded markets in order to squeeze out profits of others. Beijing has "poured billions of dollars into its steel industry—hurting the interests of workers in the US and around the world," Ms. Tai explained. "We all know this is not sustainable."[315]

Chinese firms fleeing US regulators, maritime operators turning off their AIS to hide operations, and dumping cheap steel all demonstrate troubling and often illegal activity. These actions happen in the face of China's twenty-year membership in the World Trade Organization, yet the regime consistently violates the organization's principles. Other nations confirm China's violations of its pledge to play by trade rules.

Australia's ambassador to the WTO, George Mina, criticized Beijing's use of economic coercion and warned its behavior hurts the global trading system. Specifically, Beijing has made little progress at adopting WTO principles that it needs "to adhere more closely to market-oriented principles."[316]

The ambassador wrote, "China has increasingly tested global trade rules and norms by engaging in practices that are inconsistent with its WTO commitments." His statement outlined activities by the CCP that target Australian exporters in violation of the rules such as "arbitrary border testing and inspections, the imposition of tariffs, and the unwarranted delays in listing export establishments and issuing import licenses."[317]

Evidently, according to the ambassador, China's actions are politically motivated, a Leninist practice of linking trade with ideology. In July 2021, China's foreign minister was asked how Australia should handle relations with Beijing given the squabbling over trade. The minister answered: "We will not allow any country to reap benefits from doing business with China while groundlessly accusing and smearing China and undermining China's core interests based on ideology."[318]

In 2020, the Chinese delivered a list of grievances about "core interests" it has with the Australian government. That list, according to Ambassador Arthur Culvahouse, Jr., the US ambassador to Australia, "reflects instances of the government of Australia standing up for its own interest and furthering the national interest of Australia." China listed such grievances as raids on Chinese journalists; academic visa cancellations; Australia's participation in multilateral forums on China's affairs in Taiwan, Hong Kong, and Xinjiang; and Canberra's call for an independent investigation into the origins of COVID-19.[319]

Tactic #4: China leverages its foreign investment to gain access to sovereign resources and political influence. Specifically, Beijing uses its Belt and Road Initiative (BRI) as a bait-and-switch device to gain access to key resources and advance its political interests, albeit while encouraging corruption, degrading democracy, and enriching foreign autocrats. Many of BRI's activities genuinely lack any accountability.

Ambassador Alice Wells, the principal deputy assistant Secretary of State for South and Central Asian Affairs, confirms as much when she explained that BRI projects lack transparency, which leaves partner countries mostly in the dark. "China offers substantial financing, usually as loans, but Beijing is not a member of the Paris Club [an informal group of creditor nations] and has never supported globally recognized transparent leading practices," explained Secretary Wells. In fact, Chinese President Xi's BRI has become synonymous with wasteful spending, environmental devastation, crippling debt, and a global power grab by the CCP.[320]

The Kiel Institute for the World Economy is a nonprofit economic research institute in Kiel, Germany. It estimates that China is now the world's largest lender, with $5 trillion in loans, many directly associated with the BRI program. However, according to the Kiel Institute, Beijing does not publish details of its loans. That lack of transparency makes it nearly impossible for ratings agencies like the International Monetary Fund (IMF) to monitor the regime's lending practices.[321]

China's BRI program evidently doesn't consider a country's ability to repay a loan either, probably the reason for a lack of transparency. The fact is that China loans large sums of money to the world's poorest nations, likely with no expectation that they will repay the loan—and, besides, local autocratic politicians in the countries approve Chinese projects without even considering the finances of repayment. Predictably, the entire process exacerbates corruption with kickbacks, inflated costs, and worse.[322]

This corruption-plagued cycle isn't lost on some Western officials. BRI is a "debt trap," warns British MI6 chief, Richard Moore. President

Xi's 2013 program, he explained, litters mostly poor countries with half-built bridges, over-budget railways, roads to nowhere, and mountains of debt, and it leaves behind lots of very angry people.[323]

Years ago, however, President Xi promised his BRI embodies "the spirit of peace and cooperation, openness and inclusiveness, mutual learning and mutual benefit." The MI6 chief disagrees with Xi's assessment, calling out BRI's "single greatest priority" as being to "get people on the hook" to expand Beijing's influence and erode the target nation's sovereignty.[324]

At this point, 140 nations signed BRI agreements with China. Those loans come with a high interest rate and promise to deliver the country infrastructure such as highways and airports. Most of the construction work is performed under the management of Chinese firms, and the labor is performed by Chinese citizens using Chinese-produced materials. Of course, those firms and workers never pay the local government taxes.[325]

Many countries sign the BRI loan because it's their only option to fund infrastructure projects. Virtually every one of those countries is riddled with debt and plagued by a sovereign credit rating below investable grade—which means that China is their last-resort lender and Beijing is poised to take advantage of the victim.[326]

Already, 42 of the poorest BRI countries owe China 10 percent or more of their GDP. That situation leads those nations to inevitably embrace whatever Beijing demands and, more often than not, to surrender their national sovereignty in the process.[327]

Tactic #5: China mandates that all foreign companies pay a high price to access PRC's markets, but not the other way around. Foreign companies that want to do business inside China must accept the regime's totalitarian demands. No one can even criticize the regime without a reaction from the all-seeing CCP Big Brother, who is always watching.

Clyde Prestowitz, author of *The World Turned Upside Down: America, China and the Struggle for Global Leadership*, outlines the costs of doing business in the totalitarian country. "Often foreign companies must surrender their intellectual property and abandon any expectation of free speech," according to Prestowitz.[328]

Giant corporations aren't exempt, either. Communist authorities insisted that Apple pull from its app store a map used by Hong Kong's pro-democracy protestors because it showed the location of regime police patrols.

Do you want access to China's 1.4 billion population to sell your product? Then you must obey the regime's self-censoring mandates.

The Beijing Communists also expect foreign companies to self-censor when it comes to sensitive issues like the government-oppressed Uyghurs and Tibetans. And state-sponsored censorship is pervasive. Just ask The Gap, Disney, Delta Airlines, and the National Basketball Association, which have all felt the CCP's pressure firsthand.[329]

American billionaire David Sacks addressed the CCP's intimidation and censorship campaign across American businesses. For example, he called out the backlash against his friend, billionaire Chamath Palihapitiya, the former chairman of Virgin Galactic, who dared say publicly that "no one cares" about the Communist Chinese's' ethnic cleansing of the Uyghurs. Sacks said, "The CCP is essentially depriving Americans of their free speech rights—not in China, *but on American soil*—as a condition of doing business over there."[330]

Sacks attacked the CCP's malevolent influence across the world, and not just because of the persecution of the Uyghurs, their theft of intellectual property, seeding the COVID-19 pandemic, and their belligerence to their neighbors. Most importantly, access to Chinese business has a deafening impact for a cross-section of business, media, government, and other Americans. Specifically, Sacks said:

> People's willingness to speak out about these issues tends to be related to how much business they have in China. I have no business in China, so I feel fairly unencumbered in saying what I just said. But there are a lot of people who do business in China who

just won't speak out. Everyone understands that the quid pro quo of taking Chinese cash is that you never criticize them.[331]

The mainstream media are especially sensitive about offending the Communist Chinese. Alex Marlow with Breitbart News said to follow the revenue streams with China. "News conglomerates do not want to cover bad news about China. But it's not because of a grand conspiracy theory. It's simply because they make so much money [from China]," Marlow said.[332]

Marlow called out NBCUniversal, the corporate sponsor of the "Genocide Games," the title given to Beijing's 2022 Winter Olympics by Chinese human-rights watchers, which was considered a flop by many viewers. Also, ABC News, owned by Disney, makes a lot of money from its theme parks and businesses in Chinas. AT&T, which owns CNN, lobbied the US Commerce Department for sanction relief for China Telecom. Even billionaire Michael Bloomberg "has the most access [in China] of any major media conglomerate, and it's totally at the will of Beijing's propagandists," Marlow said.[333]

"Beijing has sent a clear message to the filmmaking world, that filmmakers who criticize China will be punished, but that those who play ball with its censorship strictures will be rewarded," states a 2020 report, "Made in Hollywood, Censored by Beijing."[334]

American firms accustomed to our rule of law and free speech had better think otherwise while in China or doing business with the regime, even while here in America. We can't sue the Communist regime because justice only applies to the state-controlled courts, not to the individual, as is often the case in America. But of course, the Chinese turn the tables on Westerners when there is an issue in Washington.

Yes, the Chinese embassy in Washington uses our system—lobbyists and trade groups—to get their way in our Congress and courts. In 2020, the Chinese Communist regime spent an estimated $67 million on lobbyists to persuade American lawmakers to turn a blind eye to China's malfeasance.[335]

Tactic #6: China uses American political leaders to advance the regime's interests within our government and commercial sector. There are a host of American political officials caught up in China's campaign to advance its economic interests. My 2021 book, *Give Me Liberty, Not Marxism* includes a chapter on the Democratic Party, and in particular it identifies Party leaders who flack for China. Democratic Speaker of the House Nancy Pelosi (CA) absolved Beijing for its handling of the COVID-19 pandemic. California's Sen. Dianne Feinstein, according to *Politico*, even had a Chinese spy working as her chauffeur and liaison to the Asian-American community.[336]

On the commercial front, former California US Sen. Barbara Boxer is a registered foreign agent for the Chinese surveillance firm Hikvision, according to the *San Francisco Chronicle*. That firm is "accused of abetting the country's mass internment of Uighur Muslims."[337]

More recently, in February 2022, New York Governor Kathy Hochul (D) spoke alongside New York City Mayor Eric Adams (D) and Delaware Governor John Carney (D) at a China General Chamber of Commerce annual gala. That group represents the US-based arms of several Chinese state-owned corporations, many which are sanctioned by the US for helping the Chinese military.[338]

Those notable Democrats shared the gala stage with Chinese ambassador Qin Gang and China's New York consul general, Huang Ping. Both Chinese officials sided against the US, such as Qin allegedly provided Moscow with American intelligence regarding US plans to discourage Russia's invasion of Ukraine. Mr. Huang dismissed reports of China's genocide against Uyghurs, saying what the regime is doing to Muslims is legal.[339]

The China General Chamber of Commerce, the "largest and most impactful" Chinese trade group in the US, lists as partners the National Governors Association, the US-China Business Council, and the US Chamber of Commerce. Further, the Chamber's board of directors includes executives representing China's largest banks and corporations.

The closing remarks for the Chamber's gala were provided by Steven

Xu Tan, the president of China Telecom Americas. Last year (2021), that firm lost its operating license over security concerns, because it "is subject to exploitation, influence, and control by the Chinese government," according to the Federal Communications Commission.[340]

Communist China uses American political leaders to help it leverage our government's commercial policies to advance the economic interests of PRC corporations.

Tactic #7: China employs virtually any means necessary to make money for PRC firms while oppressing political adversaries. The PRC allows some of the most despicable, morally bankrupt activities to take place to make money and suppress its enemies.

China turns a blind eye to the murder of people to support the human organ trade. Enes Kanter Freedom, the former center for the NBA's Boston Celtics, made news in late 2021 when he slammed Beijing for industrial-scale murder of prisoners of conscience for their organs. "Stop murdering for organs. It's a crime against humanity," tweeted the Turkish basketball player.[341]

Freedom's social media posts included pictures painted on a basketball sneaker depicting a doctor gripping a blood-dripping organ. "Stop organ harvesting in China," reads a slogan also painted on the side of a shoe.[342]

As an aside, it's likely not coincidental that Enes Kanter Freedom's anti-China messaging evidently cost him his basketball career. In February 2022, the Boston Celtics traded Mr. Freedom to the Houston Rockets, which immediately waived Freedom, putting him on the bench. His appearance on the court in the 2021–22 season was also scarce, perhaps because he was a liability due to the NBC financial link to the Communist Chinese market, which earns NBC an estimated $500 million annually.[343]

In spite of the PRC's efforts to suppress the truth, the regime's organs for money activities are well documented. A 2019 report from a London-based People's Tribunal found that Beijing "had engaged in forced organ harvesting for years 'on a significant scale,' and continues to do so." The main victims of such a brutal practice are practitioners of Falun Gong, a spiritual discipline based on the principles of truthfulness, compassion, and forbearance.[344]

The practice continues in China in part because outsiders fear the consequences should they protest this debauchery. Weldon Gilcrease, a gastrointestinal specialist at the University of Utah, complained that he tried to discuss the brutal practice with his university's leadership, but they expressed reservations, fearing the Communist regime would halt the flow of students.[345]

On another questionable trade front, the CCP supports and controls the development of the Chinese pharmaceutical industry, to include the shipment of illegal drugs that annually kill tens of thousands of Americans. The regime intends for China to become "the pharmacy of the world," which includes the development of addictive synthetic narcotics.[346] One of those Chinese products is fentanyl-laced heroin, which is directly linked to sixty-four thousand American deaths from May 2020 through April 2021, according to the US Centers for Disease Control and Prevention.[347]

A 2021 Congressional Research Service report, "China Primer: Illicit Fentanyl and China's Role," states:

China has been a major source of US-bound fentanyl and, more recently, precursors and production equipment. In January 2020, the DEA [Drug Enforcement Administration] assessed that…China remained the "primary source" of all fentanyl-related substances trafficked into the United States.

Further, the CRS notes:

US objectives with respect to China remain unmet. China has not taken action to control additional fentanyl precursors… [and] China has not so far approved DEA requests to open offices in the Chinese cities of Guangzhou and Shanghai, and

Chinese nationals indicted in the United States on fentanyl trafficking charges remain at large.[348]

The Communist regime also plays host to a variety of forced and
slave-labor efforts. A 2018 report by the Global Slavery Index indicates
that "on any given day in 2016 there were over 3.8 million people living in conditions of modern slavery in China," such as the treatment of
Chinese Uyghurs, a Muslim minority.[349]

China hosts forced labor against religious dissenters within its penal
system as well. The practice dates to the 1950s, and although the CCP
claims to have abolished the activity, it was reinstated to "reeducate" dissenting Chinese Uyghurs and others.

The regime's culpability is well documented. For example, the Australian Strategic Policy Institute published a study in 2020 that found
the Chinese government built nearly four hundred detention camps in
Xinxiang Province, the home region of the Uyghur population. Similarly, a 2020 report by the US-based Jamestown Foundation, titled
"Xinxiang's System of Militarized Vocational Training Comes to Tibet,"
found that half a million Tibetans were subjects of PRC forced labor as
well.[350]

The PRC's oppressive practices also affect the country's broader
population. Specifically, a 2021 report by China Labor Watch, "Silent
Victims of Labor Trafficking: China's Belt and Road Workers Stranded
Overseas Amid COVID-19 Pandemic," indicates that Chinese citizens
recruited to work on overseas BRI projects fall into what is a forced-
labor situation. Once these people arrive at the BRI country, the report
states, their passports are confiscated, they are secured by guards in poor
living and working camps, work twelve hours every day with no breaks,
and receive no medical treatment.[351]

A further aspect of the regime's by-any-means tactic is how China
short-changes (aka cheats) client states by hiring primarily Chinese citizen workers for BRI projects. For example, South Africa is a BRI client
and, as a result, welcomed China's telecommunications giant Huawei

to upgrade the country's systems. Part of that agreement requires that at least 60 percent of foreign companies' workforces be comprised of domestic workers. However, a 2020 audit by South Africa's Department of Employment and Labor found that Huawei employs approximately 90 percent of foreign nationals, virtually all Chinese nationals. The South African government filed a lawsuit to address their grievance, and Huawei executives promised to take steps to "rebalance" its hiring practices.[352]

Tactic #8: China supplants the US dollar with the Chinese renminbi (RMB) as the world's primary reserve currency. The CCP manipulates the value of its currency to grant Chinese goods an edge over their competition. Further, the regime is aggressively introducing digital currency with the aim of making the RMB the world's default reserve currency.

The US Treasury Department's semiannual report on currency manipulators found that China violated two of the department's three criteria for currency manipulation. The Beijing government earned special attention, because it is "increasingly an outlier with respect to its non-disclosure of foreign exchange market intervention."[353]

Also, the CCP's Five-Year Plan for years 2021–2025 identifies the goal to create a new digital currency to help the regime become technologically independent of the West's global technology and to "overtake the US as the world's dominant power by 2049," states an official CCP publication.[354]

Digital currency increases state control and could affect the ability of other nations like the US to level sanctions against the PRC for human-rights violations and breaches of international law. This is serious, according to historian Niall Ferguson:

> Not only are the American monetary authorities underestimating the threat posed to dollar dominance by China's pioneering combination of digital currency and electronic payments. They are also treating the blockchain-based financial innovations that

offer the best alternative to China's e-yuan [e-RMB] like gate-crashers at their own exclusive party.[355]

Tactic #9: China dictates global financial and trade policy. The CCP will garner influence by putting its representatives inside leadership positions of international financial and trade organizations and then make policy decisions that favor the regime. This tactic is yet to be fully realized by Beijing's CCP. However, China is quite involved in many international organizations, and it takes advantage of that access. In time, its representatives will rise to the top of those organizations to dictate global financial and trade policies to suit China's hegemonic ambition.

The CCP's participation in international organizations had perhaps one of its best opportunities thanks to the United States. In 2000, the US Congress naively granted the regime permanent normal trade relations, which enabled China to enter the World Trade Organization (WTO) in December 2001. This move fundamentally changed the economic role that China plays globally by granting it a huge economic boost on trade.

Peter Hoekstra, the former US ambassador to the Netherlands during the Trump administration and former US congressman, frequently addressed the issues of China's unfair trade practices and theft of intellectual property. China was "using predatory practices to drive out European competitors to Huawei so that the CCP would soon dominate this key market. Rather than following the rules, China abused its new access [thanks to WHO membership] to go into more countries and engage in market manipulation, predatory pricing, and lending, and surreptitiously to seed its national security apparatus abroad."[356]

China is also reluctant at this time to step up to more global responsibility in the financial/economic arena. David Dollar, a senior fellow at the Brookings Institution and a former Obama administration Treasury official then posted to Beijing, explains the CCP's reluctance. He acknowledges that the PRC participates in the international economic institutions, the WTO, the International Monetary Fund, the World Bank, and the Paris Climate Agreement. However, Beijing is reluctant to take a stronger role while insisting on being treated as a developing country. Why? Perhaps the regime wants to be free for now to behave differently (more responsibly) than the so-called advanced economies.[357]

What's interesting is that the PRC takes advantage of these many international organizations to advance its trading and financial interests. For example, the Center for Global Economic Development opines that China's large footprint in many multilateral development organizations serves the PRC's broader economic interests, such as receiving more grants from multilateral development banks. Further, China also benefits commercially from these institutions with Chinese state-owned corporations being among the top recipients of multilateral development bank procurement each year.[358]

China is also an important player in International Financial Institutions (IFIs). They provide the regime with financial and technical assistance for developing countries, which the PRC insists on being recognized as one. In fact, today, China enjoys the second-highest aggregate voting power in the IFIs next to the United States.[359]

What this all means is that China wants to enjoy all the perks of being an international player without exercising any responsibility. That is about to change as President Xi seeks to leverage many of these same organizations to embrace his vision for a new economic world order in China's image.

CONCLUSION

President Xi faces a host of challenges before the regime can realize an economic new world order in its image. First, he must restart China's flagging economy by addressing several very serious obstacles addressed in this chapter. Second, and simultaneously, to realize his China Dream, Mr. Xi needs to move forward with his strategy, which likely includes the nine tactical practices outlined above, so to reset the globe's financial and trade systems to match the CCP's grandiose ambition.

5

Seeking China's Ideological New World Order

"No force can stop the progress of the Communist Party of China" towards the global victory of Marxism.[360]

—Xi Jinping, Chairman CCP (2021)

The CCP uses its governing ideology to create a new world order in its image. This chapter will explore that ideology, the CCP's Marxist foundation, and the application of that ideology by especially President Xi, and then will consider how the Beijing regime employs that view within China and across the world.

Cultural theorist Terry Eagleton, the chair within the Department of English and Creative Writing at Lancaster University, United Kingdom, provides an expansive definition of ideology: "the process of production of meanings, signs, and values in social life; a body of ideas characteristic of a particular social group or class; ideas which help to legitimize a dominant political power." In China's case, that nation's governing ideology is a version of Marxism, albeit as executed from a Leninist—a dictatorship that establishes communism—perspective.[361]

At its founding (1921), the CCP embraced Marxism as its ideological foundation. In 2021, I wrote a book on Marxism as applied to America, *Give Me Liberty, Not Marxism.* I will review here the high points of classical Marxism from my previous work before addressing the particulars of Chinese, Marxist-Leninist ideology and its applications.

> [Marxism]...is a political philosophy developed by Karl Heidrich Marx, a nineteenth-century German philosopher, economist, historian, sociologist, political theorist, journalist, and socialist revolutionary. Marx's philosophy focuses on class struggle to ensure an equal distribution of wealth for all citizens and illustrates the inequality created by the ruling class in a capitalistic system that historically oppresses the lower (working) classes, thus triggering social revolution that creates a classless society, where there is no private property and every citizen gives selflessly to the good of all persons....
>
> Marx's theory is perhaps best known for its sharp critique of capitalism, which claims that workers in a capitalist system are little more than a commodity, "labor power." This economic clash, which is set forth in Marx's 1859 book, *Das Kapital*, creates a conflict between the proletariat (workers who transform raw commodities into goods) and the bourgeoisie (owners of the means of production), which has a "built-in" inequality. The bourgeoisie, with the help of government, according to Marx, employ social institutions against the proletariat. Marx argues in his writings that capitalism creates an unfair imbalance between the bourgeoisie and the workers whom they exploit for gain, and those inherent inequalities and exploitative relations ultimately lead to revolution that abolishes capitalism and reconstructs society into a socialist form of government.[362]

The Marxist worldview is especially helpful to understand when that ideology applies to Communist China because the following tenets are evidenced by the contemporary CCP cadre. A thumbnail sketch of that view/tenets includes: it promotes the abolition of all religion; it promotes naturalism—i.e., there is no spiritual component to life;

it embraces a morality that exclusively advances the "working class"; it assumes all human behavior is based exclusively on the material; it makes no class distinctions; and it posits that a Communist world government is utopia on earth and that economics determine the nature of all legal, social, and political institutions.[363]

President Xi Jinping is a serious Marxist who subscribes to the above description, which he employs to direct his so-called "rejuvenation" of China's aim as well as to create a new world order in China's Marxist-Leninist image. In fact, given his public statements, there is no doubt Mr. Xi intends to apply his Marxist-Leninist ideology to the entire world.

In the spring of 2021, the Central Propaganda Department of the CCP published the book, *Questions and Answers on the Study of Xi Jinping Thought on Socialism with Chinese Characteristics for a New Era.* That book shares Xi's vision of the world that remains rooted in classical Marxism. In fact, the world, according to Xi, is an arena for the "competition of two ideologies and two social systems"—that is, Marxist communism and bourgeois versus democratic ideology and capitalism.[364]

President Xi affirms in the book that China is at "the centre of the world stage," and leading non-Communist countries (read "especially the US") are pushed aside. This "demonstrates," writes Xi, "the vigorous vitality of scientific Socialism with irrefutable facts."[365]

Earlier, in a 2018 speech, Mr. Xi said the CCP must "lead the reform of the global governance system" and again in 2021, he explained that "a more just and equitable international order must be heeded," no doubt based on a Marxist ideology.[366]

Mr. Xi's global ambition is also outlined in a 2016 article he authored for the CCP's Central Party School, which declares it is "only a matter of time" before Communist China is among those "leading the new world order." Logically then, a leader like Xi imposes his will on the subject—the world.[367]

What might Xi's new world order be like? The 2021 Sixth Plenum communique addressed the issue by announcing China's revised history, which outlines the CCP's goals for the future. Specifically, that document calls for the creation of a Maoist Communist "model for human advancement."[368]

A Maoist-like "model for human advancement" reflects a Marxist ideology, proselytized by Chinese disciples who are "not only capable of dismantling the old world [order], but also of building a new one," states the CCP. The communique continued:

We must use Marxist positions, viewpoints, and methods to observe, understand, and steer the trends of the times, and constantly deepen our understanding of the laws underlying governance by a communist party, the building of socialism, and the development of human society.[369]

This is no joke. Communist China and its leaders—like President Xi, who already oversees the soon-to-be world's largest economy and largest military—intend to create a new world order in their Marxist image, and we had better pay close attention to what they say to appreciate how to avoid that outcome, if that's even possible.[370]

What is the ideological work President Xi promises to use to usher in his vision of a new world order within China and across the world? He outlined that vision at the National Publicity and Ideological Work Conference in May 2013.[371]

The president explained the purpose of ideological work: "to consolidate the guiding status of Marxism in the ideological field and to consolidate the common ideological basis for united struggles by the whole party and the whole people." He called on the CCP membership to "strengthen their faith in Marxism and communism, steadfastly and with unremitting efforts carry out the party's basic program...[by] systematically master[ing] the basic theory of Marxism as an essential skill, and...[by] earnestly and exactly study[ing] the basic theories of Marxism-Leninism, Mao Zedong thought, and especially Deng Xiaoping theory."[372]

Mr. Xi called for Communist cadres at that conference to "learn to use the Marxist standpoint, viewpoint, and methods to examine and solve problems and firm up their ideals and beliefs." This is a clear ideological statement and mission.[373]

Xi Jinping then explained that ideological work must be done "under the conditions of fully opening up to the outside [what] is to guide people toward a more comprehensive and objective way of understanding contemporary China and looking at the outside world."[374]

The PRC's president stressed the "entire party [CCP] must get involved" if ideological work is to be done well. He called for linking that work to "all areas of administrative management, vocational management, and social management."[375]

What is the identifiable Chinese Communist ideology? First, we need to review the maturation of the CCP's ideology to set the stage. Second, we must consider what President Xi means when he says the "entire party must get involved" in ideological work and how it touches all aspects of management.

China experts Kerry Brown and Aleksandra Bērziņa-Cerenkova write in the *Journal of Chinese Political Science* that the Maoist version of mass ideology died after 1978 to be replaced by a new version promoted by President Xi. The new version of CCP ideology is very much alive today. It links the aims of the regime "with national prosperity, historic rejuvenation, and the delivery of the political goals promised when the communist party was founded." Xi's new CCP ideology has "become more concealed, more nuanced, and in some spaces more flexible," according to Brown and Bērziņa-Cerenkova. The objective of this new ideology is simple: "the creation of a great nation with the CPC [Communist Party of China] at the heart of its governance." Underlying this notion is "creating not just a wealthy country, but also a spiritual socialist civilization."[376]

President Xi's unique ideological approach intends to sustain the CCP's one-party rule, and his choice of key words exemplifies the ways and means in which "the contemporary CPC is willing to use ideas from diverse sources, either from its own part, or from classical Chinese thinking, as a means of achieving emotional as well as intellectual impact, and to assist in the delivery of the major Party goal of the twenty-first century—the creation of a great nation with the CPC at the heart of its governance."[377]

BACKGROUND OF CCP'S IDEOLOGY

This section provides an overview of CCP ideology supported by insights into three efforts: Xi's "Four Comprehensives" strategy; Xi's twelve key-words, and Marxist "Spiritual Civilization."

Here in the US, constitutionalism and capitalism evidence important aspects of our ideology. In contrast, the PRC's ideology is based on Marxism-Leninism, which defines all the elements outlined by cultural theorist Professor Eagleton's definition: values, social groups, ideas that legitimize political power, and more. However, the CCP's ideology changed after the Mao era, as I explained above.

For the first quarter century of the CCP's rule (1949–1976), the PRC was a highly traditional Marxist society. Beijing at that time espoused a state dogma, something akin to the Soviet Union's old International Movement of Communism with a Chinese flavor. Further, that Maoist ideology espoused the achievement of utopian social goals by means of the Marxist class struggle (proletariat versus bourgeoisie) and the cleansing of society to create a truly egalitarian society. Mao's cultural revolution (1966–1976) evidenced that egalitarian struggle. However, soon after Mao died (September 9, 1976), the CCP's Third Plenum (1978) discarded the former Chairman's egalitarian Marxist ideology for something far more radical—"market socialism with Chinese characteristics."[378]

The Third Plenum's change created an ideological earthquake for China. It quickly discarded much of Mao's socialism for "non-state sector, foreign capital, and domestic markets." The shift from a command (Marxist) economic model to a more hybrid (almost capitalist) model was indeed revolutionary, and it was also very impactful for the Party's legitimacy, which came to depend on measurable material outcomes for Chinese citizens.

The shift proved to be a boon for the CCP. By 2010, the PRC had the world's second-largest economy, which significantly improved the lot of many Chinese, as evidenced by the dramatic decline of the number of people living below the poverty line. That outcome kept the CCP in power (arguably the primary goal for the change), but it didn't necessarily toss out all of the old ideology.[379]

The CCP's contemporary ideology under Xi, as Brown and Bērziņa-Cerenkova rightly argue, retains much of the old ideology. Rather, President Xi's "new" ideology serves a number of important purposes: keep the CCP in power, sustain prosperity, encourage historic rejuvenation, and make China a modern society.[380]

President Xi's refreshed ideology, according to Brown and Bērziņa-Cerenkova, is the "key means of avoiding the fracturing that the country has experienced in modern times." Like the definition of ideology shared earlier in this chapter, it provides "practices, beliefs, and language that has been bequeathed to them by previous leaders, and shows that they are part of the same historic movement that runs from 1921 [the founding of the CCP] to 1949 [the founding of the PRC], and through 1978 [the discarding of much of Maoism] until today." That ideology created, writes Brown and Bērziņa-Cerenkova, "a faith community, where tenets of Marxism-Leninism are accepted instinctively and unreflectively because they still remain an established part of the worldview and practices of the CPC."[381]

Yes, President Xi's version of Marxism-Leninism ideology is viewed as a "faith." That's a key goal of Marxist doctrine. After all, the German philosopher Marx intended to displace the prevailing religion at his time, Christianity, with Marxism, which at its core rejects God and replaces monotheism with mono-statism, whereby all authority and allegiance rests with the state.[382]

Even though there is no evidence that Mr. Xi understands the tenets of Christianity, the Christian faith was used by Marx to inform his anti-god ideology. What's important to understand is that the Chinese president is a student of Marxism, and aspects of that ideology are religious in nature, which guide the CCP and, by association, the Chinese people.[383]

In the last chapter, I indicated that President Xi, a minor political figure before his elevation to the presidency and CCP chairmanship, is really no more than a servant to the CCP. He was selected for his high posts primarily because he is a true "believer" in the tenets of Marxism-Leninism and would help the CCP wrestle China back from the post-1978 era's corrupting focus on economic performance. So, Mr. Xi's task as the new leader that began in 2012 became returning China to the primacy of politics, back from the brink in which Party officials "confused their entrepreneurial and political functions, with many (perhaps the vast majority) succumbing to corruption and larceny," wrote Brown and Bērziņa-Cerenkova. They explained that corruption was "the anomalous position of having risen to power in order to bring down inequality and injustices in Chinese society, and yet presiding over high levels of inequality and dissatisfaction."[384]

Thus, the newly sworn-in President Xi (March 14, 2013) understood that his task was to address the income gap between the Party's elite and the citizens. He had to bring back discipline by attacking corruption, which required a shift back to Party ideology, a Chinese version of Marxism-Leninism.

Ideology became the core dimension of Xi's power, explain Brown and Bērziņa-Cerenkova. Therefore, from his first day as general secretary (November 15, 2012), Xi took steps to "preserve and reaffirm ideology... to reassure the public that there existed a level of continuity and solidarity among leadership generations." To that end, Xi spoke, as mentioned above, at the Central Party School, where he invoked the memory of the Qing Dynasty by "quoting a poem by the calligrapher and writer Zheng Xie [who worked for Xi's idol Qianlong Emperor] when calling for confidence in the path, theory and system." Then, according the Brown and Bērziņa-Cerenkova, the most important message Xi delivered that day was that "correcting mistakes and learning lessons was an acceptable part of the process," an obvious reference to recent (2012) senior CCP leader mistakes associated with economic corruption.[385]

Xi's "Four Comprehensives" Strategy

Remember that Xi is a servant doing the bidding of the Party that expected him to do whatever was necessary to sustain one-party rule. To ensure that outcome, he harnessed a revised ideology labeled the "Four Comprehensives." That strategy became official in February 2015 with its four objectives: comprehensively build a moderately prosperous society; comprehensively deepen reform; comprehensively govern the nation according to law; and comprehensively, strictly govern the Party.[386]

The Four Comprehensives strategy provided purpose and direction for the regime. In part, it gave focus to the CCP's information campaigns with the message of narrowing the income gap created by the era of prosperity and demonstrating that the Party is on the people's side by building a "moderately prosperous society."[387]

The "comprehensively deepening reform" objective was about greater productivity, especially across the state-owned sector.

The third comprehensive objective addressed rule of law, albeit a Chinese version. However, this led to a socialist legal system, not something Westerners would understand as the principle whereby all citizens are equally subject to the law.[388]

The final comprehensive was a call to fight corruption within the Party. Xi made the Party a target for reform, and he intends for the CCP to operate no longer as a state within a state with uncontested sovereignty. Rather, it was to become the servant of the people—not the other way around.[389]

Xi's Twelve Keywords

How does President Xi apply his Four Comprehensives strategy across China and the world? Professors Brown and Bērziņa-Cerenkova identify

Xi's use of twelve keywords to provide clues to his underlying ideological preoccupations. These words show up in the Party's propaganda campaigns and are sprinkled across Mr. Xi's speeches.[390]

The idea to consider keywords to better understand a leader's ideology originated, according to Brown and Bērziņa-Cerenkova, with Cambridge scholar Raymond Williams, who popularized the concept in his book, *Keywords: A Vocabulary of Culture and Society*. Williams wrote that keywords "are significant binding words in certain activities, and their interpretation; they are significant, indicative words in certain forms of thought." With that in mind, Brown and Bērziņa-Cerenkova consider President Xi's keywords used to promote his ideological campaign.

The keywords or terms of the Xi era are: "strong," "democratic," "cultured"/"civilized," "harmonious," "freedom," "equality," "justice," "rule of law," "patriotism," "dedication," "trust," and "friendly." Admittedly, these words might surprise a Western audience as coming from a Marxist. However, as in any situation, the definition of the term is really what matters. That is especially true with President Xi.[391]

Consider how he uses six of these keywords to address his ideological intent.

Mr. Xi uses the term "strong" (*fuqiang*) to align with his Chinese imperial predecessors in the Qing Dynasty who called for modernizing to repel the nineteenth-century Europeans and Japanese who created for China the previously mentioned Century of Humiliation. In that context, the term "strong" was used by every Chinese leader since Mao to promise that the country would never again fall victim to foreign aggression, and for Xi today, the term is often used to rally nationalism, such as his 100th anniversary speech, where he used the term thirteen times. For example, President Xi said, "As a nation, we have a strong sense of pride and confidence," an appeal to nationalism.[392]

The term "democratic" (*minzhu*) isn't about the promotion of equal opportunity at the ballot box. No; for Xi, it means "democracy with Chinese characteristics"—or, more specifically, the "power of the people," as represented by the regime. Brown and Bērziņa-Cerenkova explain, "Democracy here means democracy for the party, by the party, on behalf of the party, all of which act as servants of the people they serve." Mr. Xi used the term "democratic" or "democracy" six times in his anniversary speech, such as: "To realize national rejuvenation, the Party united and led the Chinese people in fighting bloody battles with unyielding determination, achieving great success in the new-democratic revolution."[393]

The Chinese term for "harmonious," *hexie,* has a truly manipulated, Party-biased meaning. Former CCP General Secretary Hu Jintao (2002–12) often used *hexie* as it applied to ancient Chinese philosophers like Confucius. However, today it is often used to draw the people together, "an invitation to unity and joint purpose," Brown and Bērziņa-Cerenkova explain. It also comes with "a slight threat to those who raise any objections to the means used to achieve this. Thus, the deep irony is that the term 'to be harmonized' is applied to those who are to be silenced or simply locked up when their ideas become too contrarian." An outsider will now understand that when President Xi speaks of dissenters needing to be "harmonized," it makes sense that some citizens like the young dissenters at the 1989 protest at Tiananmen Square were killed or carted off to re-education camps, all in the name of "harmonizing" the protesters.[394]

President Xi's use of the word "freedom" (*ziyou*) is especially bizarre for the Western mind. It's not used to call for free elections or speech. No; it's applied most often to economic empowerment, the opportunity to own a home, and make personal decisions about travel.[395]

A Chinese Communist uses the term for "rule of law" (*fazhi*) in a very different way than it's used by those in the West. For the Communist, the phrase means "more predictable regulations for property, commercial issues"—and of course, Party members are exempt.[396]

The word for "patriotism" (*aiguo*) has a curious meaning as well. The CCP constantly appeals to the citizenry's patriotism, such as in education campaigns through which Party leaders advocate for a strong country with a stable Communist Party.[397]

These terms are code words that tell us much about China's ideology under President Xi. But, as Brown and Bērziņa-Cerenkova argue, they are used with "no overarching sense of the master narrative to which they belong." Rather, that "master narrative" is evidence of Xi's ideology in action to transform China into a "spiritual civilization."[398]

Marxist "Spiritual Civilization"

A Marxist-Leninist Chinese leader calling for a "spiritual civilization" is a real oxymoron; it doesn't follow that a regime that promotes atheism as a core tenet would seek anything "spiritual." However, once again, the definition is important. The phrase "spiritual civilization" really identifies the Party's grand aim; as Brown and Bērziņa-Cerenkova write, it means the "power and the contemporary discourse of ideology that drives it."[399]

The 1986 "Central Committee of the Communist Party of China Resolution on the Guidelines of the Construction of Socialist Spiritual Civilization" identifies the ideological role of "socialist spiritual civilization." It posits economic development as the core, which is then followed by reform of the economic system, political reform, and lastly, spiritual civilization construction. Brown and Bērziņa-Cerenkova write that "informing people about socialist culture can be seen as the key role of this concept." Further, as presented by Deng Xiaoping, constructing a spiritual civilization was about remaking man to promote the idea of public morality, in line with CCP ideology.[400]

Starting with Xi, however, the spiritual civilization concept morphed into something different. It became, as Brown and Bērziņa-Cerenkova write, an effort "to cultivate and practice core socialist values, to promote truth, goodness, and beauty, as well as to spread positive energy throughout the whole of society and to generate a strong spiritual power within hundreds of millions of people." Or, more precisely, it was intended "to make one party rule sustainable and to push China towards the goal of being a great and strong nation."[401]

President Xi's speeches often refer to the importance of this "spiritual civilization," a term he owns and relates to in his signature keywords: China Dream and the Four Comprehensives. The concept is often expressed with Xi's characteristic dismissal of Western values "as not being suitable for China," while spiritual civilization, Xi often explains, represents a home-grown value alternative that mixes traditional Chinese values with socialist ethos, known as the socialist core-value outlook.[402]

Therefore, the dominant features of CCP ideology under the Xi regime include a link to its socialist heritage, past ideological positions, and a broader connection with Chinese philosophical thinking from the imperial era. That ideology makes an emotional as well as an intellectual appeal that taps nationalism, aims at rejuvenation, and advocates moving the nation into a great power status.

XI'S IDEOLOGY INSIDE CHINA

Now we move to the application of Xi's ideology at home, and then across the world. Xi's twelve keywords and his Four Comprehensives strategy apply ideology to enforce unity, create a common purpose, and guide the country under the CCP's rule toward the objective "modernization with Chinese characteristics" encompassed within a Marxist-Leninist "spiritual civilization."[403]

President Xi called on his fellow Communists to apply "the Marxist standpoint, viewpoint, and methods to examine and solve problems." Evidently, that ideological foundation guides the CCP cadre to control the Chinese people and preserve one-party rule.

The following Party actions evidence how Xi's ideology is executed to realize his objective, modernization with Chinese characteristics—or, as George Orwell, the author of the dystopian novel *Nineteen Eighty-Four*, wrote: "A society becomes totalitarian when its structure becomes flagrantly artificial: that is, when its ruling class has lost its function but succeeds in clinging to power by force or fraud." That is precisely what modern China under President Xi has become—a totalitarian regime desperately clinging to power no matter the cost.[404]

Consider five examples of CCP actions that use the regime's ideology to ensure it maintains power across China.

1. Education as an Ideology Tool

The CCP educates the population to support the regime and push President Xi's vision. The CCP uses all education and especially journalism instruction to instill ideological obedience. In fact, ideological teaching is the core of Chinese curricula, and Party authorities exercise strict oversight to keep educators in check.

Numerous Chinese scholars agree that "ideology work is both a manifestation of China's adaptive governance as well as a key ingredient of its recipe for authoritarian resilience," writes Maria Repnikova in the *China Quarterly*. Specifically, the Party, explains Repnikova, a scholar of Chinese politics and an assistant professor of global communication at Georgia State University, uses a variety of tools to propagandize students and, more broadly, the population. Those tools include "public relations and polling to shape public opinion; its proactive ways of engaging with the public; the interactive nature of its digital propaganda; and its flexible approach to cultural governance."[405]

As evidence of the regime's ideological work, beginning in September 2021, the PRC announced that all students would be taught *Xi Jinping Thought* from primary school through the university. This is the CCP's way of propagandizing the next generation with Marxist belief and Communist Chinese ideology.[406]

The PRC's Ministry of Education issued guidelines to incorporate President Xi's ideology in the country's national curriculum. The intent is to strengthen the "resolve [among students] to listen to and follow the party," as well as to "cultivate patriotic feelings," according to the guidelines.[407]

Note these guidelines use two of President Xi's keywords—"strength" (a form of the word *fuqiang*) and "patriotic" (*aiguo*). The objective of the curriculum is to "gradually form" the confidence of Chinese youth in socialism and one-party rule.[408]

This move should remind older readers of Mao's Cultural Revolution (1966–1976) and the country-wide requirement to read the *Little Red Book*, aka *Quotations from Chairman Mao Tseung*. The 304-page book has thirty-three divisions that include "The Communist Party, Classes and Class Struggle," "War and Peace," "Political Work," "Democracy in the Three Main Fields," and "Building Our Country Through Diligence and Frugality."[409]

President Xi's mandate to propagandize all Chinese students through their education process is an attempt to build a personality cult similar to that of Chairman Mao. However, according to Feng Chongyi, a professor on China studies at the University of Technology in Sydney, this effort will fail because a "mockery [of Xi] is all over the internet."[410]

2. Public Information as an Ideology Tool

Manipulating public information requires journalists to support the regime, and the CCP takes extra care to clamp down on journalists that criticize them.

In late 2021, Communist Chinese authorities detained at least 127 reporters, according to Reporters Without Borders (Reporters Sans Frontières; RSF). That report indicated the CCP viewed journalism as a state propaganda tool, not a source of free public information.[411]

The RSF, a Paris-based organization, states the CCP made China a model of society in which "freely accessing information has become a crime and to provide information an even greater crime."[412]

Evidently, according to the RSF report, "The number of taboo topics keeps rising…. Not only those typically deemed 'sensitive,'" such as independence for Taiwan nation, but also subjects like censorship and even the #MeToo Movement.[413]

Reporters who address topics sensitive to the Communist regime face intimidation, harassment, and years of detention. The RSF profiled the case of Zhang Zhan, a former lawyer turned journalist who is serving time behind bars in China for covering the COVID-19 outbreak in Wuhan. She reported on the chaotic scenes in Wuhan at the beginning of the pandemic, such as her interviews at hospitals, quarantine centers, and the Wuhan Institute of Virology. The regime charged her with "picking quarrels and stirring up trouble," a serious charge that landed her in prison.[414]

It's noteworthy that the regime encourages all journalists—especially those who are foreign—to self-censor, much as the CCP insists that foreign businesses self-censor. Specifically, to renew their press cards, non-Chinese journalists must download an app to study President Xi's official ideology—the same material mandated for Chinese students, *Xi Jinping Thought*, according to the RSF.[415]

3. Crushing Dissent as an Ideology Tool

The former democratic Hong Kong demonstrates the regime's oppressive actions. In March 2021, the Beijing administration imposed on Hong Kong electoral reforms that prohibit any opposition to its power. For example, all "candidates [for office in the Hong Kong Special Administrative Region (HKSAR)] must undergo four rounds of successive vetting before being allowed to run for office." Of course, the vetting is performed by pro-Beijing personnel.[416]

The pro-Beijing vetting is only part of the regime's anti-democracy reforms. Hong Kong's new legislative council for HKSAR will now have only twenty directly elected members that join forty others appointed by the Communist regime's chief executive election committee and thirty others chosen by professional groups that also bow to Beijing's will.[417]

These changes mean that Hong Kong's democracy is dead. Further, at the end of 2021, the HKSAR was completely absorbed into the CCP's political system. This is despite Beijing's 1997 promise that the city would be allowed to maintain its political autonomy.[418]

The CCP subsumed the HKSAR by redefining the region's framework beginning with the Basic Law (1990). However, it is obvious that the CCP's long-term plan was always to exert complete political control, as evidenced by the passage in 2020 of the National Security Legislation that modified the Basic Law to make it easier for the regime to "coerce and control Hong Kong citizens and political activities based on CCP-defined prohibitions."[419]

The 2020 changes in the Basic Law grants Hong Kong police new powers to suppress dissent. Those powers include:[420]

- "Intimidation of Hong Kong leaders accused of 'politicizing the new law.'
- "Threatening to expel foreign reporters for 'misreporting' how the law is being implemented.
- "Sanctioning of foreigners for violating the law.
- "Removal of books critical of the CCP from library shelves, banning of political slogans, and censorship in schools.
- "Self-censorship by publishers fearing prosecution under the law.
- "Firing of teachers who backed pro-democracy protests.
- "Arrests of student protestors for 'inciting secession.'
- "Arrest of pro-democracy media mogul Jimmy Lai, his two sons, and several of his executives.
- "Arrest of Hong Kong opposition activist Tam Tak-chi of the group people power."

Beijing's use of these provisions to absorb Hong Kong into the Communist regime is a model to study especially for others who may face Beijing's future wrath and absorption. Similarly, to this list of new powers, in early 2022, the HKSAR accelerated the absorption process of Hong Kong by launching an effort to co-opt all civil servants. That began with an announcement by Patrick Nip, Hong Kong's Secretary for the Civil Service, who told those public servants they must complete

National Security Law training during their probationary employment period, and all new recruits for public service positions will be tested on National Security Law knowledge. Evidently, the required training ensures that all Hong Kong civil servants are "patriots only" in accordance with the National Security Law. That requirement strengthens and aligns the Hong Kong civil servants with their mainland counterparts and the importance of loyalty to Chinese President Xi and the Beijing-based CCP.[421]

Another aspect of the National Security Law empowers the Beijing regime to deny Hong Kong residents access to certain websites, a clear move to control the flow of information. Evidently, Article 43 of the law grants the police the right to "require [Internet] service providers to take a disabling action on electronic messages," such as Hong Kong Watch's website, a United Kingdom-based, human-rights group. Authorities restrict access to content that disparages the government or supports pro-democracy movements. Further, according to a September 2021 Reuters report, a website dedicated to memorializing the 1989 Tiananmen Square massacre remains inaccessible in Hong Kong.[422]

Inevitably, the CCP will use the Hong Kong template to absorb Taiwan, President Xi's primary goal.[423]

The regime also targets individual dissent across the country. For example, the Chinese Communist regime put to death 101 Falun Gong practitioners in 2021, according to minghui.org, a US-based website that follows the regime's nationwide anti-Falun Gong campaign.[424]

The majority of those cases, according to the website, were concentrated in northeastern China's Liaoning, Heilongjiang, and Jilin provinces. And some of those deaths occurred in police stations, detention centers, and prisons, according to minghui.org, with at least seventy-five of the total victims having experienced torture, forced-labor situations, and unknown drug injections prior to their deaths.[425]

Falun Gong is a spiritual practice that features three core tenets of truthfulness, compassion, and tolerance. The group first became public in 1992 and claimed up to one hundred million followers by 1999.

However, the CCP targets those practitioners because it considers them a security threat to their ideology, and as a result launched a nationwide persecution campaign to eliminate the movement.[426]

In the previous chapter, I introduced the fact that Falun Gong practitioners are also killed for their organs, an issue slammed by Enes Kanter Freedom, the former center for the NBA's Boston Celtics. In late 2021, Freedom called out Beijing's practice of industrial-scale killing of prisoners of conscience for their organs.[427]

Mr. Freedom's allegations are backed up by a report that indicates the PRC is harvesting organs from living prisoners and selling them to the transplant market. The London-based "Independent Tribunal into Forced Organ Harvesting from Prisoners of Conscience in China" confirmed the practice with its 2019 report, which alleges Beijing is engaged in the forced organ harvesting "on a significant scale." The report confirms the source of the organs are practitioners of Falun Gong.[428]

4. Marginalizing Faith Communities as an Ideology Tool

Ningyu Huang, the coordinator of China Human Rights Watch, called for the world to boycott Beijing's 2022 Olympics because "the CCP continues to do evil." Mr. Huang said, "The CCP is an imminent menace to the whole world…it commits genocide against the Uyghurs in Xingjian and right now it is expanding its power around the world."[429]

"The CCP wants to deceive not only Chinese," said Mr. Huang, "but also overseas Chinese and even western people. It uses every opportunity to whitewash its image by turning black into white and hide its atrocities and evil deeds with lies."[430]

The CCP's abusive ways don't stop with the Falun Gong and the Uyghur Muslims. Tibetan nuns also have been subjected to CCP torture. A 2018 report by the Tibetan Center for Human Rights and Democracy (TCHRD) posted firsthand accounts of a monk witnessing nuns being sexually abused by Communist officials.[431]

Tenzin Sangmo, a researcher with TCHRD, said, "This eyewitness account by the monk was obtained with great difficulty. It is understood that the monk was detained in one of the many extra-legal political re-education centers with other monks and nuns."[432]

Mr. Sangmo said that gathering such information inside Tibet is becoming "increasingly difficult" because of the "massive ramping up of censorship and surveillance."[433]

Christians are persecuted in Communist China as well. The United States Commission on International Religious Freedom (USCIRF) called on Beijing to release the imprisoned Chinese underground church leader and religious freedom advocate Hu Shigen.[434]

Hu Shigen's crime was calling on the Beijing Communists to "let Christians practice their religious beliefs without interference," said USCIRF commissioner Gary Bauer.[435]

Mr. Hu was arrested in 2015 as part of a mass crackdown on human-rights lawyers and activists across China. He was convicted of "damaging national security and harming social stability," and was sentenced to seven and a half years in prison.[436]

The above examples of people savaged for their faith illustrates the gravity of the situation in China. However, life is about to become far more difficult for Chinese religious people. In early December 2021, President Xi spoke at a state-sponsored national religious conference, during which he called on all faith groups to embrace the Chinese Communist Party. He encouraged them to develop politically reliable religious leaders and embrace strict CCP governance of all religion.[437]

Xi's speech was a warning shot across the bow of people of all faiths. It suggests the CCP is about to crack down on religion, much as it has on cultural liberalism.[438] The coming anti-religion crackdown will be in the shadow of the regime's assault on Xinjiang Uygur Autonomous Region Muslims and Tibetans, as outlined above.

Mr. Xi emphasized at the conference the need to fully "implement the party's religious work theory in the new era." That translates into the "Sini-cization of religion," which means all religion must adapt to the socialist society, improve upon the legalization of religious affairs governance, create a new situation in religious work, and "unite and strive" for the "realization of the Chinese dream of the great rejuvenation of the Chinese nation."[439]

What does the "realization of the Chinese dream of the great rejuvenation of the Chinese nation" mean in the context of the Sinicization of religion? It means, according to Xinhua News Agency, that all "religious circles promote patriotism, stress the overall situation, the rule of law, science, and love, and constantly increase their recognition of the great motherland, the Chinese nation, Chinese culture, the communist party of China, and socialism with Chinese characteristics."[440]

5. Closely Monitoring the Population to Ensure Compliance as an Ideology Tool

Part of the regime's task of monitoring the population is to keep Party members in line, which is one of President Xi's Four Comprehensives to strictly govern the Party membership. After all, some Party officials are not reliably aboard with Xi's plans for the nation.

In 2021, the CCP's Central Party School for Training reiterated in an article that some Communist officials are attempting to "leave themselves a way out and prepared to 'jump ship' anytime." The *Study Times*, a CCP newspaper, claims "this shows a loss of ideal and a lack of confidence toward the party and the nation." The article continues by stating that such officials are more prone to losing their direction and "walking further away on the wrong path."[441]

The message in this article is a warning that echoes President Xi's commitment to keep the Party in line, which is one of President Xi's Four Comprehensives to strictly govern the Party membership. These "jump-ship" Party members are also known as "naked officials," who presumably secretly secure living arrangements abroad and leave nothing at home in China.[442]

Cao Jianliao is one such naked official, according to the *Study Times* article. He was the former vice mayor of Guangzhou, also known as

Canton and the capital city of Guangdong province in southern China. Mr. Cao used his position to build a fortune of $11 million from bribes with which he purchased resident cards for himself and his family in Hong Kong and Macau.[443]

Evidently, a regime internal survey in 2012 found that the vast majority (85 percent) of the CCP's top management were naked officials with secret exit strategies, according to Xin Ziling, a retired Chinese defense official.[444]

If true, the fact that most Party members are naked officials must be very disconcerting to President Xi and the top CCP leadership. Further, keeping track of wayward officials is only a small part of the regime's surveillance effort. The Party is understandably paranoid about its own wayward personnel, but also about non-Party personnel, which explains the CCP's efforts to closely monitor all possible dissenters, troublemakers, and especially journalists.

The paranoia among Chinese authorities is evident in the province of Henan, which is located in the center of the country. Those authorities intend to carefully monitor every person, thanks to three thousand security cameras and facial-recognition technology. Every face that crosses the path of a security camera will be instantly coded as a red, yellow, or green risk level, and police are on call to act against the red-level threats, which at this point includes most journalists and all criminals.[445]

Evidently, provincial authorities in Henan requested bids for their multi-million-dollar surveillance system to help track journalists, foreigners, students, and others they label as "suspicious," according to officials. Reports by Reuters and the BBC indicate the bid documents provided by the surveillance analytics company IPVM were tendered July 29, 2021, following the foreign publication of embarrassing photos of the flood that ravaged Henan with dozens of cars floating down a highway.[446]

The bid documents for the proposed Henan surveillance system are an example of the Beijing regime's Orwellian state on steroids. "While

the PRC has a documented history of detaining and punishing journalists for doing their jobs, this document illustrates the first known
instance of the PRC building custom security technology to streamline
state suppression of journalists," said Donald Maye, the IPVM head of
operations.[447]

Evidently, China's Neusoft Company in Shenyang, near North
Korea, won the Henan surveillance system contract, which required the
cameras to be in place by the end of 2021.[448] The Henan surveillance
system will cross-reference pre-existing provincial and national text and
image files stored by the Communist regime in a national database to
help officials quickly take action against the "red" coded threats.[449]

The surveillance system will also access a massive databank of information that includes personal cell phones, social media, vehicle ownership, hotel stays, airline tickets, and photos. As if that weren't enough, the
surveillance technology docks into local police records, the Ministry of
Public Security, and the National Immigration Bureau, to name a few.[450]

The use of such artificial intelligence-powered surveillance systems
isn't confined to one province, however. In 2020, the *Washington Post*
reported that Beijing was building artificial intelligence algorithms to
recognize Uyghur Muslims to aid the police. No telling just how far the
regime will go to track others like Tibetans, Falun Gong practitioners,
Christians, and more.[451]

Put this monitoring technology into a global setting. It should be
especially sobering, given that telecom giant Huawei's 5G technology is
spreading like wildfire across the world, and once it is connected to surveillance systems like that now in Henan, it could turn the entire world
into an open-air prison controlled by the Communist thought police.
That will give new meaning to author George Orwell's statement in his
book, *Nineteen Eighty-Four*, that "Big Brother is watching you."[452]

Consider just how pervasive the Chinese surveillance system might
become when tethered to the thought police. We already know the CCP
censors any information that brings negative attention to the Party. The
suspicious disappearance of China's premier tennis star, Peng Shuai, is

typical of what happens when you cross the CCP. The regime will do anything to protect its own.

The tennis star's 2021 case drew considerable international attention after she accused a senior CCP official of sexual assault. Peng quickly disappeared, and the Chinese authorities tried to cover up her absence with a host of excuses.

The problem with trying to make Peng disappear is the fact that she was a mega tennis celebrity, especially in China. She won it all, to include ranking as the world's top doubles player. Her popularity made her the most-recognized athlete in the country, with half a million followers on Weibo, China's Twitter-like social media platform.[453]

On November 2, 2021, Peng posted on Weibo a three-year-old detailed allegation of sexual assault against CCP official Zhang Gaoli. Mr. Zhang was a member of the CCP Politburo Standing Committee, China's highest power center (2012–17).[454]

Alert CCP social media minders took down Peng's posting within twenty minutes of her Weibo posting, and then Chinese censors blocked her account. Quickly, censors also deleted all images of Peng's past posts, shuttered her input to private group discussions, and essentially made her name unsearchable.[455]

This sort of state behavior to protect one of the CCP's elite shouldn't surprise anyone. After all, Chinese authorities regard any grassroots political movement such as the global #MeToo Movement as a threat to the CCP.

What's clear is that the CCP is ruthless and cold-blooded, and the rule of law, like Xi's keyword, means something quite different in China than it does in the West. Criticism and dissent to CCP rule are never tolerated, and in China's future, never forget that Big Brother Beijing is always watching and will snuff out any dissent.

China's Ideology Applied Across the World

The tools used to enforce ideology inside China are not always available to the CCP elsewhere. However, they are becoming more common as the regime leverages authority over sovereign foreign nations. Ultimately, that leverage will grant the CCP its desired outcome, a new world order, unless the West begins to push back.

President Xi says as much in his 2021 book, *Questions and Answers on the Study of Xi Jinping Thought on Socialism with Chinese Characteristics for a New Era*, which states the world is an arena for the "competition of two ideologies and two social systems." And, the Communist leader claims, "Marxism is winning the global ideological war."[456]

XI'S IDEOLOGICAL CAMPAIGN OUTSIDE CHINA

Consider five aspects of the CCP's growing efforts to ideologically win over the world for Chinese Marxism-Leninism.

1. Manipulating Information in Foreign Countries to Serve the CCP's Ideological Agenda

Prior to the 2022 Winter Olympic Games, the CCP paid American social media influencers to promote the event. A $300,000 contract between the Chinese consulate in New York and Vippi Media, a New Jersey consulting firm, launched a marketing campaign across Instagram, TikTok, and the livestreaming platform Twitch.[457]

The goal of the media campaign was to present a favorable portrayal of the Beijing games and US-China relations. The disclosure filed with the US Justice Department under the Foreign Agent Registration Act indicated that Vippi Media received $210,000 advance payment from the Chinese consulate.[458]

The contract required Vippi to hire eight social media influencers with specified popularity levels with at least one hundred thousand followers. The influencers are required to publish at least twenty-four posts focusing on the Olympics, the Paralympics, and Chinese culture (such as "touching moments" and Beijing's history). Further, one-fifth of the posts must focus on "cooperation and any good things in China-US relations."[459]

The pro-China social media campaign with Vippi is only the latest example of the regime's use of social media. In 2020, documents obtained by the *Epoch Times* showed the CCP used proxy Facebook pages to claim Beijing's sovereignty over democratic Taiwan as well as promote the idea of a hypothetical military assault against the island nation.[460]

Meta, Facebook's parent company, in its defense, claimed that in December 2021 it took down approximately six hundred accounts of false claims about China's involvement with the release of the COVID-19 virus and anti-American messages. Meanwhile, Twitter removed a total of 2,160 PRC-linked accounts that sought to dismiss Western criticism of human-rights violations in China.[461]

On a similar note, a Human Rights Watch researcher testified before the Congressional-Executive Commission on China that Beijing uses the popular apps WeChat and TikTok to exert influence over Americans and the Chinese diaspora. Wang Yaqiu, the researcher, testified on November 17, 2021, that "it's essential to remember that all Chinese tech companies are subject to the control of the Chinese Communist Party." She explained that "there is no way for outsiders to know what information is being suppressed or promoted on TikTok that is due to the Chinese government's influence."[462]

Ms. Wang testified: "What you see on TikTok is not so much decided by who you follow, but by the company's algorithm." She explained how the regime uses these algorithms. "If you search the hashtag Xinjian, you will find many videos with smiling and dancing Uyghurs, but not so many videos that [are] about the camps and surveillance and human rights violations."[463]

The CCP's social media campaigns are a small fraction of the regime's overall propaganda efforts, however. For example, the *China Daily*, an English language newspaper published by the CCP with an annual budget of over $5.5 million, exclusively targets Western audiences with regime propaganda.[464]

The *China Daily* is one of the "mouthpieces" for the CCP, according to Ian Easton, a senior director at the Project 2049 Institute, a US-based nonprofit institute focused on human rights and national security. "What is troubling is that some respected American publications are taking money from the CCP to run *China Daily* inserts that are not clearly labeled as Chinese government propaganda," Easton said. "If American readers knew the source of their news was taking money from a genocidal regime, they might opt to boycott that source."[465]

The CCP uses the *China Daily* to spread disinformation especially about its genocide of Uyghur Muslims. Predictably, the regime argues that its policies of forced sterilization of Uyghur women benefits China, and it dismisses accusations of genocide as part of a "defamation campaign."[466]

The CCP also employs the services of US-based broadcast media to promote its disinformation. For example, the regime's International Communication Planning Bureau paid the Virginia-based Potomac Media Group $4.4 million to use commercial radio to broadcast Chinese propaganda, according to Justice Department filings.[467]

Evidently, the CCP wants to use propaganda in the Washington, DC, media market to distract attention from the regime's human-rights abuses. The contract with the Potomac Media Group covered the period from July 2019 to August 2021 and required that all programming should come exclusively from China Global Television Network content, another CCP mouthpiece.[468]

The CCP also uses commercial partners to promote disinformation across a number of Western nations. Telecom giant Huawei frequently buys so-called news-style pieces to advance its interests and pushes them in Western markets. Such as, in 2021, Reuters published two puff pieces for Huawei about its investments in the United Kingdom. The *Wall Street Journal* published fourteen sponsored (paid) articles in 2021, and *Wired* hosted virtual events that favored the Communist regime, also sponsored by Huawei.[469]

It is common knowledge that Huawei is quite close with the Beijing regime. In fact, the company's founder, Ren Zhengfei, is a former deputy regimental head in the People's Liberation Army and a member of the CCP, which is why some say the firm's links to the PRC pose a spying risk. That's why in part the Trump administration put Huawei on an economic blacklist. Meanwhile, Huawei has spent millions of dollars lobbying the US Congress to beat back blacklisting-related sanctions. For example, the CCP hired Democratic strategist Tony Podesta, a former Hillary Clinton adviser, for $500,000 to lobby the Biden White House on the issue.[470]

Huawei technology also helps many countries censor their own and Western journalists. Researchers at the firm Top10VPN found that seventeen of sixty-nine countries studied used Huawei technology to enforce censorship laws. Cuba uses Huawei's "Middlebox" devices to censor stories that criticize the Havana communists. Also, the Burundi government, which is often criticized by Human Rights Watch and Amnesty International, blocks outlets that criticize the Burundi president, according to the Top10VPN report.[471]

Unfortunately, Huawei technology is embedded in Internet networks across the world, especially in countries with close economic ties to China, more than likely thanks to Belt and Road Initiative telecommunications projects. That Huawei technology also helps gather personal data, an important aim of totalitarian regimes.[472]

Also, a report by the Committee to Protect Journalists warns about Huawei's tools that can be used to violate user privacy. Report author Vasilis Berveris, a British cybersecurity researcher, indicates that it is unclear where the user data ends up. He said that he "would not be surprised if that data was being sold or analyzed," albeit for nefarious activities.[473]

2. Leveraging Foreign Education Establishment to Serve the CCP's Ideological Agenda

The CCP invests in Western academia to influence future generations with their ideology; but also, Chinese students spy on our research or entice experts to aid China.

The regime's efforts take on a variety of approaches, especially across the academy: joint degree programs, collaboration on university-based research, and hiring of academics with expertise on US government programs.

The PRC likes to establish a joint degree program between a Western university and one in China, in which students are exposed to one another's ideology. Those programs are financed by the Chinese Ministry of Education, especially at some of our best Ivy League institutions.[474]

Consider the proposed joint degree program between Cornell University and Peking University. Professor Alex Susskind, an associate dean at Cornell's School of Hotel Administration, promoted the proposed joint degree program by the Chinese, who promised to reward the university $1 million in annual profits.[475]

Some Cornell faculty objected to the proposed program. They are concerned about academic independence, given the Communist regime's control of its own society. "When I talk to my colleagues at Peking University, there's a dean and then there's a political officer," Ken Birman, a Cornell computer science professor, told Professor Susskind. "I'm wondering how we maintain Cornell's independence and freedom of bias and our standards," Susskind said.[476]

There is good reason to be concerned about partnering with a Communist state school or business. Why would China give a total of $1 billion to approximately 115 American colleges since 2013?[477]

Chinese students at US colleges tripled over the past decade, and today they account for one-third of all the 1.1 million foreign students in American institutions of higher learning. Why? What's the incentive?

Peel back the veneer of some of these programs and the motivation becomes obvious.

Consider the program hosted by the University of Illinois at Urbana-Champaign, which received $27 million from Chinese sources to establish a partnership between its engineering school and Zhejiang University to develop a program in Haining, China. Does that joint program provide the regime access to material not available in China?[478]

A review of research taking place at the University of Illinois is a candy store for technology-hungry China. The university's list of ongoing studies boasts of many cross-cutting research themes such as artificial intelligence and autonomous systems, bioelectronics, data and information science, plasmonics, and energy. Plasmonics "follows the trend of miniaturizing optical devices…and finds applications in sensing, microscopy, optical communications, and bio-photonics."[479]

A major concern about joint programs among some American academics like Cornell's Professor Birman is that those arrangements are with a regime that sponsors the genocide of Uyghur Muslims and commits other human-rights abuses. Then again, as Magnus Fiskesjo, a Cornell anthropologist, observed, Chinese universities are under the direct control of the state, which demands they violate academic freedom. "I thought that [the dual-degree program] was not a good idea because all these universities are similar in that they are under the thumb of the government," Fiskesjo said.[480]

The CCP buys access to important research and researchers at Western universities as well. For example, a study by Australian analyst Alex Joske submitted a report to the Australian Joint Committee on Intelligence and Security that identified at least 325 participants from Australian research institutions, including government institutions, in the CCP's talent-recruitment program, with up to six hundred total academics involved in the program.[481]

Mr. Joske's August 2020 report, "Hunting the Phoenix—The Chinese Communist Party's Global Search for Technology and Talent," states: "The Chinese Communist Party (CCP) uses talent-recruitment programs to gain technology from abroad through illegal or non-transparent means." According to official statistics, China's talent-recruitment programs drew in almost sixty thousand overseas professionals between 2008 and 2016. "These efforts," according to Joske's report, "lack transparency; are widely associated with misconduct, intellectual property theft or espionage; contribute to the People's Liberation Army's modernisation; and facilitate human-rights abuses. They form a core part of the CCP's efforts to build its own power by leveraging foreign technology and expertise. Over the long term, China's recruitment of overseas talent could shift the balance of power between it and countries such as the US."[482]

"The mechanisms of CCP talent recruitment are poorly understood. They're much broader than the Thousand Talents Plan—the best known among more than 200 CCP talent-recruitment programs. Domestically, they involve creating favourable conditions for overseas scientists, regardless of ethnicity, to work in China," wrote Mr. Joske.[483]

The Chinese actively recruit inside the US as well. A prominent American academic found himself in trouble thanks to the CCP's Thousand Talents Plan. In late 2021, there was a high-profile court trial that involved the former chair of Harvard University's chemistry department, Charles Lieber.[484]

The professor was found guilty on six felony charges related to his ties to the Thousand Talents Plan while working on sensitive US government research. Keep in mind that since 2008, the Chinese program targeted high-level overseas experts and was flagged by US authorities as a threat to national security.[485]

Mr. Lieber, 62, was handsomely paid for his services as a "strategic scientist" at the Wuhan University of Technology. His five-year agreement entitled him to $50,000 per month with another $158,000 in living expenses.[486]

What was the regime's reason for recruiting Mr. Lieber? Well, since 2008, his research group at Harvard received $15 million from the National Institutes of Health and the Department of Defense. The nature of his government-sponsored research wasn't revealed in the news reports, but you can bet the Chinese knew exactly what they were buying.[487]

"Beijing's [research investment] money always has strings attached," US Sen. Ben Sassa (R-NE), a member of the Senate Select Committee on Intelligence, said about the Liber case. The senator continued, "The Chinese Communist Party is working hard to make itself the world's preeminent superpower, and the Thousand Talents Program is designed to give China an economic and military edge by contracting with scientists in the free world and stealing their research."[488]

Other Western universities are solicited by Chinese agents as well. The Chinese targeted many British universities involved in military-related research. A report, "Inadvertently Arming China? The Chinese Military Complex and Its Potential Exploitation of Scientific Research at UK Universities," authored by the British think tank Civitas, found the "pervasive presence of Chinese military-linked conglomerates and universities in the sponsorship of high-technology research centers in many leading UK universities."[489]

The report alleges British universities are unintentionally aiding China's military on topics such as hypersonic missiles. Of course, there is plausible deniability by the sponsors, because much of the research has a possible dual use that helps China's military.[490]

Evidently, according to the report, fifteen of the twenty-four Russell Group Universities and many British academic bodies have research relationships with Chinese military-linked manufacturers and universities, and some are even sponsored by the United Kingdom taxpayers.[491]

When the CCP isn't recruiting professors or contracting with universities for joint projects, it actively seeks to change student understanding about China. A keen mechanism for spreading Chinese propaganda among students is the CCP's Confucius Institutes, a program introduced earlier in this volume.

There were a total of thirty Confucius Institutes in the United States as of December 2021. Those institutes are sponsored by the Chinese government and located on college and university campuses around the world, providing Chinese language teachers, textbooks, and operating funds at no expense to the host.

They promote Chinese culture and language, and seek to forge positive bonds with both educators and students. "Confucius Institutes were established in 2004 as part of the Chinese Communist Party's intensifying propaganda drive overseas," explained Dr. Tao Zhang, a senior lecturer in international media and communications in the School of Arts and Humanities at Nottingham Trent University, United Kingdom. "They are strategically located in various foreign universities, allowing the Chinese authorities to gain a foot-hold for the exercise of control over the study of China and the Chinese language. From its organization and funding to textbooks and staff, the Confucius Institute is an extension of the Chinese education system, directly controlled by the state and having the same ideological and propaganda roles as schools and universities in China."[492]

3. Influencing Foreign Government Officials to Serve the CCP's Ideological Agenda

The CCP pulls out all stops to influence the US government officials through a variety of mechanisms.

It's a dirty secret in Washington that foreign money enjoys access within Congress and the government. That's why some members of Congress are pushing to remove the malign influence of foreign cash from the US political system.[493]

In 2021, US House of Representatives Congressman Lance Gooden (R-TX) introduced legislation to require think tanks that seek to influence Congress to disclose foreign donations. Also, Rep. Jim Banks (R-IN) called for a Truth in Testimony Resolution that requires those rendering testimony before congressional committees to divulge any foreign funding.[494]

Rep. Mike Johnson (R-LA) proposes that Congress prohibit lobbying by former members of Congress hired by Communist regimes such as China. That would require Congress to strengthen the Foreign Agents' Registration Act (FARA), however.[495]

These Republican proposals stand little chance of becoming law without the majority Democratic Party membership's support. However, it's noteworthy that Josh Rogin, a *Washington Post* journalist, wrote an opinion piece on November 23, 2021, demanding that the Democratic Party majority join the Republicans to embrace these proposals.[496]

"Dozens of D.C. think tanks and other policy organizations take money from foreign countries and corporations without ever disclosing the details," Rogin wrote. "The staffers who have received this financing then write policy papers and testify before Congress, posing as objective, disinterested experts."[497]

Representative Banks agrees with Rogin's proposal, saying that his Truth in Testimony Resolution "would allow committees to know when individuals are being paid for consulting or advising services to Chinese companies with internal CCP committees or companies such as Huawei and TenCent."[498]

"Witnesses appearing before committees are often able to skirt disclosure requirements. …This is problematic considering [the] Chinese Communist Party's disinformation operations in the United States include funding Washington D.C. think tanks," Banks said.

A US Air Force Academy professor addressed the issue of foreign influence as well. Jahara Matisek, an active-duty officer with the academy's Department of Military and Strategic Studies, said, "From a national security perspective, all foreign money (and even big corporate money) should be kept out because it skews American democracy, not to mention skewing domestic and foreign policies that benefit other countries and elites at the expense of the average American."[499]

Professor Matisek indicated the most effective lobbyists for Beijing in Washington are American corporations that export their goods to China. He continued, "US national security is not taken that seriously by either political party in the US, precisely because the incentive structures are upside down."[500]

The laissez-faire attitude displayed by some federal lawmakers about foreign lobbyists might not be as bad as one of them openly supporting the Communist Party. For example, in December 2021, US Sen. Richard Blumenthal (D-CT) spoke at a gala hosted by the Connecticut People's World Committee, a branch of the Communist Party USA (CPUSA). He was introduced as a "special surprise guest," and he said, "I am really excited and honored to be with you today and to share this remarkable occasion." Senator Blumenthal continued to explain that he was there to "honor the great tradition of activism and standing up for the individual workers that is represented by the three honorees here."[501]

Following the senator's six-minute speech, the event's Communist hostess, Lisa Bergmann, said: "If you are not already part of the Communist Party, we invite you to participate and contribute and join."[502]

4. Recruiting Foreign Non-Government Influencers to Serve the CCP's Ideological Agenda

There are numerous CCP political surrogates in the US that lobby on the regime's behalf. For example, in March 2021, senior members of the CPUSA met with CCP officials in Beijing, according to an article on the CPUSA website. The purpose of that meeting was to "celebrate and discuss the 100th anniversary" of the CCP.[503]

The CPUSA delegation to Beijing "was treated with considerable respect and interest by CCP officials," according to a US attendee. One of those delegates was Maicol David Lynch from New York, who explained to CCP officials that "most young people [in America] have a positive attitude toward socialism, especially after the political election campaigns by Bernie Sanders. The CPUSA has attracted a lot of interest from young people and increasing numbers of young people are applying for membership."[504]

Chapter 4 of my 2021 book, *Give Me Liberty, Not Marxism*, identifies numerous pro-CCP American organizations and individuals who self-identify as Communists in the United States, and more often than not they are aligned with the Democratic Party.

You don't necessarily have to openly align yourself with the CCP to support the regime's aims. Recall Josh Rogin's article in the *Washington Post*, which shined a spotlight on the possible corruption of foreign money's influence on think tanks, identified the Washington-based Brookings Institution as an example of a think tank that has indirect associations with Communist China.

Brookings is a left-of-center think tank that lobbies Congress on a host of issues. John Thornton, the chairman emeritus of the Brookings board of trustees, also serves as chairman of the Silk Road Finance Corporation, a CCP-backed fund that develops projects for the Belt and Road Initiative. He also serves on the board of China's Confucius Institutes, a propaganda outlet introduced earlier that is found on many American universities.[505]

Over the years, Brookings and other leftist think tanks have been rightly scrutinized for their lobbying for corporate and foreign government donors. For example, the *Washington Free Beacon* reported that Brookings partnered with Shanghai Academy of Social Sciences to host multiple forums to encourage Belt and Road Initiative projects in the Middle East. It's noteworthy that the Shanghai Academy was in the past investigated by the FBI for spying, according to the *Washington Free Beacon*.[506]

Think tanks are vulnerable to foreign interests because of their access to Washington officials—and this is especially true of Brookings, because at least seventeen Brookings scholars are now part of the Biden administration, such as Rush Doshi, who serves as director of the National Security Council's China portfolio.[507]

Other Brookings staff give supporting voices to Beijing. Jamie Horsley, a Brookings scholar, published an essay in 2021 defending Confucius Institutes against charges of espionage. And Cheng Li, Brookings' director of the China Center, blasted the growing dispute between US-China education exchange programs on the China-US Exchange Foundation website, a think tank affiliated with the Communist Party that has given Brookings at least half a million dollars since 2005.[508]

5. Manipulating Foreign Elections to Serve the CCP's Ideological Agenda

The CCP tries to manipulate foreign-country elections to support its agenda. A CCP adviser and leading Chinese professor has a plan for the regime to overthrow the US as the world's sole superpower. Jin Canrong, a professor at the School of International Studies at Beijing's Renmin

University of China, outlined that plan in his 2016 speech, "Sino-US Strategic Philosophy."[509]

"We want to be the world leader," Jin said in his speech at the Southern Club Hotel Business Class in South China's Guangzhou City. His plan includes: interfering in US elections, controlling the American market, cultivating global enemies to challenge the US, stealing American technology, expanding Chinese territory, and influencing international organizations.[510]

That thumbnail sketch of Jin's plan pretty well describes China's actions over the past few years. After all, Jin has considerable sway in Beijing. He is known as the "teacher of the state" and is an advisor to the CCP's Organization Department and the United Front Work Department.[511]

Mr. Jin's strategy to interfere in American elections is paying dividends, as are the other parts of his plan outlined above. He called on the CCP to interfere in US elections to bring pro-Beijing candidates to power, and in particular he advocates for singling out races for the US House of Representatives.[512]

"The Chinese government wants to arrange Chinese investments in every single congressional district to control thousands of voters in each district," Jin told the audience at the Southern Club Hotel. Then he explained, "The best scenario is China can buy the United States, and change the US House of Representatives into the second standing committee of the National People's Congress."[513]

Don't dismiss Mr. Jin as a side show. The CCP pulled out all stops to defeat Mr. Trump's reelection bid in 2020. I document in my 2021 book *Give Me Liberty, Not Marxism* many Chinese actions undertaken via its surrogates to help Mr. Biden win the presidency.

The Chinese Communists interfere in other nations' elections as well. In early 2022, the Australian Security Intelligence Organization (ASIO), that nation's FBI, announced a plot by a wealthy individual close to Chinese intelligence who was funding Australian political candidates leading up to an election in the east-coast state of New South

Wales. These developments come as the Australian-China relations sour in the wake of Canberra's decision to reject China's BRI proposals and Australia's decision to become a party to the 2021 AUKUS (Australia, United Kingdom, United States) agreement, which provides that nation with nuclear-powered submarines.[514]

ASIO Director-General of Security Mike Burgess confirmed the Chinese effort to interfere with Australia's elections. He said the "wealthy individual with deep connections…with a foreign government and its intelligence agencies" acted as "the puppeteer," but the Chinese government "called the shots."[515]

Mr. Burgess said the CCP's "puppeteer" hired someone to enable foreign interference operations and used an offshore bank to provide "hundreds of thousands of dollars for operating expenses." Those operations were "secretly shaping the jurisdiction's political scene to benefit the foreign power." Further, "The employee hired by the puppeteer began identifying candidates likely to run in the election who either supported the interests of the foreign government [China] or who were assessed as vulnerable to inducements and cultivation," Mr. Burgess said.[516]

THE CCP AIMS TO CONTROL THE GLOBAL INTERNET

Information is power, and President Xi intends to control the means by which the world's information is published—the global Internet. In January 2017, President Xi said the "power to control the Internet" is the "new focal point of [the PRC's] national strategic contest." He admitted the US was the primary "rival" standing in the way of the regime's goal.[517]

Mr. Xi described his ambition to control all content on the Internet as "discourse power" over communications. His vision of "using technology to rule the Internet" included total control over all applications, content, quality, capital, and manpower.[518]

Those remarks were delivered at the Central Cyberspace Affairs Commission on January 4, 2017. They confirm the advances Beijing made in recent years to promote an authoritarian edition of the Internet as an alternative for the globe.[519]

The year prior to that speech, Mr. Xi, according to internal documents, said the "struggle" to control the Internet required the CCP to stop playing "passive defense," but to engage simultaneously both "attack and defense." What he means by "attack and defense" is the CCP's ability to censor, spy on, and control all Internet data.[520]

Mr. Xi has a three-part strategy to take control of the global Internet. First, he intends to "set the rules" that govern the international information forum. Second, he intends to install his proxies in important positions that oversee Internet organizations; and finally, he intends to control the Internet's infrastructure.[521]

The CCP is making gains on all three fronts. Consider the Internet's infrastructure and in particular Mr. Xi's efforts to control the domain name systems (DNS) that are hosts of root servers. Those servers direct users to websites to visit. There are more than 1,300 root servers across the world, with most located in the United States.[522]

Should the CCP gain control over more servers, it could then redirect traffic to pro-regime sites, states Gary Miliefsky, a cyber expert and publisher of *Cyber Defense Magazine*. He explained that a regime DNS server could route a user to a fake page away from a site hosting information critical of Beijing.[523]

"The minute you control the root [DNS], you can spoof or fake anything," said Miliefsky. "You can control what people see; what people don't see."[524]

President Xi and his minions are well aware of the infrastructure it must control. For example, it's no wonder that CCP-friendly telecom giant Huawei proposed an entirely new Internet, which it labels "New IP" (Internet protocol), to replace the aging infrastructure. Huawei says the New IP is faster, efficient, flexible, and secure. Of course, the New IP would be built by the Chinese (likely Huawei), and the price of that new global network, according to Miliefsky, is "freedom."[525]

"There's going to be no free speech," the Internet expert warned.

"And there's going to be eavesdropping in real-time, all the time, on everyone. Everyone who joins it is going to be eavesdropped by a single government [China]."[526]

CONCLUSION

President Xi and the CCP are serious about their ideology. They intend to take captive the Chinese people and won't permit any opposition. As they close in on that goal, they are employing a host of ideological tools across the world to create a pro-CCP ideological new world order.

The next chapter addresses the CCP's sobering escalation of a new cold war on the security front. The regime intends, by mid-century, to field the world's leading military force.

6

Role of China's Military in Creating a New World Order

On the path of completely building a modern socialist country and realizing the second centennial goal, national defense and the military must be placed in a more important position, and the consolidation of national defense and a strong military must be accelerated.[527]

—Xi Jinping (2021), 94th anniversary of the People's Liberation Army (PLA)

President Xi's 2022 New Year's address stressed the importance of maintaining a "strategic focus" and remaining mindful of "potential risks" for the CCP's long-term vision of turning China into a global power by 2049, the 100th anniversary of the founding of the PRC.[528]

Evidently, the US stands in Beijing's way of achieving that goal, which explains why in 2021 Mr. Xi called for a new world order and indirectly pointed his finger at the United States as China's primary obstacle to that outcome.

"The rules set by one or several countries should not be imposed on others, and the unilateralism of individual countries should not give the whole world a rhythm," President Xi told World Economic Forum leaders in April 2021 at Davos, Switzerland.[529]

More recently, in January 2022, President Xi delivered two other speeches that called for the need to fight against hostile forces. In one of those speeches, Mr. Xi noted that "hostile forces will never allow us to realize the great rejuvenation of the Chinese nation smoothly" and "only by taking the initiative to fight can there be a way out."[530]

It's clear from Mr. Xi's words in these speeches that he intends to keep up the Cold War mindset to help China become a global superpower and his desire to establish a new world order that sets a China-like rhythm. Further, Mr. Xi's verbal barbs are all intended for the United States.[531]

"In the eyes of China, the US is still hegemonic," explained Shi Yinhong, the director of the Centre on American Studies at Renmin University in Beijing. Evidently, according to Mr. Shi and Mr. Xi, the US is the primary encumbrance to the CCP's long-term aim of reshaping the international order to create a "China-centric order with its own norms and values," a view expressed by Elizabeth Economy in her 2022 *Foreign Affairs* article, "Xi Jinping's new world order."[532]

It is also true that the US has long driven the current world order, a view established in the previous chapters of this volume. However, for at least the past century, more and more geopolitical experts warned about a new great power rising out of the Eurasian landmass that could use the great continent's vast human and natural resources to forge a "global imperium." Perhaps that's what we see now emerging from China.[533]

British thinker Sir Halford Mackinder (1861–1947) was one of those experts, a man considered as one of the founding fathers of geopolitics and geostrategy. He labeled the landmass of Eurasia-Africa—the "world-island" and warned that "who rules the world-island commands the world." Evidently that view is shared by President Xi, who believes a "China-centric order," or new world order, is achievable, which explains in part the PRC's multi-decade military buildup, which the regime intends to use to push aside the "hegemonic" US and then take the global reins.[534]

For now, President Xi employs the Asia-Pacific region, what can be argued is the "world-island" as the geopolitical heartland in his start-up bid for global dominance. The CCP chairman's vision is expansive, not limited to Asia-Pacific hegemony, however. As Ms. Economy, a senior fellow for China at the Council on Foreign Relations, explained in her *Foreign Affairs* article, Mr. Xi is seeking a "shift in the geostrategic landscape" and a "profound transformation" to create a new world order.[535]

An important ingredient in that shift is the necessity to create a globally capable, highly sophisticated armed force, albeit to counter the US military's global reach. All the ingredients for that modern military are quickly being put in place by the ambitious CCP leadership.

Why is a strong, globally capable military essential to the creation of a new world order? History tells us that a country with a strong armed forces will inevitably realize a degree of security and stability as opposed to one that is militarily weak. We also know from recorded time that a country with a robust military has the ability to seize or reduce an opponent's power.

Such a strong military can be the catalyst for a nation like China to rise to great power and, as President Xi declares, to become a global force to create a new world order.

There are many factors that determine a country's overall military power and whether its enemies will eventually bow to its will, which inevitably is President Xi's intent regarding the United States.

This chapter considers those ingredients necessary to become a globally capable armed force and provides insights into the critical question: Can President Xi's plan to build a world-class military become the primary catalyst for the Chinese to realize a new world order in the PRC's image?

In four parts, this chapter profiles the PRC's buildup of a globally capable armed force to perhaps become the decisive capability that leads to a new world order. The four segments address President Xi's military strategy to create a globally capable joint force; his global preparations for worldwide security operations; the PLA's all-domain modernization efforts; and, finally, evidence that the People's Liberation Army (PLA) is preparing to fight the US for the opportunity to create that new world order.

PRESIDENT XI'S MILITARY STRATEGY

The Pentagon's 2021 report on China states the PRC aims to achieve President Xi's much-touted goal, "the great rejuvenation of the Chinese nation," by 2049. Simply, that means China intends to displace America's alliance infrastructure and revise the world's international order to one closer to Beijing's authoritarian system.[536]

Of course, the PRC views strategic competition with the US as an ideological contest among powerful nation-states. However, it's clear from CCP writings that the Communist regime is stepping up its actions to confront the US and its allies through all elements of national power across the world, which includes economic and especially military.

At present, China's pushback against US efforts to contain the Beijing regime is met by a variety of strategic obstacles, what the PLA calls an "active defense." One of those efforts is to strengthen the PLA into a "world-class" military by the end of 2049 with the intent to "rejuvenate" the PRC into a "great modern socialist country."[537]

The timeline for the PLA's modernization goal is now 2027, according to the Pentagon's 2021 China report. The regime intends, states that report, to accelerate "the integrated development of mechanization, informatization, and intelligentization" of its armed forces in preparation for possible military confrontation, which might mean the near-term invasion of Taiwan or something elsewhere.[538]

A major part of that preparation is a November 2021 decision issued by the CCP's Central Military Commission (CMC), the highest military decision-making body in China. That CMC decision, the "Chinese People's Liberation Army Joint Operations Outline," is the regime's new "top-level law" for the PLA's combat doctrine system intended to strengthen joint operations, combat support, national defense mobiliza-tion, and much more.[539]

The CMC made clear in that document that the two million active-duty PLA personnel must improve their proficiency across all opera-tional domains (air, land, sea, space, cyber, and electronic warfare) as a joint force. The 2021 Pentagon report elaborates on that declaration. It states the PLA must be prepared to "fight and win wars" against a "strong enemy" (a euphemism for the US), "coerce Taiwan and rival claimants [like India] in territorial disputes, counter an intervention by a third party [read "the US"] in a conflict along the PRC's periphery [such as the South China Sea], and project power globally."[540]

This Chinese national strategy, perhaps for the first time in modern history, outlines the PRC's true intentions—global dominance, begin-ning with the marginalization or outright defeat of the United States. However, many readers may not be aware that the US has long been at war with the Chinese regime, starting with the PRC's founding (1949). You can be forgiven if that statement takes you by surprise. After all, the CCP has long employed what's called "unrestricted warfare" against the US—and, for the most part, Washington has been asleep at the switch.

Bradley A. Thayer, a founding member of the Committee on Pres-ent Danger China, makes three important points about China's long unrestricted war against the United States. First, Mr. Thayer argues that the Communist regime considers its past efforts to have achieved victory because it has not triggered a "response from Washington"; to wit, we've been asleep or our incredibly naïve politicians have long believed China would become a democrat capitalist nation, not an international tyrant.[541]

Second, he argues that the Communist regime's multi-front, unre-stricted warfare has yet to lead to direct military confrontation—i.e., fighting—because it involved only non-kinetic (non-shooting) assaults, which were a very strategic means to weaken and confuse the United States, via mostly economic, ideological, and geopolitical actions.

Mr. Thayer calls out the textbook that details such warfare, a doctri-nal book written by two Chinese colonels, *Unrestricted Warfare*,[542] which profiles the forms of attack (means) the CCP has long used against the United States. Specifically, those efforts include:

> 1) Political warfare, which involves influencing the domestic political systems of other countries, including the United States, but also winning a global narrative so that Communism is seen as the wave of the future; 2) there is legal warfare or lawfare to hinder or delegitimize individuals, organizations, or countries; 3) network warfare, which involves attacking computer networks, but also communication and infrastructure networks such as the US electrical grid; 4) the use or sponsorship of terrorism against the United States or its global interests; 5) economic warfare, which involves weakening the enemy's economy and financial markets, or hijacking them to support China's growth; and 6) kinetic, which is the employment of military force.[543]

Finally, Mr. Thayer believes the US is vulnerable to the continuation of unrestricted warfare because it (the US leadership) "does not perceive the many avenues of attack." After all, the CCP uses all elements of national power—economic, ideological, legal, fake news, and of course, most recently, the armed forces—to attack. Even the export to the US of highly deadly, addictive fentanyl-heroin and the devastating release of COVID-19 are biological weapons used in this undeclared war.[544]

Unfortunately, the CCP has an upper hand over the US, in part because our response is weak or nonexistent. We've been attacked and have consistently failed to respond; further, in some respects, we've embraced those attacks, such as by allowing the PRC's economic takeover of our industrial production base along with millions of American jobs.

We are now at a tipping point. It is clear that the CCP's unconventional, unrestrictive warfare strategy is beginning to be complemented by China's military actions, which are quickly rising in capability across the globe to threaten US interests. Hopefully, our past failure to respond to unconventional, indirect attacks won't cause us to be blind to the more conventional, kinetic threats posed by the PLA now at our doorstep.

Further, now that the CCP is becoming bolder in confronting the US, it's time to recognize the global nature of the threat. In fact, in 2021, the US intelligence community described China's "push for global power" as real. The Office of the Director of National Intelligence reported that Beijing will continue its "whole-of-government [read "unrestricted warfare"] efforts to spread China's influence, undercut that of the United States, drive wedges between Washington and its allies and partners, and foster new international norms that favor the authoritarian Chinese system."[545]

"Beijing is increasingly combining its growing military power with its economic, technological, and diplomatic clout [whole-of-government] to preserve the CCP, secure what it views as its territory and regional pre-eminence, and pursue international cooperation at Washington's expense," states the ODNI report.[546]

"China, increasingly, is a near-peer competitor, challenging the United States in multiple arenas—especially economically, militarily, and technologically—and is pushing to change global norms," states the ODNI, noting that the East Asian country will seek to use coordinated, whole-of-government tools to demonstrate its growing strength and compel regional neighbors to acquiesce to Beijing's preferences, including its claims over disputed territory and assertions of sovereignty over Taiwan.

The CCP strategy is clear, and so are the regime's efforts to put in place a global infrastructure for the PLA to effectively realize President Xi's long-term aim, a "profound transformation" to create a new world order.[547]

PLA PREPARATIONS FOR WORLDWIDE SECURITY OPERATIONS

The PLA must create a global security infrastructure before it can expect to be a credible contributor to China's effort to become a world hegemon and to then create a new world order. There are a number of key ingredients required to attain that status. Specifically, the PLA must develop the capability to project power to quickly secure its overseas interests, which means it needs strategic lift (air and sea), access to foreign facilities, a network of allies, and space-based communication/spy networks.

There is no doubt the PRC wants the PLA "to become capable of operating anywhere around the globe and contesting the US military if called upon to do so," according to the US-China Economic and Security Review Commission (USCC). In fact, the USCC suggests a timeline for the PLA's ability to project military power globally.[548]

Acquiring a global expeditionary capability may take the PLA decades, according to the USCC. First, in the next five years, the PLA "will focus on consolidating the capabilities that would enable it to conduct large-scale military operations around its maritime periphery." In the medium term (next ten to fifteen years), "the PLA aims to be capable of fighting a limited war overseas to protect its interests in countries participating in the Belt and Road Initiative." And in the long term, by mid-century, "the PLA aims to be capable of rapidly deploying forces anywhere in the world."[549]

The first element of a global capability to project and sustain military forces is possessing sufficient long-haul air and sea lift.

PLA's Strategic Lift Capability

The 2021 Pentagon report indicates the PLA is quickly acquiring a robust strategic lift capability. Specifically, "The CCP has tasked the PLA to develop the capability to project power outside China's borders and its immediate periphery to secure the PRC's growing overseas interests and advance its foreign policy goals." That's precisely what the PLA is doing.[550]

The PLA is rapidly growing its lift capability in terms of ships and aircraft added to its inventory each year. In fact, the fastest-growing lift platform are China's airlifters, heavy aircraft (mostly the Xi'an Y-20) for hauling both troops and supplies long distances. Right now, the PLA operates 11 percent of all strategic airlifters in service across the world, and it is set to grow to almost one in five (18 percent) by the end of the 2020s, according to *Aviation Week*.[551]

Timothy Heath, a senior international defense researcher at the RAND Corporation, said "fundamentally," China's airlifters are "important for carrying troops long distances quickly." He continued to state that these transport aircraft provide the PLA options "to respond to some crisis across a broad geographic range quickly." And it appears, Heath said, the PLA is expanding into more combat missions for these aircraft, such as paratrooper operations, special airborne control, and intelligence gathering.[552]

The PLA Navy boasts the largest naval force in the world, according to the Pentagon's 2021 report on China. That fact is sobering, but it's not the entire story. The PRC's 2017 National Defense Transportation law requires all of China's transport infrastructure, which includes ships, to be available for military operations. One report finds that the PLA Navy has access to 1.5 million tons of shipping, whether it uses that lift to invade Taiwan or to go anywhere in the world. By comparison, the PLA's sealift capacity equals in total tonnage the entire US Navy's Military Sealift Command's one hundred active transport vessels.[553]

Yes, the PLA has a growing ability to project forces worldwide, and it has the potential to surpass the US military's strategic air and sea lift capabilities.

PLA's Overseas Basing and Access

There is evidence that the PRC seeks to establish a more robust overseas logistics and basing infrastructure to support global military operations. The 2021 Pentagon report indicates that beyond China's Djibouti (northern Africa) base, the PLA is negotiating for access to a host of basing facilities in countries such as Cambodia, Myanmar, Thailand, Singapore, United Arab Emirates, Kenya, and elsewhere.[554]

The regime's far-ranging ambitions became evident in December 2021 with the *Wall Street Journal* report that China intends to set up its first permanent military base on the Atlantic coast of Africa at Bata, Equatorial Guinea. This is a major concern for the US, because such a facility would rearm and refit Chinese warships across from the eastern coast of the US, a major step toward global influence and dominance.[555]

The exact access and support capability the PLA negotiates with foreign partners provides insight into the regime's thinking about the future. For example, do they seek deep-water ports, extended airfields with hangars, warehouses, fuel depots, communication systems, and more? The US grew such a global network for almost a century, and now there is evidence that China is planning something similar.

Of course, part of the PRC's foreign policy intends to negotiate access to such facilities but also to influence foreign populations and their leaders. That's why the PRC uses influence operations that target cultural institutions, media, businesses, academic institutions, and policy communities to achieve their strategic objectives. The latter group—the policy community—is especially important, because the PRC needs to influence those foreign decision-makers to grant access to Chinese troops and agree to the PLA's use of their infrastructure as well as participate in collaborative military activities.

Although the PLA has no permanent facilities in the Latin American region, it does have personnel assigned to various Latin countries. For example, it has personnel located in at least three Soviet-era monitoring facilities in Cuba. Also, a Chinese "shipping" firm is purchasing an island off the coast of El Salvador, which will no doubt be dual-use, and there are numerous Belt and Road Initiative projects in Latin countries like Cuba, Argentina, Uruguay, Cuba, Mexico, and Panama. Those facilities include dual-use ports, which by design will accommodate PLA naval vessels and PLA aircraft.[556]

One of the most recent acquisitions is an example of just how Beijing intends to grow its footprint across Latin America. On February 5, 2022, Argentinian President Alberto Fernandez officially joined China's

BRI and "pledged to deepen strategic cooperation on trade and currency with China," according to a report by La Jornada. Argentina's BRI agreement will streamline trade agreements with China and help that country to address its economic problems—and, in exchange, grant the Chinese access to a variety of strategic facilities. However, should Argentina default on existing International Monetary Fund debt, it may lose access to foreign markets and therefore make the country more vulnerable to Chinese manipulation and become one of Beijing's new strategic vessels.[557]

In conclusion, the PLA, with the help of the PRC's Foreign Ministry, is making inroads across the world by cobbling together a network of foreign facilities and financial relationships that help make China's military a truly globally capable force. A unique aspect of that network are the nearly one hundred ports owned by Chinese state-owned enterprises. These facilities without exception are fully dual-use logistics bases, which the PLA counts as part of their foreign infrastructure.

PRC's Expanded Network of Allies

The PLA's global influence comes in a variety of forms. One tracked closely is international arms sales and training of foreign military personnel.

Chinese companies are among some of the world's leading arms dealers. Five Chinese firms account for 13 percent of all arms sales by the one hundred largest producers, according to a report by the Stockholm International Peace Research Institute.[558]

The five leading Chinese arms dealers—NORINCO, AVIC, CETC, CASIC, and CSGC—are state-owned, conducting more than $66 billion of annual overseas business for the CCP. Those firms, which rank near the top of all global arms dealers, may only be the tip of the preverbal iceberg because the CCP hides much of the information about arms sales from the public.[559]

An example of China's secretive arms sales took place on April 10,

2022, albeit during the war in Ukraine. On that day, Russian ally Serbia accepted the delivery of a sophisticated Chinese anti-aircraft system (HQ-22), flown into Belgrade's Nikola Tesla airport aboard six marked Chinese Air Force Y-20 transport planes. The aircraft flew over two NATO member states en route, Turkey and Bulgaria, an indication of China's growing global reach. In 2020, the US warned Belgrade against purchasing the Chinese systems, indicating that any such deal would influence their bid to join the European Union and NATO.[560]

Of course, the PRC uses those arms sales as a tool to grow its access across the world. Consider its efforts to grow that influence in Latin America, in part thanks to weapons sales.

A Chinese military white paper published in the *China Daily* indicates the Latin American region is one of the focus areas of the CCP's global influence strategy. That may explain the increased emphasis in that region on trade (not just in arms), investment, geopolitics, and overall Chinese influence operations. The PRC employs influence operations in the region complemented by security cooperation—e.g., arms sales, military training, and bilateral military exercises; Belt and Road Initiative sales/investments; and the purchase of foreign raw materials, outlined in a previous chapter.

Consider Chinese arms dealings with the Bolivarian Alliance for the Peoples of Our America (ALBA), an association of socialist governments (Antigua, Barbuda, Bolivia, Cuba, Dominica, Grenada, Nicaragua, Saint Kiits and Nevis, Saint Lucia, Saint Vincent and the Grenadines, and Venezuela). These countries are targets of the PLA's security cooperation engagements that include the sale of Chinese weapons. In some countries, PLA arms sales are substantial, which include K-8 military training jets, radars, self-propelled artillery, and armored personnel carriers.[561]

The largest Chinese arms buyers in the Latin region are Venezuela, Bolivia, Trinidad and Tobago, Peru, and Ecuador. In fact, Venezuela has by far the largest account—85 percent of all Chinese weapons sales across Latin America.[562]

Military influence operations across Latin America include PLA staff visits and bilateral military exercises. Other, less militaristic, "good-will" engagements include the PLA's band performing in Grenada and the PLA's acrobatics team performing in Peru and Ecuador. Meanwhile, PLA fighter jets participated in air shows in Chile, Argentina, and Brazil.[563]

Military bilateral exercises are becoming commonplace across the region. The first notable bilateral exercise was called Angel de la Pac, which was the deployment of the PLA's hospital ship to Peru. Since that mission, the PLA sent troops to conduct training and humanitarian missions across the region, such as participating in the United Nation's Peacekeeping Force in Haiti (2004–2012).[564]

Those engagements earned the PLA goodwill, defense agreements, and often contracts with their Latin counterparts, such as Uruguay's purchase of Chinese L-15 fighters and Z-9 helicopters. Further, Uruguayan officers attended China's National Defense University in Beijing; others attended staff courses in Nanjing.[565]

Venezuela is very much in the PLA's camp. Its personnel participate in PLA-hosted instruction and joint exercises, such as the Chinese exercise known as "Clear Sky."[566]

Officers from across Latin America have graduated from PLA academies such as the PLA (Navy) command college and the PLA's National Defense University. Much like the US military, foreign officer attendance at PLA schools has a strategic purpose: to build relationships among those officers who in time will lead those foreign militaries and perhaps those same countries.[567]

The PLA even developed the International College of Defense Studies outside of Beijing that is specifically for foreign military personnel. Officers from across the world, not just Latin American personnel, attend those courses, and then the PLA nurtures those relationships to influence the officers' foreign governments.[568]

The PLA is growing allies across the world, not just in Latin America. That process takes years of relationship building, arms sales, educating future generations in Chinese military schools, personnel exchanges, and recurring military-to-military exercises to build mutual trust. Such investments will pay off in time, much as they have built a host of allies for the United States.

PLA's Space-Borne Infrastructure

A globally capable military requires a constellation of satellites, something China now has operational. The final satellite required for global coverage was launched in June 2020 aboard a Long March 3b three-stage carrier rocket, which achieved the desired orbit.[569]

That last satellite to complete China's BeiDou Navigation System (BDS), which began with a March 2015 launch, will provide the PLA full global position, navigation, and timing (PNT) functionality from a constellation of thirty satellites. BDS joins three other navigation satellite systems: the US Global Positioning System; Russia's Global Navigation Satellite System; and the European Union's Galileo.[570]

The primary requirement for BDS is to provide the PLA with PNT data that is independent of any other system and cannot be denied in times of hostilities. For example, modern long-range missiles require updates of a weapon's position during flight to achieve accuracy, something a world-class military requires.[571]

A modern, globally capable armed force also requires surveillance satellites. In July 2021, the PLA launched three more Yaogan 30-series military surveillance satellites from China's Xichang Satellite Launch Center. The PLA described the function of these satellites as "conducting electromagnetic environmental detection and other experimental observations." Predictably, the PLA did not confirm the inevitable military uses of those satellites.[572]

IHS Janes, a global source for defense intelligence information, indicates the Yaogan 30-10 satellites are likely intended to intercept and monitor radio communications and radar transmissions, primarily on China's periphery. Other Chinese satellites are used to geo-locate emitters of interest, such as those located in Taiwan or most any location within the satellites' paths.[573]

The PLA's global infrastructure is rapidly maturing, and constellations of PNT and "spy" satellites provide critical capabilities to a globally capable military.

Evidence of the regime's intention to sustain an ongoing investment in space came in early 2022. On January 28, 2022, according to Xinhua News Agency, China's Space Council released a white paper outlining the PRC's space goals for the next five years. That document pledges to accelerate China's space effort to include: "upgrade heavy-lift launch capabilities, bolster the Beidou Navigation Satellite System (China's answer to GPS), build out China's space station, launch two lunar probes and an asteroid probe, work toward an international lunar research station and develop technology for space debris cleanup."[574]

The PRC is heavily investing in a global infrastructure to create a persistent military capability. As the Space Council's white paper indicates, the regime is rapidly maturing the elements of that infrastructure. Those goals are ambitious, but given China's track record, they will be met. Further, expect the PLA to exercise that infrastructure with modernized military forces to support the PRC's expansive foreign policy.

PLA's Modernized Joint Force: The Key to PRC's Global Hegemony

The CCP's grand strategy is essentially global hegemony, but to attain that outcome it must strengthen its military and then push the US to the side. That's exactly what's happening, and at an accelerated pace.

"The CCP goals of global hegemony are real, not just propaganda," said Anders Corr, a principal at Corr Analytics, a strategic political risk and mitigation group. "They are moving forward with laws that have global extraterritorial effect, tied to aggressive extradition efforts, along with increasing influence, trending towards control, of UN and other international institutions and multinational corporations."[575]

That strategic vision is made believable because, as Mr. Corr writes, "The CCP is more willing to risk war than we [the US] are, which it can use as a form of brinkmanship to force us into retreat." He continued, "War in the nuclear age against a nuclear-armed enemy is almost unthinkable for citizens in democracies, which from Beijing's perspective is a weakness to be exploited."[576]

Is President Xi willing to go to war to get what he seeks? Yes. He spoke at the anniversary of the Korean War in 2020 to say, "A victory is needed to win peace and respect." That's a very serious statement, especially given the massive buildup of the PLA in recent years.[577]

The CCP's buildup of the PLA is real. In fact, Beijing is heavily investing in modernization to bring its armed forces military to Western standards and then beyond. The PRC's official defense budget for 2021 was $210 billion, which is in line with the regime's new five-year plan to accelerate military modernization.[578]

China's defense budget is supplemented by several additional sources of funding, which makes it difficult to make a one-on-one comparison with that of the United States. For example, payments for military pensions and benefits, civilian research, and development approximate an additional 25 percent of the public defense budget. Other examples of a lack of transparency include aspects of the military-controlled space program, defense mobilization funds, recruitment, provincial military base operations, and much more.[579]

The PLA's 2021 defense budget increased 6.8 percent, over the previous year, and marks the largest growth in military spending since 2019. This was the sixth year in succession when defense spending increases fell below the 10 percent mark, an indication of China's economic resilience to the impact of the COVID-19 pandemic, unlike most militaries that cut such expenditures at the time.[580]

In 2021, China's premier Li Keqiang said of the PRC's defense spending that it will be aimed at modernizing the PLA. In his address to the National People's Congress in Beijing, Mr. Li said the government would "thoroughly implement [President] Xi Jinping's thinking on strengthening the armed forces and the military strategy for the new era [and] ensure the [CCP] absolute leadership over the people's armed forces."[581]

"We will boost military training and preparedness across the board, make overall plans for responding to security risks in all areas and for all situations, and enhance the military's strategic capacity to protect the sovereignty, security, and development interests of our country," Mr. Li added.[582]

At the same time as Mr. Li's address, the PRC released the 14th Five-Year Plan in which the regime claims it will enable the PLA to accelerate its transition toward "informationization" and "intelligentization." These key words represent a commitment to adopting digital and networked military systems and the integration of "intelligent" systems using artificial intelligence and more.[583]

PLA Modernizing Its Military Services and Support Commands

The PLA Army (PLAA) has a standing force of 975,000 active-duty personnel in combat units. In recent years, the PLAA matured its readiness by accelerating "fight and win" training and fielding modern equipment to include increasing combat-like, force-on-force exercises with effective "blue force" opposition units that employ realistic US combat doctrine.[584]

The PLA Navy (PLAN) is the largest blue-water naval force in the world, with approximately 355 ships and submarines. The current force can conduct long-range precision strikes against land targets and maritime platforms using cruise missiles. Also, the PLAN has a growing anti-submarine warfare capability to protect both surface vessels and its ballistic missile submarine fleet.[585]

The PLA Air Force (PLAAF) and PLAN aviation are the largest aviation force in the Asia-Pacific and third largest in the world, with 2,800 total aircraft, which includes 2,250 combat aircraft. (The Russian air force is the second largest, with 3,914 aircraft, and the US Air

Force is the world's largest, with 13,362 aircraft.)[586] In 2019, the PLAAF announced the inclusion of a nuclear bomber capability thanks to the refuellable H-6N bomber.[587]

The PLA Rocket Force (PLARF) mans the PRC's conventional and nuclear forces. Specifically, those forces include new intercontinental ballistic missiles (ICBMs) that will improve the regime's nuclear capability thanks in part to the incorporation of multiple independently targetable reentry vehicle (MIRV) capabilities, as well as solid-fuel ICBMs. The PLARF already fields road-mobile, intermediate-range ballistic missiles, which are capable of delivering both conventional and nuclear warheads. Finally, the PLARF operates the PRC's new hypersonic weapon system, the DF-17 hypersonic glide vehicle.[588]

The PLA Strategic Support Force (SSF) underpins the other services with theater-level capabilities that include space, cyber, electronic, information, communications, and psychological warfare capabilities. The SSF is subdivided into a Space Systems Department and a Network Systems Department that oversees information operations.[589]

PLA's Joint Theater Commands

Modern forces fight jointly, not as individual service units. President Xi directed the Central Military Commission (CMC) to reorganize the PLA by streamlining and reducing structure while increasing firepower to realize joint service capabilities.[590]

Today, the PRC has five joint theater commands—Eastern, Southern, Western, Northern, and Central—based in seven military regions across China. These commands are subordinate to the CMC, which is similar to the US Joint Staff that operates out of the Pentagon in Washington, DC. President Xi, at the time of the restructuring, said the theater commands will "focus on combat" and "should be prepared to fight at any time."[591]

Much like the relationship between the US Joint Staff that issues orders for the US president to the five geographical combatant commands—e.g., the Indo-Pacific Command in Oahu, Hawaii—the CMC issues war plans that the five theater commands execute and all that implies, such as blending forces in theater to support the CMC's intent.[592]

The formation of China's joint staff and theater commands is a major step toward the modernization of the PLA.

Modernizing PLA Capabilities

President Xi's direction to modernize the PLA impacts all sectors of that military. A number of those capability areas are highlighted below.

Counter intervention capabilities: The PLA has in its inventory a host of anti-access/area-denial (A2/AD) capabilities, mostly rockets, missiles and anti-surface capabilities, intended to dissuade, deter, and defeat adversary intervention, such as in the case of a Taiwan contingency. These platforms are especially robust within the first island chain—the first chain of major archipelagos out from the East Asian continental mainland coast such as the Kuril Islands, the Japanese archipelago, Taiwan, the Philippines, and Borneo.[593]

Nuclear capabilities: The PLA is modernizing and expanding its nuclear forces. Specifically, it is investing in a triad—land, sea, and air delivery platforms—as well as building the infrastructure to support those forces. Further, to supply the required nuclear fuel for new warheads, the regime has increased its capacity to produce and separate plutonium through a network of fast-breeder reactors and reprocessing facilities. Plutonium-239 is the primary fissile isotope used in nuclear weapons.[594]

The 2021 Pentagon report on China indicates that the regime's accelerated pace of nuclear weapon production may provide the PLA with up to seven hundred deliverable nuclear warheads by 2027 and at least one thousand warheads by 2030.[595]

Part of the PLA's effort is evidenced by the construction in three locations of 345 total missile silos to accommodate the Dongfeng-41 (DF-41, CSS-20) intercontinental ballistic missile (ICBM). The

DF-41 has a range of approximately 9,300 miles, which can reach the entire United States. The missile also has the potential to carry ten warheads.[596]

A new development noted in 2020 was the regime's intent to increase the readiness of its nuclear forces to something not seen since the end of the Cold War (1991). That is, it moved to a launch-on-warning posture and dramatically expanded its silo-based forces for solid-fueled ICBMs.[597]

We can't say for certain about this possible development, because ambiguity continues to cloud the PRC's policy regarding weapons of mass destruction. That policy focuses on "maintaining a nuclear force structure able to survive an attack and respond with sufficient strength to inflict unacceptable damage on an enemy," according to IHS Janes.[598]

Dating back to China's 1992 decision to sign the Non-Proliferation Treaty, Beijing said at the time it would prohibit the first use of nuclear weapons. However, according to IHS Janes, in recent years, the regime's ambiguity over "how it may or may not use nuclear weapons in the struggle to control Taiwan" put the no-first-use pledge in question.[599]

New technology further confuses PRC's no-first-use pledge. Specifically, China's fielding of the hypersonic weapon system might indicate that the PRC is shifting away from its pledge, according to the Pentagon's former second-highest-ranking officer.[600]

"They look like a first-use weapon," then Joint Chiefs of Staff Vice Chairman General John Hyten said in an interview with CBS News. "That's what those weapons look like to me."[601]

General Hyten explained that the operation of the hypersonic weapon is radically different than a traditional ICBM. He said that a July 2021 test of the missile "went around the world, dropped off a hypersonic [nuclear-capable] glide vehicle that glided all the way back to China, that impacted a target in China."[602]

"We just don't know how we can defend against that technology," admitted US Disarmament Ambassador Robert Wood, referring to

China's hypersonic missile. That's because, unlike a traditional ICBM with a predictable trajectory, the hypersonic glide vehicle is released from the upper atmosphere and then can fly at a lower altitude than an ICBM—and, besides, it can change its target and trajectory repeatedly during the flight.[603]

Possible chemical and biological weapons capabilities: The Pentagon's 2021 China report indicates that the PRC continues biological activities with possible dual-use applications. That is worrisome, because it potentially suggests the regime is abrogating its obligations under the Biological and Toxins Weapons Convention (BWC) and the Chemical Weapons Convention (CWC). Specifically, studies by PRC military medical institutions indicate ongoing work with potent toxins, albeit with dual-use applications.[604]

China has an advanced biotechnology infrastructure and munitions-production capabilities to weaponize biological agents. Although the regime claims it complies with the BWC, the US government reports that, in the past, China had a small-scale offensive biological weapons program, according to IHS Janes. Further, states IHS Janes, Western intelligence agencies indicate that China's active biological weapons program included dedicated research and development activities funded by Beijing for this purpose.[605]

It remains an open question whether the PLA has an active biological weapons program. However, official statements indicate strong suspicion that the regime continues such work. For example, Dr. Dany Shoham, a researcher at the Begin-Sadat Center for Strategic Studies, Bar Ilan University, Israel, and a former senior intelligence analyst in the Israeli Defense Force, reported there are four facilities in China that possess parts of that nation's biological weapons program:[606]

1. Institute of Military Veterinary, Academy of Military Medical Sciences, Changchun
2. Center for Disease Control and Prevention, Chengdu Military Region

3. Wuhan Institute of Virology, Chinese Academy of Sciences, Hubei

4. Institute of Microbiology, Chinese Academy of Sciences, Beijing

The work at the Wuhan Institute of Virology drew international attention because of the COVID-19 pandemic. Former US Secretary of State Mike Pompeo and others are suspicious about the regime's continued work with contagious pathogens. He said:

> There are multiple labs that are continuing to conduct work, we think, on contagious pathogens inside of China today. And we don't know if they are operating at a level of security to prevent this [pandemic] from happening again. Remember this isn't the first time that we've had a virus come out of China.[607]

The PRC also claims it abides by the CWC, and it does not possess chemical weapons, nor does it transfer CWC-controlled chemicals or equipment to other state parties, like North Korea, which may have an active program.[608] However, the PLA invests in chemical defense capabilities and, according to IHS Janes, a 2001 US Department of Defense report states: "Beijing is believed to have an advanced chemical warfare program, including R&D [research and development], production, and weaponization capabilities." Of course, China has a large chemical industry with the capability to produce chemical weapons.[609]

Emergent capabilities: In late 2021, President Xi spoke at a conference on military equipment and weapons in Beijing. He claimed at the time that China achieved "leapfrog development" in military technologies during the country's 13th Five-Year Plan, which ended in 2020.[610]

The plan's progress served "the material and technological underpinning for the country's strategic capabilities," according to Mr. Xi. He went on to say during China's 14th Five-Year Plan (2021–25), progress is needed to support the PLA's stated goal to "build a modern military" by 2027. He called for China's defense industry to "step up" the development of a "modern management system" for weapons and equipment. He added, "This [will] make a positive contribution to the realization of the 100-year goal of building the PLA."[611]

Some of those "positive contributions" are on the horizon, which are profiled below.

Hypersonic missiles

These platforms were much in the news beginning in 2021, primarily because there was public acknowledgement by US officials that we are "behind" China and Russia in the deployment of hypersonic missiles.

In October 2021, then Vice Chief of Staff General John Hyten acknowledged that the US military researched a hypersonic glide vehicle system similar to the one tested by China, but after two failed tests, the project was canceled. He went on to explain that the Pentagon's complicated bureaucracy and risk-averse culture prevented the US from developing more advanced technologies to counter China's advancing military capabilities.[612]

Meanwhile, in 2019, the PLARF first deployed the Dongfeng-17 (DF-17) medium-range ballistic missile, which carries the DF-ZF hypersonic glide vehicle. That platform was displayed in the fall of 2020 to help mark the anniversary of the CCP's rule.[613]

"The DF-17 is the first deployed hypersonic strike weapon for the PLA and can travel at speeds of more than 7,000 miles per hour—enough to outrun current US anti-missile interceptors," according to an article in the *Washington Times*. "Additionally, the missile is said to be maneuverable, a feature that allows it to further avoid electronic detection."[614]

Most disconcerting is the fact that hypersonic missiles significantly decrease defensive reaction times. Specifically, it's hard to detect the pre-launch actions because the missile does not require easily detected launch preparations and, as a result, defensive commander decision-making is radically shortened.[615]

Understandably, the missile is a potential game-changer. "It will play a vital role in safeguarding China's territorial integrity, as regions including the South China Sea, the Taiwan Strait and Northeast Asia are all within its striking range," wrote Yang Chengjun, a Chinese missile expert.[616]

Mr. Yang explains that the missile can change trajectories midflight to avoid interceptors, and even though US defense systems like the Terminal High Altitude Area Defense (THAAD) system and the Standard Missile-3, part of the Aegis Weapon System, can detect a launch, such detection would be difficult because the "launch in actual combat will be done secretly."[617]

PLAN's Blue-Water Fleet

The PLAN is directly challenging the US Navy on many fronts, and surpasses the American force in the size of the overall fleet. As noted earlier in this chapter, PLAN has 355 ships and submarines, including 145 major surface combatants. That fleet, according to the Pentagon's 2021 report, will grow to 420 ships by 2025 and 460 ships by 2030, and much of that growth will be in major surface combatants. Meanwhile, by comparison, in June 2021, the US Navy had 251 active ships in commission.[618]

PLAN's submarine force is rapidly modernizing as well. In 2021, it operated six nuclear-powered ballistic-missile submarines, six nuclear-powered attack submarines, and forty-six diesel-powered attack submarines. The Pentagon estimates PLAN will maintain between sixty-five and seventy submarines through the balance of the decade. The US Navy boasts sixty-eight active submarines as of June 2021.[619]

A third PLAN aircraft carrier is expected to be launched no later than 2024. That ship is reported to be equivalent in size to America's new Ford-class nuclear aircraft carrier, with a catapult launch system. Expect additional PLAN carriers to follow. Meanwhile, the US Navy has eleven active aircraft carriers.[620]

Future carrier-based aircraft are in the works as well. The J-15 catapult-capable variant is in development. Another variant, the J-15d, a two-seat platform with electronic support measures/electronic intelligence-gathering pods, is a necessary ingredient for a modern, forward-deployed (globally capable) carrier system.[621]

The PLAN is augmented by China's coast guard, the largest by far of any country in the region, which includes the twelve thousand-ton China coast guard cutter, the largest coast guard vessel in the world. It is noteworthy that the Chinese empowered their coast guard to use actual "military force" against foreign vessels, a critical combat multiplier across the nation's periphery, such as the South China Sea.[622]

PLA Air Force Expanding

The PLAAF, the world's third-largest air force, serves as the PRC's strategic air force that is capable of long-range airpower projection. In fact, the PRC's 2019 defense white paper described PLAAF's missions and tasks as transitioning to conduct "offensive and defensive operations." Lieutenant General Ding Laihang, who assumed the post as PLAAF commander in 2017, told his service to build a "strategic" force capable of projecting airpower at a long range.[623]

The Pentagon report indicates that the CMC directed PLAAF to transform into a more effective and capable force able to conduct joint operations. That transformation includes PLAAF hosting most of the PLA's aviation, airborne, air defense, radar, electronic countermeasure, and communication forces and the formation of five theater-command air forces.[624]

Regarding emergent platforms, the J-20 fighter jet is PLAAN's fifth-generation stealth aircraft that is a near copy of the US' J-35 stealth fighter. Likely, as widely reported, blueprints and other technology for the J-20 were obtained illegally from US defense firms.[625]

PLA in Space

Earlier in this chapter, we reviewed the PLA's new navigation satellite constellation and its space-based intelligence-gathering network. What needs to be profiled here is China's offensive space capability and its counterspace system.

In 2021, China launched what it claims to be a "classified space debris mitigation technology satellite." The reality is that the system's technology is dual-use and could easily act as an anti-satellite capability. That satellite, known as the Shijian-21, has a robotic arm used to move space junk, but it could also be used to crush an enemy (read "US") satellite.[626]

It is noteworthy that the Shijian-21 was launched into a geosynchronous orbit, alongside many of the United States' most sensitive satellite systems, such as the US Nuclear Command, Communications, and Control and the US Military Communications System.[627]

"The Shijian-21 satellite is a game-changer," said Brandon Weichert, author of *Winning Space: How America Remains a Superpower*. "It is a real-world offensive capability that can hunt and destroy American systems and render the US military on earth deaf, dumb, and blind."[628]

Counter-space capabilities are more than just anti-satellite. Dean Cheng, a Heritage Foundation senior research fellow on Chinese affairs, said: "China views counterspace capabilities as not simply anti-satellite but also anti-terrestrial." This means these space-based systems hold at risk American "launch sites, mission control facilities, tracking stations, and the datalinks that tie them all together."[629]

The PLA's space- and ground-based offensive capabilities are reported by others as well. A 2020 Secure World Foundation report, "Global Counterspace Capabilities: An Open-Source Assessment," states that China is beginning to more strongly assert its interests and sees counterspace capabilities as a crucial enabler. In fact, Brain Weeden, the SWF director of program planning, said that China is refining technologies it has been working on during the past five to ten years, including direct-ascent anti-satellite (DA-ASAT) capabilities, rendezvous proximity operations, potential co-orbital technology, and ground-based laser systems. Mr. Weeden acknowledged that China's DA-ASAT capabilities may have reached operational deployment.[630]

In April 2022, the Defense Intelligence Agency acknowledged that

China has an impressive collection of anti-satellite systems that target US systems. "China has multiple ground-based laser weapons of varying power levels to disrupt, degrade, or damage satellites that include a current limited capability to employ laser systems against satellite sensors," said the DIA. "By the mid- to late-2020s, China may field higher power systems that extend the threat to the structures of non-optical satellites," as well.[631]

The DIA also reported that China's satellite fleet includes more than 250 systems, second only to that of the U.S., "and nearly doubling China's in-orbit systems since 2018."[632]

There is also China's new space station, which Richard Fisher, with the International Assessment and Strategy Center, indicates, may well "incorporate additional large military modules that can be equipped with lasers, microwave, or missile-based anti-satellite systems."[633]

"They're going counterspace in a big way," explained then Vice Chief of Staff General John Hyten in 2021. General Hyten, who previously commanded the US Air Force Space Command, said Chinese officers "are doing all those things because they saw how the United States has used space for dominant advantage."[634]

Don't forget about China's civil-military fusion strategy that requires the collaborative effort by all defense and civilian efforts to support CCP goals, which includes the goal of Chinese dominance of space.

The PRC's civil-military fusion strategy resulted in a heavily militarized Chinese space program. "The launch sites, control centers, and many of the satellites are directly run by the PLA," according to Defense One.[635]

In conclusion, the PRC is producing a massive number of new aircraft, ships, missiles, satellites, weapons systems, surveillance capabilities, a space arsenal, and much more. Its modernization campaign fuels Western belief that the CCP indeed has global ambitions and intends to employ its giant, very sophisticated military to help create a new world order in its image.

IS THE PRC REALLY PREPARING TO FIGHT THE UNITED STATES?

We established earlier in this chapter that the PRC is fighting an unrestricted war against the United States and believes it is winning because we've never responded. Expect that effort to continue, but simultaneously anticipate the PLA to become very serious about a future shooting war with the US, and there's plenty of evidence supporting that view.

The previous section of this chapter indicated that the PLA already trains its soldiers to engage in exercises that closely simulate fighting US forces. That's how armies train; that is, they exercise their combat skills to high standards against a capable proxy force that uses their likely opponent's doctrine.

Meanwhile, the PLA Air Force and PLA Navy practice shooting at full-scale mockups of major US warships like aircraft carriers, according to a 2021 news report.[636]

From the air, those Chinese military-built targets look like an American aircraft carrier and an Ardleigh Burke-class destroyer, which are found in the Taklamakan Desert, located in southwestern Xinjiang in Northwest China, as part of a new target-range complex, according to USNI News that references satellite imagery provided by the company Maxar.[637]

The site of the full-scale targets is near a training range that China uses for testing its carrier killer DF-21D anti-ship ballistic-missile practice, according to a 2013 *Business Insider* report.[638]

The extent of the PLA's investment in giant, US-type ship targets at remote ranges is evidence of their concern. And, according to Pentagon reports, "A primary objective of the PLARF will be to keep carriers at risk from anti-ship ballistic missiles throughout the western Pacific," writes USNI News.[639]

There is more to the warning that the PLA is preparing to go to war with United States forces. Evidently, the US can no longer be assured of victory in the event of such a conflict, according to a December 2021 report by the US-China Economic and Security Review Commission (USCC).

The USCC expressed concern that the US could be drawn into a war with China over the future of Taiwan, which the PRC considers a breakaway region.[640]

The bipartisan report found that, for the first time, the PLA was prepared to successfully invade Taiwan regardless of a US intervention. Further, the USCC found that China's modernization efforts and expanded nuclear capabilities have increased the risk of such a war.[641]

This is perhaps the first time the feasibility of an American victory in a war with the PLA has been questioned. In fact, US Rep. Mike Gallagher (R-WI) said in October 2021 that the US would "probably lose a war" with the PRC if such a conflict happened prior to the fielding of America's new naval fleet in the 2030s.[642]

"I am very concerned about our failure to build a bigger navy," Gallagher said. "I think you're seeing a less favorable balance of power by the day."[643]

The congressman said the ships and accompanying capabilities being budgeted for the Navy today won't be delivered until 2025 or 2026. Meanwhile, he echoed concern that China is likely to invade Taiwan long before that time frame.[644]

Risk of a US-China shooting war is not limited to a possible Taiwan assault. The USCC report also details the PRC's global ambitions and its increased nuclear capabilities.

The USCC agrees with the Pentagon's 2021 report on China that the CCP is in a "sprint" to nuclear superiority. Further, and unfortunately, Beijing has no interest in nuclear non-proliferation, a view expressed by US Sen. Angus King (I-ME).[645]

The USCC report states: "China's nuclear buildup puts it on a path to become a qualitative nuclear peer of the United States in around a decade, with a similarly diversified, precise, and survivable force." It concludes that Beijing would not engage in arms control agreements, believing they are a "trap" designed to prevent China from achieving global dominance, the CCP's ultimate goal.[646]

More frightening (if that's possible), the USCC report found that the risk of nuclear conflict with China was increasing, especially given the possible first use with hypersonic weapons, as well as the PRC's new military posture that "suggests it could also be intended to support a new strategy of limited nuclear first use."[647]

"Such a strategy would enable Chinese leaders to leverage their nuclear forces to accomplish Chinese political objectives beyond survival, such as coercing another state or deterring US intervention in a war over Taiwan," the USCC report states.[648]

So, given the escalated nuclear threat, what should the US do? The USCC recommends the US increase investments in diplomatic strategy, organize more non-proliferation agreements, and modernize our nuclear arsenal. After all, "the risks of a nuclear exchange between China and the United States are higher today than in the past," the report states.[649]

Now back to our original question: Is the PRC really preparing to fight the United States? The answer is "yes," and we must stop being so naïve and get ready.

CONCLUSION

The PRC is building a world-class military, and it has almost put in place an infrastructure to help the CCP realize a new world order in China's authoritarian image. Yes, a modern, globally capable armed force is part of the catalyst to deliver President Xi's desired outcome; turning China into a global power by 2049. However, hand in hand with a fully capable armed force is a foreign policy, a geopolitical agenda, that must be in sync with other Chinese national elements of power to deliver the desired new world order. That's the topic of the next chapter.

7

Kings of the East: Geopolitical Agenda

Most Americans are close to total ignorance about the world. They are ignorant. That is an unhealthy condition in a country in which foreign policy has to be endorsed by the people if it is to be pursued. And it makes it much more difficult for any president to pursue an intelligent policy that does justice to the complexity of the world.[650]

—Zbigniew Brzezinski (1928–2017)
Counselor to Presidents Lyndon B. Johnson and Jimmy Carter

This chapter addresses the PRC's geopolitical efforts to help create a new world order. The Chinese regime attacks the current US-led world order by targeting international bodies like the United Nations to leverage them to oppose Western ways in favor of the CCP's authoritarian model. Further, the Chinese use their economic and other sources of national power such as the PLA and BRI to win over sovereign nations to the regime's way of thinking and the acceptance of a China-friendly world model.

We begin this chapter, however, with a brief explanation of the term "geopolitics," and then explore in two sections the CCP's geopolitical efforts to reshape the international system in its image.

WHAT IS "GEOPOLITICS"?

The term "geopolitics" comes from the Greek words for "earth, land" (γῆ gê) and "politics" (πολιτική politikē). Until recently, the term was understood as "a method of studying foreign policy to understand, explain, and predict international political behavior through geographical variables" such as area studies and demography.[651]

The word "geopolitics" was first attributed to Swedish political scientist Rudolf Kjellen at the beginning of the twentieth century. Since that time, others—such as Halford Mackinder, a British scholar—advanced the "heartland theory," which states "who rules east Europe commands the heartland. Who rules the heartland commands the world-island. Who rules the world-island commands the world." Evidently, Mackinder's theory was embraced by Adolf Hitler, who invaded Russia (the heartland) in 1941, seeking to dominate the world. Hitler failed to understand the Soviet people's resilience, which contributed to the demise of the Third Reich, a geopolitical failure.[652]

America's Alfred Thayer Mahan (1840–1914), a naval officer and historian, saw geopolitics through the significance of navies in world conflict. Nicholas Spykman (1893–1943), an American political scientist and one of the founders of the classical realist school in American foreign policy, believed it was important to control the "Rimland" to command the world, which consisted of Western Europe, the Middle East, and much of Asia. Both men believed naval power was critical—especially the supremacy of key straits, isthmuses, and peninsulas that dominated ocean trade routes such as the Strait of Gibraltar and the Panama Canal.[653]

The Vietnam War era (1955–1975) was famous for the geopolitical "domino theory," the concept that communism would incrementally spread to adjacent countries like falling dominoes. In 1961, then Vice President Lyndon B. Johnson endorsed the domino theory to President John F. Kennedy by arguing that the US must hold the line in Vietnam; otherwise, communism would topple other countries across that region. That view was endorsed by then Secretary of State Dean Rusk, Secretary of Defense Robert McNamara, director of Central Intelligence John McCone, and the Pentagon's Joint Chiefs of Staff.[654]

"We have no further fallback position in southeast Asia...strengthening other areas of Asia, in the context of our having been pushed out of SVN [South Vietnam], would be a thoroughly non-productive effort militarily, and politically it seems dubious we'd even be offered the opportunity to attempt it," wrote the Joint Chiefs of Staff. They strongly endorsed drawing the line in Vietnam and supported President Johnson's escalation of forces to 536,100 personnel by 1968.[655]

More recently, geopolitics was understood as an explanation of world conflict among global movements focused on the premise that all countries struggle to survive by competing for limited resources. One such view was expressed by Harvard Professor Samuel Huntington (1927–2008), in his 1996 book, *The Clash of Civilizations and the Remaking of World Order*, which argued that, with the fall of the Soviet Union (1991), Islam would become the biggest obstacle to Western domination of the world.[656]

Aspects of these geopolitical theories remain germane today. However, as the world has shrunk, thanks to instant communication and radically shortened global travel time, geography is not as important to understanding the concept. Rather, in its place, geopolitical issues today tend to revolve around ideologies, cultures, crass power, and other differences among countries, which explains the latest application of the term.

Today, contemporary researchers employ the term "geopolitics" most often to describe a broad spectrum of concepts such as "a synonym for international political relations" and "to imply the global structure of such relations."[657]

CCP'S GEOPOLITICAL INTENTIONS ARE CLEAR

On January 17, 2022, President Xi addressed the World Economic Forum to outline his geopolitical view of the future "international

political relations" and "global structure for such relations." He introduced that view with a Chinese saying: "The momentum of the world
either flourishes or declines; the state of the world either progresses or
regresses."[658]

The implication of Mr. Xi's statement is that the PRC's geopolitical
vision for the future is best for the world—a progressive aim. He then
outlined that vision in appealing terms:

> We should follow the trend of history, work for a stable interna-
> tional order, advocate common values of humanity, and build
> a community with a shared future for mankind. We should
> choose dialogue over confrontation, inclusiveness over exclu-
> sion, and stand against all forms of unilateralism, protectionism,
> hegemony or power politics.[659]

Mr. Xi's speech advocates change, an inclusive, big-tent view, arguably a new world order—albeit with China at the helm. The problem
is his words are not consistent with his actions. Yes, he intends to reach
the lofty goal of putting China at the lead of a future new world order.
However, long ago he enlisted his geopolitical warriors to fight for that
outcome using a very different—a far less liberal—approach.

Years ago, Mr. Xi sent his "wolf warrior" diplomats across the world
to use their positions, but not to seek dialogue, inclusiveness, and plu-
ralism. Rather, these Marxist-Leninist evangelists were sent abroad to
threaten foreign governments, businesses, private institutions, and
elected leaders that menace CCP interests. The only values, community,
and politics that mattered were those that elevated Beijing to the forefront of the world.

Those Marxist-Leninist diplomat evangelists were on a deadly mission. Their explicit orders came in November 2019 from Foreign Minister Wang Yi, who emphasized to his diplomat warriors they must display
a stronger "fighting spirit." Further, the CCP's top diplomat echoed

President Xi's warrior aim when Wang said that Beijing would ensure that its "bottom lines are never violated," and then he warned, "[China] will never accept unilateral sanctions or any acts of bullying."[660]

CHINESE COMMUNIST INTERPRETATION OF CCP GEOPOLITICS

We saw firsthand what Mr. Wang meant by "never accept...bullying" during the March 2021 bilateral meeting in Anchorage, Alaska, between the Xi and Biden administrations. That confrontation demonstrated a paradigm shift in the PRC's geopolitical behavior, what is considered "evidence of its rise to great-power status which entitles China to a new role in world affairs—one that cannot be reconciled with unquestioned US dominance."[661]

That view is expressed by a CCP sycophant, Yan Xuetong, a professor at the Chinese Institute of International Relations at Tsinghua University. "The US-led unipolar order is fading away, its demise hastened by China's rise and the US' relative decline. In its place will come a multipolar order, with US-Chinese relations at its core," said Mr. Yan.[662]

Professor Yan helps us understand the regime's geopolitical thinking. Specifically, he explained the new order view among Chinese political leadership when he wrote in *Foreign Affairs* that the CCP seeks to become "a global power that can meet the rest of the world on an equal footing." Then he argued, somewhat unconvincingly, that China "thinks of itself as a developing country and rightly so, considering its GDP per capita remains far behind those of advanced economies." He continued by stating the "developing country" label affects Beijing's geopolitical alignment, which means "its loyalties will still lie firmly with the developing world."[663]

Professor Yan went on to explain that, from an ideological perspective, China "is anxious not to frame relations with the west as a new cold war" that could "trigger a backlash that might hinder their country's continued growth." Nor does the CCP expect their Communist ideology to become as popular as Western liberalism, because the Chinese "political system and governance model cannot merely be exported to other countries." However, even though the CCP will try to shape the ideological environment to favor its rise, it will push "back against the notion that western political values have universal appeal and validity."[664]

"Beijing does not reject multilateral rules and institutions out of hand," posited Professor Yan. However, the CCP will not "accept rules that the United States makes without consultation with China." Beijing seeks international norms that are truly inclusive and multi-lateral—or, more precisely, those norms acceptable to the CCP's authoritarian view of the world.[665]

Then Mr. Yan called out examples of Beijing's international cooperation, such as the meeting between Xie Zhenhua, China's climate envoy, and his US counterpart, John Kerry, as well as Chinese Foreign Minister Wang's willingness to work with the Biden administration's efforts to relaunch the 2015 Iran nuclear deal.[666]

Professor Yan, Foreign Minister Wang, and President Xi spin quite a fairytale for the gullible world. They say one thing but do something entirely different. However, not everyone is fooled by their smooth-tongued talk.

WESTERN INTERPRETATIONS OF CCP'S GEOPOLITICAL SHIFT

There is no doubt about President Xi's ambitions, writes Jude Blanchette, the Freeman Chair in China Studies at the Center for Strategic and International Studies. Blanchette writes that Mr. Xi "is a man on a mission," which includes forcefully asserting China's influence on the international stage, and that means he "picked fights with many of his neighbors and antagonized countries farther away like the United States." In fact, Blanchette warned, "Xi is impatient with the status quo, possesses a high tolerance for risk, and seems to feel a pronounced sense of urgency in challenging the international order."[667]

Mr. Xi is determined, wrote Blanchette, in his belief that the Chinese political system may well "enable China to overcome long-standing domestic challenges and achieve a new level of global centrality." Past Chinese leaders such as Hu Jintao took a slower, more deliberate path to achieving change. However, Mr. Xi began to reorder the home front and now has turned to realigning global affairs to his liking. He reasoned that the Soviet Union collapsed due to corruption and a failure to embrace Marxist ideology. President Xi noted, according to Blanchette, that when the Soviet Union collapsed, there were at the time more Soviet Communist Party members than today's CCP has in its ranks, yet "nobody was man enough to stand up and resist." President Xi is committed to making sure that won't happen to the CCP.[668]

So, according to Blanchette, now that President Xi put affairs inside China in place, he has turned to the global stage. He quickly reclaimed the South China Sea as sovereign Chinese territory, established an air defense identification zone in the East China Sea (an affront to Japan and Taiwan), launched the New Development Bank, established the Belt and Road Initiative, and then proposed the creation of the Asian Infrastructure Investment Bank. All these actions were breathtaking moves that caught the staid West-led international community off guard, clear evidence, as Blanchette said, of "a man on a mission."[669]

Then geopolitical events started to speed up in 2021, thanks to the Biden administration's fumbling. President Xi perceived a window of opportunity thanks to weakness demonstrated by President Biden, specifically, the across-the-world retreat of the US from global affairs in places like Afghanistan. So, Beijing advanced boldly, using "gray zone" tactics, practices via the elements of national power by sending Chinese wolf-warrior diplomats to further intimidate and harass countries, manhandle international organizations, seize economic opportunity, and establish a global military presence.[670]

USCC REPORT: EXAMPLES OF CCP'S GEOPOLITICAL PARADIGM SHIFT

Kerry Brown, a professor of Chinese studies at King's College London, testified before the USCC to state that the CCP's nationalism is "great for domestic politics…and lies at the heart of the Xi leadership, in terms of [China's] external messaging, it is deeply, and increasingly problematic." No doubt, Mr. Xi's aggressive, nationalist tone has become very obvious to the international audience.[671]

The USCC's 2020 annual report illustrates the "problematic" point made by Professor Brown. In November 2019, "after the Swedish branch of an international free speech organization gave an award to a Swedish bookseller kidnapped by China in 2015 and [then] Stockholm passed a law calling for a national security review of Huawei in Sweden's 5G [network] rollout, the response from China's diplomatic corps was gangster-like," said Brown. Specifically, China's ambassador reflected on the kidnapping and the Huawei review to the Swedish authorities, saying: "We treat our friends with fine wine, but for our enemies, we have shotguns."[672]

The "shotguns" comment, according to Chinese state media, was the embodiment of Foreign Minister Wang's diplomatic wolf-warrior ethos. The contemporary cultural reference to the term "wolf warrior" is attributed to the 2015 Chinese movie by the same name, which was introduced earlier in this volume. However, from ancient times in China, a person described as a wolf is someone known for savagery, destruction, and greed; it is a term that fits many contemporary Chinese diplomats.[673]

The CCP-inspired wolf warrior-like comments were directed at the US, such as when its representatives threatened to respond to China's passage of the liberty-killing Hong Kong national security law (2020). At the time, according to the USCC report, "The head of China's Hong Kong and Macau affairs office replied, the era when the Chinese cared what others thought and looked up to others is in the past, never to return."[674]

There's no doubt the wolf-warrior diplomatic ethos is top-driven. In fact, the CCP took steps to deepen what it called the "party-ification" of the ministry of foreign affairs (the CCP's diplomatic corps) "to ensure its ideological commitment to CCP directives." Qi Yu, an ideological training specialist appointed to the ministry of foreign affairs, wrote an essay that called for Chinese diplomats to "firmly counterattack against words and deeds in the international arena that assault the leadership of China's communist party and our country's socialist system." That aggressive ethos aims to export China's totalitarian governance model to the rest of the world, said Miles Yu, the China adviser to former US Secretary of State Mike Pompeo. "So, the challenge that [the] CCP poses to the world is not only a technological challenge, it's not just an economic challenge, not merely a military challenge," said Mr. Yu. "But more importantly, it's a moral challenge. Because the moral nature of the communist rule is antithetical to all the major foundations of modern society."[675]

Mr. Yu is a Chinese-born academic who is now a visiting fellow at Stanford University's Hoover Institute. He explains the CCP's model of governance is denying the unalienable rights of individuals. "That's why they have to lock up the millions of Uyghurs into concentration camps, not just to physically torture them, but, most importantly, to brainwash them so that they will get rid of their religious belief."[676]

Mr. Yu put the CCP's persecution of Falun Gong and Uyghurs into historic context. "If Soviet communism focused more on physical elimination of dissent, Chinese communism focuses far more on the conformity of everybody to communism by eliminating individual thoughts, [and] individual freedom to worship," he said. Thus, Mr. Yu argues, the China challenge is in a sense a moral challenge to the world.[677]

Then Mr. Yu put the China moral challenge into a geopolitical perspective. A CCP-led global world order would be very different from the current free and democratic situation. Under a CCP order, people would be "subjected to the will of the state." They would be required, as outlined in an earlier chapter, to study *Xi Jinping Thought* and bow to the CCP's interpretation of history and individual freedoms, Yu explained.[678]

REALITY CHECK ON CCP'S GEOPOLITICAL AIM

The USCC's 2021 annual report on China indicates that the CCP seeks to undermine the current international system and replace it with a Beijing-approved Marxist order, not the propaganda Mr. Xi pushed at the 2022 World Economic Forum. Rather, the truth is "the Chinese Communist Party's ambitions for global leadership became ever clearer in this, the CCP's centennial year," said USCC commission chair Carolyn Bartholomew.[679]

The CCP's growing aggression is a concern among the international community, said Bartholomew. She continued, "Announcing its goal to provide the world with a 'new model of human advancement,' the Chinese government deepened its embrace of aggression, wolf warrior behavior, and coercion, heightening concerns throughout the Indo-Pacific and elsewhere in the world about China's rise."[680]

That concern is real and growing. In fact, the USCC report indicates the CCP asserts that it is preparing for a confrontation between the "order of China" and the "chaos of the West." Further, the Party states it has a growing commitment to fight "strong enemies," a Communist Chinese synonym for the United States.[681]

Similar words came from the Sixth Plenum communique, which announced that CCP leaders intend to fight the United States. Specifically, the document states the CCP is dedicated to the development and proliferation of Marxism-Leninism, albeit with "Chinese characteristics," which they promise will create "a new model for human advancement," replacing the current (read "US-led") world order.[682]

USCC commission member Jim Talent, a former US senator, described the CCP's aim as "global" and said the regime's authoritarian ideology was intended to replace the United States, "not coexist with it." "Their intent…is to advance towards their 'community of common human destiny,' which it's pretty clear they define as replacing the existing rules-based international order with one that resembles a hierarchy, with China at the top," Talent said.[683]

The CCP aims to rebuild the international order in its own image, according to the USCC report, something the regime has repeatedly declared and its foreign policy (geopolitics) are grounded, the Communists claim, in principles such as "universality," "constructive dialogue," and "win-win cooperation."[684]

The Pentagon's 2021 China report indicates much the same about the CCP's grand strategy, which calls for "the great rejuvenation of the Chinese nation" by 2049. That means, according to the Pentagon report, matching or surpassing the US in global influence and power, displacing US allies, and revising the international order to be "more advantageous to Beijing's authoritarian system and national interests."[685]

Chinese leader Xi's words echo the interpretations shared by the USCC and the Pentagon about the regime's global ambitions. In 2018, President Xi said the CCP must "lead the reform of the global governance system," and again in 2021 he said that "a more just and equitable international order must be heeded" and led by China. That's not dissimilar from the views expressed in Mr. Xi's 2022 Economic World Council speech outlined earlier in this section.[686]

The Sixth Plenum's communique also called for taking action to create a "new model for human advancement," words often expressed in official Chinese documents. That communique called for proselytizing Marxist ideology across the world—not unlike the old domino geopolitical theory of the Vietnam era—as the sole political philosophy "not only capable of dismantling the old world, but also of building a new one [albeit under Chinese oversight]."[687]

Remember, the March 2021 US-China meeting in Alaska demonstrated this new approach when China's top diplomat scolded the US delegation by telling them they did "not have the qualification…to speak to China from a position of strength." That statement was interpreted by world media and the politicians in Beijing to mean that China has become "ambitious and outspoken in its claims to global leadership."[688]

Does China's new aggressiveness really make the regime an adversary? That's a helpful question, because in 2019, when Joe Biden was running for the presidency, he said of China: "They're not competition for us." However, by mid-2021, Mr. Biden expressed quite a different view when he said the relationship with China is like a "battle between democracies and autocracies" and warned that the CCP was seeking to dominate the United States. Biden continued, "[Xi] firmly believes that China, before the year '30, '35, is going to own America because autocracies can make quick decisions."[689]

Many Western Chinese experts agree that the CCP is hegemonic, ambitious to displace the United States. Anders Corr, a principal with the advisory firm Corr Analytics, said, "The CCP's goals of global hegemony are real, not just propaganda…. They are moving forward with laws that have global extraterritorial effect, tied to aggressive extradition efforts, along with increasing influence, trending towards control, of U.N. and other international institutions and multinational corporations."[690]

Mr. Corr says the CCP is pursuing a whole-of-nation strategy and is almost certainly committed to go farther than the US in pursuing conflict. Previously in this volume, Mr. Corr said China is "willing to risk war," even nuclear war which is "unthinkable for citizens in democracies." However, the PRC considers that a weakness to exploit.[691]

President Xi evidently believes, as does Mr. Corr, in the CCP's propaganda. In November 2021, General Secretary Xi argued in a speech reprinted by *Qiushi,* a bimonthly publication that addresses China's governance and perspectives, that Beijing's model of "socialism with Chinese characteristics" had brightened the prospects for the global socialist movement following the collapse of the Soviet Union. He explained that the CCP must remember its duty is to "liberate all of humanity" and serve as the "gravediggers of capitalism." Further, at the annual forum on Chinese diplomacy, Foreign Minister Wang said Beijing must propagate China's "way of governance" around the globe to "guide" the world in its "thinking" on historical progress. He went on to state that Beijing must make new efforts to increase the PRC's international influence and create a global "community of common human destiny," or the regime's preferred term, a Sino- (Chinese-) centric world order.[692]

There should be no doubt that the CCP intends to propagate its Marxist-Leninist views across the world, albeit under the guise of President Xi's "rejuvenation" and not his transparently hypocritical call at the World Economic Forum for "dialogue over confrontation, inclusiveness over exclusion, and stand against all forms of unilateralism, protectionism, hegemony or power politics."[693]

CHINA'S MANIPULATION OF MULTINATIONAL ORGANIZATIONS & AGREEMENTS

China manipulates multinational organizations of all varieties by ignoring obligations, flagrantly dismissing rules, and planting its diplomatic agents in leadership positions to advantage the regime. This approach is a significant aspect of President Xi's aim to create a new world order in China's image.

In recent years, many Communist Chinese diplomats moved into key international positions. Specifically, these agents of President Xi occupy leadership positions in standard-setting bodies through the use of economic and political leverage to reshape the international order.

The regime's influence comes at a strategic point. "Beijing believes that China has arrived at the point where it is the ascendant power and no longer needs to hide its intentions," explained, Brett Schaefer, the Jay Kingham fellow in International Regulatory Affairs in the Margaret Thatcher Center for Freedom, at the Heritage Foundation in Washington, DC. He said in his 2021 speech that the PRC perceives "the United States, which China sees as its primary competitor, is a waning power—or at least losing power relative to China."[694]

Soberly, according to Schaefer, "China has taken full advantage of the open, rules-based international system." Schaefer summarized how China took "full advantage" of the international system below.[695]

- "It has enriched itself, dramatically increasing its per capita GDP.
- "It has become a central cog in the international manufacturing and trading system.
- "It has used its huge market to leverage concessions from investors and tech companies.
- "Arguing that it is still a developing country, it demands special treatment to avoid the commitments expected of developed nations.
- "It has participated in the international system with intent to defend and advance its interests but dismissed criticism or adverse outcomes, such as the 2016 UNCLOS [UN Convention on the Law of the Sea] tribunal ruling on its claims in the South China Sea."

Mr. Schaefer concludes this summary by stating that "China has shrewdly applied diplomatic and economic pressure to advance its interests, maximize its benefits, and minimize its costs under the current system."[696]

In fact, China's international influence is breathtaking in its scope and was gained in a short period, which serves the regime's long-term goal, according to Schaefer. The regime's primary aim "is for China to supersede the United States as the preeminent global power and reorder the international system to its benefit." This is significant because Chinese values are radically different from Western values and principles, which "threaten the illiberal government of Beijing," explained Schaefer.[697]

Understandably, given the above, when there is a conflict between China's interests and Western values, Beijing's wolf-warrior diplomats fight to win within international organizations—and, more frequently than ever before, China is succeeding, because its sphere of influence is quite broad across the international community. Consider some daunting facts about the CCP's diplomatic reach into the international arena.

The PRC's footprint within the United Nations system is extensive. In 2009, the UN system hosted 784 Chinese—read "Communist"—diplomatic agents. By 2019, there were 1,336 Chinese nationals at the UN, a 68 percent increase. That change grew thanks to the PRC's expanding financial contributions to the organization; i.e., it bought influence in the New York-based international forum.[698]

For a listing of Chinese Communist diplomats in key leadership positions of international organizations, not just the UN, see the 2021 USCC report, "PRC Representation in International Organizations."[699]

Understand that it is Beijing's primary objective for diplomats it sends to the UN to advance China's self-serving goals. For example, former Under-Secretary-General Wu Hongbo explained in a video how he abused his UN position to remove a "Xinxiang [Muslim] separatist." Mr. Wu said, "I think being a Chinese diplomat means one can't be careless, when it is about protecting China's [read "CCP's"] national interest and safety. We have to strongly defend the motherland's interests." That Muslim activist was ejected from the United Nations.[700]

The PRC's influence is indeed substantial, more so than sheer numbers of diplomats. In 2021, Chinese Communist personnel led four of the fifteen UN specialized agencies. By contrast, the US leads one such agency. Expect the PRC's diplomatic agents to continue to increase their hold on the reins of international power at the United Nations.[701]

Chinese Communist leaders within the UN hierarchy also help the regime economically. Consider that China's Houlin Zhao, Secretary-General of the International Telecommunication Union (ITU), who "has encouraged China to advance its proposals for internet governance at the ITU, dismissed US concerns about Huawei's involvement in 5G networks, and explicitly endorsed the Belt and Road Initiative." Controlling the Internet is one of President Xi's international goals, as outlined in the previous chapter.[702]

Chinese diplomats use their UN positions to further support President Xi's goal of isolating Taiwan, the Chairman's primary domestic political aim. Its agents increasingly use their power to block Taiwan's participation in the UN system, such as denying the democratic state's participation as an observer in the World Health Organization (WHO).[703]

Other Chinese UN diplomats use their power in much the same manner. The Chinese Communist Secretary-General Fang Liu, the head of the International Civil Aviation Organization, rejected Taiwanese efforts to attend that organization's meetings even though the democratic island is a major Asian air traffic hub.[704]

On the broader front at the UN and elsewhere across the international arena, the PRC has a reputation for working closely with like-minded authoritarian regimes. Specifically, it works with regimes like Iran and North Korea to revise and work around international institutions to advance mutual interests, according to Jessica Chen Weiss, an associate professor of government at Cornell University. Ms. Weiss writes in *Foreign Affairs* that China "is a disgruntled and increasingly ambitious stakeholder…not an implacable enemy" of the US-led international order." However, the professor argues that Beijing's "attempts to squelch overseas opposition to its rule have had a corrosive influence on free speech and free society, particularly among the Chinese diaspora."[705]

Predictably, according to Professor Weiss, China has made it easier for other authoritarian regimes to thrive. To illustrate her point, she cites Toronto University political scientist Seva Gunitsky, who explains that economic growth doesn't require democracy: "Material success…often creates its own legitimacy: regimes become morally appealing simply by virtue of their triumph." That view indicates how the CCP maintains control and why it is so concerned about continued prosperity.[706]

China routinely uses its UN Security Council vote to shield authoritarian-run countries from international demands to protect human rights as well as block international interventions to force governments to end abuses. Those efforts encourage states such as some in Africa and Latin America to join Beijing in opposing human-rights resolutions.[707]

Beijing also uses its membership in the Security Council to defend authoritarian states, but on occasion it has favored sanctions against rogue regimes like Iran and North Korea. Political scientist Joel Wuthnow, an adjunct associate professor with the Center for Security Studies at Georgetown University, points out that "China cannot be simply described as a patron of rogue regimes." For example, it favored sanctions against Libya and was "in favor of referring the Libyan dictator Muammar al-Qaddafi to the International Criminal Court."[708]

Noteworthy is China's rich association with the UN's leading authority for health, the World Health Organization, which illustrates the regime's maligned influence. In early 2020, as the COVID-19 pandemic became widely apparent, the WHO refrained from criticizing Beijing's cover-up about the origin of the virus, generally attributed to a virology laboratory in Wuhan. Rather, the PRC failed to release critical information to help contain the crisis. In fact, CCP censors went into overdrive to delete information from the Internet to keep the world in the dark. Meanwhile, WHO Director-General Adhanom Tedros Ghebreyesus praised Beijing for its transparency and response to the virus, all which turned out to be far from the truth.[709]

CHINA ABUSES ITS WTO MEMBERSHIP

The PRC refuses to abide by the letter and spirit of its World Trade Organization (WTO) membership since its admission in 2001. The regime earned many complaints from fellow member nations for its continued reliance on heavy-handed and non-market-oriented trade and labor practices. Those complaints are not incidental, but accuse the Chinese of practices that are antithetical to WTO rules and founding principles.[710]

"When China joined the WTO, it agreed to join a global trade organization predicated on tenets of private enterprise-led, market-based rules governed trade, in accordance with the foundation principles of non-discrimination, reciprocity, and transparency," said Stephen Ezell, vice president for Global Innovation at the Information Technology and Innovation Foundation.[711]

"And China has never been further away than it is today from generally adhering to those principles," said Ezell. "They're as far away as they've ever been."[712]

An ongoing problem with China's WTO compliance is the significant role the CCP plays in the global trade markets thanks to state-owned enterprises (SOE). A 2021 study by Information Technology & Innovation Foundation, "False Promises II: The Continuing Gap Between China's WTO Commitments and Its Practices," found there are 150,000 Chinese state-owned or controlled enterprises that employ 30 million workers and hold assets totaling $15.2 trillion. Further, the study claims China's direct management of SOEs violated WTO rule.[713]

CHINA IGNORES INTERNATIONAL LAW

The PRC ignores the 2016 ruling by the International Tribunal in The Hague that rejected China's claim of sovereignty over 90 percent of the 1.4 million-square-mile South China Sea. The tribunal sided with the Philippines, citing the UN Convention on the Law of Sea (UNCLOS) to judge the Chinese assertion of sovereignty as null. Beijing challenged the maritime claims in the region by the Philippines, Vietnam, Taiwan, and Malaysia, as well as the limitations of international law. However, without an international enforcement arm, and in spite of the Tribunal's clear ruling, the Chinese are sticking by their claim and even accelerated their activities in the South China Sea.[714]

The lack of an enforcement mechanism makes other claims of little consequence. Philippine President Rodrigo Duterte explained that he doesn't have the capacity to enforce the ruling and Washington failed to shoulder the responsibility as well. Evidently, China also believed the US wasn't willing to use its military forces to push the Chinese off the artificial islands created in the disputed areas.[715]

Meanwhile, the Chinese continue their expansion by building more military facilities and constructing more islands. In April 2022, US Indo-Pacific commander Admiral John C. Aquilino said the PLA has fully militarized at least three islands in the disputed South China Sea by arming them with anti-ship and anti-aircraft missiles, laser and jamming equipment, and fighter aircraft.[716]

CHINA IS A GLOBAL CLIMATE OFFENDER

The PRC is all talk, taking no meaningful action when it comes to climate change. The regime promises the rest of the world that it will achieve "net-zero emissions" by 2060, and published a flurry of press releases and white papers attesting to that commitment. Meanwhile, it continues to lead the world in building coal-fired energy plants while ignoring the escalating pollution problems associated with Chinese deaths. And the only people pleased with China's empty climate promises are Western environmentalists, "greenies," and naïve leftist politicians who buy CCP propaganda.[717]

Much of China's "commitment" to green objectives is only window dressing, as the evidence suggests. For example, a report by the Gatestone Institute suggests China's real aim with its public green goal is continued enrichment. Specifically, the PRC seeks to "reduce US competitiveness while increasing China's competitive advantage." The Institute made the following points: "1) Beijing's seriousness about reducing emissions is not manifested in its latest five-year plan, which contains no concrete goals or actions required to reduce carbon dioxide emissions; and 2) the Paris

Agreement gives China (and India) a 'free carbon ride' for the near term, while China is in fact rapidly *increasing* carbon dioxide emissions."[718]

Some facts about China's carbon footprint are helpful here. A Rhodium Group report in May 2021 found that China's 2019 greenhouse gas emissions represented a 25 percent increase from 2009, which means Chinese claims to reduce emissions is nonsense. Meanwhile, "China commissioned more coal-fired capacity in 2020 than the rest of the world retired," which led to the "first increase in global coal capacity development since 2015.… China's coal boom accounted for 76 percent of the global 50.3 GWT [gigawatt] of new coal capacity," according to a report by OILPRICE.com.[719]

The regime's hypocrisy and the West's gullibility regarding China's promised carbon footprint reduction were on full display when, on November 2021, China's ministry of ecology and environment released a US-China joint Glasgow Declaration on enhancing climate action in the 2020s. That declaration affirmed the importance of certain climate issues and offered vague pledges, such as Beijing's promise to gradually reduce coal consumption. The US and China also pledged to cooperate on deploying green technologies, forming standards for reducing greenhouse gas emissions, and convening meetings to discuss the reduction of methane emissions.[720]

As an aside, the PRC expects the West to "go green," which suits Beijing's interests. After all, the West's push for renewable, carbon-free energy provides more fossil fuel-based energy for China, and besides, the Chinese profit from the production of green products like wind mills and solar panels. Further, China dominates the global lithium battery market, the energy source for all-electric automobiles.

In conclusion, it is clear from China's negligence, willful actions, and involvement in most major international organizations that the regime intends to do whatever it must to deflect responsibility while leveraging every organization to support the regime's ambitions to create a new world order in its totalitarian image.

LEVERAGING SOVEREIGN NATIONS

Professor Audrye Wong, an assistant professor of political science and international relations at the University of Southern California, writes that Beijing's country-specific efforts tend to be more transactional, short-term, as opposed to seeking significant geopolitical gains; that is, its "long-term strategic influence remains limited." In fact, "most of the countries China has targeted have not made major shifts in their geopolitical alignment; at best, they have offered rhetorical and symbolic commitments," states Professor Wong.[721]

Evidently, according to Ms. Wong, President Xi's wolf-warrior diplomatic corps are "tone-deaf, leaving the regime particularly vulnerable to the vicissitudes of democratic politics." The professor continued, "China has provoked backlash instead of garnering support…[and its] investments [in countries] have often become politicized, with out-of-power parties criticizing the incumbents who signed the deals for caving in to Beijing."[722]

Consider some examples of China's geopolitical missteps identified by Professor Wong in her *Foreign Affairs* article. The China-Pakistan Economic Corridor, a BRI effort, ran into significant political and economic obstacles with local Pakistanis regarding energy infrastructure projects, "and then bickered over their allocation." There is also the grand project in Sri Lanka that exposes the PRC to the failings of the "debt-trap" BRI diplomacy. Sri Lankan politicians embraced China's proposal for the Hambantota Port, but that project became a bust, both economically and geographically, a true white elephant hung around Beijing's geopolitical neck.[723]

The CCP's malign geopolitical activities have the attention of many countries, and some governments are calling out the growing Chinese threat. Canada's foreign affairs minister, Melanie Joly, said: "There's a growing influence of China in the world and every single country needs to [make] a decision as to what their relationship will be with China, and what our relationship as a country will be with China." Ms. Joly continued, "We need to be able to have a clear strategy in the region when it comes to trade, when it comes to also our relationship economically speaking, but also on human rights and democratic values and issues."[724]

"On the question of foreign interference. It is clear that as a democracy, we will never accept any form of foreign interference," Joly said. However, Canada remains the only country in the Five Eyes—an intelligence alliance among Canada, the United Kingdom, the United States, Australia, and New Zealand—that hasn't banned Huawei's 5G telecommunication networks, which poses an intelligence threat.[725]

It's clear from these examples that China uses a variety of ways to target countries across the world to leverage them into the PRC's orbit. What are Beijing's common practices used to leverage foreign countries to the PRC's new order? Consider eight practices with examples of just how the Communist regime seeks to expand its global influence across sovereign states.

Practice #1: The CCP pressures sovereign governments to support the regime's geopolitical aims, especially regarding Taiwan. That includes forcing countries to extradite Taiwanese to chill any contrary view.

The most obvious example of this strategy is the CCP's use of pressure, forcing countries to bow to the regime's demands regarding Taiwan. In 2021, the PRC demanded that countries deport citizens of Taiwan to mainland China, according to a Madrid-based human-rights group, Safeguard Defenders. That group published a report on November 30, 2021, "China's Hunt for Taiwanese Overseas," indicating the Communist giant is targeting for deportation or extradition Taiwanese nationals suspected of having committed crimes outside of Taiwan.[726]

The CCP considers Taiwan part of the PRC, which will in time be united—and by force if necessary. Therefore, the regime believes the Taiwanese government has no right to engage internationally with other nations, much less participate in international organizations such as the International Criminal Police Organization.[727]

The Safeguard Defenders' report indicates that more than six hundred citizens of Taiwan were extradited to mainland China from across the world between 2016 and 2019. Spain deported 219 Taiwanese nationals to China, the largest number among eight countries, according to the report. The balance came from Cambodia, the Philippines, Armenia, Malaysia, Kenya, Indonesia, and Vietnam.[728]

Michael Caster, a senior adviser at Safeguard Defenders, indicated: "The fundamental issue here is that the denial of fundamental human rights in China, namely the right to a fair trial and to be free of torture, are systematically denied." He continued, "Of concern, there have been cases of forced confessions. In other cases, Taiwanese nationals have been denied visitation or communication with their family members in Taiwan."[729]

Forcing countries to extradite Taiwanese suspected of crimes to Communist China supports the regime's claim that the democratic island nation is not a legitimate nation, but a renegade province of the PRC. This is the tacit acknowledgment by extraditing countries that Taiwan is not a legitimate country, Beijing's aim.

Practice #2: Beijing sanctions defense contractors and individuals that sell goods and services to Taiwan. Communist China sanctions US defense contractors that sell arms to Taiwan. In early 2022, Beijing's Foreign Affairs Ministry spokesperson cited a 2021 law, the Anti-Foreign Sanctions Law, that allows the regime to target foreign firms that help Taiwan. Specifically, the PRC responded to a $100 million deal for Raytheon Technologies and Lockheed Martin to help maintain Taiwan's missile defense systems.[730]

"China once again urges the US government and relevant parties to…stop arms sales to Taiwan and sever military ties with Taiwan," said Wang Wenbin, the PRC's Foreign Affairs Ministry spokesman. Further, Wang said, "China will continue to take all necessary measures to firmly safeguard its sovereignty and security interests in according with the development of the situation."[731]

Beijing routinely pressures American firms to influence US policies as well. In October 2020, the year prior to the new Anti-Foreign Actions law, Beijing sanctioned both American citizens and defense contracting firms for their roles in arms sales to Taiwan. For example, some of those sanctions were announced the day prior to the Trump administration's notification to Congress that it planned to sell Harpoon attack missiles to Taiwan.[732]

Evidently, Beijing's spies monitor all US sales to Taiwan and then try to circumvent normal policy channels to punish American firms and corporate leaders that refuse to support the Communist regime's dictates.

Practice #3: Beijing uses market access to 1.4 billion Chinese to manipulate countries to support the regime's political aims. In 2021, China threatened the small Baltic country of Lithuania because the government in Vilnius (the nation's capital city) approved Taiwan to open a representative office under the name of Taiwan. As a result, Beijing targeted Lithuanian businesses by telling them either to persuade their government to retract the pro-Taiwan action or be denied access to the Chinese market.

Lithuanian President Gitanas Nausėda refused to capitulate to Chinese bullying and said he remained committed to defending democratic values from attack.[733]

Beijing's action against Lithuania is clear. "China is trying to make an example out of us—a negative example—so that other countries do not follow our path. Therefore, it is a matter of principle how the Western community, the United States, and European Union react," said Arnoldas Pranckevičius, Lithuania's vice minister of foreign affairs.[734]

Beijing uses this carrot-and-stick routine across the world, and to date persuaded many countries to abandon Taiwan. At present, Taiwan has full diplomatic relations with 13 out of the 193 UN member states. However, the PRC will continue to use whatever mechanism necessary to marginalize Taiwan in the eyes of other countries.[735]

Practice #4: Beijing exports its brand of justice to gain leverage over sovereign countries. The PRC exports a brand of justice across the world through law enforcement exchanges, and as a result builds allies for future purposes.[736]

China's brand of justice comes in many forms. One notable means is Beijing's well-established population surveillance systems, used as part of its national justice efforts. For example, in 2011, Ecuador installed a Chinese human surveillance system financed by the PRC. That system is used to monitor the population for police and internal intelligence reasons. The system includes more than three thousand public security officers, in sixteen monitoring centers, reviewing footage from 4,300 cameras. Ecuador, like the PRC, has a history of monitoring, threatening, and disappearing political rivals.[737]

The export of human surveillance systems is modeled after that created by China's Central National Security Commission and the National Supervision Commission, which report directly to the CCP on "overall national security," guarding against external and internal security threats. The intent of these government agencies is to both combat internal threats from terrorists and criminals, but also to expand Beijing's surveillance and intelligence-gathering capabilities. Also, the export of these systems is a form of diplomacy, to "co-opt foreign governments, to win friends, and to assign pro-China officers in high positions in foreign security forces."[738]

The PRC exports its brand of justice thanks to the conduct of police training as well. Foreign law enforcement members, much like military personnel, are offered free or deeply discounted police training in China. For example, the police academy in Shandong province hosts annual training for African nation law enforcement officers. Another training program in Kunming hosts a Southeast Asian nation law enforcement academy; once again, that is provided at no cost to personnel from Association of Southeast Asian Nations countries. Also, the Beijing municipal public security bureau has an agreement with ten central Asian cities and hosts annual police symposiums for those officers.[739]

Practice #5: Beijing buys political leverage. The PRC buys leverage in nations across the globe. For example, Beijing has the allegiance of two nations of islands in the South Pacific. The first island nation is Kiribati, which is bowing to Beijing's illiberal influence in exchange for cash. Evidently, according to an October 2021 report, the Kiribati government deregistered a world heritage site, the Phoenix Islands Protected Area (PIPA), to make it available to China for commercial fishing and possible use by the PLAAF and PLAN to threaten the US military facilities in Hawaii.[740]

Chinese fishermen, known for illegal fishing globally, will likely benefit from the deregistering of the PIPA, home to pristine fishing grounds. That's not a surprise to people like Alex Gray, a former US National Security Council chief of staff and an expert on the Pacific Islands. He said:

> China is the world's greatest ecological menace, from its devastating illegal, unreported, and unregulated fishing around the world, to its consistent undermining of global norms that protect delicate ecosystems like Antarctica and the deep seabed. The US and its partners must confront China's attack on the ecology of the world's most vulnerable places and not remain silent on this defining issue.[741]

Beijing's influence in the Pacific Islands is also political in nature. The regime, according to Mr. Gray, is inclined "to exert leverage over these tiny islands." That view is shared by reporter Barbara Dreaver, who wrote:

> There's deep concern that the move [to deregister the PIPA] has been driven by China. PIPA is attractive to China not only for its fishing wealth but its strategically significant location near US military installations.

For example, Kanton Island previously hosted a US military base, just 1,900 miles southwest of Hawaii, which was used as an emergency air base and anti-ballistic missile tracking station.[742]

The Solomon Islands is the second island nation to succumb to China's influence. In March 2022, the PRC struck an agreement with Solomon's Prime Minister Manasseh Sogavare and without public consultation, according to Cleo Paskal of the Foundation for Defense of Democracies.[743]

The Solomon Islands' government announced the security pact with China, "Framework Agreement Between the Government of the People's Republic of China and the Government of Solomon Islands on Security Cooperation," an agreement that moves Beijing's military arm within striking distance (3,600 miles) of Hawaii.[744]

The renewable, five-year bilateral deal allows Beijing to use the Solomon Islands to base military personnel and their equipment. The pact states that China "may, according to its own needs and with the consent of Solomon Islands, make ship visits to, carry out logistical replenishment in, and have stopover and transition in Solomon Islands, and the relevant forces of China can be used to protect the safety of Chinese personnel and major projects in Solomon Islands."[745]

The agreement also provides that the "Solomon Islands may… request China to send police, armed police, military personnel, and other law enforcement and armed forces to Solomon Islands to assist in maintaining social order, protecting people's lives and property, providing humanitarian assistance, carrying out disaster response, or providing assistance on other tasks agreed upon by the Parties."[746]

Practice #6: Beijing interferes in foreign domestic politics. The CCP seeks to sway foreign elections to then leverage incumbents to support pro-China policy and public opinion.

Consider the situation in Italy, whereby the CCP's activities sought to expand its influence in that country, according to a 2021 report by researchers at Sinopsis, a project by AceMedia z.u., in collaboration with the Department of Sinology at Charles University in Prague, Czech Republic.[747]

The report, "Hijacking the Mainstream," exposes the CCP's foreign agencies and its operations to influence Italian politics by "targeting

members of parliament, political parties, officials, as well as leading figures from the media and think tanks."[748]

The CCP's efforts in foreign countries helps the regime further its
foreign policy objectives and cements its "authoritarian monopoly of
power" in China.[749]

The fruits of that effort are self-evident. "Italian influential voices
have been used as proxies to echo CCP propaganda while normalizing
Chinese totalitarianism and global expansion," according to the report.
Members of Parliament have also passed on "propaganda whitewashing
the party's human rights abuses," says the report.[750]

Evidently, the PRC has "a dedicated apparatus embedded in party,
state, army and satellite structures [that] uses proxies and neutral-look-
ing platforms to coopt [sic] elites abroad into alignment with the party's
external and domestic policies," the report states.[751]

**Practice #7: Beijing negotiates agreements to buy access to stra-
tegic resources and facilities, which brings countries into the PRC's
sphere of influence.** In 2021, Chinese and Iranian foreign ministers
signed a twenty-five-year cooperation agreement dubbed the Comprehensive Strategic Partnership. "Our relations with Iran will not be
affected by the current situation, but will be permanent and strategic,"
Chinese Foreign Minister Wang Yi said at the signing ceremony. The
agreement promises Chinese investments in key Iranian sectors such as
energy and infrastructure.[752]

Iranian President Hassan Rouhani said the accord is an example of
"successful diplomacy." He continued, "A country's strength is in its ability to join coalitions, not remain isolated." Saeed Khatibzadeh, a spokesman for Iran's foreign ministry, described the agreement as a "roadmap"
for trade and transportation cooperation, with a "special focus on the
private sectors of the two sides." The bilateral trade is projected to grow
tenfold to $600 billion over the next decade.[753]

Beijing gains new strategic infrastructure with the agreement, a
"critical node of its Belt and Road Initiative given its strategic location."

Specifically, it gains access to the Chabahar Port and investments in sectors including oil and gas and petrochemicals.[754]

There is a national security aspect to the agreement as well. After all, China and Iran have both taken part in joint naval exercises with Russia in the northern Indian Ocean. Similar military exercises are likely in the future, given their sweeping "strategic accord."[755] Further, according to Jonathan Fulton, an assistant professor at Zayed University, United Arab Emirates, who testified before the USCC, the China-Iran agreement goes beyond the parameters set by China's current partnership with Iran and "represent a dramatic departure from China's approach to the Middle East."[756]

On a related issue, and during the 2022 Beijing Olympics, President Xi met with leaders from across the world. The Communist leader used those meetings to garner more support for his BRI and to stress the regime's role in the economic growth of developing nations. Interestingly, Mr. Xi met with Serbian President Aleksandar Vucic to advance the idea that Serbia could become China's gateway to Central and Eastern European countries. President Xi also pledged to "turn Poland into a China-Europe industrial and supply chain hub" at a meeting with Polish President Andrej Duda, a move that might undermine the US relationship with Warsaw.[757]

Practice #8: Beijing buys influence across entire regions through debt obligations and development projects. Beijing's efforts to gobble up entire regions are especially sobering, a view expressed by General Stephen Townsend, Commander of the United States Africa Command. "The Chinese are outmaneuvering the U.S. in select countries in Africa," he said in Senate Armed Services Committee testimony on March 15, 2022. "Port projects, economic endeavors, infrastructure and their agreements and contracts will lead to greater access in the future. They are hedging their bets and making big bets on Africa.[758]

Evidence of China's efforts across Africa are pervasive. Specifically, Beijing grew its trade across the African continent from $67 billion in

2020 to $254 billion in 2021, according to Stratfor, an American geo-politics publisher and consultancy. In fact, there appears to be a shift in Beijing's African strategy from one that focused almost exclusively on resources for infrastructure, vis-à-vis BRI, to a model focused on trade and growing indebtedness by African nations to Beijing. At this point, it appears as if China is significantly increasing exports to African countries and, in response, many of those nations are irrationally larding their mushrooming deficit with Beijing, which leads to more dependence and, by association, vulnerability to the Asian Communist regime.[759]

Beijing's Africa strategy's ultimate goal does appear to be geopoliti-cal dominance across the continent's fifty-four countries. That's a view shared by Nathaniel Luz, a Nigeria-based author and expert on African economic and political affairs, who wrote for the Middle East Media Research Institute about what he called the "Chinese power play" in Africa. Basically, we are seeing the replay of Africa's historical subjection to foreign political dominance (read "China") and economic subservi-ence to Beijing, thanks to African leaders trading away their nations "on the altar of so-called foreign aid and bilateral relations," wrote Mr. Luz. That's precisely Beijing's aim in Africa.[760]

Communist China is never the solution to Africa's aspirations, wrote Mr. Luz. He indicated that the PRC does a "lot to build relationships with countries in Africa. However, healthy relationships ought to be mutually beneficial, but the relationship between China and Nigeria is parasitic when considered deeply." In 2021, Nigeria imported $23 bil-lion in Chinese goods and it exported less than $4 billion.[761]

Mr. Luz cited a number of examples of Beijing's "parasitic" practices across the continent beyond the Nigeria situation. For one, the African Union's building was donated by the PRC as a "Greek gift," Mr. Luz explained. Chinese hackers then accessed the Union's computer systems at the Addis Ababa-based headquarters to download confidential infor-mation. Why? Likely, to gain insights into which countries and leaders are vulnerable to CCP manipulation.[762]

China donated another building to a leading African organization, the Economic Community of West African States (ECOWAS), an institution based in Abuja, Nigeria. Mr. Luz argued, "African leaders are again selling the continent at a low price [$31.6 million for the ECOWAS building] to the future master in Asia."[763]

Consider a much broader issue now enveloping Africa to China's favor. According to Mr. Luz, Nigeria embraced China's yuan (aka renminbi, the national currency) in that African country's currency reserve, evidence of one of the CCP's international ambitions and a step toward global hegemony. This further strengthens China's involvement in Africa's political and economic system as well.[764]

A new target for Beijing's influence is the entire Middle East region. The Communist regime is spending a lot of money across the Mideast to buy influence, and it's not just about access to energy, wrote Anchal Vohra for *Foreign Policy*. In January 2022, as alluded to above, China and the Islamic Republic of Iran are forging a new relationship. As evidence of that relationship, Iran's foreign minister visited Beijing in 2021 to discuss a $400 billion investment to help the Islamist regime mitigate the impact of US sanctions on that country's flagging economy. Further, in December 2021, a CNN report indicated that Beijing plays both sides of the Mideast Shia-Sunni conflict by continuing to sell the Saudis ballistic missiles—ostensibly to protect the kingdom from Iranian missiles.[765]

Yes, the Saudis' ballistic missile inventory came from China dating back to 1987 when the US barred the Saudis and other countries from purchasing ballistic missiles via the Missile Technology Control regime, which aimed to prevent the sale of rockets capable of carrying weapons of mass destruction. As recently as 2019, the Trump administration determined that Saudi Arabia significantly escalated its ballistic missile program thanks to help from the PRC. The kingdom expanded both its missile infrastructure and its rocket technology via purchases from Beijing.[766]

China's extensive involvement in the Mideast is a relatively recent decision, which is broader than the two countries of Iran and Saudi Arabia. This is a dramatic shift. After all, prior to President Xi coming to office, the PRC avoided getting embroiled in the Middle East because, as a Chinese scholar described the region, it is a "chaotic and dangerous graveyard burying empires." However, that all changed, thanks to President Xi, who vowed to double trade with the region by 2023.[767]

Perhaps the strangest development is what China is doing in Iraq. In January 2022, Beijing announced plans to build thousands of schools and healthcare centers, as well as nearly ninety thousand homes in Iraq's Sadr City, the stronghold of Shia cleric Muqtada al-Sadr. Why is China investing in the troubled country?[768]

Ms. Vohra indicates in her article cited above that "Xi Jinping has transformed China's Middle East Policy." The PRC seeks to replace the US in the region, or at least carve out another section of the globe for Beijing's growing influence.[769]

Evidently, along with Beijing's investments in the region comes the message that authoritative regimes like the PRC (Iran, Saudi Arabia, and others) are legitimate, and Western democracy isn't necessarily the only alternative for all nations. That is music to the ears of the mostly authoritarian regimes across that region.[770]

Of interest, Shaojin Chai, a Chinese political scientist at the University of Sharjah, United Arab Emirates, believes China's development approach in the Mideast is more attractive than the West's diplomacy of "values and democratic peace." He continued: "Based on Chinese political philosophy and the mentality of the ruling elites, only development and economic prosperity can bring peace, civilization, and good governance."[771]

These eight strategic practices employed among many of the world's sovereign nations illustrate Beijing's efforts to take captive those countries to help build a new world order in its image.

CONCLUSION

The CCP is geopolitically active across the world, working within most international organizations and most sovereign countries. Its ambition is to leverage by hook or crook the necessary influence to bolster the legitimacy of the Beijing regime. So far, the Communist regime is making considerable headway geopolitically, and if not stopped, it may in fact reach its goal of building a new world order in its image—at the cost of most sovereign nations.

8

Kings of the East: Technology

The Chinese government does not engage in theft of commercial secrets in any form, nor does it encourage or support Chinese companies to engage in such practices in any way.[772]

—Xi Jinping
2015 interview with the *Wall Street Journal*

This chapter exposes the PRC's technological ambitions and how it plans to use its growing sophisticated scientific and illicit efforts to transform every aspect of human life—and to eventually dominate the world.

A major aspect of President Xi's "rejuvenation" revolution is the fusion of all technological centers that greatly benefit its armed forces and that nation's global competitiveness. All military, business, and academic enterprises in China work collaboratively to advance the nation's technological edge to become the world's dominant high-technology state using every modern invention: artificial intelligence, autonomous systems, advanced computing, quantum information sciences, biotechnology, and advanced materials and manufacturing. What Beijing can't achieve with the fusion of all elements of national power or through

211

collaborative agreements with foreign partners it will steal from the West through espionage using a global enterprise of agents.

In three sections, this chapter provides an overview of the contemporary technological revolution—what emerging technologies promise for mankind. Then we explore the evidence that the CCP seeks to lead the world in technology, and finally, we examine the PRC's primary means for satisfying its technology thirst.

GLOBAL TECHNOLOGICAL REVOLUTION AND THE IMPLICATIONS

We are entering the Fourth Industrial Revolution, aka 4IR, a period of rapid change whereby technology, industries, and societal patterns in the twenty-first century take place thanks to increased interconnectivity and smart automation. The concept was popularized by Klaus Schwab, the World Economic Forum founder, who argues that the changes are a real shift in industrial capitalism that joins technologies like artificial intelligence, gene editing, and robotics and blurs the lines between what is physical, digital, and biological—a true, Aldous Huxley-like *Brave New World* at our doorsteps.[773]

Few people would have guessed at the beginning of the twentieth century the radical transformation now happening. The past century began with the infancy of airplanes, automobiles, and primitive radio. By the turn of the century, mankind routinely used space rockets, manned space stations, relied upon computers in their homes, conversed on mobile phones, and connected with virtually the entire world though the advent of the wireless Internet.

The twenty-first century began with a host of dizzying new technologies: the launch of the mobile Internet and third-generation (3G) wireless mobile telecommunications and, today, the explosion of social media, e-readers like Dynabook, streaming video, touchscreens, and the marvels of 5G with the Internet of things, which virtually connects every aspect of life by putting it at our fingertips.

Of particular importance is the avalanche of information thanks to artificial intelligence (AI), the study of so-called intelligent agents, or, as defined by leading AI textbooks: "any system that perceives its environment and takes actions that maximize its chance of achieving its goals." Yes, AI may sound futuristic, but according to the computer software developer and marketer HubSpot, most Americans (63 percent) already use AI without realizing it. For example, Apple's Siri and Amazon's Echo help with our schedules, and Alexa (Google) smart speakers play our favorite tunes upon command. A Google application (app) guides us through traffic jams while we go to work, and much more. These are everyday examples of AI in action.[774]

AI technologies are rapidly proliferating, replacing humans in manufacturing, service delivery, recruitment, communications, military service, the financial industry, and more, according to the *Harvard Business Review*.[775] And, according to Deloitte, a global professional services network, AI will add as much as $15.7 trillion to the global economy by 2030.

AI developments are creating serious geopolitical contests, however. Back in 2017, Russian President Vladimir Putin, according to the Associated Press, warned the world: "The one who becomes the leader in this [AI] sphere will be the ruler of the world."[776]

Obviously, much is at stake as individuals and nations battle to capture the latest technologies, because control of the entire world may rest on the outcome of that competition.

Consider a number of emergent technologies and how they will soon impact our lives.

Emergent Transportation Technologies

The "Hyperloop" is a new mode of transportation technology in which commuters will travel through pods in a pipe at speeds reaching 745 miles per hour, which is two to three times faster than high-speed rail, or traveling 186 miles in just twenty minutes. *Digital Journal* indicates that "the global hyperloop technology market is expected to grow at a significant CAGR [compound annual growth rate] of 47% by 2028."[777]

Autonomous—self-driving—vehicles are very much in the news and soon will become commonplace, according to many reports. These driverless cars will be capable of operating on their own without any human interference, sensing their environment and moving safely through clogged traffic. They will combine a variety of detectors such as "Lidar" (a method for determining ranges), sonar, radar, GPS, odometry, and others to perceive their surroundings.

Not far behind the autonomous ground vehicles are flying cars. Evidently, Uber is working on pilotless flying vehicles, teaming with the National Aeronautics and Space Administration to develop an air traffic control system for these "aircraft." It's noteworthy that NBC News reports that Uber anticipates rolling out its air vehicles by 2023 in certain cities. "This technology is intriguing, and it seems it's finally going to arrive in our lifetime," said Karl Brauer with Cox Automotive.[778]

Evidently, the world's first proven flying car gained certification in early 2022. The Slovakian Transport Authority granted certification for AirCar, according to creator Stefan Klein, the founder and CEO of KleinVision. The AirCar flew two hundred times across seven hundred hours of flight to earn certification, as "the car can reach 100 miles per hour on the road, and 8,000 feet of altitude, while needing only around 2 minutes and 15 seconds to deploy or store its wings." Morgan Stanley, a global leader in financial services, estimates the flying car market over the next twenty years will be worth over a trillion US dollars, similar to the buzz that arose around the recent boom in private spaceflight.[779]

Emergent Workplace-Related Technologies

The workplace will radically change in the near future, thanks to technologies like 3D printing, which can bring to life ideas—not literally, but it can transform a digital design into a solid, real-life product with few limitations.

As mentioned earlier, AI is both science and engineering that make machines intelligent thanks to what's called "machine learning," which will revolutionize many aspects of life. Jim Baker, the legal counsel at Twitter, Inc., and lecturer on law at Harvard Law School, defined AI as four components:

(1) hardware (usually very fast computer processors); (2) software that runs on the hardware (including instructions and algorithms that allow the machine to follow a series of steps and act "intelligently"); (3) input and output devices for the machine to take in and communicate information and instructions; and (4) data that the machine can store, process, and analyze.[780]

Simply, AI is a kind of software and some hardware that automates work and should reduce human effort. Two AI-related technologies will seriously impact our future: augmented reality (AR) and mixed reality (MR).

Mixed reality is an extension of AR that allows virtual and real elements to interact in an environment. In other words, the AR is overlaid digitally on a real-world environment, while MR brings the two together—real and digital elements.

Consider that AR technology combines the real-world environment with computer-generated 3D graphics to supplement visual, auditory, olfactory, and other senses in the real world using computer-generated images, videos, and information presented in 3D graphics, albeit overlaid on the real world.

AR systems offer three primary features that can exist in AR programs, such as blending real with virtual worlds, providing real-time interaction, and providing 3D alignment of computer-generated and real objects. For example, a customer using AR can see select pieces of furniture in their actual homes, while other AR users can virtually interact with digitally created dinosaurs—like cartoons coming to life.

Another emergent and exciting technology is the robot. They are already quite popular in our homes (vacuums, security systems, voice-activated appliances, and more), and they're a growing reality across most of the world. For example, the Kuri Home Robot plays music, takes photos and videos, answers questions, engages in conversation and moves around a house at will. On the near horizon, expect other robots to perform as waiters in restaurants, help construction companies with many tasks, and further ease physical work for humans at most manufacturing plants. Literally, the sky is the limit for our robotic future.[781]

On other fronts, our food supply will benefit from the use of new technologies as well. Expect that by mid-century (2050), there will be two billion more people in the world than the current 7.8 billion, which means there will be a demand for much more food than today. Further, most (80 percent) of all mid-century people will live in megacities (cities with populations exceeding ten million). So, to feed those billions more efficiently, we are likely to see what's known as "floating farms" crop up inside cities. A single smart floating farm might measure 350 by 200 meters and is estimated to be able to produce 8.1 tons of vegetables, a real boon against common food-risk problems as well as against the need for a massive transportation infrastructure to move that food from distant farms to our homes.[782]

Emergent Medical Technologies

Many hospitals and associated medical service companies are rapidly redefining what's medically possible. What only a few years ago was the stuff of science fiction novels is today becoming routine healthcare and/or elective procedures.

Militaries around the world fund research on healthcare and performance-enhancing technologies with great potential outcomes, such as brain microchips that enhance brain power and create bionic eyes that give users infrared and night vision. Other military-related developments that could eventually come to the civilian sector include super hearing, cyborg implants to monitor efficiency, enhanced limbs to increase strength, exoskeleton legs to increase productivity by up to twenty-seven times, and synthetic blood to prevent users from getting out of breath and make combatants immune to pain.[783]

On a broader medical front, there are a host of new technologies such as CRISPR (clustered regularly interspaced short palindromic repeats). This technology allows medical scientists to create a type of wheat that contains less gluten and could soon mean that people with celiac disease will be able to safely consume wheat because CRISPR makes modifying DNA much faster, cheaper, and more accurate.[784]

AI is also a boon to medical science, especially in helping diagnose disease. For example, a sixty-year-old Japanese woman was diagnosed with acute myeloid leukemia, but none of the treatments worked. So, her doctors turned to IBM's Watson, an AI system, that in minutes compared the woman's genetic information with twenty million cancer studies. Watson saved the woman's life because her doctors had misdiagnosed her cancer. She was actually inflicted with a rare form of treatable leukemia.[785]

Implications of the Technological Revolution

It should be clear at this point that our emergent, frightening technological revolution of capabilities and devices will inevitably impact every aspect of life and could create serious challenges. Perhaps philosopher Bernard Rollin best captured the threat posed by the arrival and impact of these technologies in his book, *Science and Ethics*, stating: "Any major new technology will create a lacuna [gap or space] in social and ethical thought in direct proportion to its novelty." The pregnant question for us to ponder is: Who will fill those important thought gaps going forward?

Inevitably emergent twenty-first century technologies will impact every aspect of life, and some will recreate lacunas, thought gaps. Consider the sociological risk for the family.

Many modern technologies already reduce the burden of household work, thus create more free time for family members, which can drive members farther apart. For example, some parents with more free time thanks to technology will pursue interests outside the home, away from their children. Even while at home, many of these same parents will be distracted by time-robbing technologies like social media, the latest electronic games, and other forms of entertainment. Children will be similarly distracted by new technologies and opportunities driven by the latest devices. As a result, the family—parents and children—will too easily be cast to the side with all the adverse social pathologies that might impact future generations.

On a broader scale, technologies will limit our sphere of freedom and, in fact, when our civil liberties are manipulated by government policies, humanity could become virtually imprisoned thanks to Big Brother's constant surveillance. Yes, big government will intrude upon every aspect of life by monitoring our social networking, our voice and message transmissions, and our every movement, thanks to AI-powered facial recognition. The authorities will know every aspect of our lives thanks to intrusive devices in our homes and technology we carry in our pockets, as well as monitoring technology used when we appear in public, while we are recreating, where we shop, and where we work.

Constant surveillance will stretch the boundaries of permissible conduct by law enforcement while tracking, securing, and prosecuting those it suspects. Meanwhile, government and even individual citizens with monitoring technologies either known to us or not can selectively watch our every move and potentially create misinformation to attack our character, empty our bank accounts, or worse.

Yes, it is technically possible to monitor every aspect of someone's life without their knowledge, thanks to tiny microchips called "smart dust." Evidently, in the 1990s, Dr. Kris Pister, a professor of electrical engineering at the University of California, Berkeley, was funded by the Defense Advanced Research Projects Agency to develop smart dust, which can read our brain waves and signals, exposing unexpressed thoughts and moods—a true merging of humans with machines that has the potential of gaining complete control over our lives.[786]

Smart dust consists of hardly visible microchips that can be causally passed with a handshake and remain active on the human body for up to fourteen days to track the individual worldwide and monitor medical data like blood pressure and biometric information. Thus, total surveillance of people is possible. Further, Klaus Schwab, the World Economic Forum leader and a transhumanism enthusiast, believes these chips could come to provide a "direct communication between our brains and the digital world," what he explains is a kind of "fusion of the physical, digital and biological world."[787]

More sobering is that smart dust is a tool of the "brave new world," according to Klaus, who states:

> [Smart dust] will change not only what we do but also who we are. It will affect our identity and all the issues associated with it: our sense of privacy, our notions of ownership, our consumption patterns, the time we devote to work and leisure, and how we develop our careers, cultivate our skills, meet people, and nurture relationships.[788]

Emergent technologies might also make us dumber. After all, our over-reliance on technology has the potential to reduce our intelligence. Consider how many of us drive our automobiles while blindly following the Global Positioning System's (GPS') voice instructions guiding us to an unfamiliar destination, rather than studying a paper map for directions. We trust spell-check on our computers, but the program often mangles our meaning while we're texting or writing a school paper; and many of us no longer do simple math computations in our heads because of our dependence on calculators. Our nearly total reliance on smart devices to do our thinking makes us brain-lazy and arguably dumber.

The impact of relying on all these AI-empowered machines rather than our personal gray matter—our brains—has a serious consequence, according to late scientist Stephen Hawking (1942–2018). "The development of full artificial intelligence could spell the end of the human race," said Hawking, an English theoretical physicist, cosmologist, and author.[789]

"[AI] would take off on its own, and re-design itself at an ever-increasing rate," explained Hawking. "Humans, who are limited by slow biological evolution, couldn't compete [with AI], and would be superseded."[790]

Mr. Hawking warned of the possibility that AI could outstrip humans' ability to keep pace, a term known as "technological singularity." In other words, technology becomes so advanced that it radically changes civilization.[791]

The frightening possibility is that AI reaches a level of superintelligence; then, at some point, human biology and technology become intertwined so that man becomes part of the machine. Some scientists even argue that the concept isn't that far into the future. After all, as pointed out earlier in this section, we're already artificially augmenting soldiers to radically strengthen their physical endurance and their ability to think, make better decisions, see what is not comprehended by the naked eye, and much more.

Some futurists even speak of nanobots (robots that operate at a microscopic scale) that will plug our brain into the cloud, flooding our minds with some sort of virtual reality and expanding our neocortex (the part of the brain concerned with sight and hearing) into the cloud. "Cloud storage is a model of computer data storage in which the digital data is stored in logical pools, said to be on 'the cloud.'"[792]

Elon Musk, founder of Space-X and Tesla, also warned about uncontrolled advances in AI. There are clear dangers, he said, "potentially more dangerous than nukes." Perhaps AI "machines" come to the point that they consider humans as a lower form of "life" and are therefore expendable, a view Musk shares with Hawking.[793]

Mankind's challenge when facing a serious future AI threat is to answer the question posed by Thomas Kochan, a professor at the

Massachusetts Institute of Technology: Who will define the problems that AI is asked to solve? After all, writes Kochan, "machines, unlike humans, have no objectives of their own, we give them objectives to achieve." We humans feed objectives into machines that are then released to do the task.[794]

Most often the developer defines the problem and programs the objective(s) into the "machine" as well as determines how the technology is ultimately deployed. Professor Kochan makes it clear that "how AI is received by and affects society will depend on who participates in the key decisions influencing its design and use." The professor's article on the AI-control topic focuses on the commercial sector—how AI will replace workers, human judgment, and the over-automating of tasks, as well as the inequality in the distribution of benefits and costs and the abuse of personal data.[795]

These commercial applications provide important cautions, but in the future, AI-driven, highly technological world, the ideology of the inventor is most critical. After all, AI-driven machines seek only those objectives programmed in them, as Kochan said, and if they are purposely focused on unethical behaviors, then guess what? The machine acts, and perhaps many humans inevitably suffer.

That should scare us all, especially when we understand that the PRC officially states that it intends to "become an AI leader, both in terms of developing and deploying the technology as well as governing it with appropriate standards, laws, and regulations," according to the regime's New Generation Artificial Intelligence Development Plan (代人工 发展籶划). Further, Google's former China leader, Lee Kai-Fu, warned about the scope of the threat: "AI is going to change everything. To not understand the coming AI revolution is to risk getting left behind."[796]

Not getting left behind, especially by Communist China in the AI revolution, was the topic Secretary of State Antony Blinken addressed in July 2021 when he spoke at the National Security Commission on Artificial Intelligence's Global Emerging Technology Summit. He warned about rogue regimes like China manipulating AI technologies, explained what's "fundamentally" at stake, and called on democratic states to "put forth and carry out a compelling vision for how to use technology in a way that serves our people, protects our interests and upholds our democratic values." Blinken then cautioned about the "horrors of techno-authoritarianism, to point to what countries like China and Russia are doing." At that point, Blinken acknowledged, "We know China is determined to become the world's technology leader. And they have a well-resourced and comprehensive plan to achieve those ambitions."[797]

Secretary Blinken continued to explain the danger that China might eventually lead the world technologically and how menacing that could be for the rest of us:

> Today we also know that it's harder to ensure that American innovations are used for commercial purposes only. Countries like China don't differentiate between civilian and military in the same way, and emerging technologies, including AI applications, blur that line too. So, we've got to think differently about how to protect our innovation and industries against that kind of misuse.[798]

After all, China sees AI as a tool to realize its goal of creating a new world order, explained current affairs commentator Richard Hui to the *Epoch Times*. After all, Mr. Hui argued:

> Communism [the PRC's ideology] seeks to destroy all human beliefs, morals, and culture in order to achieve world hegemony and global control. The development of artificial intelligence technology has enabled the Chinese Communist Party to see the possibility of using new scientific and technological forces to achieve its global dominance.[799]

"Thirty years after the disintegration of the Soviet Union, people suddenly discovered that the Chinese Communist Party had replaced the Soviet Union as a new threat to Western society," explained Mr. Hui. "In many areas, the CCP has more global control than the Soviet Union back then."[800]

He continued:

During these three decades, the CCP took advantage of the negligence of the free world. Through unfair trade and intellectual property theft, it turned China into the world's second-largest economy and a manufacturing superpower. The authoritarian regime monopolizes social resources to rapidly develop AI technology seeking to surpass the United States in the new technological era.[801]

If the CCP wins the AI race, the destiny of mankind will face a huge turning point. AI technology can give birth to a new generation of intelligent weapons such as cyber weapons, which may be more threatening than nuclear weapons. These technologies can control and destroy a country's infrastructure and weapon systems instantly. This will be the mode of future warfare, completed by touching a few buttons on the computer. This is no longer a scene from a science fiction movie but real threats facing mankind.[802]

Then Mr. Hui asked: "The most important question is who will control such technology?" That is similar in purpose to the implied query posed earlier in this section attributed to philosopher Bernard Rollin: Who will fill those important (social and ethical) lacunas, thought gaps, going forward?[803]

As an aside, it is noteworthy that the US is pursuing AI-related technologies to prepare for future battlefields, much as is the PLA. At this writing, the Pentagon has 685 AI projects associated with major weapons systems, target recognition, battlefield analysis, smart sensors, and many more. In February 2022, the Government Accountability Office wrote to the Senate Armed Services Committee that "AI capabilities will enable machines to perform tasks that normally require human intelligence, such as drawing conclusions and making predictions. Moreover, AI-enabled machines can be expected to maneuver and change tactics at speeds that human operators cannot."[804]

It is also important, according to the National Security Commission on Artificial Intelligence, to understand that the US government concluded in 2021 that it "must take AI seriously—the powerful technology 'is going to reorganize the world.'" Further, the commission concluded that "America must lead the charge," in part because of the significant challenges from both Russia and China.[805]

There is no doubt that President Xi's government understands the stakes—that AI is an economic game-changer and something that will profoundly change human social life and the world. Therefore, it shouldn't surprise anyone who follows the Beijing regime that the CCP intends to do whatever necessary to "control" AI, which in part is why the regime stated that "by 2030, we shall make artificial intelligence theory, technology, and application at the world's leading level."[806]

The next section explores how China is tapping the technological revolution to become the world's leader.

CHINA SEEKS TO LEAD THE WORLD IN TECHNOLOGY

The CCP made it clear the regime intends to become the world's leader in emergent technologies and all that implies. China is serious about its focus on and investment in emerging technologies and presents the "greatest threat to US technology superiority," said US Army Lieutenant General Scott Berrier, the director of the US Defense Intelligence Agency, on April 29, 2021.[807]

General Berrier testified to Congress that China is already a "peer or near-peer" competitor to the US in many areas, and it aspires to be the world leader in those technologies by 2030–35. He specifically called out important examples of critical technologies such as "highly advanced" quantum key distribution (a secure communication method that uses cryptographic protocol) as well as the fields of AI, advanced robotics, high-performance computing, quantum information sciences, and biotechnology. Further, the general said Beijing plans to advance these technologies and "develop military capabilities that outpace those of the United States."[808]

Until the last couple of decades, the US has led the world in technology, but that is changing. Christopher Darby and Sarah Sewall write in *Foreign Affairs* that America's technology lead is changing because Communist China "has undertaken an impressive effort to claim the mantle of technological leadership, investing hundreds of billions of dollars in robotics, artificial intelligence, microelectronics, green energy, and much more." Darby and Sewall state that "Washington has tended to view Beijing's massive technology investments primarily in military terms, but defense capabilities are merely one aspect of great-power competition today." They contend that "Beijing is playing a more sophisticated game, using technological innovation as a way of advancing its goals without having to resort to war."[809]

Washington needs to do far more to "broaden its horizons and support a wider range of technologies," write Darby and Sewall, both with IQT, a not-for-profit investment firm that advises the Defense Department. "It needs to back not only those technologies that have obvious military applications, such as hypersonic flight, quantum computing, and artificial intelligence, but also those traditional thought of as civilian in nature, such as microelectronics and biotechnology."[810]

Darby and Sewall argue that Washington's investment in technologies is critical because the world is no longer "unipolar." In fact, they state:

Over the past two decades, China has evolved from a country that largely steals and imitates technology to one that now also improves and even pioneers it. This is no accident; it is the result of the state's deliberate, long-term focus. China has invested massively in R&D [research and development], with its share of global technology spending growing from under five percent in 2000 to over 23 percent in 2020. If current trends continue, China is expected to overtake the United States in such spending by 2025. Central to China's drive has been a strategy of "military-civil fusion," a coordinated effort to ensure cooperation between the private sector and the defense industry.[811]

One of the CCP's propaganda mouthpieces, *China Today*, echoes what Darby and Sewall wrote in *Foreign Affairs*. Specifically, the regime claims the 19th Central Committee proposed in its 14th Five-Year Plan (2021–2025) the "urgent need for high-quality science and technology achievements." It continued, "General Secretary Xi Jinping has placed scientific and technological innovation at the center of China's overall development plan."[812]

The *China Today* piece continued to argue that "China has made unprecedented efforts in fully implementing the strategy of innovation-driven development by strengthening its national R&D capacity, significantly improving the overall efficiency of the country's innovation system." In that regard, "China's total expenditure on R&D in 2019 amounted to RMB [Chinese yuan/renminbi] 2.21 trillion (equivalent to US $321.3 billion)…[which has translated into]…China [ranking] first in the world for the number of invention patents granted for many consecutive years."[813]

China's R&D efforts are significant. Darby and Sewall point out that the Chinese "support [for R&D] might come in the form of research grants, shared data, government-backed loans, or training programs." They illustrate how Beijing's system works by citing the example of 5G technology. "China's investment in 5G technology shows how the process works in practice," wrote Darby and Sewall. The Chinese firm Huawei "has emerged as a world leader in engineering and selling it—offering high-quality products at a lower price than its Finnish and South Korean competitors." That company has enjoyed massive support from Beijing, by one estimate as much a $75 billion in tax breaks, grants, loans, and discounts on land. Further, Huawei benefits from President Xi's Belt and Road Initiative, through which the government provides generous loans to countries and Chinese companies to finance infrastructure construction projects like 5G networks.[814]

Importantly, "Massive state investments in artificial intelligence have also paid off. Chinese researchers now publish more scientific papers in that field than American ones do," explained Darby and Sewall. Why? Those Chinese researchers are generously funded by government and are also given access to enormous amounts of government data.[815]

Meanwhile, the *China Today* article states, Beijing's "scientific and technological innovation system continues to improve." Specifically, it calls out China's progress "in building international science and technology innovation centers in Beijing, Shanghai, and the Guangdong Hong Kong Macao greater bay area. Efforts were expedited in building hubs of science and technology innovation that have global influence, and in fostering core engines to drive high-quality development."[816]

The *China Today* article highlights the "significance of building a leading national R&D force." It states that, because the "world is undergoing profound changes" and "innovation has become the key variable that influences changes," then "China urgently needs stronger support from technological innovation. China aims to become a global leader in innovation in 2035, and emerge as a country with strong strengths in science and technology by the middle of the century."[817]

Of course, much of America's past concerns about China's technological progress are attributed to worries about its growing defense capabilities. However, "China's push for technological supremacy is not simply aimed at gaining a battlefield advantage; Beijing is changing the battlefield itself." Rather, as Darby and Sewall point out, "although commercial technologies such as 5G, artificial intelligence, quantum computing, and biotechnology will undoubtedly have military applications, China envisions a world of great-power competition in which no shots need to be fired." They explain that "technological supremacy promises the ability to dominate the civilian infrastructure on which others depend, providing enormous influence." Then they make the logical connection to explain that "the countries buying Chinese systems [read "Huawei's 5G"] may think they are merely receiving electric grids, health-care technology, or online payment systems, but in reality, they may also be placing critical national infrastructure and citizens' data in Beijing's hands. Such exports are China's Trojan horse."[818]

The PRC employs three primary means to satisfy its thirst for the latest technology: it steals, it fuses all elements of industry/government/academia to advance the CCP's technology agenda, and it "collaborates" with foreign partners.

China Steals Technology It Doesn't Create or Acquires Otherwise

The CCP engages in significant economic espionage against the United States. One-third (32 percent) of 206 US federal cases between 1996 and 2019 involving charges related to the Economic Espionage Act of 1996 implicated Chinese agents. In fact, China was second to all other American companies, accounting for 37 percent of all cases over the same period. FBI Director Christopher Wray acknowledged that Chinese espionage is a growing threat, noting the agency opens a new China-related counterintelligence case every ten hours, and half have a direct China connection. Further, the economic impact of the theft is estimated at $400 billion per year, according to the US Director of National Intelligence.[819]

Although the US established a variety of sanctions intending to prevent Chinese espionage, those efforts only slow the pace of transfer. This is in part because of the significance of the trade between the US and China, which was $558 billion in 2019. That level of trade requires the sustainment of the flow of information between the countries, and therefore makes counterintelligence enforcement policies quite expensive as a result.[820]

There is no denying that President Xi incentivized espionage thanks to a number of initiatives such as Made in China 2025 and his Thousand Talents Plan. His Made in China 2025 program targets "a transition in China's labor-intensive manufacturing economy to a leader in more value-added technology production," according to Stratfor. That plan seeks to achieve "70 percent self-sufficiency in high-tech industries by 2025 and dominating global tech markets by 2049."[821]

The PRC's Thousand Talent Plan, introduced earlier in this volume, seeks to recruit top-tier scientists, researchers, and industry professionals from other countries who then bring their know-how—and, in some cases, industrial secrets—to China. The foreign talent is offered cash bonuses and other incentives for specific trade secrets as they relocate. Stratfor called out the case of a "disgruntled engineer at energy technology company AMSC" who received $1.7 million to provide trade secrets that would save the partially Chinese government-owned company SINOVEL $800 million in contracts it had with AMSC.[822]

Stratfor points out that Chinese agents also offer a variety of other incentives, not just cash, to entrepreneurs. Evidently, the Chinese modus operandi is to identify an individual inside a target company who has access to trade secrets and then encourage him/her to leave that firm and start their own rival business, and in the process to share the former employer's intellectual property with Chinese agents in exchange for helping set up the new business. One such case cited by Stratfor indicates that Chinese investors encouraged a biochemist working on monoclonal antibodies to take sensitive information and then leave GlaxoSmithKline to start a rival business in China. Also, China's interest in pharmaceutical trade secrets tracked with the COVID-19 pandemic and the massive potential profits.[823]

Unfortunately, espionage is easier today because of modern technology such as the accessibility of digitally stored information. Would-be spies/traitors with access to intellectual property can transfer terabytes of information onto concealable hard drives or thumb drives and then steal away with the data, often without notice for long periods. As Stratfor explains, "Cyberespionage techniques allow collectors access to sensitive information without the logistical complications of sending officers or informants on long, expensive missions through hostile territory."[824]

Some Chinese spies get away with stealing intellectual property because our Department of Justice bungles the cases or otherwise there is a political issue at stake. The *Epoch Times* profiled the criminal cases of scientists involved in biomedical and cancer research in California as well as a doctoral candidate studying artificial intelligence in Indiana.[825]

One such case involved Tang Juan, a biology researcher at the University of California who was to appear for trial in July 2021, but suddenly her case was dismissed and the woman immediately left for China. She was arrested in 2020 for allegedly lying about her Chinese military service in order to enter the United States.[826]

This case and others like it in recent years were launched by the Justice Department based on the 2018 Trump administration "China Initiative" to tackle threats posed by Chinese espionage. After all, as pointed out above, most (80 percent) of all economic espionage charges brought by federal prosecutors since 2012 implicated China, according to our Justice Department.[827]

Sam Faddis, a retired Central Intelligence Agency (CIA) operations officer, said a number of federal cases started by the Trump administration involving Chinese researchers accused of having PLA ties were mysteriously dismissed by the Biden administration's Justice Department. Mr. Faddis said, "Right now, there's a serious debate as to whether the FBI's China Initiative, which was put in place to get tough on Chinese espionage, is racist." He added that "this is obviously a preamble to—at a minimum—watering it down, if not doing away with it entirely."[828]

It is noteworthy that the Biden Justice Department dropped charges against a number of Chinese nationals suspected of violating the China

Initiative. US Rep. Jim Banks (R-IN), in response to these dropped cases, said the Biden administration is not serious about "challenging China in any meaningful way."[829]

It was pretty obvious that the Biden administration didn't like President Trump's get-tough-on-China Initiative. In fact, on February 23, 2022, the Biden Department of Justice (DOJ) ended the program. Matthew Olson, the head of the DOJ's National Security Division, "claimed that the DOJ would [now] focus on the broader threat landscape from China, North Korea, Russia and Iran, while still prioritizing countering China's efforts," according to Stratfor. Meanwhile in a very telling statement, Olsen cited so-called "civil rights concerns—including racial discrimination allegations—about the [China] Initiative, as well as the negative effects it had on academia and the scientific community."[830]

Previously, in late 2021, the CIA joined the FBI in sounding the alarm about Chinese spying. According to a Bloomberg report, the CIA is considering establishing a new mission center focused on the Communist Chinese regime, perhaps because the FBI dropped their program. Evidently, William Burns, the agency's director, wants to elevate the United States' focus on China as our number one strategic rival, and with good reason.[831]

The proposed "mission center for China" would address what Mr. Burns described in his confirmation hearing before the US Senate as threats to our national security. He said that "an adversarial predatory Chinese leadership" is our "biggest geopolitical test."[832]

Mr. Faddis agrees with the CIA director. "If you haven't been in a coma for the last 30 or 40 years, you should be aware that the Chinese Communist Party is the number one geopolitical strategic threat to the United States."[833]

Mr. Burns echoes that view to indicate we need to "out compete" the CCP because of the regime's "growing number of areas in which Xi's China is a formidable, authoritarian adversary—methodically strengthening its capabilities to steal intellectual property."[834]

China Fuses National Resources to Speed Up Technological Developments

The PRC outlined its commitment to accelerating military-technology development in its 14th Five-Year Plan (2021–25). The plan's communique states its target is to "make major strides in the modernization of national defense and the armed forces." Further, the plan calls this strategy "civil-military fusion."[835]

The Pentagon's 2021 report on China elaborates on the PRC's military-civil fusion (MCF;军民融合), a development strategy that fuses the nation's economic, social, and security development strategies to build an integrated national strategic system and capabilities" that support President Xi's "rejuvenation" goal.[836]

DIA Director General Berrier called out the MCF in his congressional testimony, noting that "Beijing's long-term strategy of rapid, indigenous…development of cutting-edge technology, combined with licit and illicit foreign technology acquisition, very likely has positioned China at the forefront of numerous scientific fields." He noted that open sharing of resources and transfer of technology between Chinese civilian and defense entities "intentionally blurs the distinction" between commercial and defense supply chains.[837]

Beijing and Moscow view "the development of emerging and disruptive technologies as a 'race' in which leaders in a technology area could potentially develop military capabilities that outpace their adversaries," a perspective attributed to General Berrier. The general said the CCP's milestone to achieve modernization by 2027 signals "an intent [by the PRC] to accelerate some modernization efforts to ensure that the PLA achieves its goals of completing military modernization by 2035 and transforming into a dominant military by 2049."[838]

This is a true existential threat to America's way of life. Former US Director of National Intelligence John Ratcliffe echoed General Berrier's statements to say that Beijing is launching "unethical" military experiments and "there are no ethical boundaries to Beijing's pursuit of power."[839]

Mr. Ratcliffe continued by saying that China is developing "soldiers with biologically enhanced capabilities" that will serve the CCP's goal of taking over "the planet."[840]

Further, China's MCF, according to the Pentagon 2021 report, encompasses six interrelated efforts that demonstrate the comprehensive threat:

(1) Fusing China's defense industrial base and its civilian technology and industrial base; (2) integrating and leveraging science and technology innovations across military and civilian sectors; (3) cultivating talent and blending military and civilian expertise and knowledge; (4) building military requirements into civilian infrastructure and leveraging civilian construction for military purposes; (5) leveraging civilian service and logistics capabilities for military purposes; and, (6) expanding and deepening China's national defense mobilization system to include all relevant aspects of its society and economy for use in competition and war.[841]

The MCF manifests itself in a variety of ways outlined below.

MCF diverts foreign dual-use technologies to the PLA. In 2020, the US State Department accused China of using MCF to "explicitly" divert foreign dual-use technologies to military end-uses. Evidently, the aim is to help transform the PLA into the world's most technologically advanced military.[842]

A senior State Department official said the PRC's use of MCF helps China acquire and divert foreign technologies, "specifically emerging and advanced technologies—and particularly those related to artificial intelligence (AI)—to incorporate them into the PLA's next-generation military capabilities."[843]

After all, the MCF is a policy to help develop the PLA's capabilities, said the official, by eliminating barriers between defense and civilian entities; by circumventing Western military sanctions imposed on the regime since the late 1980s; and to "gain access to sensitive and advanced commercial technologies for military gains." The State spokesman elaborated: The CCP "is determined to be the first to weaponize these technologies, and it is targeting international collaborations to do so." Further, the official said the CCP "recognizes that the world is on the cusp of a technology revolution, and that AI-enabled technologies will deeply impact the development of future military capabilities.[844]

The PRC created SASTIND to support the development of military technologies. The PRC launched a project that provides financial incentives and grants to private industry to gain their support developing military technologies. That project, the State Administration for Science, Technology and Industry for National Defense (SASTIND), answers to the Chinese Defense Ministry.[845]

The rules governing the SASTIND outline the technology requirements and guidelines for local entrepreneurs who want to participate in the project. Most of the technologies developed by this effort are passed to China's state-owned defense industrial enterprises, especially the China Aerospace Science and Technology Corporation and its sister organization, the China Aerospace Science and Industry Corporation.[846]

China reinforces its protection of rare-earth minerals. Earlier in this volume, we considered how the PRC seeks to monopolize certain important resources, which includes rare-earth minerals. This resource is critical to the PRC's long-term goal of dominating technological development because these minerals are the essential building materials for most high-technology devices.[847]

Beijing's Ministry of Industry and Information Technology (MITT) reinforced protection of its rare-earth minerals by setting in place a host of new rules, "Regulations on Rare Earth Management." China produces approximately 80 percent of the world's total supply of rare-earth elements and intends to maintain a strict control of the resource.[848]

The MITT wrote:

Rare earths are important strategic resources that are not renewable, and it is necessary to reinforce the full industrial chain regulations, targeting activities that are currently disrupting the healthy development of the industry and damaging the environment, such as illegal, destructive, unplanned and excessive mining, and illicit trading.[849]

China "collaborates" with other nations to access sophisticated technologies and to fund development that aids the PLA. What China can't steal or develop via its MCF network it seeks through a growing international technology network. In fact, the PRC has established science and technology (S&T) links with more than 150 countries, a key aspect of the regime's civil-military integration strategy to leverage advanced technologies.[850]

The Ministry of Science and Technology claims the PRC has at least 158 S&T partnerships with a like number of "countries and regions." These agreements enable China to "integrate into the global network of scientific and technological innovation." Further, China has at least 70 S&T offices across embassies, consulates, and diplomatic missions in some countries and regions with more than 146 accredited Chinese diplomats working to build inter-government cooperation and establish networks of S&T contacts.[851]

Below is a sampling of the many technology agreements that help fuel the PRC's thirst for S&T.

"Trojan Horse" Arrangements

The PRC and the Republic of Armenia established an agreement that covers military-technical cooperation such as training and logistical support. "Ministers expressed confidence that Armenian-Chinese bilateral military cooperation [will] develop in a wide range of perspectives," the Armenian Ministry of Defense wrote in a statement.[852]

There is likely a dual purpose for such an agreement, however. No doubt, Beijing will assist Armenia's "army-building" program by selling weapons and conducting associated military training. However, in all likelihood, the agreement opens the door to expand commercial export sales to Armenia and more importantly to reach additional agreements regarding oil and gas supplies as well as access to that country's mineral resources such as copper, zinc, gold, and lead—all which Armenia has in large deposits.[853]

Technological Collaboration

China loves to "collaborate" with other countries because more often than not such relationships provide Beijing opportunities to associate with high-tech corporations and then to capture the entity's technology for home use. That's exactly what China's SASTIND did with Russia's Central Institute of Aviation Motors (CIAM).[854]

SASTIND and CIAM signed a memorandum of understanding that created a "long-term cooperative partnership between the two institutions." Further, the agreement outlined collaboration in a range of aero-engine activities to include simulation technologies, distributed control systems, engine health management, thermal management, and fluid control.[855]

The clear beneficiary of this collaborative effort is the Aero Engine Corporation of China (AECC), which is state-owned. Thanks to a network of other Chinese firms and the agreement with CIAM, AECC benefits technically by "boosting China's capability in developing and producing aero-engines for military and commercial applications."[856]

Other Chinese-Russian collaborative agreements include those between China North Industries Corporation (NORINCO) and Russian industries working on military navigational and communications equipment; yet others involve aerospace manufacturing of aircraft, engines, and defense electronics.[857]

Technological Entanglements

The PRC's intentional corrupting purposes include its quest for new technology by increasing "entanglements" between Chinese agencies and foreign counterparts. There are numerous examples, such as those with Australia and the United States.[858]

The Australian Strategic Policy Institute's International Cyber Policy Centre (ICPU) published a paper that claims "strategic technology" partnerships create a "dual-use dilemma" for countries like Australia and the US that help their capability but also support the PLA.[859]

China's Electronics Technology Group Corporation (CETC), a government entity managed by the Minister of Information Industry, claimed in 2017 a "new record for the number of UAVs [unmanned aerial vehicles] launched in swarm utilizing AI technologies." The ICPU claims that China's close relationship with Australia and the US aided the PLA's UAV swarming capability. Specifically, the ICPU states:

> Despite the genuine advantages [partnerships] may offer, [they] can result in the transfer of dual-use research and technologies that advance Chinese military modernization, perhaps disrupting the future balance of power in the Indo-Pacific, or facilitate the party-state's construction of surveillance capabilities that are starting to diffuse globally.[860]

The ICPU paper continues:

> The core dilemma is that the Chinese party-state has demonstrated the capacity and intention to co-opt private technology companies and academic research to advance national and defense objectives in ways that are far from transparent.[861]

There are a number of such "partnerships" that result in aiding the modernization of the PLA. For example, a subsidiary of the CETC, a PRC-owned defense group, established an "innovation center" in Silicon Valley in 2014. Also, the CETC's joint venture with the University of Technology Sydney, Australia, established in 2017 a center for advanced research with a focus on AI and autonomous systems. The

ICPU also highlights collaboration between PLA researchers and Australia's National University of Defense Technology, Huawei's research with a variety of partnerships in both the US and Australia; and Germany's engineering group Siemens' collaboration with CETC inside China on "smart manufacturing" technologies such as digitization, networking, robotics, and AI.[862]

The ICPU paper called on Western countries to introduce policies that "balance the risks and benefits of these partnerships, collaborations and entanglements." Further, the ICPU cautioned policymakers to "examine closely research, academic and commercial partnerships that may prove problematic, and then consider updates and revisions to national export controls, defense trade controls, and investment review mechanisms as targeted countermeasures."[863]

Getting the West to Finance Research That Benefits the PLA

As recently as 2021, the European Union and the PRC agreed in principle to accept greater levels of EU investments in China. That agreement helps the PRC develop military capabilities through advanced commercial technologies.[864]

The EU-China Comprehensive Agreement on Investment (CAI), announced December 30, 2020, is intended to "significantly improve the market access conditions for EU companies in China." It shouldn't surprise anyone that the CAI contains a section "that is likely intended to address China's efforts to leverage investment to gain access to foreign technologies," an aspect of the agreement that supports the PRC's MCF strategy.[865]

Although the CAI includes rules against the forced transfer of technology, it invariably happens—and the PLA benefits. Even though there is no record of EU investment helping China's defense sector, EU-based firms such as Airbus and Safran have invested in China with the state-owned Aviation Industry Corporation of China (AVIC), a firm that operates a forced technology-transfer policy.[866]

It is also well-established that AVIC and a number of Chinese firms "have acquired stakes in several EU aerospace companies," such as the Austria-based Fischer Advanced Composite Components, the United Kingdom firm AIM Altitude, and the German company Theiler Aircraft Engines.[867]

Perhaps most disturbing is how the US helped the Chinese gain a strategic advantage. In 2021, the PLA tested a nuclear-capable hypersonic missile Pentagon experts contend can evade US missile-defense systems.[868]

"The People's Liberation Army now has an increasingly credible capability to undermine our missile defenses and threaten the American homeland with both conventional and nuclear strikes," said Rep. Mike Gallagher (R-WI), member of the House Armed Services Committee. "Even more disturbing is the fact that American technology [and money] has contributed to the PLA's hypersonic missile program."[869]

The hypersonic missile capability depends on microchips and semiconductors, which until recent years the CCP didn't possess. However, the CCP made acquiring those microchips a high priority and put Vice Premier Liu He in charge of national chip development. The vice premier turned to US companies for help.[870]

An investigative report funded by the *Wall Street Journal* found that American companies filled China's microchip gap. Specifically, the research firm Rhodium Group found that in the years 2017–2020, "US venture-capital firms, chip-industry giants and other private investors participated in 58 investment deals in China's semiconductor industry…more than double the number from the prior four years."[871]

The Rhodium Group reported that "billions of dollars have been raised for Chinese companies producing computer chips." In fact, between 2013 and 2016, "China-based firms leveraged…state funding to attempt to acquire or invest in at least 27 US semiconductor firms totaling more than $37 billion," according to the USCC.[872]

Those American funds are key to the regime's semiconductor ambitions. Although China currently possesses less than 10 percent of the global semiconductor industry, the CCP's ambitious "Digital Silk Road" initiatives, which are part of the regime's Made in China 2025 goal, indicate the regime intends to dominate the global industry, a view expressed by the regime's top leaders.

In 2016, President Xi said, "the fact that core technology is controlled by others is our greatest hidden danger." Vice Premier Ma Kai echoed that sentiment at the 2018 Nation People's Congress: "We cannot be reliant on foreign chips." Today, China produces only 16 percent of the semiconductors used in China. Therefore, it's understandable why the regime intends to end that dependence by the early 2030s, which explains its " total planned investment in semiconductors is $118 billion over five years," according to a report by the Center for Strategic and International Studies.[873]

CONCLUSION

In three sections, this chapter demonstrates the PRC's technological ambitions and how it licitly and illicitly acquires technologies that are intended to help bolster the PLA's capabilities, China's global competitiveness, and, by association, the PRC's goal of creating a new world order in its image.

Section III

WHAT TO DO: CHINA'S NEW WORLD ORDER AMBITIONS AND PROPHETIC IMPLICATIONS OF THE COMMUNIST REGIME'S HEGEMONY

We must always keep a long-term perspective, remain mindful of potential risks, maintain strategic focus and determination, and "attain the broad and great while addressing the delicate and minute."[874]

—Xi Jinping
New Years' Speech from Beijing, December 31, 2021

It should be clear by now that Communist China is dead set on scuttling the current US-run international order and replacing it with one in Beijing's favor. After all, President Xi and his Communist compatriots believe their Middle Kingdom has a better plan for mankind and thus are pulling out all stops to remake the world in their image.

We began this volume by setting the historic context for the present time. In Section I, we explored the Chinese dynastic period that spanned millennia, which created a mostly proud legacy for the Chinese people. However, since the advent of the Chinese Communist Party (1921) and their elevation to power in Beijing (1949), the regime distorted the nation's rich history to serve its totalitarian and bankrupt ambitions.

Section II of this volume outlined in great detail the five tools the CCP uses to reshape the world order to its image: economy, ideology, security, geopolitics and technology. Each of these instruments of Chinese national power is decisively employed to advance the CCP's goal of realizing world hegemony. As explained in those chapters, President Xi—with the full support of the CCP—is succeeding, because much of the West and especially the US have until recently naively embraced a fairytale-like view of the People's Republic of China.

This final section of *Kings of the East* begins with chapter 9, which outlines what the US and, by association, the freedom-loving sovereign democratic nations across the world must do to counter the CCP's rising threat. We will consider each of the five instruments of Chinese power—economy, ideology, security, geopolitics, and technology—and how to deny, if possible, the Chinese Communists' aim of transforming the world order using these instruments.

The final chapter takes a global view of the threat to consider the emergence of Communist China from a biblical perspective. We contemplate whether the CCP's actions might just be leading mankind to the prophetic end times. Further, we answer perhaps the most daunting question: Does Scripture tell us whether Communist China plays a role in the emergence of the Antichrist, the coming Tribulation, and the return of our Lord?

9

The China We Wanted and the One We Got:
Resetting That Relationship

Whether China and the US can properly handle their relations...
is critical for the future and destiny of the world.[875]

—Xi Jinping regarding his message to
President Biden, September 2021

This chapter acknowledges that Communist China is a rogue regime, hegemonic, and not easily ignored. It's a threat to world peace. Of course, that's not what much of the West hoped would become of Beijing once it was fully embraced with all the opportunity to grow into a full-fledged economic and geopolitical world partner. However, hope is never a strategy, and China today is far from being a liberal democracy. That leaves us with two choices: adjust to the reality of an authoritarian Asian superpower that seeks to dominate the world, or reset our relationship with the PRC and press for a less-threatening Middle Kingdom. Alternatively, we can continue to stick our collective heads in the sand and naively cling to a hopeful metamorphosis of the Communist regime into something akin to a Jeffersonian democracy. Let's be pragmatic and "reset" our relationship with the tyrants in Beijing.

This chapter in three parts charts the way ahead—that is, assuming the best recourse for America is to reset our relationship with the rogue regime in Beijing. Therefore, we begin with a review of history by looking back at the fairy-tale promises (the empty hope strategy) of previous diplomats and senior American government officials who were certain that welcoming China into the community of modern nations would result in the transformation of the regime's worst nature into something akin to Western liberal democracies.

Second, we briefly review the character of China, warts and all. It is certainly not the country our fairy-tale-seeking diplomats promised for much of the past half century, but it is a totalitarian, mostly fascist regime glued to its Marxist-Leninist ideology, albeit partially capitalist in its self-serving lust that is power-hungry and ultimately seeks to take over the world and transform our globe in the CCP's image.

Finally, we consider the mechanics of a real policy reset with China using the five instruments examined in the previous chapters of this volume—ideology, geopolitics, economics, security, and technology. That reset proposes what our policies ought to become when dealing with a modern authoritarian China, especially if we are to prevent the Chinese Communists from becoming what they seek to be: the dominant world power that destroys the freedoms of liberal democracies, and, as explored in the next chapter, the power that might usher in the prophetic end times.

THE FAIRY-TALE CHINA

For more than half a century, Western policymakers hung onto the hope that the integration of China into the global economy would benefit the Communist regime and the West. After all, they believed trade with the West was associated with commercial freedom inside the PRC and that, in time, that relationship would mellow the regime's totalitarian character as well as spark domestic freedoms and calm the tyrants' aggressive impulses. That hasn't happened, although Beijing has grown wealthy at our expense.

Consider a brief outline of the US government's efforts post-World War II that intended but failed to influence China to join the West and then become part of the liberal democratic league of nations. Yes, that is a fairy-tale spun by many who, for decades, whispered in the ear of every president, promising engagement would defang the Beijing rogues. However, it wasn't until Donald Trump came to the Oval Office that we finally had an administration that pushed back against Beijing's malign behavior.

The former Trump administration displayed a rather sanguine view of contemporary China as opposed to the upstart and failing Biden administration. For example, the Trump National Security Council wrote a National Security Strategy that soberly defined China as a "competitor," the first genuinely negative expression about Beijing from a US administration since the late 1960s.

Mr. Trump's National Security Strategy gave voice to those concerned about the Communist Chinese. That 2017 document stated a new consensus among many China watchers that past efforts with the regime failed because they were "based on the assumption that engagement with rivals [read "China"] and their inclusion in international institutions and global commerce would turn them into benign actors and trustworthy partners." However, the strategy concluded, "For the most part, this premise turned out to be false."[876]

Mr. Trump's tough policy stance became a whole-of-the-government approach regarding actions with the People's Republic of China, and those efforts were not limited to trade but also addressed national security and cyber defense, as well as human rights and much more. No doubt, Mr. Trump oversaw a historic reversal for US policy after many decades of turning a blind eye to China's maligned behavior.[877]

To be fair, the US government did, on occasion over more than the past half century, criticize the Chinese Communist regime. Certainly, the US was critical of China during the Korean War (1950–1953), when we fought the Chinese that sent three million troops to fight alongside the North Koreans. Some American diplomats publicly called out the regime's human-rights violations during China's Cultural Revolution (1966–1976). Further, Washington was critical of Beijing when the Communists rushed to aid their fellow Marxist regime in North Vietnam during our war (1954–1975) with Hanoi. However, much of our foreign policy attention from the 1950s to the early 1970s was reserved for the former Soviet Union—that is, except when President Richard Nixon decided to change the policy dynamic with Beijing.

President Nixon came to the White House in 1969 with a different view of China. He considered the sleeping Asian giant a country with which the US could deal, and he intended to prove his view with a surprise visit to Beijing in 1972. Nixon meant to mark the culmination of his presidency by the resumption of a harmonious relationship with the Communist regime after a quarter of a century of no communication or diplomatic ties between the two countries. Allegedly, Nixon's true aim with the Beijing visit was less charitable. Rather, he wanted to leverage that new relationship in order to bait Moscow into taking a less confrontational position toward the United States. Meanwhile, it wasn't until 1979 that then President Jimmy Carter formally established full diplomatic relations with the PRC and restored "most favored nation" status to Communist China, a regime with a nonmarket economy.[878]

The eventual collapse of the Soviet Union (1991) went a long way toward mitigating concerns in the West about communism, even the Marxists in Beijing. In fact, soon after the demise of the Communist regime in Moscow, many in Washington and other Western capitals encouraged Moscow—and, by association, Communist China—to embrace "free-market" globalization. Specifically, in 1991, President George H. W. Bush said he was "more determined than ever to press for open markets, free and fair trade around the world, and open investment opportunities everywhere…to benefit every country that participates in achieving these goals," which presumably included the recently freed Russian people and the newly welcomed Communist China.[879]

President Bush's expansion of capitalism in the wake of the Cold War wasn't a victory for many Americans, however. After all, his effort encouraged transnational corporations to move their production abroad, especially into the open-armed Chinese. Soon, America bled millions of jobs that rushed to cheaper labor markets in mostly Asia. As a result, the US middle class began to feel the effects of a lopsided trade relationship that favored the Asian dictatorship.

Understandably, Beijing greatly benefited from Bush's expansion of capitalism because it sparked a true revolution of growth for the Chinese economy. However, the collateral effects of rapid economic expansion were the corruption of the CCP, as well as the creation of a legion morally tainted Chinese millionaires. Meanwhile, those effects had no impact on American business leaders, and Washington focused like a laser on the benefits of more trade, albeit while turning their collective blind eye to the regime's malevolent human-rights behavior, Marxist ideology, and saber rattling against democratic Taiwan.

In 1993, Bill Clinton came to the Oval Office promising to take a hard line with China, especially on the growing trade imbalance as well as human rights. Mr. Clinton tried to entice the regime to correct its appalling human-rights record by offering the possibility of Most Favored Nation Status, the key to the regime's entry into the World Trade Organization (WTO), something the tyrants in Beijing desperately sought. Even though Clinton insisted on a human-rights-related quid pro quo with Beijing, in the end, it never happened, even though the US did reward China with a favorable trade relationship.

On May 28, 1993, the newly minted President Clinton celebrated China's victory. "Today, members of Congress have joined me to announce a new chapter in United States policy toward China," Clinton said. He continued:

China occupies an important place in our nation's foreign policy. It is the world's most populous state, [it's the] fastest growing major economy, and a permanent member of the United

Nations Security Council. Its future will do much to shape the future of Asia, our security and trade relations in the Pacific, and a host of global issues, from the environment to weapons proliferation. In short: our relationship with China is of very great importance.[880]

At the signing ceremony for the so-called Most Favored Nation Status for the PRC were numerous representatives of the business community along with congressional leaders. President Clinton expressed a common hope at the time:

We are hopeful that China's process of development and economic reform will be accompanied by greater political freedom. In some ways, this process has begun.

He continued:

The question we face today is how best to cultivate these hopeful seeds of change in China while strongly expressing our clear disapproval of its repressive [human-rights] policies.[881]

On the last point, Mr. Clinton's "hope" for Chinese change failed miserably. After all, Beijing didn't give an inch on human rights, but gleefully embraced its new trade status with the United States, which ultimately opened the door to the regime's accession to the WTO (2001).

Yes, Mr. Clinton was a key sponsor for China's accession to the WTO. He argued at the time that:

China would have to change its policies to adhere to WTO rules…[that] the WTO would act as a check on China's communist government, speeding up its transition to a market economy and encouraging it to have a greater stake in setting global rules…. [and] it would legitimize the WTO itself: China was the biggest trading country outside the organization, and the WTO could not really claim to be a global organization without it.[882]

The subsequent two decades demonstrated that President Clinton's claims about Communist China were terribly wrong. Beijing used the WTO for its gain and today continues to violate most every rule and principle. The regime has never come close to living up to Mr. Clinton's enthusiastic endorsement that the WTO would become a genuine check on communism.

President Clinton was also wrong about Beijing's ongoing dispute with Taiwan. In 1996, he sent two aircraft carriers to the Taiwan Strait as a show of support for the democratic island nation. That show of force was a warning to Beijing that PLA military exercises at the time in the Taiwan Strait were "unnecessarily risky" and "unnecessarily reckless" actions that could have "grave consequences," according to Clinton's Secretary of State Warren Christopher. However, Clinton's subsequent rapprochement with Beijing likely communicated to the Communist leaders an entirely different message than originally intended. China was emboldened, not deterred.[883]

Like his predecessors, President George W. Bush came to the Oval Office promising to also be tough on China, with emphasis on issues such as selling weapons to Taiwan, holding the regime accountable for human-rights violations, and concerns that the regime wasn't part of the US-Russia Anti-Ballistic Missile Treaty of 1972. Like Clinton, Mr. Bush supported China's WTO membership for what he said were three compelling reasons:

> Trade with China will promote freedom.… Trade with China serves our national interest.… Trade with China serves the economic interests of America.[884]

Before being elected president, Mr. Bush claimed in his campaign documents that "our relationship with China" needed to change, something most past presidents said but never did until Mr. Trump entered the White House. "I believe our relationship needs to be redefined as competitor," said Bush. He continued:

> Competitors can find areas of agreement, but we must make it clear to the Chinese that we don't appreciate any attempt to spread weapons of mass destruction around the world, that we don't appreciate any threats to our friends and allies in the Far East.[885]

Unfortunately, Mr. Bush never redefined our policy or issued an executive action to alter our relationship with China, and meanwhile, the regime continued to engage in a variety of human-rights violations and to cheat on trade—and all without suffering any meaningful push-back. Then Bush's promise to right our relationship with China flew out the window after the 9/11 terrorist attacks on America, because all of a sudden Beijing became an erstwhile "ally" in the global war on terrorism.

President Barack Obama wasn't successful at modifying China's malign behavior either. For example, at the White House in 2015, Obama sternly lectured President Xi about Chinese cyberattacks on American institutions. Obama said with the Chinese president at his side:

> I raised once again our very serious concerns about growing cyber-threats to American companies and American citizens. I indicated that it has to stop. The United States government does not engage in cyber economic espionage for commercial gain. And today, I can announce that our two countries have reached a common understanding on the way forward. We've agreed that neither the US or the Chinese government will conduct or knowingly support cyber-enabled theft of intellectual property, including trade secrets or other confidential business informa-tion for commercial advantage. In addition, we'll work together,

and with other nations, to promote international rules of the road for appropriate conduct in cyberspace.[886]

Obama's strong statement was never backed by follow-up action. Evidently, President Xi judged Obama's threat of action as empty, and the regime's cyber espionage continued. That hollow warning was similar to Obama's so-called Operation Freedom of Navigation in the South China Sea in 2015. The US president called out the Chinese for seizing islets in the South China Sea, which included the construction of military facilities hundreds of miles from the Chinese mainland, in those international waters. However, Obama never followed through with his promise of action other than to sail a few warships through the disputed region.

Trump Administration Was Different

The Trump administration came into office threatening to take action against the Chinese and, unlike his predecessors, he followed through and kept his promises. He began by issuing a flurry of documents targeting China: "National Security Strategy," "National Defense Strategy," and the "Nuclear Posture Review." Then Vice President Mike Pence outlined the administration's policy intent in an October 2018 speech focused on China, a comprehensive verbal assault on the regime. What Mr. Pence said was echoed by the Trump diplomatic and security teams that included Trade Representative Robert Lighthizer and National Trade Council Director Peter Navarro, who were without exception hawkish toward China.

With no exceptions, the Trump administration took a hard look at China and held the regime accountable beginning with trade. For years, the US had a huge trade deficit with China, and all the challenges associated with that outcome were carefully examined by Trump officials. As a result, Mr. Trump energized trade negotiations with Beijing that were tough, and arguably for the first time, the regime felt the pressure on issues such as intellectual property rights, state-owned enterprises, the Chinese attempts to weaken the renminbi, and much more.

Mr. Trump held the Chinese responsible on many fronts, such as cyberattacks. He issued warnings and then prosecuted Chinese agents and some leaders within the PLA. Further, the administration worked with the Congress to publish within the National Defense Authorization Act for Fiscal Year 2019 a law named the "Foreign Investment Risk Review Modernization Act" (FIRRMA) that strengthened the authority of the Committee on Foreign Investment in the United States (CFIUS), which closely monitors whether the acquisition of a US company by a foreign entity like China presents a threat to America's national security. This act opened up the opportunity to go after Beijing's corporations like Huawei Technologies, which used a variety of tools to steal American technology.

Biden Administration Backtracks on China

President Joe Biden had a much easier task than other new presidents over the past half century. He could have built upon President Trump's China policy by keeping up the momentum against the regime. However, Mr. Biden chose the easier course, squandered the opportunity, and returned America's China policy to one similar to those of Clinton, Bush, and Obama.[887]

Early in the Biden administration, it demonstrated a willingness to accommodate Beijing with the new president's vacillating rhetoric. After all, his messages were mostly confused or weak on support for Taiwan, trade, holding China accountable for the coronavirus pandemic, and much more. Rather than be tough on China like President Trump, Mr. Biden claimed the challenges of COVID-19 and the global climate crisis required both the US and China "to come together with the international community to solve."[888]

Mr. Biden's actions and words failed to hold Beijing accountable for its actions. The facts, according to Bradley Thayer, a founding member of the Committee on Present Danger China, are noted in his statement that follows:

> Beijing caused the COVID-19 pandemic, and it is the driving force behind climate change. Rather than coming together as Biden suggested, the interests of the United States and China are diametrically opposed. To resolve both problems, it would be far better if the Biden administration led the international community to sanction the Chinese regime for both problems, either one of which should compel Beijing's eviction from international society.[889]

Mr. Biden's accommodation to Beijing was reckless, because it gave the Communist regime encouragement to further suppress freedom with its authoritarian approach as well as escape accountability. This is wrongheaded, and not the strategy that previously succeeded at confronting and eventually defeating China's former partner, the Communist Soviet Union. Rather, Biden's return to the Clinton-Bush-Obama naïve approach with Beijing weakened the US against the Chinese tyrants, and that might not be a mistake.[890]

It is possible but not yet proven that President Biden's decisions regarding the PRC are influenced by the under-investigation, unethical business dealings of his son, Hunter, which were made with the Communist regime. Specifically, the *New York Post's* Miranda Devine wrote a book, *Laptop from Hell*, which declares:

> The Biden family offered their services to a huge, Chinese government-linked energy consortium to expand its business around the world. How do we know? Because of hundreds of emails documenting the deal found on Hunter Biden's laptop, left in a Delaware repair shop in April 2019.[891]

Others are sounding off about the Biden family's dealing with the Communists in Beijing as well. In 2021, Peter Schweizer, a long-time investigative reporter, released a bombshell book, *Red-Handed: How American Elites Get Rich Helping China Win*, which documents how leading American political families helped the CCP's quest for global hegemony. A large part of Schweizer's book calls out the Bidens, "and not just because the head of the Biden crime family is the current occupant of the White House." But, as Schweizer writes, the Biden "family's dealings with China were 'unprecedented' because they entered into deals with persons connected to the highest levels of Chinese intelligence."[892]

"One of the most startling things we uncovered is the simple fact that the Biden family, while he was vice president of the United States and continuing when he became president, received some $31 million from Chinese individuals who are linked to the highest levels of Chinese intelligence," Schweizer said on the Fox News Channel's *Life, Liberty & Levin*.[893]

Internal Party Agendas Distort Our China Policy

It is helpful to consider the reasons past presidents like Clinton, Obama, and even Bush, to a certain extent, chose to be soft on China. After all, US-China policy is really an internal ideological and trade debate within both the Republican and Democratic parties. This is an important point, because there are real political forces within both parties that pressure the White House, no matter the party of the president at the time, regarding the China policy, which explains in part why most past presidents were seldom tough with Beijing.

Traditionally, the Democratic Party has a constituency that includes labor unions, environmental groups, and human-rights organizations that collectively have a grievance with the Chinese Communists. Specifically, labor unions are jealous of jobs leaving America for cheaper labor inside China. Therefore, they lobby Democratic administrations for policies that require equal competition that favor the US worker.

However, business leaders often deliver a contrary request while simultaneously lining the pockets of Democrat candidates with campaign contributions, which too often results in a soft-shoe policy toward China.

There are also the environmentalist Democrats who seize on China's lax climate regulations and the country's high pollution rates. They often seek action against Beijing, but seldom get more than weak promises and agreements that address the problem, but in the end nothing changes. The Chinese promise and never deliver.

On the human-rights front, Democratic Party constituents complain vociferously about the lack of freedom of speech and the oppression of people of faith in China. Once again, all recent Democratic administrations have promised to take a tough stand against oppression, but without exception, nothing happened to change China's behavior toward its own citizens.

The Republicans have similar internal challenges and generally nothing to show for administration promises to reset the China relationship. After all, not all Republicans are Nixon/Kissinger realists about China. Rather, the Reagan-type Republicans believe in foreign policy through strength, because they tend to see Beijing as a threat on many levels. They pump up military forces in the Pacific to send a strong message to the PRC. Neoconservative Republicans, who lost credibility since the Iraq war, take a tough stance with China on a host of moral issues, undemocratic, human rights, religious persecution, security issues, and more.

Perhaps the most influential group within the Republican establishment are the pro-China, big-money businesspeople who typically trump all the others in influence. They have made a fortune working with China since the 1990s and expect the party to maintain free trade with China no matter the costs. Therefore, Republican presidents typically, much like the Democratic presidents, talk tough on China, but consistently fail to reset that relationship to address many legitimate concerns.

What's clear from this political influence across both parties is that there are pro- and anti-China factions that significantly impact the policies of the occupant in the White House. Evidently, the most persuasive voices across both parties are the businesspeople who want the status quo relationship with Beijing, which explains our failed China policy.

Chinese Communists Dismiss Washington Elite

Little wonder the Chinese haven't changed over the decades. Every US president in the post-Cold War era, perhaps with the exception of Trump, failed to deliver a China reset. Simply, the Chinese listened to our words and measured them by our non-actions. The general tendency among the Communist regime's elite was understandably that the US is in decline primarily because nothing the Chinese did ever earned more than a diplomatic tongue-lashing or slap on the wrist.

THE REAL CHINA

US-China relations are in a tailspin and are unlikely to improve in the near future. The list of challenges to that relationship is long—from Taiwan to AI to hypersonic missiles. Further, there are many potential flashpoints between Beijing and Washington. At best, the Biden administration's policy regarding China is about avoiding open conflict, albeit while doing little more than tolerate the regime's behavior.

The American people are awake to China's dangerous conduct. Specifically, more than half (52 percent) perceive the threat emanating from Beijing, a significant change since 2018 when only 21 percent expressed that view. "For the first time in our [Ronald Reagan Presidential Foundation & Institute] survey, a majority of the American people identify a single country as the greatest threat facing the United States: China," according to the 2021 survey, which polled 2,500 US adults between October 25 and November 7, 2021.[894]

Self-identified Republicans were more alarmed about China than

Democrats, however. Almost two-thirds (64 percent) of Republican respondents said China was their top concern, compared to less than half of Democrats and independents (each at 44 percent).[895]

This survey comes in the wake of back-to-back administrations (Trump and Biden) that labeled China a serious competitor for the US on the world stage. The Trump administration called out the CCP on a range of issues: unfair trade practices, espionage, malign influence in the US., security threats posed by Chinese technology, and human-rights abuses.[896]

Even President Biden, who has demonstrated a mix of confrontation and engagement with the PRC, said in February 2021 that China is "the most serious competitor" to the United States' prosperity, security, and democratic values.[897]

Survey respondents, according to the Reagan Foundation, also identified the most important Chinese challenges. For example, one in five (20 percent) said China's economic trade practices were the greatest concern, closely followed by 19 percent who identified Beijing's military buildup, and 17 percent identified human-rights abuses as the most significant issue.[898]

These and other issues were on the agenda for a December 2021 meeting between Presidents Biden and Xi. However, according to the White House, that session produced little of substance, and certainly no breakthroughs on the many contentious issues between the countries.

Yes, both men exchanged pleasantries. Mr. Xi called Biden his "old friend," even though Mr. Biden previously asserted on June 16, 2021, "We're not old friends.… It's just pure business." Perhaps that's a deflection to the leverage China may have on the Biden family thanks to the alleged shady business deals with China reportedly made by son Hunter Biden, as outlined earlier in this chapter.[899]

The two leaders' late December 2021 three-and-a-half-hour meeting did little for either side, and the lack of any details released to the press speaks loudly. Had the meeting been substantive, then the White House would have published the particulars with great fanfare. However, the best the Biden team could muster about that meeting was that the administration is "not trying to change China through bilateral engagement [because] we don't think that's realistic." Evidently, the Biden administration isn't about to try to reset that relationship; the status quo will prevail, and that's not encouraging.[900]

Therefore, perhaps the best we can expect from Mr. Biden going forward is to manage competition with Beijing and install some "common-sense guardrails" to avoid armed conflict. After all, the tensions—flashpoints—between the two superpowers are real and escalating.

Evidently, underlings from the two countries can't even have a civil conversation. The bilateral mood for the future was set at the first meeting between senior US and Chinese officials that took place in March 2021 in Anchorage, Alaska. The Chinese diplomats used that session to lecture the US diplomats. China's top diplomat at the conference, Yang Jiechi, spoke for sixteen minutes to deliver broadsides against the Biden administration, denouncing them as bullying, racist, and hypocritical. Nothing of substance came from that initial confrontation, yet the list of flashpoints grows unabated.[901]

At the top of that list is Taiwan, which was constantly harassed in 2021 and 2022 by Chinese bombers violating that nation's airspace and at sea by Chinese warships that shadow the Taiwanese navy. Meanwhile, the US policy regarding Taiwan remains fixed and governed by the Taiwan Relations Act, enacted by the US Congress in 1979 to define the relations between the US and the people of Taiwan. The act declares it is the policy of the US "to preserve and promote extensive, close, and friendly commercial, cultural, and other relations between the people of the United States and the people on Taiwan, as well as the people on the China mainland." The act also states the US "shall provide Taiwan with arms of a defensive character and shall maintain the capacity of the United States to resist any resort of force or other forms of coercion that would jeopardize the security, or social or economic system, of the people of Taiwan."[902]

Beijing's increased belligerence toward Taiwan arguably voids the act's so-called One China policy. In fact, on October 21, 2021, President Biden vowed to defend Taiwan against any future PRC attack on the island. The president called our commitment "sacred," and Taiwan's foreign ministry labeled the "commitment" a "long-time promise."[903]

It should be obvious that past agreements with Taiwan need updating. After all, President Xi warned Biden over US support for Taiwan that China was not going to sit by and watch other nations support Taipei such as Japan, which expressed a willingness to get involved in any future Taiwan crisis.[904]

Unfortunately, time has not mellowed the PRC's aggressiveness regarding Taiwan, making it a key hot-button issue. On January 29, 2022, the Chinese ambassador to Washington, Qin Gang, told National Public Radio the following:

> If the Taiwanese authorities, emboldened by the United States, keep going down the road for independence, it most likely will involve China and the United States, the two big countries, in a military conflict.

The issue of Taiwan is "the biggest tinderbox between China and the United States," Qin said.[905]

Another tinderbox issue concerns protecting American technology. Evidently, the US remains toothless against the aggressive Chinese cyber espionage and other CCP spying. Mr. Biden needs to come up with a serious plan to protect our technology from Chinese thievery, and not something like his pork-laden so-called infrastructure bill that does nothing to protect our digital infrastructure from PLA attacks.

We need to focus on developing American counters against our Chinese adversary. After all, Mr. Biden's own CIA director, Bill Burns, argued in his confirmation hearing that Beijing aims to neutralize the US in Asia, while dominating the global economy and preserving authoritarian Leninism under Beijing's watching control.[906]

Meanwhile, and understandably, much of the West has come to

agree that China is not a friend, and likely will never be as long as the CCP rules that country. For example, rather than warn the world about the release (accidental or not) of the coronavirus that killed more than six million people worldwide over the past years, the Chinese regime kept silent and let the world suffer. And on trade, the CCP's gradual entry into the global marketplace has been massively disappointing although it has enriched itself, and yet political, religious, and civil freedoms inside China are harshly quashed by the authoritarian regime.

Even President Xi's "rejuvenation" of that country isn't what many starry-eyed Westerners hoped for, argued Samuel Gregg, research director at the Acton Institute. Rather, the PRC puts on full display the continuation of the regime's authoritarian character, which means, according to Gregg:

> Centralizing of political authority, a crack-down on internal dissent, radical curtailments of already-limited religious freedoms, the mass imprisonment of "suspect" groups like Uyghur Muslims, and an increase in the party's control over Chinese military and security forces.[907]

That behavior pattern is also true for the Chinese economy. As indicated in the previous section, China's accession into the WTO did not move the regime toward market-liberalization. Rather, the Heritage Foundation's 2020 Index of Economic Freedom classified "China's economy as 'mostly unfree.'"[908]

Mr. Gregg goes on to point out:

> China increasingly behaves in a manner akin to an 18th-century mercantilist-state: the Chinese communist party not only integrates economic and military power on a scale which dwarfs that of Louis XIV's France, but it also pursues policies which have been called "colonialism with Chinese characteristics."[909]

On another front, the regime's buildup of military forces in the South China Sea fuels the integration of military, strategic, and economic policy—actions that expose the regime's arrogance and disregard for international civility. This collusion of PRC sectors is "driven by strategic and military concerns," according to Gregg, and that includes China's Belt and Road Initiative, which is all about geopolitics and especially the need to control strategic corridors in central and southeast Asia.[910]

The previous chapter in this volume identifies another economic powder-keg issue. Specifically, it profiles how Chinese technology companies, many state-owned, blur "commercial imperatives" with what Gregg calls "the strategic imperatives of the party-state," which means such actions as the compulsory theft of intellectual property from Western companies.[911]

Therefore, it is obvious that the PRC is not a friend of the US and much of the West given all the evidence—flashpoints—outlined above, and the regime can't be trusted on anything: coronavirus, trade, finance, military, human rights, cyber operations, and much more.

It is past time for clear-eyed pragmatists to exercise economic and political statesmanship regarding our collective relationship with Communist China. We must not allow this cancerous regime to continue to exercise its malignant free will in an imploding world. The West—especially the United States—must reset its relationship with the tyrants in Beijing, and none too soon.

RESETTING OUR RELATIONSHIP WITH CHINA

How should the US and the West in general respond to the PRC? After all, China is "steadily becoming richer, stronger, and aggressively self-confident," wrote Walter Clemens, professor emeritus of political science at Boston University and an associate at the Harvard University Davis Center for Russian and Eurasian Studies. The professor indicates there are many people with recommendations as to how to address the China problem, and some, like me, believe we need a total reset of that relationship.[912]

Most of those personnel will agree that the United States' history with China is checkered at best, especially during the post-World War II era. The Communist regime hasn't changed into a respectable member of the global league of nations as many hoped. In spite of our best efforts, the regime kept to its authoritarian ways, its self-serving views, and now it has become hegemonic, insisting that the world bow to its expansive ambitions. It is past time to reset our relationship with Beijing before its tyranny gets totally out of hand.

But what are the ingredients of that proposed "reset"?

Our current relationship with China is one of "mutual distrust," a view attributed to David Shambaught from the Elliott School of International Affairs, who expressed that perspective in his book, *Tangled Titans: The United States and China*. Another view called out by Professor Clemens is articulated by Arvind Subramanian, the former chief economic advisor to the government of India and a current fellow at Brown University, who, in his book, *Eclipse: Living in the Shadow of China's Economic Dominance*, wrote that unless the US puts aside its dysfunctional ways, the PRC will dominate.[913]

There are other writers who express quite a different perspective about the US-China relationship, however. Ye Zicheng at Beijing University addresses China's internal problems that will inevitably impact Beijing's relationship with Washington. Specifically, the 1.4 billion Chinese population faces growing unemployment to dangerous levels of pollution to a future ratio of two workers for every retiree by 2040, an outcome that threatens to consume the country's entire GDP. Mr. Ye indicates in his book, *Inside China's Grand Strategy*, that "democracy could help reduce these problems," a view also called out by Clemens.[914]

Yes, China faces some daunting problems, and there is no shortage of recommendations about how to address them, much less how to guide our relationship with that Communist powerhouse. I'll offer my own outlook about the challenging US-China relationship that corresponds with the five issue areas addressed in the previous section of this volume: economics, ideology, security, geopolitics, and technology.

Below I recommend specific actions the US—and, by association, the Western world governments—must take in order to right the ship to keep Communist China from reaching its aim of realizing a new world order in its image, albeit by keeping a liberal world order.

Resetting Our Economic Relationship with China

The US must disentangle itself from the PRC. At this point, our economy is indisputably intertwined with China's, and much of that outcome is of our own making. That entanglement no longer serves America's best economic interests—that is, to remain tethered to the PRC's 1.4 billion people and that government's authoritarian policies that negatively impact our economic future. After all, the tyrants in Beijing advance a mercantilist set of policies that are incompatible with America's future prosperity.

According to the Merriam-Webster dictionary:

> [Mercantilism is] an economic system…to unify and increase the power and especially the monetary wealth of a nation by a strict governmental regulation of the entire national economy usually through policies designed to secure an accumulation of bullion, a favorable balance of trade, the development of agriculture and manufactures, and the establishment of foreign trading monopolies.[915]

The PRC changed its economic strategy in 2006 away from commodity-based production facilities of foreign multinational corporations to a "China Inc.," a development model focused on helping Chinese firms, or what came to be known as "indigenous innovation," with a focus on helping Chinese firms move to higher-value-added production activities.[916]

Beijing embraced economic mercantilism to advance that strategy, which is "using a wide array of policies to assist Chinese firms while discriminating against foreign establishments attempting to compete in China," according to the magazine *Industry Week*.[917]

The result of adopting an economic mercantilist strategy included the many mandates that countries like the US complain about when trading with China today: "'forced localization' measures became prevalent such as mandatory intellectual property or technology transfer, entrance into joint ventures, or domestic production as a condition of market access."[918]

A 2022 study by the Victims of Communism Memorial Foundation, "Corporate Complicity Scorecard," echoes those complaints and nails the impact of China's mercantilist strategy for some of America's leading corporations. Specifically, some of our largest companies chase Chinese business, and in the process grant the Communist regime support for "Beijing's military modernization, surveillance state, domestic securitization, and attendant human rights violations." In fact, some of those same corporations engage in political lobbying inside the US to promote Beijing's policy interests while undermining the very values and principles that undergird the Western democratic order.[919]

Nathan Picarsic and Emily de La Bruyère, the authors of the seventy-three page report, "Corporate Complicity Scorecard," call out eight well-known American firms—Amazon, Apple, Dell, Facebook, GE, Google, Intel, and Microsoft. The authors considered indicators of each company's Chinese operations and partnerships based on an extensive study of hundreds of sources to produce a final grade based on their support of Beijing's interests. Those grades are: Amazon—D; Apple—D; Dell—F; Facebook—B; Google—B; Intel—F; and Microsoft—F.[920]

This report makes it crystal clear that American corporate ties to the CCP have "grown alongside attention to the normative, economic, and security threat of Beijing's global authoritarianism." The US Congress and the American people must demand accountability from these corporations. Their bottom line must never jeopardize our national security, economic competitiveness, and democratic values.[921]

The US—and, by association, other Western nations—must do the following regarding China's economic mercantilist ways:

1. The US should not pursue a mercantilist approach, which is associated with that pursued by Beijing. That policy hasn't paid off, according to Professor Clemens. The professor argues that President Xi's Belt and Road Initiative backfired. It has earned little real return for Beijing's significant investments—and, in some cases, China suffered significant political backlash in countries like Pakistan and Sri Lanka. Further, BRI accelerated corruption among Chinese political and business elite, something President Xi promised his comrades that he would fix.[922]

2. We must encourage only legitimate economic activity that equally shares the prosperity from free trade. Specially, as outlined in the previous section of this volume, Chinese theft of intellectual property must stop, because it fuels China's economy and helps its military. After all, much of the stolen Western technology ends up advancing the PLA's quest to become the most sophisticated military in the world—all at our expense. We must slow that theft in part by limiting Chinese immigration and escalating our investigations and judicial actions.

Meanwhile, there must also be an effort to decouple our economy from China's. That's a view shared by our best trading partner, Canada, and most of its citizens. In 2022, an Angus Reid poll found that 61 percent of Canadians favor trading less with China, and almost nine in ten (88 percent) believe "it's realistic to do so without negatively affecting" their economy.[923]

That view is especially embraced by Canadian conservatives, who have long been hostile to China. However, both political parties in Canada have a growing distaste for the PRC, with only 16 percent expressing a favorable view.[924]

Decoupling can come in a variety of ways. For example, the Canadian government invests heavily in Chinese firms through its Canada Pension Plan Investment Board, a risky proposition. By comparison, the US government pension fund also channels tens of billions of dollars into funding Chinese companies.[925]

US Senators Marco Rubio (R-FL) and Jeanne Shaheen (D-NH) wrote a letter to Michael Kennedy, chairman of the Federal Retirement Thrift Investment Board, stating the fund is supporting Chinese state-owned companies with "the paychecks of members of the US Armed Services and other federal government employees." They called on Kennedy's board to shift its more than $50 billion away from Chinese firms before those funds become exposed to the "severe and undisclosed" risks of being invested in Communist-controlled companies.[926]

3. We need to remove from the trading shelf items that have a national security nexus. This issue goes deep into our extensive supply chain with China, and we need only remember that items like surgical masks during the COVID-19 pandemic actually had a national security relationship. Also, on the services front, we should think about Huawei's 5G service that is popping up across the globe, and the Pentagon classifies that capability as a national security vulnerability. After all, communication networks with servers under the CCP's control like Huawei are vulnerable to data slaving and manipulation.

4. There must also be an expanded effort to target specific Chinese companies and industries, many of which are identified by the USCC, that pose national security and/or economic threats and then prohibit those firms and their products from participating in our economy.

5. We previously discussed the PRC's rank failure to abide by World Trade Organization rules. Therefore, the US Congress ought to revoke the 2000 legislation granting the PRC normal trade relations. That legislation enabled China to enter the WTO, which fundamentally changed the economic role the regime plays globally, and unquestionably propelled it to the second-largest economy in the world today. Then we ought to petition the WTO to expel China from its membership rolls.

6. Failing to jettison the PRC from the WTO, we must do what the US Trade Representative's 2021 annual report on China's WTO compliance claims. Specifically, it calls for the US to "strengthen existing trade tools" as well as "develop new ones to combat China's state subsidies and financial heft." After all, China and the US have made virtually no progress on easing trade tensions since the Trump administration.[927]

7. We ought to impose tariffs on a long list of Chinese products and services that violate WTO rules. In 2018, the Trump administration put tariffs on $16 billion worth of Chinese imports, and by 2019, it increased that burden to almost half of all goods that America imports from China. That regime hasn't changed its behavior, and there is no reason to expect it to improve.[928]

8. The USCC's 2021 annual report includes a number of recommendations for both Congress and the US government regarding China. Those recommendations are wide-ranging, from a call for a report and research plan "outlining a project for the collection and sequencing of nonhuman genomic data, analogous to the human genome project" to the requirement for "publicly traded US companies with facilities in China [to] report on an annual basis whether there is a CCP committee in their operations" to the call for "comprehensive legislation to ensure Chinese entities sanctioned under one US authority be automatically sanctioned under other authorities unless a waiver is granted."[929]

Resetting Our Ideological Relationship with China

Ideologically, China has a Marxist-Leninist government that oversees the massive Chinese population. The ideology chapter in this volume outlined what that means for the Chinese people and highlighted what it could mean for a future world dominated by the PRC as well.

So, what ought to be done to push back against China's ideological agenda that seeks to change the world order?

1. Cut off Chinese Communist propaganda inside the United States. This can be difficult in an open, free society like the US, where our adversary China can easily buy media space. Therefore, we must be smart about efforts to call out Chinese propaganda and educate the public.

    Citizen groups, media outlets, and the government must identify CCP-financed speech, no matter the platform, and make the public aware through many of those same platforms. Education is key. However, where the CCP is seeding insurrection or civil disobedience that serves the PRC's interests, then law enforcement ought to act to protect the public, and if our laws are insufficient, then we must pass new legislation that protects us from China's malicious conduct.

    My 2021 book, *Give Me Liberty, Not Marxism,* includes a chapter on the media, and in particular the Chinese Communist efforts to purge Hollywood productions of any criticism of the regime. The CCP effectively controls many American movie studios because they seek access to the Chinese market, and to gain that opportunity, they must avoid producing any movies that criticize the Communists in Beijing. This must be countered through education and, as appropriate through our laws, Hollywood ought to be of help to a higher ethical standard.

2. This volume established in chapter 5 that the CCP invests in our academy in order to influence future Americans, such as by

locating PRC-funded Confucius Institutes on college campuses. Those institutes must be exposed as propaganda platforms, and therefore must be denied access to our next generation.

Further, the US government can control some of this Marxist proselytizing by strictly regulating the number of visas issued to Chinese students and academics. Once again, this objective requires close scrutiny by the public, the educational establishment, and the government to ensure that Chinese personnel granted visas are here for reasons that advance American interests and not to steal our intellectual property to enable the PLA, nor to teach Communist ideology/propaganda to our youth.

3. Silence CCP dirty money from its malign influence on the US political and financial systems. We established earlier that Chinese money fills the pockets of some Washington think tanks and lobbyists who influence the US Congress and government to favor the Chinese regime. We need to strengthen laws like the Foreign Agents' Registration Act and embrace legislation such as what Rep. Jim Banks (R-IN) called the Truth in Testimony Resolution (2021) that requires so-called expert witnesses appearing before Congress to divulge any foreign funding that supports their organization.[930]

Far worse than Chinese influence within Washington think tanks is the CCP's dangerous influence called "elite capture," a truly diabolical manipulation of America's rich and powerful. Peter Schweizer, the president of the Governmental Accountability Institute, explains that elite capture, according to the CCP's intelligence apparatus, involves "quasi-private business ventures.... The idea is simple enough: by tempting another country's elite with money, access and [sexual] favors, you move them to see their interests and China's interests as intertwined or even the same."[931]

Mr. Schweizer explores in his book, *Red Handed: How American Elites Are Helping China Win*, "how elites in academia, high-finance, sports and entertainment, and the technology sector became apologists for China's deplorable human rights record, industrial and military espionage, and increasingly aggressive behavior."[932]

Schweizer's book investigates public activities of America's "elite," to call out how they have become purposely blind to help China. He writes:

From the world of Silicon Valley, we explore Mark Zuckerberg of Facebook, Tim Cook of Apple, and Bill Gates of Microsoft. From the world of Wall Street, we looked at Ray Dalio of Bridgewater, the largest hedge-fund investment company in the world, and Larry Fink of BlackRock. From academia we explored the actions of Harvard and Yale universities. We surveyed the relationship histories of the Bush family, the Trudeau family of Canada, the Pelosi family, and of course, the Biden family.[933]

China successfully co-opted these elites at an alarming rate, and no wonder. After all, the business slogan that "the customer is always right," is appropriate here, because power is wielded "by those who succumb to the temptation." Indeed, too many of America's elite were bought and sold out our nation, an idea captured by the twentieth-century novelist Upton Sinclair, who wrote, "It is difficult to get a man to understand something when his salary depends on his not understanding it."[934]

4. The CCP tries to manipulate foreign elections, and that must be addressed. There are federal laws against foreign government interference in our elections, such as 52 USC 30121: Contributions and donations by foreign nationals, which must be rigorously enforced. The American people must also be made aware of the malign influence and misinformation governments like the PRC purposely seed to confuse and disrupt our free-election process. Both the US government and citizen groups must educate

the public about this threat and, as appropriate, use legal means to stop the Communists.[935]

5. We must stop the CCP from ever controlling the global Internet and using the levers of international organizations to deny our rights. President Xi expressed his intent to control the Internet in 2017, and since then, he has grown the PRC's control of cyberspace. This effort must be tackled by the US government as well as other free-speech-loving countries.

Our efforts to deny the PRC control of the Internet begins by keeping the CCP from gaining a position to "set the rules" governing cyberspace, such as leading international organizations that govern cyberspace, nor should the regime and its proxies exercise oversight of the network's infrastructure, such as by allowing the Communist State-controlled Huawei 5G network to dominate any country's communications.

The regime must never be in the position to set rules that impact any of our other precious freedoms, such as the right to bear arms. Unfortunately, Communist China is the largest funder of the UN's Small Arms Treaty, which aims to regulate international trade in conventional weapons and globalize gun control. Dubley Brown, the president of the National Association for Gun Rights, sounded the alarm that should the Biden administration sign the Small Arms Treaty, the CCP could use its authority to undermine Americans' Second Amendment Rights. Specifically, Mr. Brown calls attention to Article V of the treaty, which encourages countries to create a "National Control List," a recordkeeping system to track owners; it could become the first step in a future gun-confiscation scheme.[936]

6. We must sustain and arguably increase a pro-freedom message reaching the Chinese people, such as the ongoing Voice of America Mandarin service that "reaches the Chinese-speaking population in the People's Republic of China.... VOA Mandarin

has provided uncensored and fact-based news about significant developments in China and around the world that empowers its audience to make informed decisions."[937]

7. We must expose the CCP's lack of transparency regarding human-rights practices. In the past, the US State Department called out nations that oppress people for their religion, ethnicity, or other defining characteristics. China has a long history of persecuting—and, in some cases, committing genocide against—its citizens, such as the Falun Gong and the Muslim Uyghurs. This ideologically driven persecution must always be exposed, and the regime must continue to pay a high price. Further, the PRC's efforts to oppress the Chinese diaspora must be vigorously opposed.

Resetting Our Security Relationship with China

The Chinese government has the right to defend itself and to build a military to accomplish that mission. However, it does not have a right to our help in that process. Therefore, the US and other freedom-loving nations must vigorously deny the Beijing regime the means and relationships it seeks to dominate the world using its military.

The Biden administration has done little to call out the PRC for its aggressive and threatening security agenda, except it did prioritize China as the Pentagon's pacing challenge in its 2023 budget. That's a small step given the many significant actions needed to check the PLA, such as those listed below.[938]

1. We must cut off the PRC's access to technologies that contribute to the PLA's growing capabilities. For example, we know the regime is growing its strategic lift—aircraft and ships—to move military personnel and their equipment to distant destinations in order to carry out the Communist regime's hegemonic agenda. The West must stop the flow of any technologies that might contribute to the modernization of the PLA.

2. The PRC seeks to establish overseas bases and access to foreign facilities. The West can actively discourage and incentivize foreign partners to deny the PLA access to sovereign facilities. This may require both financial and geopolitical support for foreign governments to turn away from China's manipulative incentives such as the Belt and Road Initiative program and the potentially disastrous outcomes that program often delivers.

3. The PLA seeks to develop foreign partners for future coalition operations. The US and its allies must vigorously oppose this effort using existing security cooperation programs to incentivize foreign militaries through education, equipment, and joint-exercise opportunities. We must make it clear to those nations that training with the US and its partners is a far superior opportunity as opposed to trusting the unreliable Chinese Communists.

It is reassuring that some allies and foreign partners are stepping up their security cooperation to push back against the aggressive Chinese. In April 2022, Japanese Defense Minister Nobuo Kishi and his Philippine counterpart, Delfin Lorenzana, agreed to increase cooperation in defense equipment and technology transfer over concerns about China's escalating assertive military actions.[939]

In recent years, Japan significantly increased its joint exercises with the US and other partners like Australia, India, France, Britain, and Germany. Tokyo is especially concerned about China's territorial claims across the region—in particular, those within the busiest sea lanes in both the South China Sea and the East China Sea near the Japanese-controlled Senkaku Islands.[940]

Also, as evidence of the seriousness of the PRC threat, Japan's ruling Liberal Democratic Party announced its intention to double the defense budget to two percent of Japan's gross domestic product, raising their budget to about $94 billion in

2023, according to Kyodo News reported April 27, 2022. This increase is "due to Japan's concerns surrounding China and North Korea, and the increase will push the bounds of Japan's pacifist constitution."[941]

4. A modern military like the United States armed forces relies upon a space-borne infrastructure. Earlier in this volume, we established that the PLA is rapidly expanding its use of space to include a satellite navigation system. Further, the regime appears to be developing capabilities that could be used for offensive purposes in earth orbit and beyond. The US and its foreign partners must respond to this growing threat by maintaining a modern, space-borne capability aimed at marginalizing China's space capabilities while advancing our own—i.e., denying Beijing control of outer space.

5. The USCC outlines numerous recommendations for our security, to include conducting "an interagency review of any Chinese universities that maintain research or training arrangements with China's nuclear weapons research institutes." The purpose of that effort, as indicated by the USCC, is to deny the Chinese access to US technologies and research that might aid the Communists' effort to further develop their nuclear arsenal. Similarly, the US must deny the Chinese access to conventional technologies as well.

6. US security policymakers should avoid an armed collision with China. This is a recommendation proposed by Professor Clemens that warrants emphasis. As he wrote, "The same analyst who articulated Washington's policy to contain Soviet expansion, George F. Kennan, later warned US policymakers not to assume that Stalin's successors would necessarily follow his example." Yes, Mr. Kennan wrote in the mid-1950s, "If Washington treats the Kremlin's new leaders as if they are inexorably committed to aggressive policies, they will have no choice but to act according to our predictions." The same warning applies to US-China relations today.

Professor Clemens develops Kennan's warning. "If Washington or Beijing acts as though both sides must collide, confrontation or even war will be more likely." He then calls for "sober personalities" to "avoid the worst and promote mutual gain policies." Further, he warns about a classic security dilemma:

The United States sees China modernizing its armed forces and decides it must beef up US assets across the Pacific Ocean. In response, China believes it must do still more to counter the US buildup. In other words, Clemens argues, this resembles the old US-Soviet arms race—"dangerous, expensive, and (some would say) pointless."[942]

7. Finally, the US military must focus on winning and fighting the Chinese, not on being "woke," slang for being politically left-leaning. Unfortunately, the Biden administration is pushing a radical, woke agenda across the armed forces that undermines our fighting ability. For example, the Biden administration pushes a radical social agenda within our ranks, such as calling for more women in direct-ground combat positions—albeit contrary to the scientific evidence—and insists that the military totally embrace transgender personnel without justification, refuse to grant religious exemptions to members who oppose COVID mandates, host a controversial "stand down" in 2020 to address so-called extremism in its ranks, and much more.[943]

An early 2022 example of Biden's woke social agenda for military personnel was especially disturbing. In early February, the Pentagon hosted an event titled, "Responding to China: The Case for Global Justice and Democratic Socialism." That presentation took place at the National Defense University and featured speaker Thomas Piketty, a French economist who, according to the announcement, "will argue that the right answer" to responding to China's rise "lies in ending Western arrogance and promoting a new emancipatory and egalitarian horizon on a global scale, a new form of democratic and participatory, ecological and post-colonial socialism." The invitation continued, "If they stick to their usual lecturing posture and a dated hyper-capitalist model, western countries may find it extremely difficult to meet the Chinese challenge," Mr. Piketty wrote, the author of the book *Time for Socialism.*[944]

The Pentagon event drew criticism from a top Republican on the House Armed Services Committee. US Rep. Jim Banks (R-IN) said the Biden administration is politicizing our armed forces to a fault. "Thanks to Joe Biden, our military is more political than ever and the world is less stable than it's been in decades," Banks told the *Washington Free Beacon*. He continued, "The Pentagon has a lot on its plate. They need to focus on their mission: keeping all Americans safe from foreign threats."[945]

Representative Banks said events like the French socialist's presentation are becoming too common at the Pentagon. He called attention to a 2021 report requested by members of Congress, "A Report on the Fighting Culture of the United States Navy Surface Fleet" that determined the military "is distracted by political and cultural trends, impacting its warfighting readiness."[946]

The seriousness of a politicized military was highlighted in that report. An unidentified US Navy lieutenant said, according to the report, "Sometimes I think we care more about whether we have enough diversity officers than if we'll survive a fight with the Chinese navy." She continued, "It's criminal. They think my only value is as a black woman. But you cut our ship open with a missile, and we'll all bleed the same color."[947]

The report also included a statement by a recently retired senior enlisted officer who said, "I guarantee you every unit in the Navy is up to speed on their diversity training. I'm sorry that I can't say the same of their ship-handling training."[948]

"We face real threats across the world, yet the Biden administration is more focused on promoting its leftist social agenda in the military instead of countering China, Russia and Iron or creating an effective counterterrorism plan," said US Sen. Roger Wicker (R-MS). He continued, "Our military is not an extremist organization, and our service members, by and large all good people, are dedicated, faithful patriots."

How bad is the US military's readiness today? As China grows its military capability, America's military readiness is declining. An April 2021 report by the US Government Accountability Office (GAO), "Military Readiness: Department of Defense Domain Readiness Varied from Fiscal Year 2017 through Fiscal Year 2019," indicates that only in one area, ground forces, did the US armed forces increase their total readiness between 2017–2019. Further, in 2020, the GAO found that, on average, US Navy ships were undermanned by 15 percent, and other important vessels such as attack submarines lost ten thousand operational days between 2008–2018.[949]

"For the US to be poised for success in facing threats from China, DoD will need to take timely actions and congressional oversight will be important as these efforts proceed," the GAO report concludes.[950]

Resetting Our Geopolitical Relationship with China

Beijing is a geopolitical pariah, willing to do whatever necessary to remake the world order in its image. Below are four mega-areas that warrant US geopolitical action.

1. The US policy regarding China must be balanced with our interests across the globe. We are in danger of an unbalanced approach to the upstart Asian Communist tyrant.

   Richard Fontaine, the chief executive officer of the Center for a New American Security, argues in *Foreign Affairs* that, "to be fair, even the most ardent China hawks are not calling on the United States to abandon other regions in favor of the Indo-Pacific." The US should not disengage from Europe, Africa, and the Middle East to create an "unbalanced engagement" in the world because that would have "damaging consequences," according to Fontaine.[951]

Mr. Fontaine argues for keeping a geopolitical balance in our approach to China. He admits there is justification for devoting new resources to meet the Chinese challenge. However, the consequence is we pay less attention to other regions, which could be a mistake. After all, any shift in resources to the Indo-Pacific must be warranted, and with "as much specificity as possible—on the basis of a particular set of policy tools or military deployments—rather than on the abstract basis that doing more is better," writes Fontaine.[952]

Both the Trump and Biden administrations ignored the balance principle. For example, in 2020, the Trump administration pushed to move US troops from Africa to the Indo-Pacific. That move left our ally, France, in a lurch regarding ongoing operations in the Sahel, Northern Africa, because the troops we relocated had provided valuable intelligence and reconnaissance support to the French. Also, that ongoing counter-terror operation serves our security interests and must be maintained.[953]

In 2021, the Biden administration recklessly withdrew 2,500 US troops from Afghanistan to allegedly relieve pressure on the military seeking to build up forces in the Indo-Pacific arena. However, that was a serious error, not just because of the debacle that ensued with our poorly planned, troubled exit and the immediate takeover by our enemy the Taliban, but also it resulted a catastrophic famine that ensued across Afghanistan. Meanwhile, our departure helped China geopolitically in the region by providing the regime more leverage, albeit while increasing the terrorist threat to America's interests.[954]

Mr. Fontaine also advances the view that we must maintain a balanced US-Chinese relationship by keeping a strong relationship with our European partners. "China needs to understand that the United States and its allies [in Europe] are united in countering its [China's] economic and military pressure, and both Europe and the Middle East require US leadership to provide effective long-term stability," wrote Fontaine.[955]

Fortunately, America's European partners are stepping up to the plate when it comes to countering the PRC. Specifically, the European Union adopted a regional strategy that is based on a "free and open Indo-Pacific"; in addition, France launched freedom-of-navigation exercises in the South China Sea, and the United Kingdom's "tilt" to Asia is helpful as well.[956]

2. The USCC recommends a number of common-sense geopolitical actions to push back on the hegemonic Chinese. The commission calls for an increase in our competitiveness to build infrastructure in regions like Latin and South America. We must also increase educational exchanges, as well as monitor PRC activities across those regions to help guide our national response.

3. We know the CCP seeks to undermine the current international system and replace it with a Beijing-approved Marxist world order. Beijing's participation in international organizations ought to be suspended if the regime fails to comply with the governing rules and principles.

The evidence of the PRC's failure to be a good international partner in many organizations is detailed in chapter 7. China's participation must be allowed only as long as it abides by the rules. For example, we established earlier that Beijing abuses its membership in the WTO. And, at the United Nations, the regime uses its positions in leadership to advance a political advantage by marginalizing the rights of the sovereign nation of Taiwan. Further, it consistently violates international law, such as at the UN Convention on the Law of Sea, vis-à-vis building military bases in the South China Sea, which is a recognized international waterway.

4. Beijing uses harsh practices with sovereign nations to leverage resources and political power. Chapter 7 identified eight practices the PRC uses to advance its interests and most are truly tyrannical. The West must expose those practices and counter them with alternatives to wean away victim nations from Beijing's malign influence.

Beijing deals most harshly with Taiwan, a sovereign state President Xi frequently reminds the world he intends to return to Communist rule. Therefore, the Biden administration must clearly state US interests in Taiwan. Should the administration communicate it is in the US interest to support a sovereign Taiwan and oppose the PRC's announced aim of returning the island nation to Communist control, then a number of actions are needed.

The best deterrence against Chinese aggression is to recognize, arm, and stand with Taiwan before the Communist giant acts. That will require Washington to work with Asian allies like Japan and Australia to offer a multilateral defense treaty to Taipei, and to recognize Taiwan as a sovereign state. Simultaneously, those same countries should begin arming the island nation with urgently needed weapons, such as long-range missiles that can hold Beijing hostage and even take the next logical step as an ally, base forces on the island.

Resetting Our Technological Relationship with China

The technology chapter outlines the CCP's intent to become the world leader by military-civil fusion, collaborating with foreign partners or by stealing what it can't acquire otherwise.

The US must proactively address all three of these efforts, because should China become the world leader in technology, it will likely turn that capability to its advantage to gain world dominance.

1. The US and the balance of the Western world must use its laws and investigative resources to stop the CCP and its agents from stealing western technology. This is a significant, dangerous problem and one our FBI, CIA, and other agencies confirm. Other than identify spies and put them away, we ought to limit China's access to our educational institutions and research facilities. Only when we aggressively go after these Chinese agents will we stem the flow of technology to the PLA.

    We must also use our cyber capabilities to eliminate cyber espionage, a boon for China's PLA cyber-warrior army. The US has an offensive cyber capability and ought to use it when the evidence supports doing so, especially against nation-states like China that consistently stage attacks on our infrastructure and steal our secrets.

2. We must undermine the effectiveness of China's military-civil fusion strategy by eliminating any US firm's connection with a Chinese company that participates in the fusion program. Specifically, many American firms working with Chinese companies may not be aware of China's MCF arrangement. This must stop. The US government can help identify the culprits, and then American firms must be required to sever that relationship.

3. The PRC casts a wide net across the world to grow its international technology network. As pointed out in chapter 8, more than 150 countries are part of the PRC's science and technology network, which is nothing short of a technology fishing expedition.

    Many of these links are veiled behind legitimate civilian efforts. However, again, as explained in the technology chapter, China consistently leverages civil enterprises to advance its military efforts. The US government must carefully vet every collaborative relationship a Chinese firm has with an American enterprise. Further, the US must work with its foreign partners to compel them to do the same, and international organizations must address technology transfer to help prevent spillage of civil technologies into China's security establishment.

4. Western intelligence agencies must closely collaborate to recruit Chinese students, visitors, and others from the Communist regime to turn on Beijing. This is the lifeblood, sometimes the unpleasant—albeit necessary—work of the cloak-and-dagger community. Turning people against their country to help the West regarding technology and security issues is absolutely essential to keep the Communist regime from its hegemonic goal.

CONCLUSION

Decades ago, the US set out to curry favor with the Chinese and facilitate their entrance into the international community. We had great aspirations for a modern PRC. However, in spite of our best efforts, the Communist regime took advantage of their new status and soiled virtually every well-meaning opportunity. Today, the PRC is a rogue state, albeit with an oversized economy and geopolitical and military might, and it intends to replace the current international order with a Chinese version. This chapter addresses along five lines of effort—through economy, ideology, security, geopolitics and technology—numerous actions the US and its Western allies must undertake in order to prevent the Beijing regime from succeeding.

10

China's Prophetic End-Times Role: How Should We Then Live?

And the sixth angel poured out his vial upon the great river Euphrates; and the water thereof was dried up, that the way of the kings of the east might be prepared.

—Revelation 16:12

This chapter identifies the PRC's possible prophetic end-times role. Is China a key biblical end-times player? Or will Beijing's economic and military might fade, to be replaced by another, more sinister tyrant who opens the final earthly abyss? Is President Xi's "rejuvenation" goal reflective of the Qing Dynasty's Manchu ethos that stirs to "trembling" not just the Chinese people, but a broad swath of the world—a true Antichrist-like entity? Alternatively, is the CCP regime a precursor to the biblical end times that sets the stage for the coming Antichrist? Perhaps President Xi is the Antichrist himself—or might the Antichrist be a yet unidentified Communist Chinese leader, or a European surrogate?

No one this side of Heaven can answer whether China will come to dominate the world, much less play a decisive role in the end times. Certainly, all the elements of national power and ambition are in place in Beijing to reach that lofty goal; Katy, bar the door! should that happen.

However, if it does happen, then our world could become a nightmarish hell governed by Chinese totalitarians who come to dictate every aspect of our lives, deny our freedoms of speech and worship, and freely kill and incarcerate the disobedient. That's a scary proposition that ought to motivate especially those in the West, who are so accustomed to freedom.

Certainly, the West ought to resist that outcome by embracing the recommendations in the previous chapter. Those recommendations across the five issue areas will go far toward defanging the tyrants in Beijing and perhaps could prevent the worst outcome—a new world order under the Communist rogue regime. However, we may fail, and China may already be written in the Bible as a key player in biblical end times. Although that role may seem veiled by biblical inference and metaphor, perhaps that position is more obvious via a closer consideration.

The following section reflects the interpretation of God's prophetic Word based on a number of wise and somewhat differing views by theologians. Should we interpret the end-times Scriptures literally or understand them in a spiritual context? There is disagreement. I view the prophetic Word regarding the "kings of the east" account believing some of it as quite literal while understanding other aspects spiritually. However, I do believe that China is found in the Scripture, albeit obscure, and there is a real possibility that, yes, China, the Asian giant, is a key end-times player. Further, I believe the giant army from the East that joins the final battle at Armageddon is a spiritual force, not one with human ranks, even though there are a couple of very interesting alternatives explored in this chapter.

The balance of the chapter addresses the rapidly growing Christian Body in Communist China—all in spite of Satan's vigorous resistance. Then we conclude the chapter with the role the Body of Christ outside of China ought to play, particularly regarding their duty to pray, encourage, and take specific actions to help defang the tyrants in Beijing to enable fellow believers who find themselves under the Communist regime's boot and to hopefully prevent those same tyrants from creating a new world order in their evil image.

CHINA'S POSSIBLE END-TIMES ROLE

Numerous theologians have weighed in on whether China is mentioned in the Bible and whether it has a role in end-times prophecy. For example, the late John Walvoord (1910–2002), the long-time president of Dallas Theological Seminary, was considered in his time one of the foremost interpreters of biblical prophecy. His book, *The Nations in Prophecy*, is a compilation of his lectures on the topic. In it, he states that "with one-fourth of the Bible prophetically future when it was written, the interpretation of prophecy is one of the most challenging areas of biblical study." The theologian explains that "because prophecy is scattered from the early chapters of Genesis to the last chapter of Revelation and deals with so many different situations and subjects, interpreters of prophecy have too often abandoned any detailed interpretation and reached only general conclusions."[957]

One of the chapters in Walvoord's prophecy book is entitled "The Kings of the East: The Oriental Confederacy." Somewhat uniquely, Dr. Walvoord's interpretation of Scripture is literal, which for some theologians is a stretch because they may tend to spiritualize hard-to-understand prophecies. However, perhaps Dr. Walvoord is correct, as you will see, especially with regard to what other theologians refuse to see—that China is part of end-times biblical prophecy.[958]

Dr. Walvoord acknowledges that the twentieth-century awakening of the Orient, the nations of Asia east of the Euphrates River—which means every nation to include Iran stretching all the way to Japan—are "now beginning to stir and to become a major factor in the international situation." Further, he points out that the "geographic immensity and the millions of humanity involved make it inevitable that any future development embracing the entire world must take the Orient [the countries of Asia] into consideration."[959]

Even though Dr. Walvoord wrote those words decades ago, recent developments across the Orient, especially in China, as indicated in previous chapters, are relevant today. He argued that people interested in

Bible prophecy must pay close attention to Asia, because "even if there were no Scripture bearing on the place of the Orient in end-time events, it would be only natural to expect them to be part of the world-wide scene."[960]

He points out what historians know, that the "great nations of eastern Asia have had no important part in the history of Israel...there is no record of any past war between Israel and the nations beyond the Euphrates." However, that doesn't mean we are to discount an Asian role in prophecy, because "the future...in view of modern rapid communications and transportation and the world-wide character of any military effort in the missile age, will be a different story," wrote Walvoord.

After all, Dr. Walvoord points out, we've been surprised by powers in the Orient during the twentieth century. He mentioned the Japanese attack on Pearl Harbor on December 7, 1941, then the emergence of Red China in 1949, as well as the war with Vietnam (1955–1975).

In World War II, the Japanese were just as hegemonic as the present-day Chinese leadership, if not more so. Specifically, the famed Japanese Admiral Isoroku Yamamoto allegedly boasted that he was "looking forward to dictating peace to the United States in the White House," even though, in reality, the admiral "never made this boast," according to some historians. Rather, "It was a product of Japanese propaganda, but Americans took it as the gospel truth." The effect was to instill fear across America—and it worked.[961]

Communist China displays the same hubris today in its propaganda and, as indicated earlier in this volume, officials beginning with President Xi threat, boast, and communicate true belligerence toward the West and especially the United States. Therefore, as Walvoord wrote:

In this confused situation that has so many omens of future disaster for western civilization, a student of the scriptures may well ask whether prophecy has any sure word concerning the role of Asia [especially China] among the nations of the world in the end time.[962]

Dr. Walvoord sees plenty of scriptural evidence that China is found in God's Word and will play a key role in the prophetic end times. We begin with the identity of China.

Sinim = China

The Hebrew word *Sinim* is translated *Qin*, which means "China" in biblical prophecy. The Scriptures seldom mention people or geography beyond the boundaries of the ancient Roman Empire. However, there is an exception found in Isaiah 49:12 that is relating to the ultimate regathering of the nation Israel: "Behold, these shall come from far: and, lo, these from the north and from the west; and these from the land of Sinim."

Dr. Walvoord admits, "Although it is not possible to be dogmatic as to the precise reference of 'the land of Sinim,' conservative scholarship has generally agreed that the most probable explanation is that this refers to the ancient land of China."[963]

The professor speculates that it is possible there were ancient commercial relationships with China reaching as far away as the Mediterranean Sea, and "there is also evidence that some of the history of the Old Testament was known in China." Further, he indicates that "prophecy assumes a logical and natural interpretation, namely, that in the end time some of the Jews who will be regathered will come...from the east."[964]

Anecdotally, the World Jewish Congress states "China is home to about 2,500 Jews. A small ethno-religious minority, the Chinese Jewish community has deep historical roots that go back centuries. There is currently no Jewish community representative body in China, although there are small active communities of expatriates in Beijing, Hong Kong and Shanghai."[965]

Other references and scholars agree about the perspective. There are biblical clues that help discern whether modern China is part of the "Table of Nations" found in Genesis 10 and descendants from Ham, one of Noah's three sons who survived the Great Flood. After all, Ham's son Canaan (Genesis 10:6) had a son, Heth, who allegedly started the "Sinites" (Genesis 10:17), who might be the progenitors of the people known as Chinese.[966]

Theologian Henry Morris acknowledges the people in the Far East named "Sinim" (Isaiah 49:12) and calls out secular histories that reference people in the Far East called "Sinae," which to him suggests the possibility that some of Sin's descendants migrated eastward. Further, he argues, "It is significant that the Chinese people have always been identified by the prefix 'Sino'. The name 'Sin'" is frequently encountered in Chinese names in the form 'Siang' or its equivalent."[967]

"The evidence is tenuous but, of all the names in the Table of Nations, it does seem that two sons of Canaan, Heth (Hitties = Khittae = Cathay) and Sin (Sinites = Sinim = China) are the most likely to have become ancestors of the Oriental [Asian] peoples," according to Morris. "Since it seems reasonable that divine inspiration would include in such a table information concerning the ancestry of all the major streams of human development, it is reasonable to conclude that the Mongoloid peoples (and therefore also the American Indians) have come mostly from the Hamitic line."[968]

Further, the word "Sinim" from Isaiah 49:12 means, according to *Strong's Concordance*, "a distant oriental region." *Young's Concordance* indicates that "Sinim is a people in the far east; the Chinese?"[969]

Samuel Wang and Ethel Nelson write in their book, *God and the Ancient Chinese*, that the meaning for "Sinim" isn't quite clear from the concordances, however. So, they turned to an English dictionary and found that the word "Sino" indicates Chinese and Sinophile. Then they point out: "French, from late Latin 'Sinae;' the Chinese, from Greek 'Sinai;' from Arabic 'Sin;' China, from Chinese (Mandarin) 'Ch'in' [Qin], [the] dynastic name of the country."[970]

So, conclude Wang and Nelson: "The Hebrew word 'Sinim' means China, as can be seen…in the word 'Sinology'—a study of things Chinese." Further, they indicate "all Chinese roots meet in the Qin Dynasty (221 to 206 BC). However, the Hebrew alphabet does not have the equiv-

alent of 'ch' in English and 'q' in Chinese. Thus 'Qin' has been phoneti-
cally translated as 'Sinim.'"[971]

Further, "Qin" has a special place in China's history. The ancient
Chinese state of Qin emerged as "one of the 14 major states under the
Zhou Dynasty," which was approximately five hundred years after Isa-
iah Qin Shi Huangdi established the Qin Dynasty, and from that time
forward, Qin came to represent what is known today as the Middle
Kingdom, or China.[972]

Alternatively, "Sinim" from Isaiah 49:12 has also been interpreted
to mean "Land of the South" in the Aramaic Translation and the Vul-
gate Latin versions of the Bible as "Australia." Allegedly, there are reports
of Egyptian and Phoenician remains found in Australia, according to
Yair Davidiy, a spokesman for Brit-Am/Hebrew Awareness. In fact, Mr.
Davidiy writes that the History Research Projects' book by Craig White,
In Search of…the Origin of Nations (2003), discusses the possibility that
Australian aborigines came from Egypt and then further moved to South
America, India, and Australia.[973]

Another view is expressed by Dr. Dale A. Brueggemann with
Redemption Seminary, who calls out the name "Kittim" (כִּתִּים, kittim;
כִּתִּיִּם, kittiyyim), the descendants of Javan (Genesis 10:4; 1 Chronicles
1:7), which are the descendants of Noah's son Japheth. Evidently, the
Syriac Peshitta, the standard version of the Bible translated from biblical Hebrew for churches in the Syriac tradition, identifies "Kittim" as
"Cathay"—i.e., China, or it may be used as an idiom for distant lands.[974]

There is further suggestion that people from the Far East are in the
Scripture.

The Magi

The Christmas story speaks of visiting magi from the Far East who
brought gifts to the Christ child. Matthew 2:1–2 calls these visitors "wise
men from the east," asking "where is he that is born king of the Jews?"
Dr. Walvoord indicates that early church fathers believed these men

came from "the area east of the Euphrates and probably from ancient Persia [Iran]." Evidently the messianic hope spurred the ancient men from a distant land to know to follow the star that brought them to Bethlehem to inquire about the birth of the king of the Jews."[975]

"The fact that they wanted to worship him and recognized him as the king of the Jews reveals that the basic facts concerning the Old Testament were more widely known than is commonly realized," according to Walvoord. He goes on to assert that, regarding Isaiah's reference to the "land of Sinim," the story of the wise men from the East supports the "conclusion that the Bible includes the orient [countries of Asia] in its world-wide view."[976]

End-Times Invaders from the Far East

Daniel 11:35 is a prophecy about "the time of the end," when a king in the Mediterranean Sea region fights with the kings of the south and north, as well as a military force from the east. Walvoord believes this "king" is the head of the revived Roman Empire and the world dictator. Further, the period mentioned is just prior "to the second coming of Christ in the latter part of the great tribulation."[977]

Next, Walvoord calls out the prophecy in Daniel 11:44, "But tidings out of the east and out of the north shall trouble him: therefore, he shall go forth with great fury to destroy, and utterly to make away many." These tidings concern a military invasion from the Orient (likely China), evidently a late arrival to the growing global conflict that already engulfs the north and the south with the world dictator. So, the fight continues because, as the world experiences the Second Coming of Christ, a great war is underway "in which the armies are deployed over much of the holy land with the valley of Armageddon as its focal point."[978]

Dr. Walvoord states that the Daniel 11 prophecy is evidence that "the orient will have a place in the great world conflict of the end time."[979]

Gigantic Army from the Orient

Passages from Revelation 9 and 16 indicate that one of the large armies deployed in the final world conflict will come from the Orient. Consider Revelation 9:14–16, which states the Apostle John heard a voice from four horns of the golden altar:

> Saying to the sixth angel which had the trumpet, Loose the four angels which are bound in the great river Euphrates. And the four angels were loosed, which were prepared for an hour, and a day, and a month, and a year, for to slay the third part of men. And the number of the army of the horsemen were two hundred thousand-thousand [200,000,000]: and I heard the number of them.

This is a sobering, perhaps hard-to-believe number. However, geographically, the giant army would come from the eastern boundary of the ancient Roman Empire. Anecdotally, the Euphrates River flows through present-day Syria and through Iraq, emptying into the Persian Gulf. Therefore, the lands to the east of the river begin with Iran and ultimately include present-day China before reaching the coast of the Pacific Ocean.

The staggering size of a two hundred-million-man army mounted on horses is hard to fathom. After all, the number of men by comparison under arms in World War II on both sides was never more than fifty million. Therefore, the tendency for the prophecy interpreter is to spiritualize the number or to infer it really means an army of demonic beings, not humans. Then again, given the PLA's aggressive robot and super-soldier efforts, an army of robots and cyborgs is another possibility that could explain the giant force. Keep in mind that a robot is an advanced machine, while a cyborg is a combination of machine and living organism, not necessarily a human being.

I'm inclined to believe the giant army is filled with demonic beings, a view expressed by Arnold Fruchtenbaum, who writes in *Footsteps of the Messiah* that the two hundred million-man army is filled with demons, not men.[980] At the end of this section, I'll address the robot/cyborg possibility, but for now, there is a view shared by Dr. Walvoord, who believes the immense army might be filled with human beings. He writes:

> With the twentieth century and its attendant population explosion, however, the number of an army of two hundred million men becomes increasingly a possibility and with modern transportation and means of supply, for the first time in history such an army is plausible.[981]

Dr. Walvoord soberly called attention to a statement by the former chief of staff of the People's Liberation Army, General Lo Juiching, which is recorded in a 1965 *Time* magazine article. That article, "Red China: Firecracker No. 2," quotes General Lo as describing then US President Lyndon Johnson as "more insidious and deadly than Hitler." His anger was over America's "imperialist threat" in Vietnam. "Whoever wants to satisfy his greed at the expense of others, is lifting a rock that will inevitably fall on his own toes," said General Lo in a threatening manner.[982]

About the time of General Lo's bluster, the Communist Chinese government released a statement that "its 200 million-man (and woman) militia had gone into serious training," according to *Time*. Further, according to *Time*, "the mainland press reported shrilly that units on the Yunnan border were engaged in intensive bayonet and machine-gun drill; men and women in blue boiler suits marched briskly through Peking [now Beijing] streets with rifles slung."[983]

Clearly, as I thought initially, this statement was hyperbole, a claim not meant to be taken literally. However, Dr. Walvoord argues that, given the numbers associated with China's militia, there is "the possibility that the number [200,000,000] should be taken literally." Then he mentions the deadly fate of the army, which, according to Revelation 9:18, lost a "third part of men killed."[984]

I wasn't satisfied with Dr. Walvoord's explanation regarding the two hundred million number, however. So, I further researched and came across a 1960 *Foreign Affairs* article, "Everyone a Soldier: The Communist Chinese Militia." Evidently, General Lo's bluster had some credibility, as did the propaganda flowing from the CCP.[985]

Briefly, years ago, the Communist Chinese slogan, "Everyone a Soldier," was a call to militarize the general population by enrolling "immense numbers in the militia," in what was described as creating a "human sea" or "steel wall," according to Ralph L. Powell in the *Foreign Affairs* article.[986]

The CCP, in its civil war with the Kuomintang (1927–1949), needed replacements for the Red Army, wrote Powell. So, in 1945, the Party created a force of over 2,200,000 (2.2 million) militiamen that grew to 5,500,000 (5.5 million) strong. Once the CCP won its war with the Kuomintang and established the PRC (1949), it passed a law that required the military to continue "to preserve order and protect production," which mandated the continuation of the militia.[987]

By 1958, the beginning of Mao's Great Leap Forward in economic development, the PRC launched a drive to vastly increase the militia, under the slogan "Everyone a Soldier." The objective of the larger militia was "to consolidate still further the totalitarian controls of the communist party over every aspect of Chinese life; to make China a great industrial and military power at a superhuman rate of speed; and to hasten the transition from 'socialism' to a Chinese version of 'communism.'"[988]

Soon Mao organized the rural populace into more than 26,400 communes, which essentially became political, economic, social, and military units under the leadership of the CCP. About that time, the PRC bombarded Quemoy Island, a Taiwanese possession 1.5 miles from the Chinese mainland, which led to the first of many Taiwan Straits crises and aroused Chinese nationalism. That triggered a further growth in the Chinese militia, to 120,000,000 (120 million) young men and women who had some basic military training and "based on statistics from part of the provinces, one author has estimated that by the end of 1958 there already were more than 200,000,000 [200 million] on the militia rolls."[989]

Responsibility for the surge in the size of the militia was attributed to the campaign to make "Everyone a Soldier," which rested with Mao Zedong. Might the current president-for-life Xi Jinping launch an "Everyone a Soldier" campaign in the future? After all, he is often revered—much like Mao—with all the requisite power and vision. Further, during the Cultural Revolution, the CCP mandated every citizen carry and study the *Quotations from Chairman Mao Tsetung* [Zedong] (aka the *Little Red Book*); today the Party requires citizens beginning with children in school to study the textbook entitled *Xi Jinping Thought on Socialism with Chinese Characteristics for a New Era*, more commonly abbreviated as *Xi Jinping Thought*, a collection of policies and ideas taken from Mr. Xi's writings and speeches.[990]

Is it possible that President Xi, like Mao, has an "Everyone a Soldier" vision for the twenty-first century?

Yes, a two hundred-million-man army (militia) is possible. That doesn't necessarily mean the future army from the East mentioned in Revelation 9 comes from China. However, the fact that there is a historic precedent for the figure two hundred million at least should cause some reconsideration among skeptical prophecy students.

Finally, I indicated earlier there is yet another possible explanation for the massive army, a force filled by either robots and or cyborgs. My 2016 book, *Future War, Super Soldiers, Terminators, Cyberspace & the National Security Strategy for 21st Century Combat*, includes a chapter, "Transhumanism and Super-Soldiers," that elaborates on such developments. I explain that every modern military—especially the PLA—is working on soldier enhancements (cyborgs), as well as building a corps of robots to join future battles.[991]

The possibility of a cyborg or robotic army can't be completely ruled out, given the technological advances across the world, and their numbers could easily rise to the level mentioned above.

Keep in mind that John Ratcliffe, President Trump's director of national intelligence, soberly wrote in the *Wall Street Journal* that "US intelligence shows that China has even conducted human testing on members of the People's Liberation Army in hope of developing soldiers with biologically enhanced capabilities [cyborgs]."[992]

Future cyborgs, "biologically enhanced" soldiers, will demonstrate truly superior capabilities. Some will have brain implants that permit telepathic communication with other soldiers; eye implants that allow sharp vision using both infrared and ultraviolent sight; skin sensors that increase strength and endurance; and exoskeletons that increase soldier core and leg strength. Also, these "super-soldiers" may in fact be controlled externally by their "commanders," and not guided by their own brains, much less influenced by their own moral system, but by an artificial intelligent agent—aka "commander"—that manipulates armies of "soldiers" from the cloud. Yes, it may sound unrealistic, but it is a true future possibility.

The PLA and other military forces including the US armed forces are rapidly adding robotic platforms to their arsenals. For example, the PLA is testing a tracked war robot armed with machine guns, night vision, missile loaders, and camera sensors ready to attack while its human masters are out of sight and danger. Evidently, Chinese humans remain in the decision loop for such robots, but it's only a matter of time before such killing machines are able to act autonomously, especially given the PRC's exploitation of all things AI.

Is it possible to man a giant army of robotic and cyborg "soldiers" that follow commands from a remote, safe command center? Unfortunately, the answer, given modern technology, is a firm "yes."

So, how do we interpret the army of two hundred million mentioned in Revelation 9? Is that future army filled with humans, robots, and cyborgs or all demons? Or is that end-times army a combination of all four?

"KINGS OF THE EAST"—ARE THEY FROM CHINA?

The sixth vial is opened (Revelation 16:12–16) and poured "upon the great river Euphrates; and the water thereof was dried up, that the way of the kings of the east might be prepared." The drying is evidently done to facilitate the movement of a worldwide gathering of the "kings of the earth and the whole world," as Walvoord wrote, "in order that they might participate in 'the battle of that great day of God almighty.'" Of course, the Valley of Jezreel, known as the Plain of Megiddo in present-day northern Israel, is known as Armageddon, the location where the end-times battle will be waged when Christ returns to destroy His enemies.[993]

One of the nonliteral interpretations for the phrase "the kings of the east" is "identified with the Dacians, who conquered Rome, and the Euphrates is then taken to represent the Danube. Others relate the kings of the East to the Parthians, who contended against Rome at the Euphrates, according to Walvoord. Yet others "think it refers to the ten kings of Revelation 17:12; others have related it to the apostles or to the four angels of Revelation 9:14,15…or to Gog and Magog, or Turkey."[994]

There is also the view that, if China is involved, then this immense (two hundred-million-man) army identified as the kings of the East allies with the Russian-led (Gog and Magog from Ezekiel 38–39) alliance.[995] Does Russia join with the Chinese to make up the kings of the East? Jack Wellman, a Christian author and pastor in Udall, Kansas, argues in his blog that "Russia is typically believed to be Gog and Magog to the north but still more east than north. Many Bible scholars believe that Gog and Magog in Ezekiel 38 and 39 refer to Russia although we cannot know with 100% certainty."[996]

That possibility isn't a new concept for me. My 2018 book, *Alliance of Evil*, establishes the close geopolitical relationship between China and Russia, which since that time has only grown closer. For example, Russia and China have a long history of working together, and in early 2022, China's Ministry of Foreign Affairs referred to Russia's "legitimate security concerns" in places like Ukraine and then called for the US to end the "Cold War mentality." Yes, said Evan Feignebaum with the Washington-based Carnegie Endowment for International Peace, "The Chinese have moved progressively closer to Russian positions."[997]

It's noteworthy that Russian President Vladimir Putin welcomed President Xi's invitation to attend the 2022 Beijing Olympics after the US announced a diplomatic boycott of the games over Beijing's human-rights record. In accepting the invitation, Mr. Putin praised the "truly unprecedented character" of China-Russia relations, which he described as a "dignified relationship that helps each of us develop."[998]

A Chinese-Russian alliance appears to be emerging and could well satisfy the prophecies in Ezekiel and Revelation. Whether those nations do align, no matter, because, as Dr. Walvoord said, the simplest interpretation of the phrase "kings of the east" is to take the verse literally. The river becomes the eastern boundary of the ancient Roman Empire, and the "kings of the east" come from the East or "of the sunrising," in the distant Orient (China).[999]

Euphrates River Dries Up to Permit Passage

The Euphrates River plays an important role in the passage of the kings of the East and their armies. Scripture (Revelation 16:12) states that "the water thereof was dried up, that the way of the kings of the east might be prepared" much like God dried up the Red Sea to allow Moses and the Israelites to escape Pharaoh's wrath. Exodus 14:21 states:

> Then Moses stretched out his hand over the sea, and all that night the Lord drove the sea back with a strong east wind and turned it into dry land.

Scripture mentions the Euphrates River nineteen times in the Old Testament and twice in the New Testament. It's an important river referenced in Genesis 2:10–14, one of the four rivers that drew its water from the Garden of Eden. The kings of the East will have to cross this barrier to invade the Promised Land; they need a miracle.[1000]

It is noteworthy that the Euphrates River is associated with a number of events in the Bible. In Daniel 5, we learn the armies of Darius the Mede took Babylon following Daniel's message to Belshazzar. That fall of Babylon is recorded by ancient historians Herodutus, Berosus, and Xenophon. Their account reads:

> Cyrus then dug a trench and diverted the flow of the Euphrates River into the new channel which led to an existing swamp. The level of the river then dropped to such a level that it became like a stream. His army was then able to take the city by marching through the shallow waters…. The Babylonians at the time were celebrating intensely at a feast to one of their gods and they were taken totally by surprise.[1001]

We should understand the drying-up of the Euphrates as a literal miracle, according to Walvoord. It is a 1,700-mile-long obstacle that divides the region geographically—east from west—much like the Mississippi River divides the continental United States in half.

A literal interpretation of this Scripture would be that an act of God permits the armies from the East (presumably China) to cross unimpeded to speed up their march to Armageddon. After all, a world war would no doubt involve armies from Asia, which, as mentioned earlier, will be the last to join the war.

SUMMARY OF PROPHETIC SCRIPTURE AND CHINA

An act of God will dry up the Euphrates River bottom that helps the Chinese army (likely mostly a demonic force) quicken its pace to join the final battle at Armageddon, which ushers in the Lord's return. However, until that time arrives, we must ask ourselves: What then ought to be done?

Chinese Christians and the Future

There are an estimated 150 million Chinese Christians, making them that country's largest religious minority. They are severely persecuted for their faith, and in spite of that repression, their numbers continue to grow against the anti-Christian tyranny of President Xi.[1002]

The persecution of Christians is real, but the faith is exploding across Communist China, as sociologist Rodney Stark explains, because Christianity has answers to modern scientific technology and for life in general.[1003]

Mr. Stark and co-author Xinhua Wang explain in their book, *A Star in the East: The Rise of Christianity in China*, that in "1980 there were 10 million Christians in the People's Republic of China and…in 2007, the figure was 60 million. These numbers yield an annual growth rate of 7%," which means by 2020 there were nearly 150 million Christians in China, and by 2040, given the same growth rate, there will be 579 million believers in Christ inside the PRC by 2040, according to Stark and Wang.[1004]

Why is there such a phenomenal growth of Christians in China? Stark and Wang indicate that expansion includes the "better educated, who are experiencing 'cultural incongruity' between traditional Asian culture and industrial—technological modernity, which results in spiritual deprivation, which Christianity is able to answer."[1005]

Stark explains that Eastern religions like Taoism and Confucianism are "all anti-progress; they all proclaim the world is going downhill from a glorious past and that we should look backwards, not forwards… [which] doesn't fit with the world that modern Chinese are experiencing having happened around them."[1006]

"But the question of 'What does the world mean, and how do we live in it?' persists—and so that's a major motor in the Christianization of China, and it explains why it's the most educated Chinese who are the most apt to join," according to Stark.[1007]

The rapid growth of Christianity across the Communist regime terrifies the CCP to the point that drastic measures are being taken. The

Xi regime launched a systematic campaign to reduce China's Christian demographic in order to control them within a "birdcage," a term attributed to Hong Kong's Catholic Cardinal Joseph Zen, who blames the Chinese Communists for the growing oppression in the name of ideological conformity.[1008]

At this point, it's important for the reader to appreciate that Marxists like President Xi are deathly afraid of religion-inspired ideology, and they will do whatever is necessary to destroy people of faith. I wrote in my 2021 book, *Give Me Liberty, Not Marxism*, about the deep-seated hatred Karl Marx, the founder of the Marxist ideology, had for all religion, especially Christianity. Specifically, in 1844, Marx wrote:

> The abolition of religion as the illusory happiness of the people is required for their real happiness. Religion is the sigh of the oppressed creature, the heart of a heartless world, and the soul of soulless conditions. It is the opium of the people.

Marx also said religion is a "spiritual booze," and called for making government god—the provider, sustainer, protector, and lawgiver—and Marxism the state religion.[1009]

After all, to make Marx's ideology function, there must be no god (deity) for the people to depend upon. We've seen this played out by former Soviet leader Vladimir Lenin, who used the machinery of state (the Soviet Union's government) to launch a campaign to eliminate all religion in order for the Marxist revolution to succeed.

I write in *Give Me Liberty, Not Marxism*:

> Lenin's attack on religion used high-pressure tactics to oppress all faiths in order to force people to abandon God. From the start, he passed a resolution that ordered the confiscation of all valuables from churches and religious institutions "with ruthless resolution, leaving nothing in doubt, and in the very shortest time."[1010]

That resolution continued:

The greater the number of representatives of the reactionary clergy and the reactionary bourgeoisie that we succeed in shooting on this occasion, the better because this "audience" must precisely now be taught a lesson in such a way that they will not dare to think about any resistance whatsoever for several decades.[1011]

Soviet dictator Joseph Stalin, who ruled the Soviet Union from 1929 to 1953, picked up where Lenin left off to pursue a campaign to eliminate all religion in communist Russia. Stalin launched a Five-Year Plan of Atheism with the goal of closing all churches and ending with the Soviet Union embracing communist atheism. Although he wasn't completely successful, Stalin by 1941 reduced the number of orthodox churches from 46,000 before the revolution to 4,225 after it. Further, 95 percent of all orthodox monasteries were destroyed, and most of the religious elite were either in gulags or executed.[1012]

President Xi's anti-Christian tactics are similar to those found in the former Soviet Union under both Lenin and Stalin. Specifically, according to Nida Shea, a senior fellow with the Hudson Institute, the CCP's anti-Christian tactics range from prison to social marginalization, closure of churches, censorship of Christian teaching, "black" jails for brainwashing, and Maoist "struggle sessions," torture, and even execution by means of organ excision, similar to the horrendous procedures famously used on Falun Gong practitioners.[1013]

President Xi is rabidly anti-Christian, which explains his 2018 directive to "Sinicize" all religion, which requires all places of worship to embrace CCP dictates, essentially making Chinese Marxism the official Chinese religion. Those dictates prohibit children from church, much less from exposure to any religion. Bibles are scarce, as are religion-based websites. Most recently, on May 1, 2021, Beijing issued fifty-two new rules mandating that religious leaders must actively support CCP practices, even in their sermons.[1014]

In 2020, according to the *Aquila Report*, a publication for Reformed and Presbyterian churches, President Xi's "Sinicize" policy resulted in:

> …the removal of over 900 crosses from churches; the confiscation of Bibles across China as the police raided and closed down many house churches, including state-run churches; churches were also bulldozed and destroyed; and for the first time in 40 years, as attested by Bob (Xiqiu) Fu, a Chinese Christian who fled to the United States, the demand for Christian children to renounce their faith, simultaneously prohibiting them from reading or hearing the Bible read to them by their parents.[1015]

Yes, the CCP is Sinicizing Christianity, in part, by rewriting the Bible. The Communist-approved rewrite of the Scripture includes the Gospel of John, chapter 8. That chapter describes an adulterous woman brought to Jesus, and her accusers ask Him whether she should be stoned for her sins.[1016]

In the King James Version of John 8:7, Jesus responds to their question:

> So when they continued asking him, he lifted up himself, and said unto them, "He that is without sin among you, let him first cast a stone at her."

At that point, the woman's accusers left, and in John 8:10–11, the Word says:

> When Jesus had lifted up himself, and saw none but the woman, he said unto her, "Woman, where are those thine accusers? Hath no man condemned thee?" She said, "No man, Lord." And Jesus said unto her, "neither do I condemn thee: go, and sin no more."

The CCP's version of this passage is radically different. It states that the crowd departs, but Jesus turns to the woman to admit:

> "I too am a sinner. But if the law could only be executed by men without blemish, the law would be dead." Then Jesus picks up stones to kill the woman.[1017]

The CCP's version of the account in John teaches that forgiveness is rejected and the law must be obeyed. After all, that's the regime's message to all citizens—the CCP is to be obeyed above all, which is what it means to Sinicize the Bible.

Similarly, members of the laity must be compliant with CCP directives. Consider that Catholic Bishop Vincent Zhan Silu is a CCP-approved Christian leader for the Mindong diocese. As the leader, the bishop appointed thirty-three priests to attend a "formation course" hosted by the Central Institute of Socialism, which is associated with the CCP's local United Front Work Department, a state security operation. The purpose of the course was "to carry out the Sinicization of religion with determination[;] we will continue to follow a path that conforms to socialist society."[1018]

Further, President Xi's "May [2021 Sinicization] rules provide for high-tech enforcement: active Christians will be subject to state surveillance through 'strict gatekeeping, verification of identity, and registration," writes Ms. Shea for *National Review*. She indicates the Xi regime maintains a database of all church members that is used to assess their compliance and lists their "rewards" and "punishments."[1019]

Pastor Ezra Jin and his daughter understand the consequences of disobeying these new rules and the compliance "rewards" and "punishments." For example, they were barred from boarding international flights because the pastor rejected the placement of facial-recognition cameras inside his church. Bishop Vincent Guo also understands the state's rules regarding the demand to affiliate with the Chinese Patriotic Catholic Association, the CCP's approved Catholic Church. After all, he resigned as a bishop after the government turned off his heat, water, and electricity to pressure him to submit to the new rules and join the association.[1020]

The CCP's so-called social-credit system is designed to force Christians to obey. Low scores result in denial of state-regulated goods and services, as Bishop Guo came to understand. In other words, the Communist regime treats religion "as state institutions" and religious workers as "civil servants" who must comply with CCP policies.[1021]

Even though many Christians bow to CCP rules, thousands of churches, even some that are registered with the government, have been shuttered. There are reports of government agents destroying large churches like the Golden Lampstand Church in Shanxi Province, as well as Zion Church and Sichuan's Early Rain Covenant Church.[1022]

All told, at least four hundred Protestant churches were demolished, closed, or repurposed in 2020 alone, according to the website Bitter Winter. "In April 2020 alone, 48 Three-Self Churches were closed in Yugan County, Jiangxi," according to Ms. Shea. She explained that "a local government official was cited as saying that all churches built after 2014, even those holding required permits, were ordered closed there."[1023]

The punishment for Christians who refuse to comply with CCP directives can be stiff, much worse than the treatment experienced by Bishop Guo. Some believers are subjected to confinement, prison, house arrest, and detention centers called "black jails." Most of those Christians arrested for practicing their faith are placed in extrajudicial detention, which "go undocumented, and all are deprived of basic due process," wrote Ms. Shea. There are thousands of underground church members being held for long periods, perhaps even decades. Meanwhile, they are brainwashed by CCP officials and subjected to beatings, drugs, sleep deprivation, and often worse.[1024]

Radio Free Asia confirms that some Chinese Christians are being detained in CCP-run "brainwashing camps." That report cites the story of Li Yuese, a pseudonym, a Chinese Christian who described his ten-month detention in a "transformation facility" after a CCP raid at his house church in Sichuan Province in 2018. He explained the "prisoners" were held in mobile facilities operated by the United Front. Mr. Li said he was subjected to verbal and physical abuse that included intimidation, threats, and beatings intended to coerce him to renounce his faith. "After you've been in there a week, death starts to look better than staying there," he said.[1025]

A 2021 Radio Free Asia broadcast reported on the case of a Sichuanese Christian held in a CCP-run black jail for many months after a raid on his house church. The man told his story of being locked with other Christians in a basement where there were "no windows, no ventilation, and no time allowed outside." They were subjected to brainwashing and long periods of solitary confinement for refusing to "admit their mistakes."[1026]

Earlier in this volume, I reported about the horrendous CCP practice of organ harvesting for profit and for punishment of Falun Gong practitioners. Christians, according to leading UN human-rights experts, are also subjects of CCP-hosted organ harvesting. Specifically, as Ms. Shea reports, there are credible reports of "detained Christians" who, as a punishment, are killed in the process: "after ultrasound checks, surgeons excise detained believers' hearts, kidneys, livers and corneas."[1027]

Former Canadian Cabinet minister David Kilgour and others conclude:

> The source for most of the massive volume of organs from transplants is the killing of innocents: Uyghurs, Tibetans, house Christians and primarily, practitioners of the spiritually based set of exercises Falun Gong.[1028]

President Xi's anti-Christian campaign, his policy of Sinicizing the church, in part also relies on Chinese cultural identity to remain in power and limits what the CCP perceives as a threat, such as Christianity and religion in general, to control society.

Besides the horrendous activities outlined above, the regime also restricts religious-based content on the Internet and social media and from nongovernment organizations. In fact, Xi's new laws require neighbors to report the practice of Christian activities to authorities, and those reports often earn monetary rewards for the informers.[1029]

Miss Shea concludes her *National Review* article with a call for action:

Christians, along with other religious-minority communities, are now being severely repressed by President Xi and reinvigorated CCP. The new religious-affairs rules ensure that the crisis will deepen. China's Christians need much greater Western help.[1030]

WESTERN CHRISTIANS' RESPONSE

How should Western Christians respond to the dire situation facing believers in Communist China?

The persecution of Chinese Christians should be anticipated. Across history, the Christian Church faced assaults, because Satan's mission until the Lord returns is to undermine Christ and His Church. The rapidly growing Chinese Body is no exception.

History demonstrates that the Body of Christ grows when persecuted, and God knows that's happening in China today. That should be a reason to praise the Lord as well as an urgent call to action for Christians around the world.

There are at least three things the Body of Christ can do to help the Chinese Church.

1. We must commit together to pray for the Body of Christ in China as it faces tyranny. Encourage them in prayer to persevere in spite of the persecution. After all, we read in Hebrews 12:1–3 that believers are to: "lay aside every weight, and the sin which

doth so easily beset us, and let us run with patience the race that is set before us, Looking unto Jesus the author and finisher of our faith; who for the joy that was set before him endured the cross, despising the shame, and is set down at the right hand of the throne of God. For consider him that endured such contradiction of sinners against himself, lest ye be wearied and faint in your minds," knowing fully well that God promises, "I will never desert you, nor will I ever forsake you" (Hebrews 13:5).

2. We can support ministries that help the Chinese Christian Church. Like in the Cold War days of the former Soviet Union, there were ministries that managed to help persecuted Christians behind the Iron Curtain. Similarly, whether through broadcasts into Communist China or other more clandestine means, such as supplying Bibles, we need to help those believers who risk it all to spread the Word of God to the Chinese people.

3. We should support efforts to hold the PRC accountable by advocating for the objectives outlined in the previous chapter. Although those efforts are secular in nature, they are intended to restrain the Communist regime and pressure it to act more responsibly across the world and at home. That would include the appropriate treatment of people of faith.

CONCLUSION

This chapter introduced an interpretation of the end-times prophecies that advance the view that China is mentioned, albeit indirectly, in the Scripture, and it is involved in the final battle, Armageddon. Certainly, the shared information and scriptural interpretations advance that view, but we can never be dogmatic. However, what is clear today is that the number of Christian believers is exploding across China in part because Christianity provides answers to life and hope for eternity through the saving knowledge of Jesus Christ. Yes, as the Body of Christ grows in

Communist China, so does the persecution, something warned about in God's Word (e.g., 1 Peter 4:12). However, those believers have a cross to bear this side of Heaven, as do we in the West. Our obligation, as outlined above, is to do what we must to help those brothers and sisters separated by great distances, language, and culture to remain faithful to the end.

Afterword

For I know the plans I have for you, declares the LORD, plans to prosper you and not to harm you, plans to give you hope and a future.

—Jeremiah 29:11 (NIV)

I recognize that *Kings of the East: China's Plan to Eliminate America and Impose a Communist World Order* is not uplifting; that was not my intent. Rather, it is my sobering call to action before it is too late and an encouragement, especially to Christians, that God has plans, but not necessarily to save America, the West, and fellow believers from persecution before the return of Christ.

Although I don't claim to be a prophet, nor am I the son of one, this volume warns the free world about the real threat posed by Communist China, which isn't that different in the possible consequences from the prophecy delivered by the prophet Jeremiah to the Israelites 2,600 years ago to prepare that nation for a dramatic fall.

God communicated through Jeremiah (25:11, NIV): "This whole country [Israel] will become a desolate wasteland, and these nations will serve the king of Babylon seventy years." That warning shouldn't have surprised the Jews at the time, because King Nebuchadnezzar had already removed some Hebrews to Babylon. Further, the total destruction of Jerusalem and the Temple were still future at that writing, yet Jeremiah reassured those frightened Jews that God would not forsake them, and ultimately their nation would return to the land, albeit after the prophesied exile.

Today, many people are fearful about the present tumultuous times, and more than a few Christians are growing anxious about the numerous prophetic end-times indicators firing up the heavens, such as threats of war coming from the Communist tyrants in Beijing. However, even though our collective angst is real, we can garner some encouragement from Jeremiah's prophecy for the sixth-century BC Israelites. Understand that prophecy was exclusive to the ancient Jews; however, the general principle applies to modern Christians thanks to the assurance we have in the sacrifice of Jesus Christ for our sins.

Contemporary Christians find that assurance in New Testament verses like Romans 8:31–39 that indicate we are justified through Christ, and even though our challenges may be similar to those of the Israelites of old, our Babylon-like hardships and persecution will never separate us from God. Thus, Christians should be confident in Christ that all things will work together for our good, and that God has a plan for us, even though that plan may not deliver us from the present-day evil intentions of contemporary Nebuchadnezzars.

Yes, Communist China and its tyrant leaders may well be our most threatening Babylon, led by tyrants like Nebuchadnezzar, aka Xi Jinping. Or, others may arise in time to take their place to threaten our very existence. For now, however, *Kings of the East* is a wake-up call for Western readers to appreciate the threat posed by the PRC, both to our national existence and as an instrument leading to the prophetic end times.

The threat from Communist China for us today is no less real than that posed by the Babylonians for the ancient Israelites. That's why this volume provides the reader with a foundational understanding of the Middle Kingdom's long history, the Chinese Communists' agenda, insights into their leadership, and a detailed outline of their five-part strategic plan (instruments) to remake the world in its image.

The volume began by reviewing China's 3,500-year history and how that great people became the modern victims of an incendiary ideology, Marxist-Leninism, and the tyrants with a stranglehold over that nation. However, we must not blame ordinary Chinese citizens for the corruption plaguing their country. Rather, all the fault rests with the Chinese Communist Party, which long ago embraced the worst instincts of mankind, and its evil ideology to gain control and steer the ship of that state in an evil—arguably satanic—direction.

The first section of *Kings of the East* concludes by identifying the strategic tools the Beijing regime uses to remake the world order. The first tool is the most obvious: economy and trade. Yes, the engines of work, finance, and resources rocketed the Communist regime into the world's prosperity spotlight, and soon that country may have the globe's largest economy. In part, that outcome is thanks to the malfeasance of greedy Western capitalists who turned a blind eye to corruption, but also of many Chinese Communists who compromised the history and reputation of that great nation to leverage their personal prosperity. Meanwhile, in their lust for wealth, the CCP is rapidly coming face to face with existential demographic challenges that truly threaten to totally compromise their so-called successes. They have themselves to thank for these crises. Specifically, decades ago, they promoted the failed one-child policy that is now reaping an imploding population—a very low fertility rate—which is coupled with a crippling abundance of older citizens who must depend on the state for their livelihood, and insufficient working people to pay the taxes that are necessary to sustain the country. This combination, as explained, could bankrupt China.

Second, ideologically, the CCP is pushing its Marxist-Leninist agenda within the giant Asian country, and it is most recently doing so aggressively across the world. The PRC seeks to make big Marxist government everyone's "god" while attacking faith in the True God. Currently, virtually every aspect of the average citizen's life—housing, jobs, school, marriage, family, and much more—in China is monitored by the state and totally controlled. Nothing is outside the government's all-knowing oversight. Further, through the regime's tentacles abroad, it seeks to influence the entire world's population much as it does the lives of 1.4 billion Chinese. Yes, ideology is Beijing's mechanism to dominate, and the regime is making rapid gains.

Third, what the Chinese Communists can't accomplish through economic and ideological manipulation, they intend to realize through the use of military force. Their security might demonstrates how Beijing is rapidly fielding an armed force to match the US military in size, sophistication, and global reach. In fact, there is evidence announced by the Pentagon in 2021 that China's People's Liberation Army already outpaces America's armed forces in important areas such as hypersonic missiles, artificial intelligence, some weapons of mass destruction, and much more. These significant developments could well result in the CCP having the upper hand to humble the US military and the balance of the world if a future kinetic war happens.

Fourth, geopolitically the Chinese are expanding their influence lightning fast. They advanced their persuasion across most major international organizations such as the United Nations, where today their proxies exercise considerable influence on rules and programs that impact us all. Further, using the tentacles of their Belt and Road Initiative, the CCP has a network to manipulate more than half of all sovereign countries, and that control grows each year to the point that, by association, China could soon enjoy authority over most international decisions—either directly or through a rainbow of leveraged representatives.

Finally, China's President Xi made becoming the world leader in technology a critical Chinese aim. Of course, the regime requires all components of that society—academic, government, business, scientific, military—to closely collaborate in order to lead the world in frightening technologies that will inevitably shape our collective future. They are succeeding more than many in the West understand, and what they lack in know-how, the regime's global network of spies steals, buys, or coerces from those with special knowledge about high-technologies that are then transferred to China.

The third section of *Kings of the East* begins with specific actions the US and the West must undertake if there is any hope of reversing the CCP's radical global agenda. Specifically, I propose very specific objectives across each of the five strategic mechanisms used by Beijing to seize global control—economy, ideology, security, geopolitics, and technology. A concerted effort to embrace and execute those recommendations could significantly degrade the CCP's progress and just perhaps might preserve the West's world order established in the wake of World War II that gave much of the globe freedom and prosperity.

Stopping Communist China's assault on world order may not be God's plan, and thus humanity may well continue down the path to radicalism and the eventual prophetic end times. The final chapter in *Kings of the East* demonstrates that the Middle Kingdom may in fact be an end-times player. However, and especially for Christians both inside China and those elsewhere across the modern world, there are things we must all do, and soon. We must do our part to defeat the Chinese Marxist global agenda by following the formula outlined in chapter 9, but also, we are spiritually obligated to help our brothers and sisters inside the Chinese regime. We do that out of love for our Lord.

No one really knows whether the PRC will succeed at destroying the current West-favoring world order and replace it with one in Communist China's image. However, there is no doubt the tyrants in Beijing are seeking that outcome, and we must awaken to that reality and prepare for the worse, much as Jeremiah warned the Israelites about the coming seventy-year exile, while realizing the plans are in God's hands. Finally, whether China fails or succeeds in its horrible aims, we must remember what the Apostle Paul wrote in Romans 8:28 (NIV): "And we know that in all things God works for the good of those who love him, who have been called according to his purpose."

Notes

1. Robert Maginnis, *Alliance of Evil* (Crane, MO: Defender, 2018) https://www.amazon.com/Alliance-Lieutenant-Colonel-Robert-Maginnis/dp/1948014068.

2. Reagan National Defense Survey, Ronald Reagan Institute, November 2021, rndf_survey_booklet.pdf (reaganfoundation.org).

3. Carrie Gracie, "The Credo: Great Rejuvenation of the Chinese Nation," BBC, November 7, 2014, https://www.bbc.com/news/world-asia-china-29788802.

4. Ibid. Note: The term "rejuvenation" is "the action of rejuvenating or the state of being rejuvenated: restoration of youthful vigor." Marriam-Webster, https://www.merriam-webster.com/dictionary/rejuvenation.

5. Ibid.

6. "Chinese Dynasties in Order," Worldatlas, accessed February 27, 2022, https://www.worldatlas.com/articles/chinese-dynasties-in-order.html.

7. "Xi Zhongxun," accessed February 15, 2022, https://en.wikipedia.org/wiki/Xi_Zhongxun.

8. "Isoroku Yamamoto's Sleeping Giant Quote," accessed February 15, 2022, https://en.wikipedia.org/wiki/Isoroku_Yamamoto%27s_sleeping_giant_quote.

9. Stephen Kotkin, "The Cold War Never Ended: Ukraine, the China Challenge, and the Revival of the West," *Foreign Affairs*, May/June 2022, https://www.foreignaffairs.com/reviews/review-essay/2022-04-06/cold-war-never-ended-russia-ukraine-war?utm_medium=newsletters&utm_

source=twofa&utm_campaign=The%20Cold%20War%20Never%20
Ended&utm_content=20220415&utm_term=FA%20This%20Week%20
-%20112017.

10. Barend Biesheuvel, Alexander Haig and J. William Middendorf, Nixon
Library, 656–10 Excerpt 2 (1:02) January 26, 1972 RN, https://www.
nixonlibrary.gov/sites/default/files/virtuallibrary/tapeexcerpts/china-656-10b.
pdf.

11. Allen Ellender, Michael Mansfield, J. William Fulbright, Henry
Kissinger, et al 92–1, Nixon Library, Excerpt 2 (1:35) February 29,
1972 RN, https://www.nixonlibrary.gov/sites/default/files/virtuallibrary/
tapeexcerpts/china-92-1b.pdf.

12. Alexander Zhang, "China 'Single Greatest Priority' for UK's
MI6 Intelligence Agency," *Epoch Times*, December 1, 2021, https://
www.theepochtimes.com/china-single-greatest-priority-for-uks-mi6-
intelligence-agency_4130712.html?utm_source=ChinaDaily&utm_
medium=email&utm_campaign=2021-12-01.

13. Ibid.

14. Covid-19 Coronavirus Pandemic, Worldometre, https://www.
worldometers.info/coronavirus/, accessed April 20, 2022.

15. Deidre McPhillips, "Drug Overdose Deaths Top 100,000 Annually
for the First Time, Driven by Fentanyl, CDC Data Show," CNN, January
12, 2022, https://www.kdrv.com/content/news/Drug-overdose-deaths-
top-100000-annually-for-the-first-time-driven-by-fentanyl-CDC-data-
show-575762501.html.

16. "Full text: China's New Party Chief Xi Jinping's Speech,"
BBC, November 15, 2012, https://www.bbc.com/news/
world-asia-china-20338586.

17. "China is called Zhongguo in Mandarin Chinese, [which] translates
as 'middle kingdom. This is because Chinese philosophy believes China is
center of the earth." "China's History and Their Role in Trade over Time,"
Laowai Career, accessed February 15, 2022, www.laowaicareer.com/blog/
china-middle-kingdom-history-trade.

18. Note: The island of Taiwan is occasionally referred to as "Formosa."
In the late nineteenth century, the Formosa Republic, a democratic state,
was formed when the Taiwanese resisted cession to Japan under the Qing
Dynasty.

"What and Where Was the Republic Of Formosa?" WorldAtlas, accessed February 27, 2022, https://www.worldatlas.com/articles/what-and-where-was-the-republic-of-formosa.html.

19. Tom Phillips, "Xi Jinping Heralds 'New Era' of Chinese Power at Communist Party Congress," *Guardian*, October 18, 2017, https://www.theguardian.com/world/2017/oct/18/xi-jinping-speech-new-era-chinese-power-party-congress.

20. "China's Xi Jinping Remakes the Communist Party's History in His Image," *New York Times*, November 11, 2021, https://www.nytimes.com/live/2021/11/11/world/china-xi-jinping-cpc.

21. Elizabeth Economy, "Xi Jinping's New World Order," *Foreign Affairs*, December 9, 2021, https://www.foreignaffairs.com/articles/china/2021-12-09/xi-jinpings-new-world-order?utm_medium=promo_email&utm_source=pre_release&utm_campaign=mktg_sub_120921_prospects&utm_content=20211209&utm_term=promo-email-prospects.

22. "Before Common Era or Before Current Era or Before Christian Era: used when referring to a year before the birth of Jesus Christ when the Christian calendar starts counting year." Cambridge Dictionary, accessed February 15, 2022, https://dictionary.cambridge.org/dictionary/english/bce and "Xia Dynasty," World History Encyclopedia, accessed February 15, 2022, https://www.worldhistory.org/Xia_Dynasty/ .

23. "A Brief History of China," Political Overview, *China Country Review*, Country Watch Inc. 2012, pp. 9–14, https://eds-s-ebscohost-com.pentagonlibrary.idm.oclc.org/eds/pdfviewer/pdfviewer?vid=4&sid=650b1420-4467-462b-bd53-8eeb14648468%40redis.

24. Ibid.

25. Elfren S. Cruz, "History of Chinese Invasions," *Philippine Star*, May 2, 2019, https://www.philstar.com/opinion/2019/05/02/1914194/history-chinese-invasions.

26. Ibid.

27. "Sun Tzu," accessed February 15, 2022, https://en.wikipedia.org/wiki/Sun_Tzu.

28. "List of Chinese Wars and Battles," accessed February 15, 2022, https://en.wikipedia.org/wiki/List_of_Chinese_wars_and_battles.

29. "Qin Shi Huang," Britannica, accessed February 15, 2022, https://www.britannica.com/biography/Qin-Shi-Huang.

30. Ibid.

31. "A Brief History of China," op cit.

32. Ibid.

33. "Opium Wars," accessed February 15, 2022, https://en.wikipedia.org/wiki/Opium_Wars.

34. "A Brief History of China," op cit.

35. Ibid.

36. Ibid.

37. "History of the Kuomintang," accessed February 15, 2022, https://en.wikipedia.org/wiki/History_of_the_Kuomintang.

38. "Warlord Era," accessed February 15, 2022, https://en.wikipedia.org/wiki/Warlord_Era#:~:text=In%20historiography%2C%20the%20Warlord%20Era%20began%20in%201916,and%20established%20the%20Republic%20of%20China%20in%201912.

39. "A Brief History of China," op cit.

40. "Yan'an," accessed February 15, 2022, https://en.wikipedia.org/wiki/Yan%27an#:~:text=Yan%27an%20was%20near%20the%20endpoint%20of%20the%20Long,2019%2C%20Yan%27an%20has%20approximately%202%2C255%2C700%20permanent%20residents.%20%3A%E2%80%8A4-5.

41. "A Brief History of China," op cit.

42. Ibid.

43. Ibid.

44. These were Chairman Mao's efforts to rid Chinese cities of corruption and enemies of the state. However, they were in reality Mao's efforts to consolidate power by targeting his political opponents. "Three-anti and Five-anti Campaigns," accessed February 15, 2022, https://en.wikipedia.org/wiki/Three-anti_and_Five-anti_Campaigns.

45. "Mao Zedong," accessed February 15, 2022, https://en.wikipedia.org/wiki/Mao_Zedong.

46. "A Brief History of China," op cit.

47. Ibid.

48. Mao's Four Pests Campaign was one of the first actions taken in the Great Leap Forward. The four pests to be eliminated were rats, flies, mosquitoes, and sparrows. However, that effort resulted in a severe ecological imbalance.

"Four Pests Campaign," accessed February 15, 2022, https://en.wikipedia.org/wiki/Four_Pests_campaign.

49. "Great Chinese Famine," accessed February 15, 2022, https://en.wikipedia.org/wiki/Great_Chinese_Famine.

50. "A Brief History of China," op cit.

51. Ibid.

52. Ibid.

53. Ibid.

54. Ibid.

55. Ibid.

56. Ibid.

57. Ibid.

58. Ibid.

59. The Great Hall of the People is an important venue for the CCP, state affairs, and diplomatic activities. It is situated on the west of Tiananmen Square, opposite the Museum of Chinese Revolution and the Museum of Chinese History on the east. "The Great Hall of the People, NPC, accessed February 15, 2022, http://www.npc.gov.cn/zgrdw/englishnpc/GreatHall/node_3072.htm.

60. "A Brief History of China," op cit.

61. Ibid.

62. Ibid.

63. Ibid.

64. Ibid.

65. "History of the People's Republic of China," accessed February 15, 2022, https://en.wikipedia.org/wiki/History_of_the_People%27s_Republic_of_China_(2002%E2%80%93present).

66. Francis P. Sempa, "The Genocide Olympics," *American Spectator*, January 25, 2022, https://spectator.org/the-genocide-olympics/.

67. "Beijing Winter Olympics: Russia Rejects 'Pointless' Diplomatic Boycott; France, Germany Call for EU Response," Reuters, December 9, 2021, https://africa.espn.com/olympics/story/_/id/32828696/beijing-winter-olympics-russia-rejects-pointless-diplomatic-boycott-france-germany-call-eu-response.

68. Lee Xin En, "China's President Xi Could Learn from Qing Emperors:

Historian Jonathan Spence," *Strait Times*, April 17, 2015, https://www.straitstimes.com/asia/east-asia/chinas-president-xi-could-learn-from-qing-emperors-historian-jonathan-spence.

69. Ibid.

70. Ibid.

71. Ibid.

72. Economy, op cit.

73. "Qing Dynasty," accessed February 15, 2022, https://en.wikipedia.org/wiki/Qing_dynasty.

74. "The House of Aisin-Gioro was a Manchu clan that ruled the Later Jin dynasty (1616–1636), the Qing dynasty (1636–1912) and Manchukuo (1932–1945).… Under the Ming dynasty, members of the Aisin Gioro clan served as chiefs of the Jianzhou Jurchens, one of the three major Jurchen tribes at this time. Qing bannermen passed through the gates of the Great Wall in 1644, defeated the short-lived Shun dynasty and the Southern Ming, and gained control of China proper." "House of Aisin-Gioro," accessed February 15, 2022, https://en.wikipedia.org/wiki/House_of_Aisin-Gioro.

75. "Qing Dynasty," op cit.

76. "The Ming Dynasty," Britannica, accessed February 15, 2022, https://www.britannica.com/art/Chinese-architecture/The-Ming-dynasty-1368-1644.

77. "Chinese History—1644–1912 AD—Qing / Ch'ing (Manchu) Dynasty," Global Security, accessed February 15, 2022, https://www.globalsecurity.org/military/world/china/history-manchu.htm.

78. Ibid.

79. Ibid.

80. Hugo Van der Merwe, "The Qing Dynasty: China's Last Imperial Age," CLI, September 13, 2021, https://studycli.org/chinese-history/qing-dynasty/.

81. "Inner Asia," accessed February 15, 2022, https://en.wikipedia.org/wiki/Inner_Asia.

82. "Qing Tributary System," Epic World History, accessed February 15, 2022, https://epicworldhistory.blogspot.com/2012/05/qing-tributary-system.html.

83. Merwe, op cit.

84. Ibid.

85. "Hong Xiuquan," Britannica, accessed February 15, 2022, https://www.britannica.com/biography/Hong-Xiuquan.

86. Merwe, op cit.

87. "Chinese History—1644–1912 AD—Qing / Ch'ing (Manchu) Dynasty," globalsecurity.org, accessed February 15, 2022, https://www.globalsecurity.org/military/world/china/history-manchu.htm.

88. Ibid.

89. Ibid.

90. Ibid.

91. Merwe, op cit. and "Taiping Rebellion (1850–1864)," Asia for Educators, accessed February 15, 2022, http://afe.easia.columbia.edu/special/china_1750_taiping.htm.

92. Ibid.

93. Ibid.

94. Ibid.

95. Ibid.

96. Ibid.

97. "Chinese History—1644–1912 AD—Qing / Ch'ing (Manchu) Dynasty," Op cit. and Kallie Szczepanski, "The Fall of China's Qing Dynasty in 1911–1912," Thoughtco, January 23, 2020. https://www.thoughtco.com/fall-of-the-qing-dynasty-195608.

98. "The Manchu," Infoplease, January 25, 2021, https://www.infoplease.com/history/world/the-manchu.

99. Ibid.

100. "China Unveils New Leaders, with Xi at Head," States News Service, November 15, 2012, Gale Academic OneFile, link.gale.com/apps/doc/A308538124/AONE?u=wash92852&sid=ebsco&xid=e943cad8.

101. Eric B. Brown and Charles Horner, "The Future of China's Past: Rising China's Next Act," Hudson Institute, February 10, 2021, https://www.hudson.org/research/16675-the-future-of-china-s-past-rising-china-s-next-act.

102. Ibid.

103. Joe McDonald, "Chinese Leaders Issue Official History to Elevate Xi," AP News, November 11, 2021, https://apnews.com/article/business-mao-zedong-xi-jinping-china-492f45c5d638ec642a63f67479091 5db.

104. Brown, op cit.

105. Ibid.

106. "Leninism," Wikipedia, accessed March 5, 2022, https://en.wikipedia.org/wiki/Leninism.

107. Chi Wang, "Why Did Xi Jinping Visit Manchuria," Diplomat, October 19, 2018, https://thediplomat.com/2018/10/why-did-xi-jinping-visit-manchuria/.

108. "Chaguan: The Party's Model Emperor," *Economist*, Vol. 440, Issue 9263, September 18, 2021, page 58, https://www.economist.com/china/2021/09/18/the-chinese-communist-partys-model-emperor.

109. Ibid.

110. Ibid.

111. Ibid.

112. Ibid.

113. Ibid.

114. Ibid.

115. Ibid.

116. Ibid.

117. Newt Gingrich, "New Gingrich Says He (and We) Were Wrong about China: It's More Dangerous Than We Wanted to Believe," *Newsweek*, April 29, 2019, https://www.newsweek.com/2019/05/10/china-newt-gingrich-xi-jinping-5g-technology-dangerous-myths-fantasy-1408874.html.

118. Ibid.

119. Ibid.

120. Ibid.

121. Shu Tong, "Chinese Communist Party's History of Violence and Deception," Minghui.org, May 23, 2020, https://en.minghui.org/html/articles/2020/5/23/185169.html.

122. Ibid.

123. Ibid.

124. Ibid.

125. Ibid.

126. Ibid.

127. Ibid.

128. "Who Are the Uyghurs and Why Is China Being Accused

of Genocide?" BBC, June 21, 2021, https://www.bbc.com/news/world-asia-china-22278037.

129. Rana Mitter and Elsbeth Johnson, "What the West Gets Wrong About China," *Harvard Business Review*, Vol. 99, Issue 3, May/June 2021, pp. 42–28, https://hbr.org/2021/05/what-the-west-gets-wrong-about-china.

130. Ibid.

131. Ibid.

132. Ibid.

133. Ibid.

134. Ibid.

135. Ibid.

136. Ibid.

137. Ibid.

138. Ibid.

139. Richard Overy, "An Economy Geared to War," *History Today*, Vol. 51, Issue 11, November 11, 2001, https://www.historytoday.com/archive/economy-geared-war.

140. Ibid.

141. Ibid.

142. Ibid.

143. Ibid.

144. Ibid.

145. Ibid.

146. Ibid.

147. "Xuexi Qiangguo," Actipedia, accessed February 16, 2022, https://actipedia.org/project/xuexi-qiangguo.

148. "Xuexi Qiangguo," Wikipedia, accessed February 16, 2022, https://en.wikipedia.org/wiki/Xuexi_Qiangguo.

149. Mitter and Johnson, op cit.

150. Ibid.

151. Ibid.

152. Ibid.

153. Ibid.

154. Ibid.

155. Ibid.

156. Jaime A. FlorCruz, "Corruption as China's Top Priority," CNN, January 7, 2013, https://edition.cnn.com/2013/01/06/world/asia/florcruz-china-corruption.

157. Chun Han Wong and Keith Zhai, "Xi Jinping Warns China Won't Be Bullied as Communist Party Marks 100 Years," *Wall Street Journal*, July 1, 2021, https://www.wsj.com/articles/xi-jinping-warns-china-wont-be-bullied-as-communist-party-marks-100-years-11625122870.

158. Ibid.

159. Ibid.

160. Chris Buckley and Keith Bradsher, "Marking Party's Centennial, Xi Warns That China Will Not Be Bullied," *New York Times*, July 1, 2021, https://www.nytimes.com/2021/07/01/world/asia/xi-china-communist-party-anniversary.html#:~:text=Mr.%20Xi%2C%20the%20most%20powerful%20Chinese%20leader%20in,on%20the%20country%E2%80%99s%20path%20to%20becoming%20a%20superpower.

161. Ibid.

162. "China: Communique for Sixth Plenum Celebrates Chinese Socialism and President Xi," Stratfor, November 11, 2021, China: Communique for Sixth Plenum Celebrates Chinese Socialism and President Xi (stratfor.com).

163. "China's Xi Jinping Remakes the Communist Party's History in His Image," *New York Times*, November 11, 2021, https://www.nytimes.com/live/2021/11/11/world/china-xi-jinping-cpc.

164. Ibid.

165. Nicole Hao, "China's Plenary Session Reveals Xi Jinping's Tenuous Hold on Power: Scholars," *Epoch Times*, November 25, 2021, https://www.theepochtimes.com/chinas-plenary-session-reveals-xi-jinpings-tenuous-hold-on-power-scholars_4114786.html?utm_source=ChinaDaily&utm_medium=email&utm_campaign=2021-11-26.

166. Ibid.

167. Ibid.

168. Ibid.

169. Ibid.

170. Gordon G. Chang, "Will Xi Jinping's 'End of Days' Plunge China and the World into War?" Gatestone Institute, February 16, 2022, https://www.gatestoneinstitute.org/18231/xi-jinping-china-war.

171. Ibid.
172. Ibid.
173. Ibid.
174. Ibid.
175. Ibid.
176. Ibid.
177. Ibid.
178. Hao, op cit.
179. Ibid.
180. Kerry Brown, "The Powers of Xi Jinping," Asian Affairs, Vol. 48, Issue 1, February 1, 2017, https://www-tandfonline-com.pentagonlibrary.idm. oclc.org/doi/full/10.1080/03068374.2016.1267435.
181. Ibid.
182. Ibid.
183. Ibid.
184. Ibid.
185. Ibid.
186. Ibid.
187. Ibid.
188. Ibid.
189. Ibid.
190. Ibid.
191. Ibid.
192. Ibid.
193. Ibid.
194. Ibid.
195. Ibid.
196. Ibid.
197. Ibid.
198. Ibid.
199. Ibid.
200. Ibid.
201. Ibid.
202. Ibid.
203. "China's Xi Jinping Unveils New 'Four Comprehensives'

Slogans," BBC, February 25, 2015, https://www.bbc.com/news/world-asia-china-31622571.

204. Brown, op cit.

205. Michael Beckley, "Enemies of My Enemy," *Foreign Affairs*, February 14, 2021, https://www.foreignaffairs.com/articles/2021-02-14/china-new-world-order-enemies-my-enemy?utm_medium=promo_email&utm_source=pre_release&utm_campaign=special_preview_021422_prospects&utm_content=20220214&utm_term=promo-email-prospects.

206. Ibid.

207. Ibid.

208. Ibid.

209. Ibid.

210. Ibid.

211. Ibid.

212. Ibid.

213. Ibid.

214. Ibid.

215. Ibid.

216. Ibid.

217. Ibid.

218. Ibid.

219. Ibid.

220. Ibid.

221. Ibid.

222. Ibid.

223. Helen Davidson and Vincent Ni, "China Attacks US Diplomatic Boycott of Winter Games as 'Travesty' of Olympic Spirit," *Guardian*, December 7, 2021, https://www.theguardian.com/world/2021/dec/07/china-attacks-us-diplomatic-boycott-of-winter-games-as-travesty-of-olympic-spirit.

224. Beckley, op cit.

225. Ibid.

226. Ibid.

227. Ibid.

228. Ibid.

229. Ibid.

230. Ibid.

231. "China's Growing Power Projection and Expeditionary Capabilities," Section II, US China Economic and Security Review Commission, 2020https://www.uscc.gov/annual-report/2020-annual-report-congress.

232. Ibid.

233. "Factbox: China-Russia Trade Has Surged as Countries Grow Closer," Reuters, March 1, 2022, https://www.reuters.com/markets/europe/china-russia-trade-has-surged-countries-grow-closer-2022-03-01/ and Fred Lucas, "Sen. Tom Cotton Wary of Chinese Spying on, DNA Tracking of American Olympians," Daily Signal, February 16, 2022, https://www.dailysignal.com/2022/02/16/sen-tom-cotton-wary-of-chinese-spying-on-dna-tracking-of-american-olympians/.

234. US China Economic and Security Review Commission, op cit.

235. Dean Cheng, "China, Russia, and Ukraine: It's Folly to Think Beijing Will Work With West," *Daily Signal*, March 2, 2022, https://www.dailysignal.com/2022/03/02/china-russia-and-ukraine-its-folly-to-think-beijing-will-work-with-west/?utm_source=TDS_Email&utm_medium=email&utm_campaign=MorningBell&mkt_tok=ODI0LU1IVC0zMDQAAAGC83DIb6i5As2J5AbS92xYdaSSLPoVIUp6PqHEp8-Mq7kLzGV3VICgfQ5AdyKJouoXuLUsdtwBIt-mwz2nzcs7jpOaCsXjROlOh6fM1Ez5oI-TW0rT.

236. Ibid.

237. Ibid.

238. Ibid.

239. Patrick Goodenough, "National Security Advisor on Putin-Xi Declaration: They Didn't Call Each Other 'Allies'," CNS News, February 6, 2022, https://www.cnsnews.com/article/international/patrick-goodenough/national-security-advisor-putin-xi-declaration-they-didnt.

240. Dimitri Simes, "'No Limits' Friendship: Putin and Xi Present Common Front Against the US," CNS News, February 6, 2022, https://www.cnsnews.com/article/international/dimitri-simes/no-limits-friendship-putin-and-xi-present-common-front-against.

241. Chris Buckley and Steven Lee Meyers, "In Beijing, Olympic Spectacle and Global Power Games," *New York Times*, February 4, 2022,

https://www.nytimes.com/2022/02/04/world/asia/olympics-beijing-xi-putin.html?campaign_id=9&emc=edit_nn_20220209&instance_id=52576&nl=the-morning&regi_id=26545726&segment_id=82087&te=1&user_id=b0f2196b18a7350fc830c0a6cc32e369.

242. "Russia and China Announce a Bid to Make the World Safe for Dictatorship," Editorial Board, *Washington Post*, February 5, 2022, https://www.washingtonpost.com/opinions/2022/02/07/putin-xi-the-dictators-meet-at-olympics/.

243. Chao Deng et al, "Putin, Xi Aim Russia-China Partnership against US, *Wall Street Journal*, February 4, 2022, https://www.wsj.com/articles/russias-vladimir-putin-meets-with-chinese-leader-xi-jinping-in-beijing-11643966743.

244. "Nato Chief Says Russia and China Seeking to 'Rewrite International Rule Book'," Agence France-Presse, February 19, 2022, Nato chief says Russia and China seeking to 'rewrite international rule book' | South China Morning Post (scmp.com).

245. "China's Xi Promises World 'Heads Bashed Bloody.' He Should Be Taken Seriously." Editorial Board, *Washington Post*, July 5, 2021, https://www.washingtonpost.com/opinions/2021/07/05/chinas-xi-promises-world-heads-bashed-bloody-he-should-be-taken-seriously/.

246. "Wolf Warrior," IMDb, accessed February 16, 2022, https://www.imdb.com/title/tt3540136/ and US China Economic and Security Review Commission, 2020https://www.uscc.gov/annual-report/2020-annual-report-congress.

247. "China's Xi Promises World 'Heads Bashed Bloody.' He Should Be Taken Seriously." op cit.

248. Ibid.

249. Oiwan Lam, "Chinese netizens rebrand Xi Jinping's international relations strategy as 'wolf warrior' style diplomacy," Global Voices, July 22, 2020, https://globalvoices.org/2020/07/22/chinese-netizens-rebrand-xi-jinpings-international-relations-strategy-as-wolf-warrior-style-diplomacy/#:~:text=The%20term%20comes%20from%20the%20-2015%20popular%20Chinese,been%20employed%20by%20a%20number%20of%20Chinese%20diplomats.

250. Rana Mitter, "The World China Wants: How Power Will—and Won't—Reshape Chinese Ambitions," *Foreign Affairs*, January/February 2021, https://www.asiascot.com/news/2021/01/04/the-world-china-wants/.

251. "Today, renminbi is the general name for the Chinese currency, while yuan is the name of a unit of that currency. One way to understand this is to imagine a country that uses gold as its currency." "What Is the Chinese Currency Called?" CLI, accessed February 16, 2022, https://studycli.org/learn-chinese/chinese-renminbi/.

252. "China Renews Push for Increased Global Role for the Yuan," *Bloomberg News*, July 12, 2020, https://www.bloombergquint.com/global-economics/china-presses-global-yuan-role-as-u-s-tensions-explode-into-fx.

253. Stu Cvrk, "Communist China Declared War on the US Long Ago," November 29, 2021, https://www.theepochtimes.com/communist-china-declared-war-on-the-us-long-ago_4124451.html.

254. Ibid.

255. "DOD Releases 2021 Report on Military and Security Developments Involving the People's Republic of China," Department of Defense, November 3, 2021, https://www.defense.gov/News/Releases/Release/Article/2831819/dod-releases-2021-report-on-military-and-security-developments-involving-the-pe/.

256. Ibid.

257. Ibid.

258. "China Cyber Threat Overview and Advisories," Cybersecurity and Infrastructure Security Agency, accessed February 16, 2022, https://www.cisa.gov/uscert/china.

259. "DOD Releases 2021 Report on Military and Security Developments Involving the People's Republic of China," op cit.

260. Gordon G. Chang, "What to Do about China," Gatestone Institute, May 1, 2022, https://www.gatestoneinstitute.org/18480/what-to-do-about-china.

261. "China's Xi Vows 'Reunification' with Taiwan, but Holds Off Threatening Force," CNBC, October 8, 2021, https://www.cnbc.com/2021/10/09/china-president-xi-jinping-on-reunification-with-taiwan.html.

262. "China's Technology Dominance Could Give it Decisive

Military Edge," Hotlifestylenews, October 10, 2021, HTTPS://
HOTLIFESTYLENEWS.COM/WORLD-NEWS/CHINAS-
TECHNOLOGY-DOMINANCE-COULD-GIVE-IT-DECISIVE-
MILITARY-EDGE/.

263. Mark Pomerleau, "Russia and China Devote More Cyber Forces
to Offensive Operations Than US, Says New Report," C4ISRNET.
com, February 14, 2022, https://www.c4isrnet.com/cyber/2022/02/14/
russia-and-china-devote-more-cyber-forces-to-offensive-operations-than-
us-says-new-report/?utm_source=Sailthru&utm_medium=email&utm_
campaign=EBB%2002.15.2022&utm_term=Editorial%20-%20Early%20
Bird%20Brief.

264. Charlie Campbell, "Xi Jinping's Party Congress Speech Leaves No
Doubts Over His Leadership Role," *Time*, October 18, 2017, p. 17.
https://eds-p-ebscohost-com.pentagonlibrary.idm.oclc.org/eds/detail/
detail?vid=6&sid=1b42263a-f99c-46b1-9a15-719a12e2750d%40redis&bda
ta=JnNpdGU9ZWRzLWxpdmU%3d#AN=125810765&db=bth.

265. Treadgold, Donald, *The West in Russia and China: Volume 2. China
1852–1949.* (New York: Cambridge University Press, 1973). Treadgold: The
West In Russia And China: Volume 2, Google Scholar.

266. Martin K. Whyte, "China's Economic Development History and Xi
Jinping's 'China Dream:' an Overview with Personal Reflections," *Chinese
Sociological Review* Vol. 53, Issue 2, 2021, Full article: China's economic
development history and Xi Jinping's "China dream:" an overview with
personal reflections (tandfonline.com).

267. Ibid.

268. Ibid.

269. Ibid.

270. Ibid.

271. Ibid.

272. Ibid.

273. Ibid.

274. Ibid.

275. Ibid.

276. Ibid.

277. Gordon G. Chang, "If Xi Jinping's Zero-COVID Olympic Coronation

Fails, His Enemies in Beijing Are Ready," *Newsweek*, February 11, 2022, https://www.newsweek.com/2022/02/11/if-xi-jinpings-zero-covid-olympic-coronation-fails-his-enemies-beijing-are-ready-1675166.html.

278. Orange Wang, "China Population: Plummeting Births in Anhui Province Underscore 'Extremely Severe' Demographic Problem," *South China Morning Post*, September 29, 2021, scmp.com.

279. Ibid.

280. Ibid.

281. Whyte, op cit.

282. Ibid.

283. Ibid.

284. Ibid.

285. Ibid.

286. Antonio Graceffo, "The End of China's High-Paced Growth," The Epoch Times, November 22, 2021, https://www.theepochtimes.com/the-end-of-chinas-high-paced-growth_4115181.html?utm_source=ChinaDaily&utm_medium=email&utm_campaign=2021-11-23

287. Ibid.

288. Ben West, "Understanding Economic Espionage: The Present," Stratfor, February 23, 2021, https://worldview.stratfor.com/article/understanding-economic-espionage-present?id=743c2bc617&e=99971e0a2b&uuid=a a6f6bbd-83b7-42e9-aa14-5b7982ae9119&mc_cid=57d40a1508&mc_eid=99971e0a2b.

289. Ibid.

290. Ibid.

291. Ibid.

292. Autumn Spredemann, "China's Resource Exploitation in South America Is 'Unstoppable'," *Epoch Times*, December 10, 2021, https://www.theepochtimes.com/chinas-resource-exploitation-in-south-america-is-unstoppable_4150018.html?utm_source=ai&utm_medium=search.

293. Ibid.

294. Fran Wang, "China Increases Rare Earth Production, Reaching New High in Yearly Quota," *Epoch Times*, October 3, 2021, https://www.theepochtimes.com/china-increases-rare-earth-production-reaching-new-high-in-yearly-quota_4029283.html?utm_source=ai&utm_medium=search.

295. Antonio Graceffo, "US and China Battle for Defense-Critical Rare Earth Metals," *Epoch Times*, September 22, 2021, https://www.theepochtimes.com/us-and-china-battle-for-defense-critical-rare-earth-metals_4008841.html?utm_source=ai&utm_medium=search.

296. Ibid.

297. Chuck Ross, "Biden Touts Chinese Backed Company at Made In America Event," Washington Free Beacon, February 23, 2022, https://freebeacon.com/biden-administration/biden-touts-this-chinese-backed-company-at-made-in-america-event/.

298. Ibid.

299. Wang, op cit. and "Afghanistan: Chinese Company to Build Industrial Complex in Kabul," Stratfor, April 29, 2022, https://worldview.stratfor.com/situation-report/afghanistan-chinese-company-build-industrial-complex-kabul?id=030c4e7823&e=99971e0a2b&uuid=c3edfa19-9cc9-4b33-b7ca-64840598916e&mc_cid=6c8df1ea0a&mc_eid=99971e0a2b.

300. Andrew Thornebrooke, "Cold Ambition: China Eyes Arctic as New Frontier," *Epoch Times*, October 10, 2021, https://www.theepochtimes.com/cold-ambition-china-eyes-arctic-as-new-frontier_4040960.html?utm_source=ai&utm_medium=search.

301. Ibid.

302. Ibid.

303. "In the Race to Boost Semiconductor Manufacturing, Global Powers Take Their Marks," Stratfor, November 11, 2021, https://worldview.stratfor.com/article/race-boost-semiconductor-manufacturing-global-powers-take-their-marks?id=743c2bc617&e=99971e0a2b&uuid=d5de7741-28bd-4058-b4c5-4fb30a887271&mc_cid=8faadc3ae7&mc_eid=99971e0a2b.

304. Ibid.

305. Ruth Lee, "China Launches State-Owned Logistics Group in Bid to Strengthen Global Supply China Dominance: Expert," *Epoch Times*, December 13, 2021, https://www.theepochtimes.com/china-reniforces-its-monopoly-in-global-logistic-chain-uses-rare-earths-resource-as-backing_4154509.html?utm_source=ai&utm_medium=search.

306. Anders Corr, "China Seeks Financial Decoupling on Its Own Terms," *Epoch Times*, December 17, 2021, https://www.theepochtimes.com/mkt_morningbrief/us-china-capital-controls_4161114.html?utm_

source=Morningbrief&utm_medium=email&utm_campaign=mb-2021-12-19&mktids=585bf3f1161077c9c10c15e77d0524b6&est=%2FpjmN6xw0Gx9iCQsPZnskMewBhIIS50nxksVpaq8ik%2FxLJm5HuHRsVpWcvjoW64n0Ic9.

307. Ibid.

308. Ibid.

309. Ibid.

310. Anders Corr, "China's Shipping Goes Dark, Enabling Criminality and Militarism," *Epoch Times*, November 29, 2021, https://www.theepochtimes.com/chinas-shipping-goes-dark-enabling-criminality-and-militarism_4127130.html?utm_source=ChinaDaily&utm_medium=email&utm_campaign=2021-11-30

311. Ibid.

312. Ibid.

313. Rita Li, "US Trade Chief Urges New Laws Targeting China's Overseas Steel Investment," *Epoch Times*, November 3, 2021, https://www.theepochtimes.com/us-trade-chief-urges-new-laws-targeting-chinas-overseas-steel-investment_4083556.html?utm_source=ai&utm_medium=search.

314. Ibid.

315. Ibid.

316. Daniel Y. Teng, "Australia Lays Bare Beijing's Coercive Trade Policy at WTO," *Epoch Times*, October 20, 2021, https://www.theepochtimes.com/australia-lays-bare-beijings-coercive-trade-policy-at-wto_4060338.html?utm_source=ai&utm_medium=search.

317. Ibid.

318. Ibid.

319. Daniel Y. Teng, "'Not the Way to Do Diplomacy': US Ambassador to Australia Criticises Chinese Embassy's Complaints Dossier," *Epoch Times*, November 25, 2020, https://www.theepochtimes.com/not-the-way-to-do-diplomacy-us-ambassador-to-australia-criticises-chinese-embassys-complaints-dossier_3592820.html.

320. Antonio Graceffo, "'Free Money' from China Promotes Corruption along the Belt and Road," *Epoch Times*, December 20, 2021, https://www.theepochtimes.com/free-money-from-china-promotes-corruption-along-the-belt-and-road_4165021.html?utm_source=ai&utm_medium=search.

321. Ibid.

322. Ibid.

323. Antonio Graceffo, "China's Belt and Road: Unfinished Projects and Huge Debt," *Epoch Times*, December 7, 2021, https://www.theepochtimes.com/chinas-belt-and-road-unfinished-projects-and-huge-debt_4139511.html?utm_source=ai&utm_medium=search.

324. Ibid.

325. Ibid.

326. Ibid.

327. Ibid.

328. Emel Akan, "US Companies Are 'Hostages' to China," *Epoch Times*, December 4, 2021, https://www.theepochtimes.com/us-companies-are-hostages-to-china_4137114.html?utm_source=ai&utm_medium=search.

329. Ibid.

330. Peter Schweizer, "Chinese Censorship on American Soil," Gatestone Institute, February 25, 2022, https://www.gatestoneinstitute.org/18268/chinese-censorship-american-soil.

331. Ibid.

332. Ibid.

333. Ibid.

334. James Tager, "Made in Hollywood, Censored by Beijing, The US Film Industry and Chinese Government Influence PEN America," accessed January 26, 2021, https://pen.org/report/made-in-hollywood-censored-by-beijing/.

335. Akan, op cit.

336. "China's PR Shop in America: The Democrat Party," States News Service, 24 July 2020, p. NA. *Gale Academic OneFile*, https://link.gale.com/apps/doc/A630477069/AONE?u=wash92852&sid=AONE&xid=b563b3df. Accessed 29 Nov. 2020.

337. Eric Ting, "Former Sen. Barbara Boxer Is Now Working for a Chinese Surveillance Firm," *San Francisco Chronicle*, January 12, 2021, https://www.sfgate.com/politics/article/Barbara-Boxer-China-foreign-agent-Uighur-Muslims-15865511.php.

338. Chuck Ross, "New York's Governor Boosts Chinese Companies Under US Sanctions," *Washington Free Beacon*,

February 28, 2022, https://freebeacon.com/national-security/new-yorks-governor-boosts-chinese-companies-under-us-sanctions/.

339. Ibid.

340. David Shepardson, "China Telecom Plans to Continue Some US Services after FCC Revokes Authorization," Reuters, December 22, 2021, China Telecom plans to continue some US services after FCC revokes authorization | Reuters.

341. Eva Fu, "'Stop Murdering for Organs': NBA Player Tells Beijing to End Forced Organ Harvesting," *Epoch Times*, November 16, 2021, https://www.theepochtimes.com/mkt_breakingnews/stop-murdering-for-organs-nba-player-tells-beijing-to-end-forced-organ-harvesting_4108211.html?utm_source=News&utm_medium=email&utm_campaign=breaking-2021-11-17-2&mktids=74230f2f8571ebd298a71620b61310ba&est=cjtLVm8fbHW%2Fhcai1g8c4sxCPMqKfSLGVou%2FYB6Hv4OT%2FykxTXL2ydkK4xWZRSQk1o01.

342. Ibid.

343. Alexjandro Avila, "China-basher Enes Kanter Freedom Gets Traded, Then Waived by the Houston Rockets. Coincidence?," Fox News, February 14, 2022, https://www.foxnews.com/sports/china-basher-enes-kanter-freedom-gets-traded-then-waived-by-the-houston-rockets-coincidence.

344. Ibid.

345. Ibid.

346. Ryan Clarke, "Chinese Synthetic Narcotics Networks in Post-NATO Afghanistan," *Epoch Times*, December 14, 2021, https://www.theepochtimes.com/chinese-synthetic-narcotics-networks-in-post-nato-afghanistan_4153754.html?utm_source=ai&utm_medium=search

347. Zachary B. Wolf, "Americans Are Overdosing on a Drug They Don't Know They're Taking," CNN, November 18, 2021, https://www.cnn.com/2021/11/17/politics/fentanyl-overdose-deaths-what-matters/index.html.

348. "China Primer: Illicit Fentanyl and China's Role," Congressional Research Service, January 29, 2021, https://crsreports.congress.gov/product/pdf/IF/IF10890.

349. Judith Bergman, "China's Belt and Road Being Built with Forced Labor," Gatestone Institute, June 2, 2021, https://www.gatestoneinstitute.org/17403/china-belt-road-forced-labor.

350. Ibid.

351. Ibid.

352. "South Africa Government Files Lawsuit Against Huawei for Employment Law Violation," Stratfor, February 16, 2022, https://worldview. stratfor.com/situation-report/south-africa-government-files-lawsuit-against-huawei-employment-law-violation?id=030c4e7823&e=99971e0a2b&uuid=6b9ba218-b693-4d4f-9ccf-c30a61ee127e&mc_cid=b6d80a9fad&mc_eid=99971e0a2b.

353. "US: Treasury Department Report Declines to Name Currency Manipulators," Stratfor, December 6, 2021, https://worldview.stratfor.com/situation-report/us-treasury-department-report-declines-name-currency-manipulators?id=030c4e7823&e=99971e0a2b&uuid=ef607692-e257-4572-9c1f-5c1878b516f7&mc_cid=c7e12dcc80&mc_eid=99971e0a2b.

354. Judith Bergman, "Communist China's New Plan: Digital Currency," Gatestone Institute, July 27, 2021, https://www.gatestoneinstitute.org/17487/china-digital-currency.

355. Ibid.

356. Pete Hoekstra, "China and a Failed WTO Accession," Gatestone Institute, December 17, 2021, https://www.gatestoneinstitute.org/18037/china-failed-wto.

357. David Dollar, "Reluctant Player: China's Approach to International Economic Institutions," Brookings, September 14, 2020, https://www.brookings.edu/articles/reluctant-player-chinas-approach-to-international-economic-institutions.

358. Scott Morris, Rowan Rockafellow, and Sarah Rose, "Mapping China's Participation in Multilateral Development Institutions and Funds," Center for Global Development, November 18, 2021, https://www.cgdev.org/publication/mapping-chinas-participation-multilateral-development-institutions-and-funds.

359. Ibid.

360. Massimo Introvigne, "Xi Jinping: 'Marxism Is Winning the Global Ideological War'," Mercatornet, May 7, 2021, https://mercatornet.com/xi-jinping-marxism-winning/71775/.

361. As cited in Kerry Brown and Una Aleksandra Bērziņa-Čerenkova, "Ideology in the Era of Xi Jinping," *Journal of Chinese Political Science*

Vol. 23, pp. 323–339, 2018, https://link.springer.com/article/10.1007/s11366-018-9541-z.

362. Robert L. Maginnis, *Give Me Liberty, Not Marxism*, (Crane, MO: Defender Publishing, 2021), pp. 10–11, https://www.amazon.com/Give-Me-Liberty-Not-Marxism/dp/1948014467.

363. "Marxist Worldview," All About Worldview, accessed January 25, 2021, https://www.allaboutworldview.org/marxist-worldview.htm#:~:text=The%20Marxist%20worldview%20is%20grounded%20in%20Karl%20Marx,of%20the%20Marxist%20Worldview%20across%20ten%20major%20categories.

364. Introvigne, op cit.

365. Ibid.

366. Andrew Thornebrooke, "Beijing Steps Up Aggression as It Seeks to Lead 'New World Order'," *Epoch Times*, December 20, 2021, https://www.theepochtimes.com/beijing-steps-up-aggression-as-it-seeks-to-lead-new-world-order_4166360.html?utm_source=ChinaDaily&utm_medium=email&utm_campaign=2021-12-21.

367. Ibid.

368. Ibid.

369. Ibid.

370. Ibid.

371. "Xi Jinping: Ideological Work Is Extremely Important Work for the Party," *Chinese Law & Government*, Vol. 48, Issue 6, November 28, 2016, https://doi-org.pentagonlibrary.idm.oclc.org/10.1080/00094609.2016.1241108.

372. Ibid.

373. Ibid.

374. Ibid.

375. Ibid.

376. Brown, op cit.

377. Ibid.

378. Ibid.

379. The percent of the Chinese population living below the poverty line in year 2000 was 49.8 percent compared to 0 percent by year 2020. "Ratio of Residents Living below the Poverty Line in China from 2000 to 2020,"

Statista, March 12, 2021, https://www.statista.com/statistics/1086836/china-poverty-ratio/.

380. Brown, op cit.

381. Ibid.

382. "Thoughts of a Living Christian," Wordpress.com, accessed January 25, 2021, https://thoughtsofalivingchristian.wordpress.com/2010/11/21/a-christian-critique-of-marxism/.

383. For similarities between Marxism and Christianity, see chapter 1, "Understanding the Isms of Contemporary American Political Discourse," in Robert L. Maginnis, *Give Me Liberty, Not Marxism*, (Crane, MO: Defender, 2021), https://www.amazon.com/s?k=give+me+liberty+not+marxism&adgrpid=1332609012638274&hvadid=83288190410322&hvbmt=be&hvdev=c&hvlocphy=58520&hvnetw=o&hvqmt=e&hvtargid=kwd-83288680885711%3Aloc-190&hydadcr=21720_10367104&tag=mh0b-20&ref=pd_sl_743i6fplva_e.

384. Brown, op cit.

385. Ibid.

386. Ibid.

387. Ibid.

388. Ibid.

389. Ibid.

390. Ibid.

391. Ibid.

392. Ibid and Xi Jingping, "Full Text of Xi Jinping's Speech on the CCP's 100th Anniversary," *Nikkei News*, July 1, 2021, https://asia.nikkei.com/Politics/Full-text-of-Xi-Jinping-s-speech-on-the-CCP-s-100th-anniversary.

393. Ibid.

394. Ibid.

395. Ibid.

396. Ibid.

397. Ibid.

398. Ibid.

399. Ibid.

400. Ibid.

401. Ibid.

402. Ibid.

403. Ibid.

404. "George Orwell Quotes," AZQuotes, accessed February 19, 2022, https://www.azquotes.com/author/11147-George_Orwell.

405. Maria Repnikova, "Thought Work Contested: Ideology and Journalism Education in China," *China Quarterly*, Cambridge University Press, May 8, 2017, https://www.cambridge.org/core/journals/china-quarterly/article/abs/thought-work-contested-ideology-and-journalism-education-in-china/23CC426BD1B9712B70F8F9CE130F05B8.

406. Rita Li, "Chinese Regime Adds 'Xi Jinping Thought' to National Curriculum," *Epoch Times*, August 25, 2021, https://www.theepochtimes.com/chinese-regime-adds-xi-jinping-thought-to-national-curriculum_3964664.html?utm_source=ai&utm_medium=search.

407. Ibid.

408. Ibid.

409. *Quotations from Chairman Mao Tsetung*, (Peking: Foreign Languages Press, 1972).

410. Ibid.

411. Dorothy Li, "The Chinese Regime Is the 'World's Biggest Captor of Journalists': Report," *Epoch Times*, December 8, 2021, https://www.theepochtimes.com/the-chinese-regime-is-the-worlds-biggest-captor-of-journalists-report_4146212.html?utm_source=ChinaDaily&utm_medium=email&utm_campaign=2021-12-09.

412. Ibid.

413. Ibid.

414. Ibid.

415. Ibid.

416. "The Mainland Finalizes and Implements Hong Kong Electoral Reforms," Stratfor, March 30, 2021, https://worldview.stratfor.com/article/mainland-finalizes-and-implements-hong-kong-electoral-reforms?id=030c4e7823&e=99971e0a2b&uuid=dca083b5-017b-4d59-b8d2-3e5296dd8ec3&mc_cid=ca36f0d383&mc_eid=99971e0a2b.

417. Ibid.

418. Stu Cvrk, "Hong Kong's Slide Into Darkness," *Epoch Times*, December 19, 2021, https://www.theepochtimes.com/mkt_morningbrief/hong-kongs-

slide-into-darkness_4165649.html?utm_source=Morningbrief&utm_
medium=email&utm_campaign=mb-2021-12-20&mktids=aa38ff747fe6edf
95b416cc78465295a&est=Ji8nz1xWhoSvK1BIvtWM%2BAux6aep7%2BX
2WhHmmz0HOxPW72vz%2BXwwCihZV38HXuUyRxva.

419. Ibid.

420. Ibid.

421. "Hong Kong: Civil Servant Training and Exchanges Align with
Mainland Politics," Stratfor, February 9, 2022, https://worldview.stratfor.
com/situation-report/hong-kong-civil-servant-training-and-exchanges-align-
mainland-politics?id=030c4e7823&e=99971e0a2b&uuid=cee0c601-4aad-
4430-ad93-6525710a922c&mc_cid=27c6c41a5c&mc_eid=99971e0a2b.

422. "Hong Kong Website Blockage Raises Questions About Internet
Freedoms," Stratfor, February 15, 2022, https://worldview.stratfor.com/
situation-report/hong-kong-website-blockage-raises-questions-about-
internet-freedoms?id=030c4e7823&e=99971e0a2b&uuid=8f1ddb6a-4380-
473b-b612-5656f37e1fa1&mc_cid=74d68ac730&mc_eid=99971e0a2b.

423. Stu Cvrk, "Hong Kong's Slide into Darkness," op cit.

424. Frank Yue, "101 Falun Gong Practitioners Persecuted to Death in Past
10 Months in China," *Epoch Times*, November 15, 2021, https://www.
theepochtimes.com/mkt_breakingnews/101-falun-gong-practitioners-
dead-in-past-10-months-amid-persecution_4100994.html?utm_
source=News&utm_medium=email&utm_campaign=breaking-2021-11-15-
2&mktids=7bd3d1c5a3011b41e32df94b71f7907b&est=49TieEyriHimH%
2Bg%2F6o0WkF3NGsFMeqvQSrmS1wQMyGcOSjZapZbWaC1NvOmE
G%2F1HOA0Z.

425. Ibid.

426. Ibid.

427. Eva Fu, "'Stop Murdering for Organs': NBA Player Tells Beijing to End
Forced Organ Harvesting," *Epoch Times*, November 16, 2021, https://www.
theepochtimes.com/mkt_breakingnews/stop-murdering-for-organs-nba-
player-tells-beijing-to-end-forced-organ-harvesting_4108211.html?utm_
source=News&utm_medium=email&utm_campaign=breaking-2021-11-17-
2&mktids=74230f2f8571ebd298a71620b61310ba&est=cjtLVm8fbHW%2
Fhcai1g8c4sxCPMqKfSLGVou%2FYB6Hv4OT%2FykxTXL2ydkK4xWZ
RSQk1o01.

428. Sir Geoffrey Nice QC, et al, "Independent Tribunal Into Forced Organ Harvesting of Prisoners of Conscience in China," Chinatribunal.com, June 2019, https://chinatribunal.com/wp-content/uploads/2019/06/China-Tribunal-SUMMARY-JUDGMENT_FINAL.pdf.

429. Limin Zhou, "Vancouver Groups Renew Call for Boycott of Beijing Olympics," *Epoch Times*, October 29, 2021, https://www.theepochtimes.com/vancouver-groups-renew-call-for-boycott-of-beijing-olympics_4076399.html.

430. Ibid.

431. Jocelyn Neo, "Anecdotal Evidence of Sexual Abuse of Tibetan Nuns While in Chinese Police Custody," *Epoch Times*, November 18, 2021, https://www.theepochtimes.com/anecdotal-evidence-of-sexual-abuse-of-tibetan-nuns-while-in-chinese-police-custody_3981264.html?utm_source=News&utm_medium=email&utm_campaign=breaking-2021-11-18-1&est=lRAuLr1zxTTPw4iE3rEqCXdjaIUB0H0dDxfLd6Js9Y19j3SNKQ8KgCzZclzZEOotsUm7.

432. Ibid.

433. Ibid.

434. Frank Fang, "US Religious Freedom Commission Urges Beijing to Release Chinese Christian Leader," *Epoch Times*, August 6, 2019, https://www.theepochtimes.com/us-commission-on-international-religious-freedom-urges-beijing-to-release-chinese-religion-activist_3031461.html.

435. Ibid.

436. Ibid.

437. "China: Speech Presages Tighter Party Control of Religion, Western Human Rights Concerns," Stratfor, December 6, 2021, https://worldview.stratfor.com/situation-report/china-speech-presages-tighter-party-control-religion-western-human-rights-concerns?id=030c4e7823&e=99971e0a2b&uuid=b9051743-e1d7-4617-b833-8567912856b6&mc_cid=3dfbb2b0e7&mc_eid=99971e0a2b.

438. Ibid.

439. "Xi Jinping: Persist in the direction of the sinicization of religions in our country and actively guide religions to adapt to the socialist society," Teller Report, December 4, 2021, https://www.tellerreport.com/news/2021-12-04-xi-jinping--persist-in-the-direction-of-the-sinicization-of-religions-in-

our-country-and-actively-guide-religions-to-adapt-to-the-socialist-society.
SkNvaLpdYt.html.

440. Ibid.

441. Winnie Han and Eva Fu, "Chinese State Media Take Aim at Officials Who Try to 'Jump Ship' and Flee China," *Epoch Times*, November 9, 2021, https://www.theepochtimes.com/mkt_breakingnews/ccp-media-admits-large-number-of-officials-lack-confidence-in-the-ccp-could-flee-at-any-time_4088265.html?utm_source=News&utm_medium=email&utm_campaign=breaking-2021-11-09-2&mktids=532daa23ba33138fcf5898938c fc6975&est=hbbko9Sb236aX2cT0o4YaV1jf3OdRfv505viyzf%2F3p7DuN bN2YwRsG5%2FOpC6KyJxo1%2FH.

442. Ibid.

443. Ibid.

444. Ibid.

445. Anders Corr, "China's New Surveillance," *Epoch Times*, December 6, 2021, https://www.theepochtimes.com/chinas-new-surveillance_4135551. html?utm_source=ChinaDaily&utm_medium=email&utm_campaign=2021-12-07.

446. Ibid.

447. Ibid.

448. Ibid.

449. Ibid.

450. Ibid.

451. Ibid.

452. Ibid.

453. Helen Raleigh, "The Suspicious 'Disappearance' of China's Tennis Star Is Right out of the Chinese Communist Playbook," *Federalist*, November 19, 2021, https://thefederalist.com/2021/11/19/the-suspicious-disappearance-of-chinas-tennis-star-is-right-out-of-the-ccps-playbook/?utm_source=rss&utm_medium=rss&utm_campaign=the-suspicious-disappearance-of-chinas-tennis-star-is-right-out-of-the-ccps-playbook?utm_campaign=ACTENGAGE.

454. Ibid.

455. Ibid.

456. Introvigne, op cit.

457. Eva Fu, "China Pays US Social Media Influencers to Promote

Beijing Olympics, 'Positive' US–China News," *Epoch Times*, December 14, 2021, https://www.theepochtimes.com/china-pays-american-social-media-influencers-to-promote-beijing-olympics-positive-us-china-news_4157726.html?utm_source=ChinaDaily&utm_medium=email&utm_campaign=2021-12-15.

458. Ibid.

459. Ibid.

460. Ibid.

461. Ibid.

462. Frank Fang, "China Exerts Influence in US Through TikTok and WeChat, Expert Says," *Epoch Times*, November 18, 2021, https://www.theepochtimes.com/china-exerts-influence-in-us-through-tiktok-and-wechat-expert-says_4111260.html?utm_source=ChinaDaily&utm_medium=email&utm_campaign=2021-11-19.

463. Ibid.

464. Fu, op cit.

465. Jack Buyrer, "Stafanik Challenger Was China Daily's Lawyer," *Washington Free Beacon*, June 29, 2021, https://freebeacon.com/elections/stefanik-challenger-china-daily/

466. Ibid.

467. Chuck Ross, "CCP Paid DC Radio Station $4.4 Million to Broadcast Propaganda," *Washington Free Beacon*, December 20, 2021, https://freebeacon.com/media/ccp-paid-dc-radio-station-4-4-million-to-broadcast-propaganda/.

468. Ibid.

469. Chuck Ross and Santi Ruiz, "Top News Organizations Run Huawei-Sponsored Puff Pieces," *Washington Free Beacon*, October 27, 2021, https://freebeacon.com/media/top-news-organizations-run-huawei-content/.

470. Ibid.

471. Santi Ruiz, "Report: Authoritarian Governments Use Hauwei Technology to Censor Journalists," *Washington Free Beacon*, December 2, 2021, https://freebeacon.com/national-security/report-authoritarian-governments-use-huawei-technology-to-censor-journalists/.

472. Ibid.

473. Ibid.

474. Yuichiro Katutani, "Cornell Faculty Revolt against China Partnership," *Washington Free Beacon*, March 15, 2021, https://freebeacon.com/national-security/cornell-faculty-revolt-against-china-partnership/?utm_source=actengage&utm_campaign=conservative_test&utm_medium=email.

475. Ibid.

476. Ibid.

477. Janet Lorin and Brandon Kochkodin, "Harvard Leads US Colleges That Received $1 Billion from China," *Philadelphia Inquirer*, February 7, 2020, https://www.inquirer.com/education/china-funding-us-colleges-universities-trade-tensions-20200207.html&outputType=app-web-view.

478. Ibid.

479. "Crosscutting Research Themes," Grainger College of Engineering, University of Illinois Urbana Campaign, accessed March 6, 2022, https://ece.illinois.edu/research/crosscutting-themes.

480. Katutani, op cit.

481. Judith Bergman, "China's Exploitation of Western Academia," Gatestone Institute, April 7, 2021, https://www.gatestoneinstitute.org/17074/china-western-academia.

482. Ibid.

483. Ibid.

484. Mimi Nguyen Ly, "Harvard Professor Charles Lieber Convicted of Lying about China Ties," *Epoch Times*, December 21, 2021, https://www.theepochtimes.com/harvard-professor-charles-lieber-convicted-of-lying-about-china-ties_4171382.html?utm_source=ai&utm_medium=search.

485. Ibid.

486. Ibid.

487. Ibid.

488. Eva Fu, "US Charges Harvard Professor, 2 Researchers with Aiding Chinese Regime," *Epoch Times*, January 28, 2000, https://www.theepochtimes.com/us-charges-harvard-professor-2-researchers-with-aiding-chinese-regime_3219520.html.

489. Bergman, op cit.

490. Ibid.

491. Ibid.

492. "China's Confucius Institutes," An Inquiry by the

Conservative Party Human Rights Commission, February 2019, CPHRC_Confucius_Institutes_report_FEBRUARY_2019-1.pdf (conservativepartyhumanrightscommission.co.uk).

493. Anders Corr, "CCP Influence in Congress," *Epoch Times*, November 27, 2021, https://www.theepochtimes.com/ccp-influence-in-congress_4124095.html?utm_source=ChinaDaily&utm_medium=email&utm_campaign=2021-11-29.

494. Ibid.

495. Ibid.

496. Ibid.

497. Josh Rogin, "It's Time to Drain the Foreign Influence Swamp," *Washington Post*, November 23, 2021, https://www.washingtonpost.com/opinions/2021/11/23/its-time-drain-foreign-influence-swamp-real/.

498. Anders Corr, "CCP Influence in Congress," op cit.

499. Rogin, op cit.

500. Anders Corr, "CCP Influence in Congress," op cit.

501. Zachary Stieber, "Democrat Senator Under Fire after Speaking at Communist Group's Gala," *Epoch Times*, December 16, 2021, https://www.theepochtimes.com/democrat-senator-under-fire-after-speaking-at-communist-groups-gala_4160985.html?utm_source=News&utm_campaign=breaking-2021-12-16-3&utm_medium=email.

502. Ibid.

503. Trevor Loudon, "Communist Party USA Affirms Loyalty to Beijing," *Epoch Times*, March 26, 2021, https://www.theepochtimes.com/communist-party-usa-affirms-loyalty-to-beijing_3749844.html?utm_source=morningbrief&utm_medium=email&utm_campaign=mb-2021-03-27.

504. Ibid.

505. Chuck Ross, "Brookings Institution Boosts China Initiatives Linked to Board Member," *Washington Free Beacon*, November 1, 2021, https://freebeacon.com/national-security/brookings-institution-boosts-china-initiatives-linked-to-board-member/.

506. Ibid.

507. Ibid.

508. Ibid.

509. Nicole Hao and Cathy He, "CCP Adviser Outlines Detailed Plan to Defeat US, Including Manipulating Elections," *Epoch Times*, March 26, 2021, https://www.theepochtimes.com/xi-jinpings-adviser-outlines-plan-for-ccp-to-defeat-us-including-manipulating-elections_3748196.html?utm_source=morningbrief&utm_medium=email&utm_campaign=mb-2021-03-27.

510. Ibid.

511. Ibid.

512. Ibid.

513. Ibid.

514. "Australia: Intelligence Foils Chinese Plot to Bankroll Political Candidates," Stratfor, February 11, 2022, https://worldview.stratfor.com/situation-report/australia-intelligence-foils-chinese-plot-bankroll-political-candidates?id=030c4e7823&e=99971e0a2b&uuid=43de93cf-24f2-437b-acd3-37bbe7eba4d2&mc_cid=4a4ec87f95&mc_eid=99971e0a2b.

515. Alex Blair, "Senator James Paterson Weighs in after ASIO Reveals Foreign Spies Are Using Dating Apps to Contact Aussies," News.com.au, February 10, 2022, https://www.news.com.au/technology/online/security/asio-reveals-foreign-plot-to-influence-aussie-election-in-annual-threat-assessment/news-story/bba40243b629747838213bfe71143dd9.

516. Ibid.

517. Nicole Hao and Cathy He, "Chinese Leader Xi Jinping Lays Out Plan to Control Global Internet: Leaked Documents," *Epoch Times*, May 2, 2021, https://www.theepochtimes.com/mkt_breakingnews/chinese-leader-xi-jinping-lays-out-plan-to-control-the-global-internet-leaked-documents_3791944.html?utm_source=News&utm_medium=email&utm_campaign=breaking-2021-05-02-3&mktids=c6f9dc97f5768015217ad36c66e5a859&est=KdRBHKH1CsL8WG73KSTy3n1VIGn2DJPx4klh%2BtUVO1ZwQebpR3i74m2sxSfbEyR0inNL.

518. Ibid.

519. Ibid.

520. Ibid.

521. Ibid.

522. Ibid.

523. Ibid.

524. Ibid.

525. Ibid.

526. Ibid.

527. Benjamin Fearnow, "Xi Jinping Urges China to Prep for 'Military Struggle' Amid Afghanistan Security Concerns," *Newsweek*, July 31, 2021, https://www.newsweek.com/xi-jinping-urges-china-prep-military-struggle-amid-afghanistan-security-concerns-1614931.

528. "Look to the Future and Stay Focused, Xi Tells China in New Year's Address," *US News*, December 31, 2021, https://www.usnews.com/news/world/articles/2021-12-31/look-to-the-future-and-stay-focused-xi-tells-china-in-new-years-address.

529. Ryan McMorrow, "Xi Warns against Economic Decoupling and Calls for New World Order," *Financial Times*, April 20, 2021, https://www.ft.com/content/096dd554-499b-468c-b5fa-38b0352941a0.

530. "China: Xi's Fiery Speeches Presage Party-led Economy Amid US Competition," Stratfor, January 4, 2022, https://worldview.stratfor.com/situation-report/china-xi-s-fiery-speeches-presage-party-led-economy-amid-us-competition?id=030c4e7823&e=99971e0a2b&uuid=975ee430-e959-4b96-a2e5-845a99c41d1d&mc_cid=066a0142e0&mc_eid=99971e0a2b.

531. Ibid.

532. McMorrow, op cit. and Economy, op cit.

533. "Alfred Thayer Mahan and Nicholas Spykman long ago warned about the rise of a great power on the Eurasian landmass that could use the vast human and natural resources of 'the great continent' to forge a global imperium." Francis P. Sempa, "The Threat of a China-Centric New World Order," *American Spectator*, December 14, 2021, https://spectator.org/china-new-world-order-geopolitics/.

534. Ibid.

535. Economy, op cit.

536. "Military and Security Developments Involving the People's Republic of China 2021," Report to Congress, Department of Defense, FY2020, https://media.defense.gov/2021/Nov/03/2002885874/-1/-1/0/2021-CMPR-FINAL.PDF.

537. Ibid.

538. Ibid.

539. Ibid.

540. Ibid.

541. Bradley A. Thayer, "The Evolution of the Chinese Regime's Unrestricted Warfare Against the US," *Epoch Times*, December 6, 2021, https://www.theepochtimes.com/the-evolution-of-the-chinese-regimes-unrestricted-warfare-against-the-us_4136881.html?utm_source=ChinaDaily&utm_medium=email&utm_campaign=2021-12-07.

542. Qiao Liang and Wang Xiangsui, *Unrestricted Warfare: China's Master Plan to Destroy America*, Paperback, November 10, 2015, https://www.amazon.com/Unrestricted-Warfare-Chinas-Destroy-America/dp/1626543054/ref=sr_1_1?adgrpid=1346902307595599&hvadid=84181465120977&hvbmt=be&hvdev=c&hvlocphy=135788&hvnetw=o&hvqmt=e&hvtargid=kwd-84181736099211%3Aloc-190&hydadcr=22565_10772412&keywords=unrestricted+warfare+book&qid=1641386042&sr=8-1.

543. Thayer, op cit.

544. Ibid.

545. Gabriel Dominguez, "Update: China's 'push for global power' Poses Greatest Security Threat to US, Says US Intelligence Community, Janes, April 19, 2021. https://www.janes.com/defence-news/news-detail/chinas-push-for-global-power-poses-greatest-security-threat-to-us-says-us-intelligence-community.

546. Ibid.

547. Economy, op cit.

548. "China's Growing Power Projection and Expeditionary Capabilities," Section II, US-China Economic and Security Review Commission, 2020, https://www.uscc.gov/annual-report/2020-annual-report-congress.

549. Ibid.

550. "Military and Security Developments Involving the People's Republic of China 2021," op cit.

551. Christopher *Woody, "China's Air Force Has Big Plans for Its Biggest Planes," Business* Insider, July 7, 2021, https://www.businessinsider.com/chinas-fast-growing-airlift-fleet-reflects-beijings-military-goals-2021-7.

552. Ibid.

553. James E. Fanell, "China's Global Navy," *Naval War College Review*,

Autumn 2020, Vol .73, Issue 4, https://digital-commons.usnwc.edu/cgi/viewcontent.cgi?article=8144&context=nwc-review.

554. "Military and Security Developments Involving the People's Republic of China 2021," op cit.

555. "Equatorial Guinea: US Intelligence Reports Point to New Chinese Military Base," Stratfor, December 6, 2021, https://worldview.stratfor.com/situation-report/equatorial-guinea-us-intelligence-reports-point-new-chinese-military-base?id=030c4e7823&e=99971e0a2b&uuid=e4951f16-dd3a-4e67-b552-591b0dcb359c&mc_cid=bff64c2051&mc_eid=99971e0a2b.

556. Antonio Graceffo, "Defense Diplomacy: Beijing's New Weapon for Expanding Its Influence in Latin America," *Epoch Times*, December 16, 2021, https://www.theepochtimes.com/defense-diplomacy-beijings-new-weapon-for-expanding-its-influence-in-latin-america_4158629.html?utm_source=ChinaDaily&utm_medium=email&utm_campaign=2021-12-17.

557. "Argentina: Buenos Aires Joins China's Belt and Road Initiative," Stratfor, February 7, 2022, https://worldview.stratfor.com/situation-report/argentina-buenos-aires-joins-china-s-belt-and-road-initiative?id=030c4e7823&e=99971e0a2b&uuid=da98a09d-4a10-4671-895e-ff8026dbc1a2&mc_cid=bc9b03f2c7&mc_eid=99971e0a2b.

558. Andrew Thornebrooke, "Chinese Arms Sellers Expanded in 2020, Second Only to US," *Epoch Times*, December 7, 2021, https://www.theepochtimes.com/chinese-arms-sellers-expanded-in-2020-second-only-to-us_4143804.html?utm_source=ChinaDaily&utm_medium=email&utm_campaign=2021-12-08.

559. Ibid.

560. Dusan Stojanovic, "China Makes Semi-Secret Delivery of Missiles to Serbia," Associated Press, April 10, 2022, https://apnews.com/article/russia-ukraine-europe-china-serbia-nato-682ab79c4239f14ecc1133ff5c7addc9.

561. Antonio Graceffo, "Defense Diplomacy: Beijing's New Weapon for Expanding Its Influence in Latin America," op cit.

562. Ibid.

563. Ibid.

564. Ibid.

565. Ibid.

566. Ibid.

567. Ibid.

568. Ibid.

569. "China Launches Final Satellite for BeiDou Navigation System," Janes, accessed February 21, 2022, https://customer-janes-com.pentagonlibrary. idm.oclc.org/DefenceWeekly/Display/FG_3209176-JDW.

570. Ibid.

571. Ibid.

572. Andrew Tate, "China Launches More Surveillance Satellites," IHS Janes, July 20, 2021, https://customer-janes-com.pentagonlibrary.idm.oclc. org/Janes/Display/FG_2254177-JDW.

573. Ibid.

574. "China: Five-year Space Plan Pledges More Rapid Developments," Stratfor, January 28, 2022, https://worldview.stratfor.com/situation-report/ china-five-year-space-plan-pledges-more-rapid-developments?id=030c4e782 3&e=99971e0a2b&uuid=79a4b621-b77c-4d24-897c-e400a7f013a8&mc_ cid=54b3a2355c&mc_eid=99971e0a2b.

575. Andrew Thornebrooke, "Beijing Steps Up Aggression as It Seeks to Lead 'New World Order'," *Epoch Times*, December 20, 2021, https:// www.theepochtimes.com/beijing-steps-up-aggression-as-it-seeks-to- lead-new-world-order_4166360.html?utm_source=ChinaDaily&utm_ medium=email&utm_campaign=2021-12-21.

576. Ibid.

577. Ibid.

578. "China Announces 6.8% Increase in 2021 Defence Budget," Janes, accessed February 21, 2022, https://customer-janes-com.pentagonlibrary. idm.oclc.org/Janes/Display/FG_3912291-JDW.

579. Ibid. and "What Does China Really Spend on Its Military?," CSIS, accessed February 21, 2022, https://chinapower.csis.org/military-spending/.

580. "China Announces 6.8% Increase in 2021 Defence Budget," op cit.

581. Ibid.

582. Ibid.

583. Ibid.

584. "Military and Security Developments Involving the People's Republic of China 2021," op cit.

585. Ibid.

586. Nancy Levin, "10 Largest Air Forces in the World," Largest.org, December 4, 2018, https://largest.org/technology/air-forces/.

587. "Military and Security Developments Involving the People's Republic of China 2021," op cit.

588. Ibid.

589. Ibid.

590. "China Announces New Theatre Commands," Janes, accessed February 21, 2022, https://customer-janes-com.pentagonlibrary.idm.oclc.org/Janes/Display/jdw60921-jdw-2016.

591. Ibid.

592. Ibid.

593. "Military and Security Developments Involving the People's Republic of China 2021," op cit.

594. Ibid.

595. Ibid.

596. Chang, "What to do about China," op cit.

597. Ibid.

598. "Strategic Weapon Systems," Janes, accessed February 21, 2022, https://customer-janes-com.pentagonlibrary.idm.oclc.org/Janes/Display/CNAA015-CNA.

599. Ibid.

600. Andrew Thornebrooke, "China's Hypersonic Weapon Could Be for Nuclear 'First-Use': Pentagon No. 2," *Epoch Times*, November 18, 2021, https://www.theepochtimes.com/chinas-hypersonic-weapon-could-be-for-nuclear-first-use-pentagon-no-2_4111527.html?utm_source=ChinaDaily&utm_medium=email&utm_campaign=2021-11-19.

601. Ibid.

602. Ibid.

603. Ibid.

604. "Military and Security Developments Involving the People's Republic of China 2021," op cit.

605. "Strategic Weapon Systems," op cit.

606. "Biological Weapons, Weapons of Mass Destruction, Global Security," accessed February 21, 2022, https://www.globalsecurity.org/wmd/world/china/bw.htm.

607. Ibid.

608. "Chemical Weapons Program," fas.org, accessed February 21, 2022, https://nuke.fas.org/guide/dprk/cw/.

609. "Strategic Weapon Systems," op cit.

610. Jon Grevatt, "President Xi Calls for Accelerated Development of Military Technologies," IHS Janes, October 28, 2021, https://customer-janes-com.pentagonlibrary.idm.oclc.org/DefenceWeekly/Display/BSP_8104-JDW.

611. Ibid.

612. Frank Dong, "Chinese Researchers Built Hypersonic Aircraft Prototype Using Design Scrapped by NASA," *Epoch Times*, December 15, 2021, https://www.theepochtimes.com/chinese-researchers-built-hypersonic-aircraft-prototype-using-scrapped-nasa-design_4159515.html?utm_source=ChinaDaily&utm_medium=email&utm_campaign=2021-12-16.

613. Stu Cvrk, "Chinese Military Improves Capabilities While America Sleeps," *Epoch Times*, November 25, 2021, https://www.theepochtimes.com/chinese-military-improves-capabilities-while-america-sleeps_4119002.html.

614. Bill Gertz, "China Shows DF-17 Hypersonic Missile," *Washington Times*, October 2, 2019, https://www.washingtontimes.com/news/2019/oct/2/china-shows-df-17-hypersonic-missile/.

615. Ibid.

616. Ibid.

617. Ibid.

618. "Military and Security Developments Involving the People's Republic of China 2021," op cit. and Hope Hodge Seck, "Active Ships in the US Navy," Military.com, June 23, 2021, https://www.military.com/navy/us-navy-ships.html.

619. Ibid.

620. Ibid.

621. Ibid.

622. Stu Cvrk, "Chinese Military Improves Capabilities While America Sleeps," The Epoch Times, November 25, 2021, https://www.theepochtimes.com/chinese-military-improves-capabilities-while-america-sleeps_4119002.html?utm_source=ChinaDaily&utm_medium=email&utm_campaign=2021-11-26.

623. "Military and Security Developments Involving the People's Republic of China 2021," op cit.

624. Ibid., p. 55.

625. Cvrk, op cit.

626. Gordon G. Chang, "China's 'Satellite Crusher': 'Space Pearl Harbor' Is Coming," *Epoch Times*, November 2, 2021, https://www.theepochtimes.com/mkt_morningbrief/chinas-satellite-crusher-space-pearl-harbor-is-coming_4082087.html?utm_source=Morningbrief&utm_medium=email&utm_campaign=mb-2021-11-04&mktids=5a6822e9a6e19 23ce6479ea95567a1c3&est=x1e5BAe%2FyKTjHqF1QshkwfNC46jHxKx BnWawNf05xaKCc8EI9gSQx18hN4KXd7qsTvpI.

627. Ibid.

628. Ibid.

629. Pat Host, "New Space Race: China Advances Its Space Capabilities for Future Warfare," IHS Janes, April 13, 2021. https://customer-janes-com.pentagonlibrary.idm.oclc.org/DefenceWeekly/Display/FG_3924979-JDW.

630. Ibid.

631. Anthony Capaccio, "China, Russia Seek Weapons to Hit U.S. Satellites, Pentagon Says," Bloomberg, April 12, 2022, China, Russia Seek Weapons to Hit U.S. Satellites, Pentagon Says - Bloomberg.

632. Ibid.

633. Chang, Op cit.

634. Ibid.

635. Taylor A Lee and Peter W. Singer, "China's Space Program Is More Military Than You Might Think," Defense One, July 16, 2021, https://www.defenseone.com/ideas/2021/07/chinas-space-program-more-military-you-might-think/183790/.

636. Emily Crane, "China Constructs Fake US Warships for Potential Target Practice, Images Show," *New York Post*, November 8, 2021, https://nypost.com/2021/11/08/china-builds-fake-us-warships-for-potential-target-practice/.

637. H. I. Sutton and Sam LaGrone, "China Builds Missile Targets Shaped Like US Aircraft Carrier, Destroyers in Remote Desert," USNI News, November 7, 2021, https://news.usni.org/2021/11/07/china-builds-missile-targets-shaped-like-u-s-aircraft-carrier-destroyers-in-remote-desert.

638. Robert Johnson, "China Successfully Tests 'Carrier Killer' Missile in the

Gobi Desert," *Business Insider*, January 25, 2013,https://www.businessinsider. com/chinas-carrier-killer-missile-test-proves-df-21d-lives-up-to-name-2013-1.

639. H. I. Sutton and Sam LaGrone, op cit.

640. Andrew Thornebrooke, "US 'Cannot Be Certain' of Military Victory Against China: Report," *Epoch Times*, December 18, 2021, https://www.theepochtimes.com/us-cannot-be-certain-of-military-victory-against-china-report_4109296.html?utm_source=ChinaDaily&utm_medium=email&utm_campaign=2021-12-20.

641. Ibid.

642. Ibid.

643. Andrew Thornebrooke, "'We'd Probably Lose' a War Over Taiwan: Rep. Gallagher," *Epoch Times*, October 29, 2021, https://www.theepochtimes. com/wed-probably-lose-a-war-over-taiwan-rep-gallagher_4076314.html.

644. Ibid.

645. Thornebrooke, op cit.

646. Ibid.

647. Ibid.

648. Ibid.

649. Ibid.

650. Zbigniew Brzezinski, "Geopolitics," accessed February 22, 2022, https://www.goodreads.com/quotes/tag/geopolitics.

651. "Geopolitics," Wikipedia, accessed February 22, 2022, https://en.wikipedia.org/wiki/Geopolitics.

652. Ibid.

653. Ibid.

654. "The Domino Theory—The 1960s: High Tide of the Domino Theory," American Foreign Relations, accessed 22, 2022, https://www.americanforeignrelations.com/A-D/The-Domino-Theory-The-1960s-high-tide-of-the-domino-theory.html#ixzz7LeIGzXkh.

655. Ibid.

656. Ibid.

657. Gogwilt, Christopher, *The Fiction of Geopolitics: Afterimages of Geopolitics, from Wilkie Collins to Alfred Hitchcock, 1860–1940* (Stanford, CA, Cambridge: Stanford University Press; Cambridge University Press, 2000) pp. 35–36.

658. "Full Text: Special Address by Chinese President Xi Jinping at the 2022 World Economic Forum Virtual Session," Xinhua, January 17, 2022, http://www.news.cn/english/20220117/d3c169b45b304f6f9176969a45480784/c.html.

659. Ibid.

660. "2020 Report to Congress of the US-China Economic and Security Review Commission 116 Congress Second Session, December 2020," https://www.uscc.gov/sites/default/files/2020-12/2020_Annual_Report_to_Congress.pdf.

661. Yan Xuetong, "Becoming Strong: The New Chinese Foreign Policy," *Foreign Affairs*, July/August 2021, https://www.foreignaffairs.com/articles/united-states/2021-06-22/becoming-strong.

662. Ibid.

663. Ibid.

664. Ibid.

665. Ibid.

666. Ibid.

667. Jude Blanchette, "Xi's Gamble: The Race to Consolidate Power and Stave off Disaster," Foreign Affairs Vol. 100, Issue 4, July-August 2021, *Gale Academic OneFile*, link.gale.com/apps/doc/A667436797/AONE?u=wash92852&sid=ebsco&xid=b46a7350.

668. Ibid.

669. Ibid.

670. Ibid.

671. 2020 Report to Congress of the US-China Economic and Security Review Commission," op cit.

672. Ibid.

673. Ibid and "30 Animals Symbolism in Chinese Culture," AboutChina, January 7, 2012, https://discover.hubpages.com/education/Animal-Symbolism-in-Chinese-Culture.

674. "2020 Report to Congress of the US-China Economic and Security Review Commission," op cit.

675. Frank Fang, "The China Threat Is a Moral Challenge to the World, Expert Says," *Epoch Times*, November 22, 2021, The China Threat Is a Moral Challenge to the World, Expert Says (theepochtimes.com).

676. Ibid.

677. Ibid.

678. Ibid.

679. Andrew Thornebrooke, "Chinese Regime Advances Global Marxism to Confront Western-Led International Order: Report," *Epoch Times*, November 17, 2021, https://www.theepochtimes.com/chinese-regime-advances-global-marxism-to-confront-western-led-international-order-report_4109499.html.

680. Ibid.

681. Ibid.

682. Ibid.

683. Ibid.

684. Andrew Thornebrooke, "Beijing Steps Up Aggression as It Seeks to Lead 'New World Order'," op cit.

685. Ibid.

686. Ibid.

687. Ibid.

688. Xuetong, op cit.

689. Andrew Thornebrooke, "Beijing Steps Up Aggression as It Seeks to Lead 'New World Order'," op cit.

690. Ibid.

691. Ibid.

692. "2020 Report to Congress of the US-China Economic and Security Review Commission," op cit.

693. "Full Text: Special Address by Chinese President Xi Jinping at the 2022 World Economic Forum Virtual Session, op cit.

694. Brett D. Schaefer, "China's Goals in International Organizations," Heritage Foundation, March 23, 2021.

695. Ibid.

696. Ibid.

697. Ibid.

698. Ibid.

699. "2021 Report to Congress of the US-China Economic and Security Review Commission," op cit.

700. Ibid.

701. Ibid.

702. Ibid.

703. Ibid.

704. Ibid.

705. Jessica Chen Weiss, A World Safe for Autocracy: China's Rise and the Future of Global Politics, Foreign Affairs, July/August 2019, http://www.jessicachenweiss.com/uploads/3/0/6/3/30636001/weiss_2019_fa_a_world_safe_for_autocracy.pdf.

706. Ibid.

707. Ibid.

708. Ibid.

709. "2021 Report to Congress of the US-China Economic and Security Review Commission," op cit.

710. Michael Washburn, "20 Years After Joining WTO, China Still 'Far Away' from Meeting Commitments: Experts," Epoch Times, December 11, 2021, https://www.theepochtimes.com/chronic-violations-chinas-20-years-in-wto-has-done-little-to-curb-its-trade-abuses-experts-say_4151801.html.

711. Ibid.

712. Ibid.

713. Stephen Ezell, "False Promises II: The Continuing Gap Between China's WTO Commitments and Its Practices," ITIF, July 26, 2021, https://itif.org/publications/2021/07/26/false-promises-ii-continuing-gap-between-chinas-wto-commitments-and-its.

714. Rodger Baker, "A Look Back at a Landmark South China Sea Ruling, Five Years On," Stratfor, July 12, 2021, https://worldview.stratfor.com/article/look-back-landmark-south-china-sea-ruling-five-years?id=743c2bc617&e=99971e0a2b&uuid=bb648b1d-53d3-4809-a0d9-5fe8141d0b76&mc_cid=d3a3000666&mc_eid=99971e0a2b.

715. Ibid.

716. Jim Gomez, "China Fully Militarized Isles, Indo-Pacific Commander Ssays," Military Times, March 20, 2022, https://www.militarytimes.com/flashpoints/china/2022/03/20/china-fully-militarized-isles-indo-pacific-commander-says/?utm_source=Sailthru&utm_medium=email&utm_campaign=EBB%2003.21.2022&utm_term=Editorial%20-%20Early%20Bird%20Brief.

717. Stu Cvrk, "China Fools Western Environmentalists," *Epoch Times*, January 11, 2022, https://www.theepochtimes.com/china-fools-western-environmentalists_4201349.html.

718. Ibid.

719. Ibid.

720. "China, US: Joint Declaration on Climate Cooperation Released," Stratfor, November 11, 2021, https://worldview.stratfor.com/situation-report/china-us-joint-declaration-climate-cooperation-released.

721. Audrye Wong, "How Not to Win Allies and Influence Geopolitics: China's Self-Defeating Economic Statecraft," *Foreign Affairs*, May/June 2021, http://cis.mit.edu/publications/analysis-opinion/2021/how-not-win-allies-and-influence-geopolitics.

722. Ibid.

723. Ibid.

724. Andrew Chen, "All Countries Need to Rethink Their Relationship with China: Canadian Foreign Affairs Minister," *Epoch Times*, January 10, 2022, https://www.theepochtimes.com/all-countries-need-to-rethink-their-relationship-with-china-canadian-foreign-affairs-minister_4203890.html.

725. Ibid.

726. Frank Fang, "Beijing Pressures Countries to Deport Taiwanese Nationals to China, Report Says," *Epoch Times*, December 1, 2021, https://www.theepochtimes.com/beijing-pressures-countries-to-deport-taiwanese-nationals-to-china-report-says_4132640.html?utm_source=ChinaDaily&utm_medium=email&utm_campaign=2021-12-02.

727. Ibid.

728. Ibid.

729. Ibid.

730. "China sanctions Raytheon, Lockheed over Taiwan deal," Associated Press, February 22, 2022, https://www.defensenews.com/industry/2022/02/22/china-sanctions-raytheon-lockheed-over-taiwan-deal/?utm_source=Sailthru&utm_medium=email&utm_campaign=EBB%2002.23.2022&utm_term=Editorial%20-%20Early%20Bird%20Brief.

731. Ibid.

732. Ibid.

733. Soeren Kern, "Lithuania Stands Up to China," Gatestone Institute, December 16, 2021, https://www.gatestoneinstitute.org/18034/lithuania-china.

734. Ibid.

735. "Foreign Relations of Taiwan," Wikipedia, accessed February 22, 2022, https://en.wikipedia.org/wiki/Foreign_relations_of_Taiwan.

736. Antonio Graceffo, "Beijing Uses Police and Security Training to Infiltrate Foreign Countries,"
Epoch Times, December 17, 2021, https://www.theepochtimes.com/beijing-uses-police-and-security-training-to-infiltrate-foreign-countries_4161229.html?utm_source=News&utm_campaign=breaking-2021-12-18-1&utm_medium=email&est=cBuAInD8vAJcaG3CIcV4mhj6Reb7IiKll5S
Anyhwe%2BZgRQI6NB0LyWTWrz7k6CUkVsns.

737. Ibid.

738. Ibid.

739. Ibid.

740. Anders Corr, "China's Aggression Is Changing the Nature of Sovereignty," *Epoch Times*, November 26, 2021, https://www.theepochtimes.com/mkt_breakingnews/chinas-aggression-is-changing-the-nature-of-sovereignty_4118213.html?utm_source=News&utm_medium=email&utm_campaign=breaking-2021-11-27-2&mktids=59e5f49f38955834f10ab635b2
b390e5&est=oyMy00X68jTORrKkMkxqZBJEpozGSsj28WHr%2FNqO6
w0yH8zU9RUXM7Fx%2BxDWxOkeAg3z.

741. Ibid.

742. Ibid.

743. Gordon G. Chang, "China Takes over the Solomon Islands—And the Pacific," Gatestone Institute, March 31, 2022, https://www.gatestoneinstitute.org/18384/china-takes-over-solomon-islands.

744. Ibid.

745. Ibid.

746. Ibid.

747. Danella Perez Schmieloz, "Report Exposes Chinese Influence in Italian Politics," *Epoch Times*, December 1, 2021, https://www.theepochtimes.com/report-exposes-chinese-influence-in-italian-politics_4132397.html?utm_source=ChinaDaily&utm_medium=email&utm_campaign=2021-12-02.

748. Ibid.

749. Ibid.

750. Ibid.

751. Ibid.

752. "Iran and China Sign 25-Year Cooperation Agreement," Reuters, March 27, 2021, https://www.reuters.com/world/china/iran-china-sign-25-year-cooperation-agreement-2021-03-27/.

753. Ibid.

754. "China, Iran: Comprehensive Strategic Agreement Signed," Stratfor, March 29, 2021, https://worldview.stratfor.com/situation-report/china-iran-comprehensive-strategic-agreement-signed.

755. "Iran, China Sign Strategic Long-Term Cooperation Agreement," Associated Press, March 27, 2021, https://abcnews.go.com/International/wireStory/iran-china-sign-strategic-long-term-cooperation-agreement-76720627.

756. "2020 Report to Congress of the US-China Economic and Security Review Commission," op cit.

757. "China: Meetings with World Leaders Amid Olympics Show Xi's Foreign Policy Priorities," Stratfor, February 7, 2022, https://worldview.stratfor.com/situation-report/china-meetings-world-leaders-amid-olympics-show-xis-foreign-policy-priorities?id=030c4e7823&e=99971e0a2b&uuid=9b479792-fd7f-4636-a52a-5d67c16b6ecb&mc_cid=8d031823fc&mc_eid=99971e0a2b and https://news.cgtn.com/news/2022-02-05/Xi-Jinping-meets-with-visiting-Serbian-President-Vucic-17oRsENft1S/index.html and https://news.yahoo.com/xi-meets-poland-pakistan-leaders-110448257.html?fr=sycsrp_catchall.

758. Judith Bergman, "China Taking over Africa: 'China's Second Continent,'" Gatestone Institute, April 11, 2022, https://www.gatestoneinstitute.org/18417/china-taking-over-africa.

759. "Africa, China: Record 2021 Trade Presages More Partnerships in 2022," Stratfor, January 19, 2022, https://worldview.stratfor.com/situation-report/africa-china-record-2021-trade-presages-more-partnerships-2022?id=030c4e7823&e=99971e0a2b&uuid=e7572cb6-239b-4254-8f71-ac762dd0b36d&mc_cid=812fc6402a&mc_eid=99971e0a2b.

760. Nathaniel Luz, "A Gradual Auctioning of Africa to China,"

Memri.org, May 3, 2021, https://www.memri.org/reports/gradual-auctioning-africa-china.

761. Ibid.

762. Ibid.

763. Ibid.

764. Ibid.

765. Anchal Vohra, "Xi Jinping Has Transformed China's Middle East Policy," Foreign Affairs, February 1, 2022, https://foreignpolicy.com/2022/02/01/xi-jinping-has-transformed-chinas-middle-east-policy/.

766. Phil Mattingly, Zachary Cohen and Jeremy Herb, "Exclusive: US Intel Shows Saudi Arabia Escalated Its Missile Program with Help from China," CNN, June 5, 2019, https://edition.cnn.com/2019/06/05/politics/us-intelligence-saudi-arabia-ballistic-missile-china/index.html#:~:text=Saudi%20Arabia%20is%20known%20to%20have%20purchased%20ballistic,even%20effectively%20deploy%20the%20ones%20it%20does%20have.

767. Ibid.

768. Ibid.

769. Ibid.

770. Ibid.

771. Ibid.

772. Mark Ward, "Does China's Government Hack US Companies to Steal Secrets?," BBC, September 23, 2015, https://www.bbc.com/news/technology-34324252.

773. "Fourth Industrial Revolution," Wikipedia, accessed February 22, 2022, https://en.wikipedia.org/wiki/Fourth_Industrial_Revolution.

774. Wyatt Massey, "The Scientific Method: How Will Technology Be Used in the Future? The Faith Community Can Remind Scientists of the Ethics at Stake," US Catholic, Vol. 84, Issue 1, Claretian Publications, January 2019.

775. David De Cremer and Garry Kasparov, "AI Should Augment Human Intelligence, Not Replace It," Harvard Business Review, March 18, 2021, https://hbr.org/2021/03/ai-should-augment-human-intelligence-not-replace-it.

776. Shi Shan and Anne Zhang, "US and China Race to Control the Future Through Artificial Intelligence," Epoch Times, November 27, 2021,

https://www.theepochtimes.com/mkt_morningbrief/us-and-china-race-to-control-the-future-through-artificial-intelligence_4109862.html?utm_source=Morningbrief&utm_medium=email&utm_campaign=mb-2021-11-28&mktids=0449f116506200f5b2546d0231069968&est=PesuaEQGm7O XE8q9NsCxZXoBnjAIQ1HawRTuibW62oJDDwAlSjhXm534aKGhwgU AKODv.

777. "Hyperloop Technology Market Analysis, Research Study with Hyperloop Transportation Technologies, Hyperloop One, TransPod," *Digital Journal*, January 19, 2022, https://www.digitaljournal.com/pr/hyperloop-technology-market-analysis-research-study-with-hyperloop-transportation-technologies-hyperloop-one-transpod#ixzz7IjizJlOz.

778. Andrew J. Hawkins, "Uber's 'Flying Cars' Could Arrive in LA by 2020—And Here's What It'll Be Like to Ride One," The Verge, November 8, 2017, Uber's 'flying cars' could arrive in LA by 2020 — and here's what it'll be like to ride one - The Verge and Alyssa Newcomb, "Flying Cars Could Take Off as Soon as 2023," NBC News, January 10, 2019, https://www.nbcnews.com/business/business-news/flying-cars-could-take-soon-2023-n957276.

779. Andy Corbley, "A Flying Car Just Got Certified as Airworthy to Fly," Good News Network, January 28, 2022, https://www.goodnewsnetwork.org/a-flying-car-just-got-certified-as-airworthy-to-fly/.

780. Jim Baker, Artificial Intelligence: A Counterintelligence Perspective: Part 1, LAWFARE BLOG (Aug. 15, 2018), https://www.lawfareblog.com/artificialintelligence-counterintelligence-perspective-part-1.

781. Venkat Vajradhar, "6 Amazing AI devices," Data Driven Investor, September 12, 2019, https://medium.datadriveninvestor.com/ai-devices-f269f3e0464f.

782. Souvik, "11 Ideas to Change Our World with Future Technology," RS Web Solutions, June 15, 2021, https://www.rswebsols.com/tutorials/technology/ideas-change-world-future-technology.

783. Paula Froelich, "France, China Developing Biologically Engineered Super-soldiers," *New York Post*, December 19, 2020, https://nypost.com/2020/12/19/france-china-developing-biologically-engineered-super-soldiers/.

784. Massey, op cit.

785. Ibid.

786. Amy Mek, "Reset: 'Smart Dust' Spying on Your Brain, Human Microchipping," Rair Foundation, February 8, 2022, https://rairfoundation. com/the-great-transhumanism-reset-smart-dust-spying-on-your-brain-human-microchipping-video/.

787. Ibid.

788. Ibid.

789. Dominique Mosbergen, "Stephen Hawking Says Artificial Intelligence 'Could Spell the End of the Human Race'," Huffpost, December 2, 2014, https://www.huffpost.com/entry/stephen-hawking-ai-artificial-intelligence-dangers_n_6255338#:~:text=In%20a%20recent%20interview%20with%20BBC%2C%20Hawking%20said,biological%20evolution%2C%20couldn%E2%80%99t%20compete%2C%20and%20would%20be%20superseded.%E2%80%9D.

790. Ibid.

791. Ibid.

792. "Cloud Storage," Wikipedia, accessed February 23, 2022, https://en.wikipedia.org/wiki/Cloud_storage#:~:text=Cloud%20storage%20is%20a%20model%20of%20computer%20data,typically%20owned%20and%20managed%20by%20a%20hosting%20company.

793. Sebastian Anthony, "Elon Musk Warns Us That Human-level AI Is 'Potentially More Dangerous Than Nukes'," *ExtremeTech*, August 4, 2014, https://www.extremetech.com/extreme/187467-elon-musk-warns-us-that-human-level-ai-is-more-dangerous-than-nukes#:~:text=Elon%20Musk%2C%20the%20mastermind%20behind%20SpaceX%20and%20Tesla%2C,humanity%20to%20closely%20resemble%20Judgment%20Day%20from%20Terminator.

794. Thomas A. Kochan, "Artificial Intelligence and the Future of Work: A Proactive Strategy," *AI Magazine*, VOL. 42, Issue 1, Spring 2021, https://www.proquest.com/docview/2515179174?accountid=6768.

795. Ibid.

796. Xinyidai Rengongzhineng Fazhan Guihua "New Generation Artificial Intelligence Development Plan," Council, July 20, 2017, http://www.gov.cn/zhengce/content/2017-07/20/content_5211996.ht m. and Ian Burrows, "Made in China 2025: Xi Jinping's Plan to Turn China into the AI World

Leader," ABC News (AU), October 6, 2018, https://www.abc.net.au/news/2018-10-06/china-plans-to-become-ai-world-leader/10332614.

797. "Secretary Antony J. Blinken at the National Security Commission on Artificial Intelligence (NSCAI) Global Emerging Technology Summit," States News Service, 13 July 2021, *Gale Academic OneFile*, link.gale.com/apps/doc/A668384913/AONE?u=wash92852&sid=ebsco&xid=4490a9a9.

798. Ibid.

799. Shi Shan and Anne Zhang, "US and China Race to Control the Future Through Artificial Intelligence," *Epoch Times*, November 27, 2021, https://www.theepochtimes.com/mkt_morningbrief/us-and-china-race-to-control-the-future-through-artificial-intelligence_4109862.html?utm_source=Morningbrief&utm_medium=email&utm_campaign=mb-2021-11-28&mktids=0449f116506200f5b2546d0231069968&est=PesuaEQGm7OXE8q9NsCxZXoBnjAIQ1HawRTuibW62oJDDwAlSjhXm534aKGhwgUAKODv.

800. Ibid.

801. Ibid.

802. Ibid.

803. Ibid.

804. Colin Demarest, "Hundreds of AI projects Underway as Defense Department Eyes Future Combat," C4ISRNET, February 22, 2022, https://www.c4isrnet.com/artificial-intelligence/2022/02/22/hundreds-of-ai-projects-underway-as-defense-department-eyes-future-combat/?utm_source=Sailthru&utm_medium=email&utm_campaign=EBB%2002.23.2022&utm_term=Editorial%20-%20Early%20Bird%20Brief.

805. Ibid.

806. Burrow, op cit.

807. "Chinese Advancements in Disruptive Technologies Threaten US Technology Superiority, says DIA chief," IHS Janes, accessed February 23, 2022, https://customer-janes-com.pentagonlibrary.idm.oclc.org/DefenceWeekly/Display/FG_3961801-JDW.

808. Ibid.

809. Christopher Darby and Sarah Sewall, "The Innovation Wars: America's Eroding Technological Advantage," *Foreign Affairs*, March/April

2021, https://www.foreignaffairs.com/articles/united-states/2021-02-10/technology-innovation-wars.

810. Ibid.

811. Ibid.

812. Bai Chunli, "Fostering R&D Force for National Growth," *China Today*, Vol. 70, Issue 3, March 2021, https://www.pressreader.com/australia/china-today-english/20210305/281543703668624.

813. Ibid.

814. Darby, op cit.

815. Ibid.

816. Chunli, op cit.

817. Ibid.

818. Darby, op cit.

819. Ben West, "Understanding Economic Espionage: The Present," Stratfor, February 23, 2021, https://worldview.stratfor.com/article/understanding-economic-espionage-present?id=743c2bc617&e=99971e0a2b&uuid=aa6f6bbd-83b7-42e9-aa14-5b7982ae9119&mc_cid=57d40a1508&mc_eid=99971e0a2b.

820. Ibid.

821. Ibid.

822. Ibid.

823. Ibid.

824. Ibid.

825. Mimi Nguyen Ly, "DOJ Drops Charges against 5 Researchers Accused of Hiding Chinese Military Affiliations: Report," *Epoch Times*, July 23, 2021, https://www.theepochtimes.com/mkt_morningbrief/doj-drops-charges-against-5-researchers-accused-of-hiding-chinese-military-affiliations-report_3916163.html?utm_source=Morningbrief&utm_medium=email&utm_campaign=mb-2021-07-24&mktids=3e351c0585f0a693aebaa3e8c1da431b&est=CNKM7rl5s7DchpNvRi%2BJOR1EdN%2F0AaQAx3tbxgoCYPgoxfHiZmzrRWIR%2FrO5MO4OrZ2k.

826. Ibid.

827. Ibid.

828. J. M. Phelps, "CIA's Bid to Throttle Down Chinese Espionage May Be Easier Said Than Done: Experts," *Epoch Times*, September 14, 2021, https://

www.theepochtimes.com/cias-bid-to-throttle-down-chinese-espionage-may-be-easier-said-than-done-experts_3996789.html.

829. Ly, op cit.

830. "US: China DOJ Ends China Initiative Counterespionage Work to Continue," Stratfor, February 24, 2022, https://worldview.stratfor.com/situation-report/us-china-doj-ends-china-initiative-counterespionage-work-continue?id=030c4e7823&e=99971e0a2b&uuid=86524928-19eb-416d-a3a9-8b3275444e21&mc_cid=f46a6561fd&mc_eid=99971e0a2b.

831. Phelps, oOp cit.

832. Ibid.

833. Ibid.

834. Ibid.

835. Jon Grevatt, "China to Deepen 'Civil-Military Fusion' in 14th Five Year Plan," IHS Janes, November 2, 2020, https://customer-janes-com.pentagonlibrary.idm.oclc.org/DefenceWeekly/Display/FG_3782985-JDW.

836. "Military and Security Developments Involving the People's Republic of China 2021," op cit.

837. Gabriel Dominguez, "Chinese Advancements in Disruptive Technologies Threaten US Technology Superiority, Says DIA Chief," IHS Janes, April 30, 2021, https://customer-janes-com.pentagonlibrary.idm.oclc.org/DefenceWeekly/Display/FG_3961801-JDW.

838. Ibid.

839. Caroline Downey, "Former Intelligence Director Urges US to Relocate Beijing Olympics to Punish COVID-Origins Cover Up," *National Review*, August 3, 2021, https://www.nationalreview.com/news/former-intelligence-director-urges-u-s-to-relocate-beijing-olympics-to-punish-covid-origins-cover-up/.

840. Ibid.

841. "Military and Security Developments Involving the People's Republic of China 2021," op cit.

842. Gabriel Dominguez, "US Accuses China of 'Explicitly' Diverting Foreign Dual-use Technologies to Modernise the PLA," IHS Janes, March 13, 2020. https://customer-janes-com.pentagonlibrary.idm.oclc.org/DefenceWeekly/Display/FG_2728238-JDW.

843. Ibid.

844. Ibid.

845. Jon Grevatt, "China Launches Technology Incentive Project," IHS Janes, December 2, 2020, https://customer-janes-com.pentagonlibrary.idm. oclc.org/DefenceWeekly/Display/FG_3808147-JDW.

846. Ibid.

847. Ibid.

848. Ibid.

849. Ibid.

850. Jon Grevatt, "China Grows Its International Technology Network," IHS Janes, January 19, 2017, https://customer-janes-com.pentagonlibrary. idm.oclc.org/DefenceWeekly/Display/jdin91289-jdw-2017.

851. Ibid.

852. Jon Grevatt, "Armenia and China Sign Military Technology Cooperation Agreement," IHS Janes, January 17, 2012. https://customer-janes-com.pentagonlibrary.idm.oclc.org/DefenceWeekly/Display/jdin84563-jdw-2012.

853. Ibid.

854. Jon Grevatt, "China and Russia to Collaborate on Aero-Engine R&D," IHS Janes, January 26, 2017, https://customer-janes-com.pentagonlibrary. idm.oclc.org/DefenceWeekly/Display/jdin91313-jdw-2017.

855. Ibid.

856. Ibid.

857. Ibid.

858. Jon Grevatt, "China's AI 'Entanglement" with Australia and US," IHS Janes, July 5, 2018, https://customer-janes-com.pentagonlibrary.idm.oclc. org/DefenceWeekly/Display/FG_969011-JDW.

859. Ibid.

860. Ibid.

861. Ibid.

862. Ibid.

863. Ibid.

864. Jon Grevatt, "EU China Sign Investment Treaty," IHS Janes, January 4, 2021, https://customer-janes-com.pentagonlibrary.idm.oclc.org/DefenceWeekly/Display/FG_3856755-JDW.

865. Ibid.

866. Ibid.

867. Ibid.

868. Judith Bergman, "How American Technology Aids China's Global Ambitions," Gatestone Institute, December 7, 2021, https://www.gatestoneinstitute.org/17945/china-american-technology.

869. "Rep. Gallagher: Statement on Reports of Chinese Hypersonic Missile Test," wispolitics.com, accessed February 24, 2022, https://www.wispolitics.com/2021/rep-gallagher-statement-on-reports-of-chinese-hypersonic-missile-test/#:~:text=Rep.%20Gallagher%3A%20Statement%20on%20reports%20of%20Chinese%20hypersonic,test%20should%20serve%20as%20a%20call%20to%20action.

870. Judith Bergman, "How American Technology Aids China's Global Ambitions," op cit.

871. Kate O'Keeffe, Heather Somerville, and Yang Jie, "US Companies Aid China's Bid for Chip Dominance Despite Security Concerns," *Wall Street Journal*, November 12, 2021, https://www.wsj.com/articles/u-s-firms-aid-chinas-bid-for-chip-dominance-despite-security-concerns-11636718400.

872. "How Chinese Companies Facilitate Technology Transfer from the United States," US-China Economic and Security Review Commission, May 6, 2019, https://www.uscc.gov/research/how-chinese-companies-facilitate-technology-transfer-united-states.

873. James A. Lewis, "Learning the Superior Techniques of the Barbarians," CSIS, January 2019, https://apo.org.au/node/222631.

874. "Look to the Future and Stay Focused, Xi tells China," Reuters, December 31, 2021, https://www.khaleejtimes.com/world/look-to-the-future-and-stay-focused-xi-tells-china.

875. "Xi Says 'Critical' to Reset Strained US Relations," *Agence France-Presse*, September 11, 2021, https://www.manilatimes.net/2021/09/11/news/world/xi-says-critical-to-reset-strained-us-relations/1814271.

876. "National Security Strategy of the United States of America," December 2017, http://nssarchive.us/wp-content/uploads/2020/04/2017.pdf p. 3.

877. Fumiaki Kubo, "Reading the Trump Administration's China Policy," *Asia-Pacific Review*, Vol. 26, Issue 1, 2019, https://www-tandfonline-com.pentagonlibrary.idm.oclc.org/doi/full/10.1080/13439006.2019.1633153.

878. "1972 Visit by Richard Nixon to China," Wikipedia,

accessed February 24, 2022, https://en.wikipedia.org/
wiki/1972_visit_by_Richard_Nixon_to_China.

879. Brian D'Haeseleer, Jeremy Kuzmarov and Roger Peace, "The Post-
Cold War Era, 1989–2001, United States Foreign Policy History and
Resource Guide, accessed February 24, 2022, http://peacehistory-usfp.org/
post-cold-war-era/.

880. William Clinton, "Statement by the President Clinton on Most
Favored Nation Status for China, 1993," USC US-China China Institute,
University of Southern California, May 28, 1993, https://china.usc.edu/
statement-president-clinton-most-favored-nation-status-china-1993.

881. Ibid.

882. Bill Clinton, What Happened When China Joined the WTO?," World
101, accessed February 24, 2022, https://world101.cfr.org/global-era-issues/
trade/what-happened-when-china-joined-wto.

883. Dana Priest; Judith Havemann, "Second Group of US Ships Sent to
Taiwan," *Washington Post*, March 11, 1996, https://www.washingtonpost.
com/archive/politics/1996/03/11/second-group-of-us-ships-sent-to-
taiwan/34280337-be79-4d6e-b859-8046682a37b3/.

884. "George W. Bush on China," Issues 2000, accessed February 25, 2022,
https://www.ontheissues.org/George_W__Bush_China.htm.

885. Ibid.

886. Barack Obama and Xi Jinping, Joint Press Conference, American
Rhetoric, September 25, 2015, https://www.americanrhetoric.com/speeches/
barackobama/barackobamaxijinpingrosegardenpresser2015.htm.

887. Bradley A. Thayer, "Trump Versus Biden on the China Threat," *Epoch
Times*, November 23, 2021, https://www.theepochtimes.com/trump-vs-
biden-on-the-china-threat_4114199.html?utm_source=ChinaDaily&utm_
medium=email&utm_campaign=2021-11-24.

888. Ibid.

889. Ibid.

890. Ibid.

891. Miranda Devine, "'More Money Than God': Chinese Titan
Lavished Hunter Biden with 3-Carat Gem, Offer of $30 Million,"
New York Post, November 28, 2021, https://nypost.com/2021/11/28/
chinese-titan-lavished-hunter-biden-with-3-carat-gem-offer-of-30-million/.

892. Steven Mosher, "Caught Red-Handed: A Review of Peter Schweizer's Exposé of the Corruption Spread by Communist China," LifeSite, February 2, 2022, https://www.lifesitenews.com/blogs/caught-red-handed-a-review-of-peter-schweizers-expose-of-the-corruption-spread-by-communist-china/.

893. Ibid.

894. Frank Fang, "Majority of Americans Consider China Top Threat, Survey Finds," *Epoch Times*, December 2, 2021, https://www.theepochtimes.com/mkt_breakingnews/majority-of-americans-consider-china-top-threat-survey-finds_4134833.html?utm_source=News&utm_medium=email&utm_campaign=breaking-2021-12-2-1&mktids=0081ebbe b4cd11994a4f24cd18f55832&est=ClRlVDxepTfLTueezMdjZghiiZOeYw6 5gOa3w1cgFWVRjoOr%2FWgRBuskPZXPO%2BghKYCg .

895. Ibid.

896. Ibid.

897. Ibid.

898. Ibid.

899. Christian Datoc, " 'We're Not Old Friends': Biden Says His Relationship with China's Xi Is 'Pure Business'," *South China Morning Post*, June 16, 2021, https://www.msn.com/en-us/news/politics/were-not-old-friends-biden-says-his-relationship-with-chinas-xi-is-pure-business/ar-AAL7imw.

900. Ibid.

901. Emma Graham-Harrison, "Will a Chilly Meeting in Anchorage Set the Tone for US-China Relations?," *Guardian*, March 19, 2021, https://www.theguardian.com/world/2021/mar/19/us-china-meeting-anchorage-tone-relations-turbulent-times-ahead.

902. Taiwan Relations Act (TRA; Pub.L. 96–8, 93 Stat. 14, enacted April 10, 1979; H.R. 2479), H.R.2479 - 96th Congress (1979-1980): Taiwan Relations Act | Congress.gov | Library of Congress.

903. Ibid.

904. "Japan's Policy Shift on Taiwan Centers on Okinawa," Global Taiwan Institute, September 10, 2021, https://ketagalanmedia.com/2021/09/10/japan-policy-okinawa-taiwan/.

905. Patrick Reilly, "Chinese Ambassador to US Warns of 'Military Conflict' over Taiwan," January 29, 2022, https://nypost.com/2022/01/29/chinese-

ambassador-qin-gang-warns-us-of-potential-military-conflict-over-taiwan/.

906. Greg Myre, "CIA Nominee William Burns Talks Tough on China," NPR, February 24, 2021, https://www.kpcw.org/2021-02-24/cia-nominee-william-burns-talks-tough-on-china.

907. Samuel Gregg, "What to Do about China?" States News Service, 20 Apr. 2020, *Gale Academic OneFile*, link.gale.com/apps/doc/A621425369/AONE?u=wash92852&sid=ebsco&xid=c9240efb. Accessed 27 Jan. 2022.

908. Ibid.

909. Ibid.

910. Ibid.

911. Ibid.

912. Walter C Clemens Jr. , "What to Do about—or with—China?," *Asian Perspective* 37, 2013, file:///C:/Users/rober/OneDrive/Desktop/V3%20 CHINA%20NEW%20WORLD%20ORDER%20-%20Copy/SEC%20 3%20CHINA%20NWO%20RESPONSE%20TO%20THREAT%20 &%20END%20TIMES/CHP%209/what%20to%20do%20about%20 or%20with%20china.pdf.

913. Ibid.

914. Ibid.

915. "Mercantilism," Merriam-Webster, accessed February 25, 2022, https://www.merriam-webster.com/dictionary/mercantilism.

916. Stephen Ezell, "China's Economic Mercantilism," *Industry Week*, July 24, 2013, https://www.industryweek.com/the-economy/public-policy/article/21960801/chinas-economic-mercantilism'

917. Ibid.

918. Ibid.

919. Nathan Picarsic and Emily de La Bruyère, "Corporate Complicity Scorecard," Victims of Communism Memorial Foundation, Washington, DC, February 3, 2022, https://victimsofcommunism.org/publication/corporate-complicity-scorecard/'

920. Ibid.

921. Ibid.

922. Clemens, op cit.

923. Patricia Adams and Lawrence Solomon, "How Canada Can Decouple from China,"

Epoch Times, February 20, 2022, https://www.theepochtimes.
com/how-canada-can-decouple-from-china_4283207.html?utm_
source=Morningbrief&utm_
campaign=mb-2022-02-21&utm_medium=email&est=Bt5EnYP%2BqZD
MLzeoew
B1bhEvSDF%2FbsXEy6VYPUPryLVyTfmO5kSG4tQGZKQziHdOZ
4wZ.

924. Ibid.

925. Ibid.

926. "US Government Pension Fund Urged to Reverse China Investment,"
Economic Review, August 27, 2019, https://chinaeconomicreview.
com/us-government-pension-fund-urged-to-reverse-china-
investment/#:~:text=Senior%20US%20senators%20are%20demanding%20
that%20one%20of,and%20domestic%20security%20efforts%2C%20
said%20the%20Financial%20Times.

927. "US China Washington and Beijing Urge New Trade Measures to
Combat Each Other," Stratfor, February 16, 2022, https://worldview.
stratfor.com/situation-report/us-china-washington-and-beijing-urge-new-
trade-measures-combat-each-other?id=030c4e7823&e=99971e0a2b&uui
d=a2fe5cd6-beb0-49f9-babf-4b21fa2e6562&mc_cid=6c3346b451&mc_
eid=99971e0a2b.

928. "Trump's China Tariffs—The List of Products Affected and What
You Can Do," EcomCrew, January 20, 2022, https://www.ecomcrew.com/
trumps-china-tariffs/#list.

929. "2021 Report to Congress of the US-China Economic and Security
Review Commission, One Hundred Seventeenth Congress First Session,"
November 2021, https://www.uscc.gov/sites/default/files/2021-11/2021_
Annual_Report_to_Congress.pdf.

930. "Rep. Jim Banks Introduces Truth in Testimony Rule," WBIW.
COM, November 23, 2021, http://www.wbiw.com/2021/11/23/
rep-jim-banks-introduces-truth-in-testimony-rule/.

931. Peter Schweizer, "Elite Capture," Gatestone Institute, February 20,
2022, https://www.gatestoneinstitute.org/18207/elite-capture.

932. Ibid.

933. Ibid.

934. Ibid.

935. "Contributions and Donations by Foreign Nationals," 52 USC 30121, https://uscode.house.gov/view.xhtml?req=(title:52%20section:30121%20 edition:prelim).

936. Jose Alberto Nino, "Communist China is Now the Largest Financial Backer of the UN 'Small Arms Treaty'," Liberty Conservative News, February 11, 2022, https://libertyconservativenews.substack.com/ communist-china-is-now-the-largest.

937. "VOA Broadcasting in Mandarin," VOA, accessed February 25, 2022, https://www.insidevoa.com/p/6440.html.

938. Emel Akan, "Biden's Budget Calls for Funding the Police, Taxing Rich, Countering China," *Epoch Times*, March 28, 2022, https://www. theepochtimes.com/bidens-budget-calls-for-funding-the-police-taxing- rich-countering-china_4366619.html?utm_source=News&utm_ campaign=breaking-2022-03-28-3&utm_medium=email&est=dAvo7OnU UhO%2F6XPkPpVk58zja5dC%2BQDW%2BGUZAo8%2Fgwd4zHAkA TyQ5cEiJRJjgGIQos2E.

939. Mari Yamaguchi, "Japan, Philippines to Step Up Security Ties Amid China Worry," Associated Press, April 7, 2022, https://news.yahoo.com/ japan-philippines-step-security-ties-154245504.html?fr=yhssrp_catchall.

940. Ibid.

941. "Japan: Ruling Party Calls for Doubling of Defense Budget," Stratfor, April 27, 2022, https://worldview.stratfor.com/situation-report/japan-ruling- party-calls-doubling-defense-budget?id=030c4e7823&e=99971e0a2b&uu id=3d664611-d07f-472a-bf67-2a773b6eef94&mc_cid=ac4ef7301b&mc_ eid=99971e0a2b.

942. Clemens, op cit.

943. Adam Kredo, "Pentagon's Latest Strategy: Promote Socialism to Combat China, *Washington Free Beacon*, February 15, 2022, https://freebeacon.com/biden-administration/ pentagons-latest-strategy-promote-socialism-to-combat-china/.

944. Ibid.

945. Ibid.

946. Ibid.

947. Ibid.

948. Ibid.

949. James R. Webb, "China Now More Willing, Able to Challenge US Military, Report Says," *Military Times*, February 16, 2022, https://www.militarytimes.com/flashpoints/2022/02/16/china-now-more-willing-able-to-challenge-us-military-report-says/?utm_source=Sailthru&utm_medium=email&utm_campaign=EBB%20 02.17.2022&utm_term=Editorial%20-%20Early%20Bird%20Brief.

950. Ibid.

951. Richard Fontaine, "What the New China Focus Gets Wrong," *Foreign Affairs*, November 2, 2021 https://www.foreignaffairs.com/articles/china/2021-11-02/what-new-china-focus-gets-wrong.

952. Ibid.

953. Ibid.

954. Ibid.

955. Ibid.

956. Ibid.

957. John F. Walvoord, "Preface," *The Nations in Prophecy*, August 27, 2007, https://walvoord.com/series/318.

958. John F. Walvoord, Chapter XII, "The Kings of The East: The Oriental Confederacy," *The Nations in Prophecy*, August 27, 2007, https://walvoord.com/article/303.

959. Ibid.

960. Ibid.

961. Joseph Connor, "Have You Heard?," World War II, January–February 2017, p. 32. https://eds-p-ebscohost-com.pentagonlibrary.idm.oclc.org/eds/pdfviewer/pdfviewer?vid=14&sid=bfe1cc95-b559-44cd-8249-2fbc4487717e%40redis.

962. Walvoord, Op cit.

963. Ibid.

964. Ibid.

965. "China," World Jewish Congress, accessed February 25, 2022, https://www.worldjewishcongress.org/en/about/communities/CN.

966. "China in Prophecy," Bible Study, accessed February 25, 2022, https://www.biblestudy.org/prophecy/china-in-prophecy.html#:~:text=Bible%20prophecy%20suggests%20that%20the%20

%22kings%20of%20the,near%20the%20mount%20of%20Megiddo%20
%28Armageddon%2C%20Revelation%2016%3A16%29.

967. "Out of Which of Noah's Three Sons Did the Chinese Race Come
From?," Bible.org, accessed February 25, 2022, https://bible.org/question/
out-which-noah%E2%80%99s-three-sons-did-chinese-race-come.

968. Ibid.

969. "China in Bible Prophecy," Passionate Generation, January 10, 2008,
https://revivekashgar.wordpress.com/2008/01/10/china-in-bible-prophecy/.

970. Ibid.

971. Ibid.

972. Ibid.

973. "Land of Sinim," Hebrew Nations, accessed February 25, 2022,
https://hebrewnations.com/articles/biblical-proof/geo/geoaustralia.
html#:~:text=Sinim%20is%20interpreted%20to%20mean%20Land%20
of%20the,Australia%20u001din%20Latin%20means%20Land%20of%20
the%20South and Craig White, In Search of... The Origin of Nations,
History Research Projects, https://www.amazon.com/Search-Nations-
History-Research-Projects/dp/141070016X/ref=sr_1_1?qid=1644523082&
refinements=p_27%3AHistory+Research+Projects&s=books&sr=1-1&text
=History+Research+Projects. Note: The History Research Projects promotes
research and publications such as national origins.

974. Dale A. Brueggemann, "Kittim," ed. John D. Barry et al., *Lexham Bible
Dictionary* (Bellingham, WA: Lexham Press, 2016).

975. Walvoord, op cit.

976. Ibid.

977. Ibid.

978. Ibid.

979. Ibid.

980. Arnold G. Fruchtenbaum, *Footsteps of the Messiah*, (Logos, 2003),
https://www.amazon.com/Footsteps-Messiah-Arnold-G-Fruchtenbaum/
dp/0914863096.

981. Ibid.

982. "Red China: Firecracker No. 2," *Time*, May 21, 1965, http://content.
time.com/time/subscriber/article/0,33009,901693,00.html.

983. Ibid.

984. Walvoord, op cit.

985. Ralph L. Powell, "Everyone a Soldier: The Communist Chinese Militia," *Foreign Affairs*, Vol. 39, No. 1, October 1960, http://www.jstor.com/stable/20029468.

986. Ibid.

987. Ibid.

988. Ibid.

989. Ibid. Powell attributes the 200,000,000 figure to Cheng Chu-yuan, "The People's Communes." Hong Kong: Union Press,1959, p. 90–91.

990. "Xi Jinpng Thought," Wikipedia, accessed February 25, 2022, https://en.wikipedia.org/wiki/Xi_Jinping_Thought.

991. Robert L. Maginnis, F*uture War: Super Soldiers, Terminators, Cyberspace & The National Security Strategy for 21st Century Combat*, (Crane, MO: Defender Publishing), p. 99. https://www.amazon.com/Future-War-SOLDIERS-TERMINATORS-CYBERSPACE/dp/0996409572.

992. Adam Gabbatt, "China Conducting Biological Tests to Create Super Soldiers, US Spy Chief Says," *Guardian*, December 4, 2020, https://www.theguardian.com/world/2020/dec/04/china-super-soldiers-biologically-enhanced-john-ratcliffe.

993. Walvoord, op cit.

994. Ibid.

995. "China in Prophecy," op cit.

996. Jack Wellman, "What Role Does China Play in Biblical End Times Studies?," What Christians Want to Know, accessed February 25, 2022, https://www.whatchristianswanttoknow.com/what-role-does-china-play-in-biblical-end-times-studies/#ixzz7JkwbeHsm.

997. William Gallo, "At Beijing Olympics, Xi and Putin Announce Plan to Counter US," *China News*, February 3, 2022, https://www.voanews.com/a/at-beijing-olympics-xi-and-putin-strive-for-unity-against-us/6426270.html#:~:text=Though%20Russia%20and%20China%20do%20not%20share%20a,border%20with%20Ukraine%2C%20raising%20fears%20of%20a%20conflict.

998. Ibid.

999. Walvoord, op cit.

1000. Ibid.

1001. "King Belshazzar and Darius The Mede," Wilmington for Christ, January 25, 2022, https://www.wilmingtonfavs.com/king-babylon/king-belshazzar-and-darius-the-mede.html and "Darius the Mede "Received the Kingdom," AMAIC, April 12, 2016, https://bookofdanielamaic.wordpress.com/2016/04/12/darius-the-mede-received-the-kingdom/.

1002. Nina Shea, "Christians Under Xi," *National Review*, Vol. 73, Issue 14, August 2, 2021, https://eds-s-ebscohost-com.pentagonlibrary.idm.oclc.org/eds/detail/detail?vid=6&sid=4e4d88a3-f6a2-4048-b5d6-a7a83ed6dd84%40redis&bdata=JnNpdGU9ZWRzLWxpdmU%3d#AN=151415242&db=mth.

1003. Carl Hunderson, "Why Is Christianity Growing So Quickly in Communist China?," *National Catholic Register*, August 18, 2015, https://www.ncregister.com/news/why-is-christianity-growing-so-quickly-in-communist-china.

1004. Ibid.

1005. Ibid.

1006. Ibid.

1007. Ibid.

1008. Shea, op cit.

1009. "Marxist Worldview," All About Worldview, accessed January 25, 2021, https://www.allaboutworldview.org/marxist-worldview.htm#:~:text=The%20Marxist%20worldview%20is%20grounded%20in%20Karl%20Marx,of%20the%20Marxist%20Worldview%20across%20ten%20major%20categories.

1010. Robert L. Maginnis, *Give Me Liberty, Not Marxism*, (Crane, MO: Defender Publishing Group, 2021).

1011. US Library of Congress, "Translation of Letter from Lenin," Revelations from the Russian Archives, accessed April 17, 2020, https://www.loc.gov/exhibits/archives/trans-ae2bkhun.html.

1012. Editorial Team, *The Specter of Communism*, Chapter Six: "The Revolt Against God," *Epoch Times*, June 20, 2018, https://www.theepochtimes.com/chapter-6-articles-of-faith-how-the-devil-has-man-revolt-against-god_2562880.html.

1013. Ibid.

1014. Ibid.

1015. Bill Muelenberg, "The Persecution of Christians in China," Aquila Report, December 2, 2021, https://theaquilareport.com/the-persecution-of-christians-in-china/.

1016. Arielle Del Turco, "China to Christians: We're Rrewriting the Bible, and You'll Use It or Else," *Federalist*, October 26, 2020, https://thefederalist.com/2020/10/26/china-to-christians-were-rewriting-the-bible-and-youll-use-it-or-else/.

1017. Ibid.

1018. Ibid.

1019. Shea, op cit.

1020. Ibid.

1021. Ibid.

1022. Ibid.

1023. Ibid.

1024. Ibid.

1025. Olivia Enos and Hannah So, "Religious Persecution in China Intensifies with Brainwashing Camps for Christians," Heritage Foundation, May, 12, 2021, https://www.heritage.org/religious-liberty/commentary/religious-persecution-china-intensifies-brainwashing-camps-christians.

1026. Ibid.

1027. Shea, op cit.

1028. Ibid.

1029. Muehlenberg, op cit.

1030. Shea, op cit.